# ORGANS
# IN SCOTLAND

## A REVISED LIST

## ALAN BUCHAN

CW00551408

The Edinburgh Society of Organists

# FOREWORD
## by David Stewart

I am glad to be writing a foreword to this significant publication by my friend and colleague, Alan Buchan. It is almost 45 years since Alan and I began researching organs in Scotland and so I am more than relieved that this comprehensive list of organs in Scotland, past and present, is now being published, thanks to the considerable efforts of Alan. He has spared no effort to unearth material through the relevant archives held in various parts of the country, through printed and unpublished sources, through contacts with churches, researchers, organists and organ builders, and through site visits to many parts of the country.

His work has been informed by his own extensive knowledge, gathered as a church organist in both urban and rural parishes, a past President of the Scottish Federation of Organists, the Edinburgh Society of Organists and the Borders Guild of Organists, as an Adviser on Organs for the advisory service provided to the Scottish Churches by the Scottish Federation of Organists, and through a practical stint many years ago working for an organ builder.

While great progress has been made in both the quantity and quality of information, the position is constantly changing, as churches continue to close, as organs are moved elsewhere or scrapped, and as new information comes to light. No such publication can ever be completely accurate. Corrections, updates and new information are always welcome.

I hope you will find this publication both interesting and informative - and that it will play a part in raising awareness of the rich heritage of organs still extant in Scotland, the importance of conserving them, especially those which remain unaltered, and of using them for their intended purpose - to provide music for public worship to lift the spirits in church, chapel and cathedral, and - for the secular organs - to inform and entertain. It is also encouraging to note the significant number of new organs installed in Scotland over the last few decades.

Thanks are due to the Edinburgh Society of Organists for funding a publication for the fourth time, this time on a much larger scale.

# Acknowledgments

I have had the nerve to claim authorship of this book, but in fact the contributors are so numerous that it would be impossible to thank them all individually. My unreserved thanks are due to all.

Many are mentioned in the "Sources" section of the book, pages 30-36, but I shall here single out only four individuals here who have constantly encouraged and provided a huge amount of information over many years. One was the late Dr. Jim Inglis whose detailed researches extended to every period of Scottish organ history, and whose thorough and discerning approach was inspirational. The second is Mr. James Mackenzie of Glasgow, whose knowledge and memory are unsurpassed. The third is Mr. Philip Wright, whose work on Wadsworth and Lawton is well known, but who has recently provided hundreds of newspaper cuttings from a subscription to the British Newspaper Archive. Finally I should thank Mr. David Stewart for all the work involved in compiling his previous publications, for hundreds of e-mails providing further information and for meticulously proof reading this publication. Without them, the present edition of the directory would never have surfaced.

**Alan Buchan**

# ORGANS IN SCOTLAND

## A REVISED LIST

# Photographs

# An Introduction to the Organ in Scotland
## Alan Buchan

The word "organ" originally meant simply a tool or contrivance which requires skill to use. The musical instrument of that name certainly reflects an impressively varied range of skills and disciplines: music, physics, architecture, fine art, history, engineering, woodwork, metalwork, as well as the physical skill and coordination required to play it.

The organ is one of the oldest musical instruments to have survived on the planet. The earliest references date from the 3rd century BC; the earliest remains date from the 3rd century AD and were found in Budapest. For at least half of its two thousand year history the organ was a secular instrument. Whether used as an accompaniment to gladiatorial Roman games, or played *outside* churches before or after weddings, it was probably not used for sacred purposes until at least the 10th century. The Benedictines were pro-organ; the Cistercians initially against. Wulstan's poem about the supposedly colossal 10th century organ at Winchester (wind supplied by 26 bellows, blown by 70 men, "*auditur ubique in urbe*" - heard throughout the town) does not actually say where the organ was located in the church, though it was clearly in some kind of structure on a floor. Its function may have been that of a signal, similar to the role already assumed by church bells.

The secular pipe organ probably moved from Eastern Europe (where it has never become a church instrument) to Western Europe in the form of gifts from Byzantine kings to Charlemagne and the Spanish or French aristocracy. Its role outside churches for weddings perhaps gives us one clue why it may have become a church instrument. As it moved north and west, and the weather became colder and wetter, the players of organs might be inclined to ask if they might come inside.

By the time the organ reached Scotland, it was almost certainly used within churches for sacred purposes. When the first organ was erected in Scotland remains speculative. The story that an organ was heard when Saint Margaret's remains were moved within Dunfermline Abbey in 1250 may be true but the source of the information was not even the 14th century John of Fordoun who chronicled the ceremony, but rather his mid-15th century text embellisher Walter Bower of Inchcolm. The evidence itself is in no way convincing.

By the time that Bower was writing, organs had certainly arrived in Scotland and they became widely used in abbeys, cathedrals, collegiate churches, town churches and university colleges. The earliest known reference, in 1437, relates to Aberdeen where there is a single payment of 26s 8d for blowing the organs in St. Nicholas' Church. Incidentally, the last pre-Reformation organ whose parts survived in Scotland was also at St. Nicholas' Church. Organ parts were unearthed in the crypt towards the end of the 18th century, and indeed again during the 20th.

As far as monastic installations were concerned, the earliest reference relates to the Cistercian abbey at Kinloss in the 1470s, which is perhaps surprising given the Cistercians' earlier reluctance to accept organs. The Benedictines at Dunfermline and Pluscarden, the Tironensians at Kelso and Arbroath, the Premonstratensians at Fearn and the Augustinians at St. Andrews soon followed suit.

Most references to organs in the cathedrals date from the 16th century. Some of the collegiate churches like Dunglass and both Trinity College and St. Giles in Edinburgh had them by the late 15th century, but the majority probably came later. They include Lochwinnoch (1504), Restalrig (1515), Seton (1544), and Biggar (1545). At Seton, it is recorded that the English army "spulyeit the kirk, and tuk away the bellis, organis and all other tursable thingis, and put thame in thair schippis..."

**1) Dunglass Collegiate Church, near Cockburnspath**

**2) Seton Collegiate Church, East Lothian**

We know very little about what the pre-Reformation organs of Scotland were like. However, a few general conclusions can be drawn. The Trinity College altarpiece by Hugo van der Goes in the National Gallery of Scotland may have been painted in the Low Countries, but the portraits of provost Sir Edward Bonkil kneeling in front of an organ and portraits of St. Andrew, James III and the young James IV scarcely have a Flemish aura about them. If the organ in the painting itself shows some Flemish influence, that need not be surprising in the Scottish context, as we know that Flemish builders worked here. The organs at Fearn Abbey were bought from Flanders in 1485 and the Bruges organ builder Joris de Buus received payment from the Scottish Exchequer in 1507. The organ painted by Hugo van der Goes does not, however, bear much resemblance to large Dutch town organs like the 1466 organ in Haarlem's Bavokerk, which can be seen in the painting by Pieter Saenredam also on display in the National Gallery. The individuality of the Trinity College organ is quite clear, even if the technical details are unreliable (since the painting shows signs of alteration). Then, as now, each organ was unique with its own size, design and specification suitable for its location and function. However, the altarpiece might have looked ridiculous if the organ depicted had been totally different from the real one standing near it in Trinity College Church. Bonkil bought an organ for this church, which stood on the present site of Edinburgh's Waverley Station, in 1466. It seems likely that the real organ might have been matched or at least complemented by the instrument in the picture.

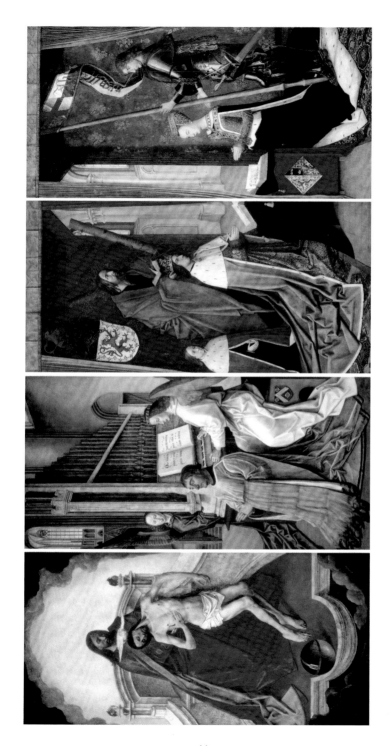

3) **The Trinity Altarpiece by Hugo van der Goes (1476) showing the organ and Sir Edward Bonkil, provost of Trinity College Church, Edinburgh.** Photo: reproduced with permission of the Royal Collections Trust/copyright Her Majesty Queen Elizabeth II 2017. Royal Collection Enterprises Ltd. RCIN 403260

11

We should not however assume that all organs in Scotland were as small as that painted by Hugo van der Goes. In 1517 the organ of Arbroath Abbey was described as *magnum et pulcherrimum* (large and very beautiful). At Linlithgow Palace eight great "glaspes" were required to bind a French-made organ to the wall in 1513. At Falkland Palace there was an "organ loft", in other words a location of some size designated for an organ. When an organ at St. Nicholas' Church, Aberdeen was put up for sale in 1591 the price demanded was high (£200) for "ane pair of organes, weill furnishit with their sang buird [soundboard] and all their tungis [pipes]". In 1542 at King's College, Aberdeen, there was "...in the loft of the organ, the organ itself, with an image of the holy virgin in the upper part thereof...", which to the Presbyterians who pulled the organ down exactly a hundred years later was merely "...ane pourtraicte of some woman..." Down the organ came and was described as "very intolerable".

Some organs, like King's College, Aberdeen, survived long after the Reformation; others, like Dunfermline Abbey, were swiftly destroyed in 1560. As the events of 1560 were relatively non-violent in comparison with later religious strife, musical canons of the various abbeys became ministers or readers in the reformed Kirk. Composers like John Angus of Dunfermline held the vicarage at Inverkeithing, and Andro Blackhall of Holyrood became minister at Inveresk. David Peebles continued at St. Andrews where he reluctantly composed four-part psalm settings for the Reformers. Part singing, now taught by the burgh authorities, continued to be widespread and it is not inconceivable that small organs were moved and used privately - though not in church - for practice. Before 1560 organs had not necessarily been used in the Mass for accompaniment; instead they are more often likely to have alternated with voices, giving the solo singers a rest from chanting. Thus after 1560, the very idea of the organ's use for accompaniment might not even have occurred to everyone and the justification for the destruction of organs (that only the human voice could legitimately praise God) may well have been both retrospective and theoretical. Despite the destruction of organs in some locations, serious music making undoubtedly continued to flourish in the late 16th century, but there were leaner and more destructive times to come.

The tragic religious and civil wars which blighted the 17th century, the resultant witch hunting, Darien and famine (leading to 1707) are reflected in the small number of pipe organs recorded. Most of the instruments related to the occasional Scottish sojourns of the Episcopalian monarchs and were thus located in the Chapel Royal at Stirling and at Holyrood. No objections were recorded to the erection of a secular organ played outside the Tron Kirk in Edinburgh when King Charles was crowned in 1633, but more than one attempt to erect an organ in the Chapel Royal at Holyrood was met with swift destruction. In 1687 James VII had another organ built at Holyrood but ".....the Mob at the Revolution pull'd it all to pieces, thinking that it smelt too rank of Popery..." Only a few secular organs survived the century, notably one recorded in inventories at Glamis Castle.

Surprisingly, the earliest surviving organs in the British Isles date from this lean century and two of them have Scottish connections. The earliest of these is a cabinet organ dating from 1602. An inscription reveals it was built by E. Hoffheimer, probably in the Low Countries, as the opening of Psalm 150 is inscribed in Flemish "*Loofe den Heere...*" (Praise the Lord...). The mechanism of the organ is straightforward, but the intricate Flemish design is an astonishing piece of carving, in which the initials of the organ's probable first owner, John Graham, 3rd Earl of Montrose are interwoven. This instrument is housed in Carisbrooke Castle in the Isle of Wight, where - according to tradition - it belonged to Charles I's sister Elizabeth, "the winter queen" of Bohemia. Given Montrose's political life under King James VI, one can easily see how this tradition may be correct. The carving of the wooden pipe stoppers in the detailed form of a Scottish thistle emblem is, to the best of my knowledge, unique. Pipe stoppers which plug pipes have been used in organs since at least the 15th century but their design, though varied, has generally been quite plain. On the Carisbrooke organ, the fronts of each key on the keyboard are decorated with thistles and the initials "J.G."

4) The organ made in 1602 for the Earl of Montrose, now
at Carisbrooke Castle, Isle of Wight
Photo: Carisbrooke Castle Museum

13

The other 17th century organ is found in Blair Castle, Perthshire with a date of 1630 and the initials "I.L." Although long thought to be the work of John Loosemore, who built an organ at Exeter Cathedral in 1665, the organ has a history which is yet to be convincingly established. It is complicated by the fact that here are references to more than one organ in Blair Castle during the 18th century. The present organ stands on a decorated walnut frame of late 17th century design, with two horizontal bellows, four wooden sets of pipes of different pitches and a set of reed pipes entitled "trumpet". The wooden pipes are very unusual in that they share walls with the neighbouring pipes, thus saving space and preventing casual or illicit removal.

**5) The organ of 1630 currently on display at Blair Castle**

A less intact example of an organ with 17th century pipes can be found at St. Adamnan's Episcopal Church, Duror. There have been different accounts of where the organ was located (Leith, Dundee, Arbroath, Aberdeen) before it arrived at the Rosse Episcopal Chapel in Fort William in the first half of the 19th century. It was moved to Duror in 1881. The organ has pipe markings attributable to "Father Smith" of London. Bernard Smith, or rather Schmidt, came from Bremen but worked in Hoorn, Holland before settling in London in 1667. In the 18th century there were additions to the Duror organ by John Donaldson of York, whose son became Reid Professor of Music at Edinburgh University. There were further alterations in the 19th century. The organ was fully restored in 1978 by Michael Macdonald of Glasgow. A photograph of the Duror organ appears on page 135.

After the (political) Restoration, Episcopacy began to flourish in Scotland again and around the year 1700 King's College, Aberdeen found itself with an Episcopalian congregation and pipe organ, "..the novelty of which brings each Lord's day a multitude of idle people.....to debauch in taverns after sermons..." The quelling of the 1715 Jacobite rising probably led to the termination of the congregation's tenure of the College chapel. In 1722 they reassembled in a new chapel, St. Paul's, Gallowgate, with an organ by Thomas Hollister whose style of case - photographed in 1866 immediately prior to the demolition of the chapel - suggests that at least the case might have come from the instrument at King's twenty years earlier. William Bristow of London completed the organ in St. Paul's in 1726. The 1866 photograph of this organ, appears with the listing of the organ on page 57.

Other London builders supplied organs for Episcopal chapels in Scotland throughout the 18th century. Banff had an organ before 1730, but the fact that the rector had sworn allegiance to King George did not prevent Cumberland's soldiers from setting chapel and organ on fire in the immediate aftermath of Culloden. Jordan of London provided a new organ for Banff in 1759. Dundee's "Qualified" chapel had an organ from Richard Bridge by 1758. John Snetzler (1710-85), who was born in Passau but was based in London from around 1740, supplied about eight organs for Scotland, mainly for chapels in Edinburgh, but some went to the west and others were subsequently moved north. Snetzler's organ of 1757 for the Lodge Canongate Kilwinning, Edinburgh survives in working order in its original location. An organ of 1778 by Samuel Green survives in the "Tartan Kirk", St. Mary's Episcopal Church, Carden Place, Aberdeen. This instrument was previously a house organ at Westhall near Oyne.

Domestic instruments like this were quite common at the time. Edward Rostrand of London supplied a small organ for Sir Archibald Grant at Monymusk in 1760, while John Byfield made an organ for Castle Grant at Grantown-on-Spey in 1766, recently sold from a museum at Finchcocks, Kent and now in France. John Donaldson of York built an organ for Altyre House, Forres in 1799. Instruments at Blair Castle and Glamis Castle have already been mentioned.

Native organ builders in Scotland were still rare, as in the 16th century, but they did exist. James Logan of Edinburgh was a spinet maker and organ tuner in the late 18th century, who produced at least one complete instrument. John Johnston of Edinburgh erected a temporary organ in St. Cecilia's Hall, Edinburgh in 1764, before becoming tuner of the Snetzler organ installed there in 1775. Richard Livingstone was another organ builder whose name features in the late 18th century Edinburgh scene. James Bristow, son of the William who completed the organ at St. Paul's, Aberdeen, settled for some years in Scotland and was organist of Montrose Episcopal Chapel around 1740. Although he rebuilt the Glamis Castle organ in the 1730s, and also worked as a "mathematician" surveying land near Forfar, he can scarcely be described as a native Scot. James Watt was however very much a native Scot, and is best known as developer of the steam engine, but he also built several pipe organs. One attributed to him is housed in Glasgow's museum store at Nitshill, after a long spell in the People's Palace Museum on Glasgow Green.

A significant figure to arrive on the Edinburgh scene was an Irishman called Samuel Letts, who, according to Sir John Dalyell of the Binns, "resorted hither" about 1802. Letts had trained with Thomas Elliot in London and features in Edinburgh Street Directories from 1802-1810. Two organs by Letts survive, one in Forest Green in Surrey, recently restored, and the other in a private house in Norham, Northumberland.

Andrew Wood (1765-1829) was the founder of a succession of music businesses in Edinburgh (Muir Wood, Wood Small, Wood & Co.) which manufactured all kinds of keyboard instruments throughout the 19th century. Wood had some practical training in organ building from both James Logan and Samuel Letts. Wood's son, John Muir Wood, perhaps better known as an amateur photographer, moved the retail side of the music business to Glasgow around 1850. Wood's earlier firms provided an opening for a young organ builder who heralded and developed what was to become a golden age in Scottish organ building: James Bruce (1786-1856). Bruce played a pivotal role in re-establishing the pipe organ as an object of wonder in all Scotland's major cities. That he did so was achieved not so much by the historical accident of being in the right place at the right time, but by an extraordinary talent and standards of workmanship arguably equal to any British organ builder of the period.

James Bruce was born in 1786 in Edinburgh, the son of a merchant. He lived in the Calton area of the city all his life. As a tuner with the Wood firm, however, he travelled widely throughout Scotland and the north of England and must have seen the new organ installed by John Avery of London in Carlisle Cathedral in 1807. This organ was designed with the newly fashionable Gothic-revival style of case and part of the Carlisle structure can still be seen in Hexham Abbey, to where the Avery organ was moved in 1857. Bruce adopted and used this elaborate Gothic style of case throughout his career. The quality of his pipework and mechanism - all manufactured "in house" at his workshop in Amphion Place - can still be judged today from his various surviving instruments. Bruce built the vast majority of new organs in Scotland in the first half of the nineteenth century. By contrast English builders such as Thomas Elliot and Henry Lincoln provided only a few. Nearly all of the Episcopal and RC chapels of Edinburgh, Glasgow, Dundee, Aberdeen, Inverness and Dumfries had organs built and installed by James Bruce. His reputation extended beyond Scotland, and he made several instruments for Northern England and Ireland. Of course, only those built for locations in Scotland are listed in this publication, and up to 1840 these all appear as the work of the parent firms for whom Bruce worked: Muir Wood, Wood Small and Small Bruce. Bruce died in 1856, and the goodwill of his business passed to fellow organ builder John Renton, a Fifer who may have trained with him in Edinburgh. Renton died in 1880 but his son, also John, continued the business in Edinburgh until 1895. After that a branch of the Renton firm continued in Glasgow until 1930 and work was also carried out in Australia. About six organs by Renton survive in recognisable form, including two in Melbourne and two in Dorset.

The finest surviving Bruce organ is located in St. Gregory's RC Chapel, Preshome near Buckie. In 1697 Preshome became the residence of the first post-Reformation Catholic bishop in Scotland. The present chapel - "the first Catholic church in Scotland to look like a church" (as a local RC guidebook describes it), dates from 1788 with a chancel designed in 1896 by P. P. Pugin. The organ was built by James Bruce in 1820. Apart from very minor alterations in the 1890s, this organ has remained exactly as it was built. It deserves to be listed as a national monument and to receive sympathetic minimal restoration. It would be marvellous if this could be achieved for the organ's bicentenary. To see and hear a properly restored Bruce organ, however, one must for the moment visit Holland, where the notion of restoring and maintaining such artefacts to a high standard is not quite so unusual as it is in Scotland. The instrument in question dates from about 1825 and can now be found in the Grote Kerk, Monnickendam, a short distance north of Amsterdam.

**6) The organ built in 1820 by James Bruce for St. Gregory's RC Church, Preshome, near Buckie**

**7) The Bruce organ of c. 1825 in the Grote Kerk, Monnickendam, The Netherlands.**
Photo: Gerard Verloop

Bruce's only serious rival was David Hamilton (1800-63), son of a piano-making wright from Musselburgh. Hamilton studied music and organ building in the Netherlands and Saxony (the only early 19th century British organ builder to train abroad), returning to Edinburgh in 1824 to turn his father's piano making business into a thriving organ building and music selling concern. His organs were highly individual, voiced on typically low Saxon wind pressures with pipes of thinly cast tin, producing a refined silvery tone. He introduced full "German" pedalboards and keyboards to Scotland (virtually universal now) and claimed to have invented the pneumatic lever for lightening key touch before it was patented by C. S. Barker in England. Hamilton was organist of St. John's Episcopal Church, Edinburgh for twenty years and wrote some interesting articles on music and organ building. Few of David Hamilton's organs survive intact, his largest being the surprisingly quiet three manual organ of 1845 in St. Mary's Episcopal Church, Dalkeith. One unusual feature of this organ is that it is still powered by a water engine, installed by David Hamilton's nephews, Charles and Frederick, in 1891. That this organ is so quiet in volume may have reflected the wishes of the patron, the Duke of Buccleuch. Hamilton's slightly altered instrument at All Saints Church, Woodhead, Fyvie is slightly more forceful in tone, perhaps reflecting more closely the organ choruses he had heard in Saxony. Like Bruce, Hamilton made all his own organ components, including metal pipes, in his workshop. From 1835 to 1863, all Hamilton's metal pipes were made of tin in the German style, instead of the usual alloy of tin and lead more widely used in Britain. From 1828-38 the Hamilton workshop was at St. Andrew Square, Edinburgh, but from 1838-88 it was based at 116 George Street.

Other early 19th century Scottish builders like Robert Mirrlees of Glasgow, Joseph Wishart of Aberdeen, and some Edinburgh-based amateurs were partly dependent on components made elsewhere. These included John Croall, a coaching proprietor in Edinburgh, and William Townsend,

17

primarily a harp maker, both of whom produced organs of quality. Amateur organ building also thrived throughout North East Scotland from about 1780, and one or two surviving instruments reflect this strong tradition, notably the small organ in Fraserburgh RC Church. Others are recorded in the lists which follow and the tradition may well have inspired George Ashdown Audsley, born in Elgin in 1838, to write his comprehensive two volume practical guide *The Art of Organ Building* (1905) after emigrating to the United States.

What is remarkable about the achievements of builders like Bruce and Hamilton is that their church instruments were inevitably confined to churches of minority denominations, particularly the Episcopal and Roman Catholic Churches. From the late 16th century until 1864, instrumental accompaniment to praise had not been tolerated in any of the Presbyterian churches in Scotland. In certain locations, at different times, organs were allowed within Presbyterian church buildings, as long as they were not heard in services of worship. The Earl of Fife for example was able to install his own organ in Macduff Parish Church in the early 1800s, and presumably use it for practice. The Glasgow Sacred Music Institution was also allowed to erect an organ for its own use in Glasgow Cathedral in the early 1800s, but only when St. Andrew's Parish Church in Glasgow tried to use an organ *for worship* in 1807, did potent controversy break out. Roxburgh Place Relief Church in Edinburgh had a similar experience in 1829. In both of these cases the individual churches were in favour of the innovation of instrumental accompaniment, but their respective Presbyteries were strongly against. Presbyterian authority prevailed and use of these instruments soon ceased. The organs were subsequently removed. Unaccompanied singing continued in all Presbyterian churches for another thirty years. It was in the year 1863 that the Rev. Robert Lee tried to use instrumental accompaniment for Presbyterian worship at Greyfriars Kirk, Edinburgh. This time the General Assembly of the Church of Scotland did debate the issue and decided to allow individual Presbyteries to make up their own minds. However, the controversy continued for decades and many a local "stooshie" was comprehensively reported in the Scottish newspapers.

The first Church of Scotland organ to be officially opened for use in worship in a Church of Scotland building was at Anderston Parish Church, Glasgow, on 15th January 1865. It was built by the eminent firm of William Hill of London and survives today in largely original condition, though moved in the early 1970s to St. Bride's Episcopal Church in neighbouring Hyndland. A photograph of the organ in its original location appears under "Glasgow Anderston & St. Peter's" in the alphabetical lists which follow.

After Anderston, St. Giles Parish Church at Dundonald, Ayrshire opened its organ on 3rd February 1865. It was built by James Hamilton of Edinburgh while his younger brother Thomas was busy completing the organ for Greyfriars Old Church, Edinburgh, where the organ controversy had originally been stirred up. The Greyfriars organ was opened on 22nd April 1865. Two organs by Peter Conacher were opened in June 1865: Duns and Skelmorlie, parish churches, though the latter had been completed some weeks earlier.

For the record, the Scottish Episcopal Church used organs from about 1700, the Roman Catholic Church from 1814, the Congregational Church from about 1853, the Church of Scotland from 1865, and the United Presbyterian Church from 1872. The Free Church of Scotland sanctioned the use of organs in 1883, but it was a year or two before the first instrument was erected. The latter two denominations came together in 1900 as the United Free Church and it in turn united with the established Church of Scotland in 1929.

The flourishing organ building trade within Scotland up to 1865 ought to have been well placed to meet the demand for new instruments which gradually mushroomed from that year. David Hamilton's younger brothers James and Thomas continued to produce new instruments after

David's death in 1863, and James's sons Charles and Frederick continued the business until the Second World War. John Renton's family also continued to build what were by now very old fashioned instruments from his workshop at Bank Street, Edinburgh. Alex Mirrlees greatly expanded his family's organ building business in Glasgow, creating facilities for the manufacture of all components. Good examples of his instruments survive in Clydebank and Greenock. It is difficult to estimate how many new organs the Mirrlees firm built, as many small instruments from the earlier years are difficult to track down, but there were about twenty five larger new organs built between the 1865 landmark "organ emancipation" year and the First World War. Alex N. Mirrlees and Adam Mirrlees continued the firm until 1948.

8) The organ at Colliston Parish Church, Angus, probably by James Hamilton, c.1875

9) The organ at Holy Redeemer RC Church, Clydebank, by J. & A. Mirrlees 1867.
Photograph: Michael Macdonald

Sadly, as it transpired, these Scottish builders could not, or did not want to, cope with the huge upsurge in demand, or indeed changes in musical style. The organs of Hamilton, Mirrlees and John Renton remained mildly voiced on quite low wind pressures throughout the 19th century, and this suited some churches. Many other clients however now preferred the more strident sounds of the national UK builders, which soon dominated the market. Some of the most prolific of these UK organ builders were in fact born in Scotland. For example, Henry Bryceson of London was born in Perth in 1775 and a branch of his firm remained in Edinburgh for a short time (the barrel organ at Portmore House is from that branch). Both Peter and James Conacher were born in Bankfoot, Perthshire in the 1820s and may have trained initially with Hamilton in Edinburgh, where they initially tried to set up business. The Conacher firms at Huddersfield, along with Forster & Andrews of Hull, exported far more organs to Scotland in the late 19th century than all the local Scottish builders managed to produce together. Each of these two firms made at least 150 organs for Scottish locations between 1865 and the 1920s. Many of these survive in original condition, for example the 1872 Conacher in the former Parish Church at Forgue near Huntly (hand blown until the 21st century) and the 1894 Forster & Andrews in Ayton Church, Berwickshire. Bryceson, in successive partnerships with Ellis, Morten and Taylor, built a smaller number of organs for Scotland, but of excellent tonal quality. Of these Aberfoyle Parish Church (1887) is now the best survival, as the instrument formerly at North Morningside is no longer intact and that at St. Andrew's, Fort William is currently out of commission.

Between 1850 and 1930 there were at least 1784 new pipe organs built in Scotland of which 1005 were partly financed by the Dunfermline-born steel magnate Andrew Carnegie. Usually Carnegie paid 50% of the cost of new organs and their installation, sometimes more. Altogether he financed a total of 7689 pipe organs throughout the English-speaking world, including British colonies in Africa. We should remember his philanthropy and the toil of the American steel workers who made this possible. Of the 1784 organs, only about 300 were built by organ builders with headquarters in Scotland. About 1400 were built by English builders, though some had more northerly workshops. Wadsworth of Manchester for example carried out a large amount of new work from a branch in Aberdeen. A healthy number of small "Waddies" can still be found in good playing condition in the North East of Scotland. Most of these owe their creation to the renowned John Wardle, Wadsworth's manager in Aberdeen and organist of St. James's Episcopal Church, Stonehaven, for fifty years. Wardle will soon be commemorated in a permanent exhibition in the church.

**10) The 1901 Wadsworth at the former church of Drumblade, near Huntly, with console at the side**

20

Although Carnegie paid 50% of the costs of pipe organ installation, the remaining 50% was in many cases not entirely funded out of the lean pockets of parishioners. Local landowners, lairds and industrialists often stepped in. The Coats family of Paisley for example paid for numerous instruments in that town, both for churches and secular locations. The family's own house organ of 1888, made in a French style by August Gern, can still be seen in a hall of Paisley Museum. Originally this organ spoke into two separate rooms in Woodside House, with pipe facades in different architectural styles facing Janus-like in both directions, similar to the organ of Windsor Castle destroyed by fire in 1992. Gern was born in Berlin and worked with the esteemed Cavaillé-Coll in Paris before settling in London in 1866.

**11) The 1888 organ by August Gern in Paisley Museum**

Another continental firm active at a slightly later period in Scotland was E. F. Walcker, from Ludwigsburg, who produced over ninety organs for Scotland, far more than they produced for the rest of the UK. Many of these were for small country churches, for which the firm's Dulsannel model organs were designed, but others like the new organ for St. Columba's Gaelic Church, Glasgow (1905) were built on a large scale. The firm continues to restore and service organs in Scotland today.

The influence of continental builders and organ building styles was widespread. We have already seen how David Hamilton of Edinburgh eagerly absorbed German tonal styles and designs. Later British builders also did so. Two of the finest London-based builders of the Victorian era were Thomas C. Lewis (1833-1915) and "Father" Henry Willis (1821-1901). Both absorbed French and German influences, but the style of their respective instruments was very different, Lewis preferring the bright, clear chorus textures of the German style and Willis more readily accepting the high wind pressures and mellower sounds of Cavaillé-Coll's French instruments. Competition between these two major firms was intense and at times bitter. This reached a peak in 1897 when Lewis published a pamphlet entitled "A Protest against unmusical Tone in Organs" in which he wholeheartedly attacked Willis's organ building style.

Lewis trained first as an architect and is likely to have designed some of the fine casework which adorns his surviving instruments, like the unaltered example in Broughton St. Mary's Church, Edinburgh (1882). By this time, Lewis had diversified into bell-founding and had made both bells and organ for the Coltness Memorial Church, Newmains in 1878. This organ survives, though the bells have now been sold. Church, organ and bells were endowed by the Houldsworth family, who were both local landowners and iron magnates. The family also commissioned an organ from Lewis for Coltness House in 1881, which was moved to Motherwell Baptist Church in 1951. One of T.C. Lewis's finest organs was built for the St. Andrew's Hall, Glasgow in 1877, but it was destroyed by fire with the halls in 1962. The brewing magnate John Courage provided financial support for the firm and in the 1890s Lewis himself was gradually frozen out of day-to-day involvement. The firm became "Lewis & Co.". It was in that guise that the firm built a large organ for the Glasgow Exhibition in 1901, which was moved the following year a short distance into Kelvingrove Art Gallery. Restored by Mander in 1989, this instrument is of outstanding musical quality and can be heard on weekdays at lunchtime and on Sunday afternoons. See a photograph on page 219.

**12) The 1878 T.C. Lewis organ in the Coltness Memorial Church, Newmains, Lanarkshire**

**13) The 1892 Lewis organ in St. Michael's, Inveresk, Musselburgh**

In the east of Scotland, Lewis & Co.'s instrument in St. Michael's Church, Inveresk (1892) is also of note and is featured on the Edinburgh Society of Organists' triple CD (2010). Throughout its existence, the Lewis firm built about sixty organs in Scotland. Richard Smith (1849-1926) was the firm's Scottish representative, and although he advertised as an independent builder in Glasgow from 1889, he continued also to act as agent for Lewis & Co. Smith and the Lewis firm seem to have co-existed happily. Smith's firm was very successful and continued until his death. His finest surviving organ is at Dennistoun Blackfriars Church (1902), now owned by an independent denomination.

Turning to Lewis's rival, "Father" Henry Willis, we are lucky to find various unaltered examples of his work still performing sterling service throughout Scotland. The earliest of these, now restored in Knightswood, Glasgow was originally built in 1866 for Townhead Church. Playfair's unique St. Stephen's Church in Edinburgh (now owned by a theatre director) houses a splendid original example of an 1880 Willis in resonant octagonal acoustics which were more friendly to music than the spoken word of its various ministers. A clutch of churches in Monklands and central Aberdeenshire also boast good examples of organs by Father Willis, the doyen of Aberdeenshire Willises being the 1881 instrument in Haddo House. The town of Largs has two unaltered "Father" Willis organs of 1892; the Clark Memorial Church has a typical Willis design, while St. Columba's instrument was influenced by the views of the renowned organist of Glasgow Cathedral, A.L. Peace. As a keen yachtsman, Willis must have enjoyed his visits to Largs and also Dunbar, where he built an organ for the Episcopal church in 1896 which survives unscathed.

Rather unexpectedly, the firms of Willis and Lewis amalgamated at the close of the First World War, and although Willis inevitably came to dominate the partnership, a good original example of the firm's combined skills can still be found at St.Ninian's Church, Nairn (1924).

Other Victorian firms which supplied organs for Scotland included Brindley & Foster of Sheffield, whose large instrument (1913) in the Freemasons' Hall in Edinburgh was restored by Forth Pipe Organs in 2009, J. J. Binns of Leeds made over 70 new organs for Scotland and restored or rebuilt others. The firm's robustly-built organs mostly survive unaltered wherever they were built, and fine examples survive at Skelmorlie (1905), Dunfermline St. Leonard's (1910), Hawick Trinity (1911) and Galston (1913). Harrisons of Durham built about thirty church organs in Scotland, notably the three manual all-mechanical organ at Beith (1886) and the small three manual pneumatic organ at Peebles St. Peter's (1909), before completing their largest organ in Scotland at the Caird Hall, Dundee in 1923.

The 20th century saw various firms springing up, often formed by employees of the national firms who decided to branch out on their own in Scotland.

Joseph Brook (1851-1914) established himself in Glasgow in the late 1870s, taking John Spring initially as a partner. Brook's father William had also been an organ builder. Joseph trained with Peter Conacher in Huddersfield and then was employed by Gray & Davison in London, where he tuned the Crystal Palace organ. Most of his new instruments (around fifty altogether) were located in Strathclyde, but of the half dozen in the East of Scotland, an original example at Crichton (1899) is a rare survival and was restored by Willis in 2012 with the inclusion of a redundant Cornopean from Brook's first organ (1879) at St. Ninian's Episcopal Church, Pollokshields, Glasgow. From 1890 the firm used pneumatic action and by 1891 was already experimenting with electric action, which however it only used on two organs. Joseph Brook's son John and grandson (also Joseph) continued the firm until the mid-1950s, carrying out much overhaul and rebuilding work, also operating a lucrative horsehair business at Busby. The firm was absorbed by Willis, who had to complete one of the firm's last installations at Craigneuk, Wishaw in 1953.

Other small firms of organ builders had sprung up in Glasgow at various times. T.W. Gardiner dealt with both piano and organ maintenance and he appears in the directories from 1835 to the 1860s. He had a partner by the name of Condi for a short period. James and Samuel Hay feature from 1853 to the late 1890s, but they dealt mainly with harmoniums. Throughout much of the 19th century, "organ" in church records often meant simply a harmonium or a reed organ. This has led to one or two erroneous entries in previous lists.

Ernest Lawton (1869-1947) trained with Brindley & Foster in Sheffield, then worked with Wadsworth under John Wardle at the firm's Aberdeen branch, before establishing his own firm in 1898 in Aberdeen. Like Brook, he used mechanical action at first, and these instruments were successful, judging by his early organs like Rhynie (1899), Barry (1902), New Pitsligo (1904) and Keithhall (1907). His output was remarkable: about 120 new organs in forty years, and many renovations. The 1923 organ in Bon Accord Free Church in Aberdeen attracted interest latterly, although it was not used in services after the Free Church regained ownership of the building. It could be heard in a short demonstration each Sunday after worship had been concluded. Lawton exported many instruments abroad, to Africa and New Zealand where he had an able partner in Donald Osborne.

The prolific firm of Arthur Ingram, based in Edinburgh, grew out of the parent company owned by Eustace Ingram in London, while Eustace Ingram jn. established his own branch in Hereford. Arthur Ingram's branch started in Edinburgh in 1894 and continued until it was absorbed by Rushworth & Dreaper in 1956. Throughout these years, the Ingram firms built about 140 new or largely new organs in Scotland, most of them with pneumatic action. The musical quality of their new instruments could be variable. Of some instruments, like the 1912 organ in the True Jesus Church in Edinburgh (formerly St. Luke's), the firm was justifiably proud. In addition to that there were many overhauls and rebuilds, generally carried out to a high standard. Their records have probably not survived. Most, but by no means all, of their work was carried out in the east of Scotland.

**14) The 1905 Ingram organ at St. Mary of Wedale Parish Church, Stow; it shows at this period the influence of the parent firm, Eustace Ingram.** Photograph by Andrew Caskie

The firm of Andrew Watt of Glasgow operated largely in the west of Scotland and started around 1900. Watt had twenty years' experience with J. & A. Mirrlees and produced around seventy new organs. Good early examples survive at Stewarton John Knox Church (1903) and one originally in Bishopton UF Church (1902) now in Lutten, the Netherlands. The firm survived until 1965 with a large number of overhauls and rebuilds to its credit. Many well-known organ builders worked for Watt, notably Bert Meek, James Mackenzie and Michael Macdonald. The Watt firm was taken over by J.W. Walker.

Like Richard Smith, George Brooksby (1875-1959) had been the local representative for Lewis & Co., but he branched out on his own when Willis and Lewis merged (1919), partly because the new firm cut his wages! Brooksby continued until 1948, when the goodwill of his business passed to Hill Norman & Beard.

David Hume was Richard Smith's tuner and became independent from 1912 until 1948. His assistant was Robert Inglis or Ingles, who continued the business until 1959, when it was absorbed by Rushworth & Dreaper

Harry Hilsdon (1873-1935), Scottish manager of Norman & Beard, was another figure who became independent and based himself in Glasgow from 1910, employing a number of staff from Norman & Beard such as Hadlow Myers. His firm built about forty new organs between 1912 and 1931, plus a number of cinema and theatre organs. The firm was later managed by Wilfred Southward and Hilsdon's daughter, Mrs. Mabel Sinclair. It continued to carry out much overhaul and rebuilding work until it was taken over by the short-lived firm of Wood Wordsworth in 1976.

Kirtley & Blossom were agents for Hill Norman & Beard who also carried out work independently. Blossom's name appears as early as 1916, and the firm continued until Kirtley's death in 1953.

Another builder to emerge from the Norman & Beard stable was Charles Percy Scovell (1873-1949). Originally from a naval family living on the Isle of Wight, Scovell trained first with Browne of Canterbury and then joined the radical firm of Robert Hope-Jones (1859-1914), whose new organs for the McEwan Hall and St. Cuthbert's Parish Church, Edinburgh, he helped to install in 1897 and 1899. Hope-Jones's firm was disbanded in 1899 and it was at that stage that Scovell joined Norman & Beard, where he met Thomas William Lewis (probably not related to T. C. Lewis, though there are one or two interesting connections). Scovell settled in Edinburgh in 1901 and Lewis joined him on the south side of Edinburgh in 1902. The partnership of Scovell & Lewis existed from 1903-09, though Lewis took his family back to Bristol in 1907. From 1909 to 1945 Scovell traded under his own name. From 1933 Scovell took as a young partner David Gay (1912-2004), whose father provided some finance for the firm. Scovell (with or without Lewis) produced about twenty five new organs and carried out many rebuilds. The Scovell firm merged into the Willis firm from 1945. David Gay later joined Rushworth & Dreaper as the firm's Dundee representative.

John Miller of Dundee (1857-1941) also had an association with Hope-Jones when the two of them collaborated over rebuilding an organ in 1894 for enthusiast J. Martin White at Balruddery, near Dundee. Miller's early training was with John Stringer of Hanley, Staffordshire, whose work at Queen Street Church, Broughty Ferry he had observed in 1876. After a spell with Stringer, Miller moved to work with J.W. Walker. At the 1881 census he was lodging with another slightly older Angus organ builder, Robert Scott (1840-1911) at Stoke-on-Trent, near where Stringer had set up shop. The organ builder Frederick Holt, after a productive spell in Edinburgh, had also moved to this area in 1876.

Robert Scott's training (along with that of his brother William) is slightly clearer, as both brothers were lodging in Huddersfield at the 1871 census. An association with Conacher of Huddersfield thus seems likely to have developed.

Both Miller and Scott started their respective Scottish-based businesses around 1884. Miller was at first based briefly in Stranraer and formed a brief partnership with Thomas Casson, a Welsh banker interested in radical new mechanisms, whom he may have met at Walker's. After moving to Perth, Casson and Miller jointly produced four organs, including that of Perth City Hall, later rebuilt and now in Australia. After going their separate ways, Casson became known in Edwardian times for his little "Positive" organs which still serve some country churches. Miller, despite his brief involvement with Hope-Jones, relied on more traditional technology, producing over fifty new organs, and carrying out rebuilds, largely in Dundee, Angus, north Fife and Perthshire between 1887 and 1932. Scott's business continued for ten years in Dundee, producing about half a dozen new organs, at which point (1894) Miller moved from Perth and took over Scott's Dundee premises at 7 Sea Wynd. Miller was later based at North Lindsay Street and latterly at Caldrum Street, with works at Dens Road. Like many organ builders, Miller enjoyed longevity, and died at the age of 84.

In addition to Robert Scott and John Miller, a third Dundonian was active - Allan Watson (1867-1950) who probably trained with Conacher, and took Ernest Conacher as partner, first in Perth, then in Dundee. His organs built in 1913 for Dundee Steeple Church and Wormit UF Church are described as the work of "Watson & Conacher". Although the partnership was wound up in 1915, he appeared on his own account in the 1896 Dundee directory and continued to be listed on his own at a business address until 1936, after which his home address in Broughty Ferry was used until his death in 1950 at the age of 83. Watson also played the double bass. A.M. Coutts, the Edinburgh organ historian (1873-1936), lists six new organs by Watson, all in Tayside, built between 1909 and 1926. To what extent the three builders collaborated at different times is still to be researched.

Frank Roberts also appears as an organ builder in Dundee directories from 1875 and had been with both Gray & Davison in London and Forster & Andrews in Hull prior to that period.

Henry Wellby worked with Gray & Davison at Usk, and worked with the Hill firm, before settling in Edinburgh as both organ builder and janitor of the Reid Concert Hall at Edinburgh University. He also is known to have worked with D. & T. Hamilton. Two of Wellby's sons, Charles and Herbert continued to operate the firm, but after Charles' emigration to South America, Herbert continued on his own. The firm was eventually absorbed by Scovell in 1942. There was little new work, but the firm was kept busy with maintenance.

Other builders have emerged from the larger Scottish firms at different times. In the early stages of the 19th century John Christie had a close association with James Bruce but also operated on his own account, both in Edinburgh and Glasgow, before and after Bruce's death. A rare picture of one of Christie's own organs can be seen in an R.H. Walker advertisement in *Musical Opinion,* October 1954. Will Ewart operated briefly during the 1870s in Edinburgh and one little organ by him survives in New Kilpatrick Church, Bearsden.

After the demise of the second "generation" of the Hamilton firm in the late 1880s, several builders emerged briefly as independent concerns in Edinburgh. One was the Hamilton brothers' nephew Alexander Macdonald (1824-98), who did his best to prolong the old style, while his much younger cousins Charles & Frederick Hamilton moved radically into the Edwardian era. Another former Hamilton employee was Herbert King, who operated in Edinburgh from 1890 to 1911, carrying out maintenance and rebuilding work. His only known surviving instrument (1892) was located at Dalry Congregational Church, Edinburgh, until 2005, when the church closed. The organ included older material from the 1840s, and was dismantled and stored. Despite its quality, it has proved difficult to relocate.

William B. Gledhill operated from 1899 to 1926 and two of his organs survive at Falkirk Camelon and Kenmore Church, near Aberfeldy. However, his name appears in various other entries in the lists which follow. The fact that he carried out further work to the D.& T. Hamilton organ in Stockbridge Church, already drastically rebuilt by C. & F. Hamilton, suggests that he may have emerged from that stable.

Arthur Catlin appears in the Edinburgh Street Directories in 1910 at Causewayside, very near to the workshop of Scovell & Lewis, which may suggest a former association with Scovell. He indicates that he had previously worked for 25 years with different firms. In 1912 he moved a short distance to Duncan Street and remained in the directories until 1926, advertising as a supplier of organ parts.

Not all the organs built in the Victorian and Edwardian eras were destined for churches. Each large city and many larger towns had civic organs of note. In Glasgow, the City Hall and St. Andrew's Hall had major instruments which no longer exist but the magnificent Lewis organ in Kelvingrove Art Gallery, already mentioned, survives. Dundee's Caird Hall Harrison of 1923 was saved from possible annihilation in 1990 by a dedicated group of enthusiasts who maintain a flourishing *Friends of the Caird Hall Organ*. FOCHO arranges events and supports the instrument in all sorts of ways. In Edinburgh the Usher Hall organ of 1914 has proved itself worthy following restoration in 2003 and subsequent appointment of Dr. John Kitchen as City Organist. In Aberdeen the Music Hall has a large Willis dating back to 1854, but once again it is in need of overhaul. There survives still a large three manual Binns organ in Aberdeen's Cowdray Hall (1925), not heard properly since the 1960s. As mentioned above, Perth City Hall's organ has now gone, but has been resurrected and enlarged in Melbourne, Australia. Ayr Town Hall's Lewis organ of 1904 works, but awaits full restoration. The Town Halls of Alloa, Greenock, Paisley and Coatbridge once boasted fine organs, but these have now disappeared. Cinema and theatre organs, once ubiquitous, can only now be seen in a few dedicated locations at Pollokshaws, Summerlee and Greenlaw. A few large country houses still retain interesting working organs, for example Scone Palace (Elliot 1813), Birkhill House in north Fife (Townsend c. 1850), Cluny Castle in Aberdeenshire (Forster & Andrews 1873), Haddo House (Willis 1881), Skibo Castle (Brindley 1904), Manderston House (Aeolian self-playing organ 1905), Fyvie Castle (Norman & Beard 1905), Mount Stuart, Bute (three organs), Beaufort Castle (Norman & Beard 1910), Marchmont House (Hill 1918), and Glencruitten House, Oban (Ingram & Welte 1928).

The depression of the 1930s, the Second World War, loss of craftsmen and financial stringency led to a severe decline in organ building. From 1939, when the superb Rushworth & Dreaper organ in the Church of the Holy Rude, Stirling, was constructed, until the 1970s there were very few new pipe organs constructed in Scotland. Apart from financial stringency after the Second World War, there was a Government ban on the manufacture of new material in the organ building trade, which meant that relocation of organs from redundant churches happily became more prevalent for a while. Churches in Wishaw, Jedburgh, Inverness and Kirkconnel (amongst others) benefitted from "new" organs during the 1950s, while the large national firms continued to provide a comprehensive maintenance service throughout most of Scotland. The Hill Norman & Beard firm was based in the west with James Wardrop and Hugh Tomlinson in succession as their representatives. Rushworth & Dreaper was based in the east, managed by Ivor Norridge from 1976 to 1999. Until the 1980s the Willis firm remained strong with a tuning service operated by Nelson Keeys in Glasgow and by John Dunbar in Edinburgh. J.W. Walker absorbed a number of craftsmen from other firms like Watt in the mid-1960s, but with changes in that firm, a number of smaller enterprises sprang up soon after. Robert Goldsmith (ex-Walker and Rushworth's Scottish manager) started in Edinburgh in 1972 and retired in 2012, and David Loosley (ex-Walker) began in 1974 and has been based in Stirling. Michael Macdonald (ex-Watt and Walker) commenced in Glasgow in 1975 and his son Andrew continues to operate the firm today. Ronald Smith (ex-Willis and Rushworth) operated from

1968-1999 in Edinburgh and Cleish. Sandy Edmonstone (ex-Walker) operated independently in Perthshire from 1983 to 2013. Paul Miller (ex-Hill Norman & Beard) has been based independently near Falkirk since 1998. James Mackenzie (ex-Watt) operated for a remarkable fifty four years (1960-2014) as an independent organ builder in Glasgow. Neil Richerby (ex-Brunzema) has built sixty five new mechanical organs from his workshop in Oldhamstocks since 1983, under the name Lammermuir Pipe Organs. David Stark of Kelso took early retirement as a teacher to concentrate on organ building from 1995. He has carried out various renovations and transplants.

The universities spearheaded a welcome revival of new work. Aberdeen University began with a Harrison in King's College in 1959 and added a small organ by R.H. Walker in Marischal College in 1972. St. Andrews followed with a large organ by Hradtezky, Austria in 1974, Dundee installed a small organ by Collins in 1978 and Edinburgh completed the trend with an organ in 17th century style by Ahrend of Leer, north Germany in the same year. Glasgow University already had three organs. Strathclyde discarded a large Harrison organ from the Barony Hall, but after experiencing an electronic instrument commissioned a brand new pipe organ by Kögler of St. Florian in 2009. Aberdeen University replaced the 1959 Harrison organ in King's College with a new organ by Aubertin, France, in 2004.

Churches began to install some major new instruments in the 1980s and engaged firms from all over Europe. These included St. Andrew's & St. George's, Edinburgh (Wells Kennedy, 1984), Greyfriars Kirk, Edinburgh (Peter Collins, 1990), St. Mary's Haddington (Lammermuir, 1990), Dunblane Cathedral (Flentrop, 1990), Palmerston Place, Edinburgh (Wells Kennedy, 1992), St. Giles, Edinburgh (Rieger, 1992), Sherbrooke St. Gilbert's, Glasgow (Lammermuir 1997) and Canongate Kirk, Edinburgh (Frobenius, 1998). Loretto School in Musselburgh installed a new organ by Kenneth Jones of Bray, Ireland in 1989.

15) The organ by Lammermuir Pipe Organs of Oldhamstocks under construction at St. Mary's Parish Church, Haddington in 1990

This amazing revival of new organs in part arose from bad experiences of some of the less successful adaptations of older organs during the 1960s, a problem not peculiar to Scotland. Extra stops had often been grafted on to older instruments without regard to their musical character or technical limitations. This was often done at the behest of over-zealous organists and at the expense of essential overhaul work to the organ's existing mechanism. The results were not only poor, but may have ultimately prevented these instruments obtaining restoration grants which became available in the 1990s. There were two consequences of the unsatisfactory work carried out in the 1960s and the failure of the Scottish organ building trade to regulate itself. One was that the

Scottish Federation of Organists (known as the SFO long before the Serious Fraud Office was established) set up an advisory group to regulate standards, offer advice to churches and to try to find homes for good redundant organs. This became the official advisory group for the Church of Scotland in 1986 and it continues today.

The other was an attempt to form a Scottish Historic Organs Trust (SHOT) on the initiative of the late Hugh Ross (1950-95). Ross had bought Leithen Lodge in Peeblesshire, and number of small organs by Scottish builders were installed there. He had grandiose plans for building a large barn up the Leithen valley to accommodate larger instruments, but financial difficulties and his early death in 1995 brought these plans to a close, although SHOT continues to operate on a limited basis. One useful initiative was a project to list Scottish organs along the lines of architectural listing, and this project is complete. Listing categories are included in the lists which follow.

Such initiatives are badly needed. While electronic organs often replaced pipe organs in poor condition from the 1960s, we have more recently been faced with situations where perfectly good pipe organs are being enthusiastically thrown out in favour of the latest digital instruments. "We had great fun breaking the organ up", as one Edinburgh church quite openly declared. The worst case to report in recent years has been Lyle Kirk (St. Paul's) in Greenock where a tonally unaltered three manual Father Willis was scrapped in favour of a cheap electronic with blatant disregard for the advice endorsed by the Church of Scotland. The sales techniques used by the digital representatives are slick and the apparent range of stops impressive, but the aftercare is at times poor and the sameness of the sound soon palls on the ear. Many churches have had cause to regret discarding their pipe organs; some have reversed the process by installing redundant pipe organs which are often available free of charge. Scoonie Kirk in Leven brought its outstanding Gern organ of 1884 back into use after using an electronic for twenty years. The redundant organ option has not been pursued as often as it might be, especially in recent years.

On the maintenance front, there are welcome signs that after a lean period, a few more younger tuners are establishing themselves in Scotland. Forth Pipe Organs emerged from the ashes of the national firm of Rushworth & Dreaper in 2002 and remain the largest concern in Scotland with about half a dozen staff, based now in Rosyth, under their directors David Page and Jim Smail. Rushworth's Aberdeen tuner John Nobes became independent in 2002. The Willis firm intends to appoint a new tuner to replace John McCarron, who has recently retired. For the first time, Harrison of Durham has appointed a Scottish-based tuner, living in Bannockburn, after the firm bought the Glasgow tuning round of James Mackenzie.

There are still over 1000 pipe organs in Scotland. Many will inevitably be destroyed during the 21st century. This is partly because so many churches continue to be closed, but there remains in places an antipathy to the pipe organ in Scotland, unusual in the wider European context, especially amongst the Presbyterian clergy of today, and still quite prevalent in the Highlands. However, the outlook is not all pessimistic and many fine organs will remain. Since 1995 grants have been available, and will continue to be available, from the Heritage Lottery Fund and other sources for the restoration of organs which faithfully reflect a particular style of organ building. These grants can provide as much as 70% of the total cost of exact restoration and are thus a stimulus to restoration. The oldest playing organ in the world was built in 1390; many of our fine instruments, with periodic restoration, deserve and can achieve similar longevity.

**This article is an expanded version of a two part article which appeared in the magazine *History Scotland* in 2011 Vol. 11, no. 6 and 2012 Vol. 12, no.1. See www.historyscotland.com**

# Sources used in researching the lists

The present volume incorporates the information contained in the three previous booklets by David Stewart, published by the Edinburgh Society of Organists, namely:

⋏ *Edinburgh Organs* 1975 (co-authored with the late David A.R. Thomson)

⋏ *An Interim List of Organs in Scotland* 1985

⋏ *Organs in Edinburgh* 1991 (a revision of the 1975 *Edinburgh Organs* publication)

The sources used have varied considerably in the last forty two years since *Edinburgh Organs* appeared. In addition, many of the organs have been rebuilt, moved or scrapped during this period.

*Edinburgh Organs* (1975) took its information from questionnaires sent to churches, two of the notebooks of the Edinburgh accountant Andrew M. Coutts, church histories in the Edinburgh Public Library and personal visits to many of the locations. The result was not yet a complete catalogue of Edinburgh organs, but it was quite thorough in light of the information then available.

The 1985 publication *An Interim List of Organs in Scotland* incorporated the research notes of Col. Godfrey Ives Burgess-Winn, who had died in 1980. Instruments in Edinburgh were not included, as they had been covered by the 1975 publication. Inevitably this survey was by no means complete or accurate, partly because Col. Winn did not have access to the notebooks of A.M. Coutts, which were still languishing in the Edinburgh Public Library when he was carrying out most of his work. Occasionally Winn mixed up church names, an unsurprising consequence of the unions of the various branches of the Church of Scotland and changes in the names of particular buildings. Entries were also included from Philip Wright's book about organs in Aberdeen and Colin Menzies' notes about many instruments in Scotland.

The 1991 revision of the survey of Edinburgh organs *Organs in Edinburgh* followed the discovery of another two notebooks of A.M. Coutts in the Edinburgh Public Library. Research carried out for BIOS on some of the Edinburgh-based organ builders also provided more detail. Between 1975 and 1991, the organ landscape had also changed considerably.

The present volume attempts to combine the information from all the previous publications and also benefits from new sources. If it purports to be a complete list of all the pipe organs which have ever existed in Scotland, it can never be complete or entirely accurate, but it is hoped that it comes closer to reaching that goal than the previous volumes. It has benefited from the National Pipe Organ Register (NPOR), and the British Organ Archive (BOA), both of which were gradually established by the British Institute of Organ Studies (BIOS) over the years since its foundation in 1976. The NPOR however is not for the moment complete or accurate for Scotland.

Here are details of the main sources used to compile the present volume:

### The Organ Notebooks of A.M. Coutts (1936)

There are four surviving handwritten notebooks, housed in the National Library of Scotland, Manuscript Department. They are kept with Col. Winn's collection of data under the deposit number 361 and the Coutts notebooks comprise items 35-38. Items 35 and 36 were donated in 1982 along with the rest of the Winn collection, while 37 and 38 were added in 1988. In format and style the Coutts notebooks completed by 1936 are surprisingly similar to the Leffler manuscript of 1800 which BIOS acquired in 2007. As with Leffler, Coutts' notebooks 35, 36 and 37 devote part of a page (or two) to each instrument: a brief statement of builder and date, stop lists written in columns and brief details of any interesting features or subsequent history. The handwriting of both compilers' manuscripts is similarly ornate and neat. Coutts' notebook 35 covers Edinburgh, while notebooks 36 and 37 mostly cover the rest of Scotland. Notebook 36 contains a large index, written in varied and more recent styles of handwriting, suggesting that Coutts' family members

30

were helping. This index also suggests that there may have been more than four notebooks. Notebook 38 is quite different and gives a chronological list of each builder's work in Scotland, very useful for providing the original names of churches and the exact dates on which their organs were opened.

Andrew Magnus Coutts was born on 10th September 1873 in Stockbridge, Edinburgh. His father, of exactly the same name, came from Unst, Shetland and traded in the grocery business. His mother Isabella Salmond came from Angus. Andrew jn. was only twenty one when he married Elizabeth Black of Edinburgh in 1895 and his occupation is given as "stockbroker clerk". By the time of the 1911 census Andrew and Elizabeth had four children and were living in Dalkeith. He must have been a practising organist, as he is known to have applied for a post at Junction Road Church in Leith, but there is no sign of him in the records of the Edinburgh Society of Organists. Soon the family moved to Woodburn Terrace in Morningside where they remained until bereavement struck hard in the early 1930s. Andrew lost his sister, mother and wife within four years and he himself died in 1936, aged 63.

The notebooks reflect a chartered accountant's meticulous care. Volume 38 records a total of 1738 organs, from the time of Snetzler to the last entry under Ingram dated October 1933. Of these instruments, 630 are recorded in more detail in volumes 35-37. This reflects a huge amount of part time work. Given that Coutts died before normal retirement age, this work was probably done in evenings or on rare holidays.

**The Col. Winn Collection (1980)**

Col. Godfrey Ives Burgess-Winn (1907-80) served with the Royal Signals during his military career. After retiral, he was a Vice-President of the Edinburgh Society of Organists, and a staunch member of St. Mary's Episcopal Cathedral, Edinburgh. In his latter years he was confined to his house in Newhaven and devoted his time to typing out copious notes on pipe organs including many stop lists, not just of organs in Scotland, but also throughout the UK and Ireland. In addition he catalogued gramophone records, biographies of organ recitalists and organ recital programmes. There were also a number of monographs on specific churches and organs, mostly in Edinburgh.

Most of the collection was given to the National Library of Scotland by the Edinburgh Society of Organists in 1982. These have formed Deposit 361 in the Manuscript Department and there are now 39 items, including the Coutts notebooks. A full contents list can be supplied by the authors of this publication.

A small part of Col. Winn's collection was given to fellow organ enthusiast Hugh L.E. Ross (1950-95) and these were left to the Scottish Historic Organs Trust's archive, housed in Newtonmore at the moment.

**The Jim Inglis Collection (2012)**

Dr. Jim Inglis (1934-2011) was a native of Kirkcaldy and studied for a degree in Law at Edinburgh University, which fostered suitable analytical skills not for a career in Law, as it turned out, but in computer science. He eventually became a lecturer in that subject at London University. His Ph.D. was however on organs: *The Scottish Churches and the Organ in the 19th Century* (Glasgow University 1987). Various articles in the BIOS Journal and *The Scottish Organist* subsequently summarised this work. Jim's research notes in both hard copy and disc were sent to the Scottish Historic Organs Trust, where they have been of enormous assistance in the revision of this volume. Jim's other publications are mentioned below; the entries in his survey of the organ in Scotland prior to 1700 have all been incorporated in the lists which follow.

**The National Pipe Organ Register**

The NPOR began in 1990 under the *aegis* of the British Institute of Organ Studies (BIOS). It is a largely online record, covering the whole of the UK, which ostensibly includes the history of each instrument, its stop list and often photographs. Initially the compilers based in Cambridge did not look to David Stewart's printed lists to compile data relating to Scotland, but rather relied on the notes of itinerant travellers from the south such as Charles Drane.

At first therefore the NPOR's coverage of Scotland was somewhat misleading, in terms of organs, denominations and individual buildings. Gradually this situation has improved; the online catalogue has appealed to Scots and visitors alike and at present the coverage is quite good. It is gradually becoming more comprehensive. Major contributors of information about Scottish organs have included Michael Macdonald of Glasgow and Kenneth Gray of Thirsk and Hawick. Andrew Caskie has also entered much information. Much remains to be added to the NPOR, including material readily available in the BOA (see below), and indeed material from the lists which follow in this publication. Equally, however, individual entries supplied to the NPOR by local organists and church office bearers have in many cases been of considerable value in updating the Stewart lists. Greater financial support is currently needed to keep the NPOR in full operation.

## The British Organ Archive

This resource was also founded and developed by BIOS, and it started about fifteen years earlier than the NPOR, from about 1974. It comprises organ builders' own records and includes such builders as Forster & Andrews, Bevington, Gray & Davison, Blackett & Howden, Wadsworth, Willis and Lewis. Unlike the NPOR, the BOA cannot so far make all its information available online. Detailed enquiries can be answered either by the BIOS Hon. Archivist or the staff at the Cadbury Library in Birmingham where the archive material is stored. However, abstracts of lists can be made available for particular areas of the UK, including Scotland. These have been of invaluable help in the revision of this publication. For the work involved in the creation of these abstracts, and the BOA as a resource, a huge amount of credit must go to David Wickens, who from a base in Oxfordshire has grasped remarkably well the complexities of Scottish church history and the changes in names of individual churches.

## Individual Church Histories

These have always been an important resource in researching Scottish church histories. Often the books or booklets can be found grouped together in public libraries throughout Scotland, in the local studies sections. They are a prime example of a resource which can seldom be found on Google. Some give only a brief mention to organs and occasionally the information has turned out to be speculative. In many cases however the authors have taken the time to research Session or Vestry minutes with great care and the results are very informative. I hope it is not invidious to single out the history of St. John's Episcopal Church in Perth by David Willington, published 2011, as the most comprehensive survey of musical instruments in any such publication. A whole chapter is devoted to the (not entirely happy) history of the church's various organs; the church now has a digital instrument!

## Individual Church Websites

Church websites are a relatively new resource and they vary enormously in style and quality. Some offer a useful summary of churches' histories. The introduction of instrumental music or the arrival of an organ is often mentioned. Others concern themselves purely with present worship patterns and spiritual care. Some which do not mention organs at all are still sometimes useful if they include photographs of the sanctuary. An organ case, even disused, can indicate that a pipe organ is or has been present and can lead the avid organ sleuth to other sources.

## The Instruments

There are two ways of studying the past: history and archaeology, the former uses documents and the latter artefacts. Inspecting an organ can tell you a lot about its history, whether it has been preserved intact, or rebuilt and altered. An experienced organ builder will be able to deduce a fairly accurate history of any organ without a single piece of written information. This type of evidence has been used in the lists on various occasions, especially where the documentary evidence has been scant.

## Newspapers and Journals

Throughout much of the 19th century, broadsheets contained a huge amount of detailed information and the openings of pipe organs were well covered, often before and after the event, especially between about 1865 and 1890. Founded in 1718, *The Edinburgh Evening Courant* was one of the earliest newspapers to appear in the UK, and gradually it started to cover organ installations. From the late 18th century, *The Aberdeen Journal* and *The Caledonian Mercury* also mentioned most organ installations or sales of small organs, either in news columns or advertisements. *The Glasgow Herald* and *The Scotsman* followed suit from 1805 and 1817 respectively. Newspaper reports were probably based on releases from organ builders and thus the detail is very accurate. Finding the exact date of an organ's opening (the best place to look is Coutts' notebook 38) can make the search for newspaper reports much easier.

In addition to newspapers, church journals provided detailed coverage, but sometimes not so accurately as the newspapers. Episcopal journals like *The Scottish Guardian* and *The Scottish Standard Bearer* are always worth consulting. The Scottish Roman Catholic Yearbooks are also quite reliable for dates of installations. By contrast, Presbyterian journals and magazines are generally of little use. Musical journals like *Musical Opinion* provide extensive coverage of openings of new organs which are generally reliable. *The Organ* has also provided some information not found in other sources.

Thanks should be recorded to Mr. Gerard Verloop, formerly editor of the Dutch organ history magazine *De Mixtuur*, for taking out a subscription to British newspapers online, which allowed him to abstract many references to organs between about 1760 and 1825. Most of these came from *The Caledonian Mercury* newspaper and relate to Edinburgh. Mr. Philip Wright, formerly of Aberdeen now living in Kilmacolm, has also taken out the subscription and has provided hundreds of useful newspaper clips.

## Records of Individual Churches

That Vestry, Kirk Session and Deacons' Court minutes have often been a last resort for updating this publication is partly due to the history of our previous publications, which for the most part did not use them. Another factor is the time it takes to scan through such minutes, which can be lengthy if you are uncertain of an exact date of an organ's installation. As a valuable primary source however, church records can and have changed many an organ's entry in the lists. They have been useful for the period following the Second World War, when nearly all installations were second hand and therefore not publicised elsewhere. It is not always clear where every church's records are located, and even the National Register of Archives for Scotland (NRAS) does not record them all. Some are still housed under the bed in the manse or rectory, or in the attic of an office bearer.

Some of the information in minutes can be vague. Where minutes refer to an "organ" this can refer to a harmonium, reed organ, pipe organ or electronic organ. Often the only way to check if the organ has sounding pipes is to look at the church accounts; if maintenance payments are made to known organ builders, then the instrument is probably a pipe organ, but if the payment is to a music shop, then the instrument may be a harmonium or reed organ. Reed organs were often quite sophisticated with two manuals, full pedalboards and even dummy pipe facades; these should not be included in this publication, but some will inevitably have slipped in, to be traced in the future.

Technical details in church records are often misapplied and names misspelt, in sharp contrast to newspaper reports where almost everything is accurately presented. A decade or two ago, consulting church records in public care was slightly more straightforward than it is now, as most of the tomes were housed in Register House, Edinburgh, in the National Records of Scotland, formerly known as the Scottish Record Office. In more recent times, many have been digitised, but others (mostly the 20th century volumes) remain in hard copy and have been distributed to local history hubs. Many are now found in the Mitchell Library in Glasgow, the Borders Archive in Hawick, Stirling Council Archives, Dundee City Archives, St. Andrews University Library, Highland Archive in Inverness and others. Some records have always been elsewhere, for example the records of some Episcopal churches in Edinburgh are housed in the Edinburgh City Archive.

Since 2015 I have been looking through as many church tomes as I can, in situations where the secondary sources conflict with each other or are silent, and this has proved to be productive in various cases.

**Churches and Parishes of the Church of Scotland**

The hitherto unpublished *Churches and Parishes of the Church of Scotland* has been (and is still being compiled) by Mr. Roy Pinkerton, a retired lecturer in Classics at Edinburgh University, and an organist himself. The publication at present only exists privately on disc or stick. It provides a comprehensive history of all 6275 buildings which have been at some point part of the Church of Scotland, including those which existed before the Reformation of 1560, but remained in use afterwards. Dates of buildings, unions or closures are provided in each case. Former names of churches and congregations are clearly indicated and each parish has at least one photograph, and often several. This represents a huge amount of work and careful compilation. It has been of great use in revising the lists of organs.

Another similar but older publication is the *Historical Directory to Glasgow Presbytery* by the late Rev. Dr. Andrew Herron, revised 2007 by Andrew Wale. This is of a slightly more speculative nature in places, but contains a lot of interesting narrative. It remains a very useful guide to the complexities of churches and denominations in Glasgow.

The online indices of the National Records of Scotland also provide a good summary of the various name changes of particular buildings, once the elusive NRS on-screen system is mastered. I am very grateful to the staff in the Historical Search Room at Register House for their patience and assistance.

**Buildings of Scotland Series**

The now complete *Buildings of Scotland* series (published first by Penguin and now Yale) "Pevsner" series has been very useful both in identifying buildings and organs. We have both Colin Menzies and the late Norman Marr to thank for encouraging Colin McWilliam and later editors to have information on organs included. The English volumes do not include this information. In the Scottish volumes, coverage of the pipe organs in churches is very good on the whole, but a little intermittent in the more recent volumes. Some of the contributors identify the builder of organs as a matter of course; others only mention the organ when it affects the architecture. Several organs have however been added to our lists from the information in the Pevsner series, which is a monumental work, covering its subject with a thoroughness hitherto unimaginable.

**Human Sources**

It would be impossible to mention every individual who has provided information from his or her own experience or knowledge for the lists. These have included the clergy, church office bearers, organists and organ builders. You will find a list of Scottish organ builders towards the close of the preceding article on the history of the organ in Scotland. They have all been helpful in providing information at different times.

I should single out organ builders James Mackenzie and Matthew Hynes of Glasgow for the time they took to meet David Stewart and myself to iron out the complexities of Glasgow and Strathclyde. This involved six full day sessions at the Cottier Centre café in Partick. Their own research and expertise generated a substantial input to the lists throughout Strathclyde and beyond. Organ enthusiasts not mentioned earlier include Dr. Peter Thornton of Carnoustie and Kerr Jamieson of Duror and Glasgow. The late Norman Marr of Aberdeen contributed a great deal of information about organs in the North East. Philip Wright of Kilmacolm and David Welch of Banchory have been similarly informative and have resulted in many new entries, especially of smaller organs such as Casson Positives and Walcker Dulsannels.

I am very grateful indeed to all who have helped by contributing information so generously.

**Bibliography** (in chronological order)

Sir John Graham Dalyell of the Binns *Musical Memoirs of Scotland,* Edinburgh 1849

Hamilton, David *Remarks on Organ Building and the Causes of Defective Instruments,* Hamilton & Müller, Edinburgh 1851

Baptie, David *Musical Scotland, Past and Present,* Paisley 1894

Thornsby, Frederick *Dictionary of Organs and Organists,* Bournemouth 1912

Mate, G.A. & Son, with introduction by Freeman, Andrew *Dictionary of Organs and Organists,* Second Edition, London 1921

Wright, Philip M.G. *Organs in Aberdeen,* Aberdeen 1966

Elvin, Laurence *Forster & Andrews Organ Builders 1843-1956,* Lincoln 1968 (supplementary volume on barrel, chamber and small church organs published 1976)

Wright, Philip M.G. *A Chapter in Scottish Organ Building: E.H. Lawton,* Aberdeen 1972

Elvin, Laurence *The Harrison Story,* Lincoln 1973

Knott, J.R. *Brindley & Foster, Organ Builders, Sheffield,* Bognor Regis, 1974

Menzies, Colin D.L. *Organ Club Tour Notes*
   ⋏   *July/August 1980 Tour of Scotland*
   ⋏   *June 1995 Tour of Southern Scotland*
   ⋏   *May 2013 Tour of Edinburgh and Lothian*

Inglis, Jim *Scotland's Earliest Organ?* Musical Times, June 1988, p.317

Thistlethwaite, Nicholas *The Making of the Victorian Organ,* Cambridge 1990

Macdonald, Robert *Churches and Places of Catholic Interest in Moray,* Elgin 1990

Inglis, Jim *The Organ in Scotland before 1700 ,* De Mixtuur, Schagen, The Netherlands 1991, distributed by Positif Press, Oxford

Williams, Peter F. *The Organ in Western Culture,* Cambridge 1993

Barnes, Alan & Renshaw, Martin *The Life and Work of John Snetzler,* Aldershot & Vermont, 1994

Bicknell, Stephen *The History of the English Organ,* Cambridge 1996

Wilson, Michael I. *The Chamber Organ in Britain, 1600-1830,* Aldershot & Vermont 2001

Jamieson, Kerr *Peace, Perfect Peace; the Life and Work of Albert Lister Peace 1844-1912* Duror 2012. The electronic version includes many specifications of organs played by Peace.

Bevington, A.P., G.G. & R.J. *Bevington & Sons, Victorian Organ Builders,* Bristol 2013

Wright, Philip M.G. *John Wardle Timeline,* Kilmacolm 2017

Journals of the British Institute of Organ Studies (BIOS) - articles relevant to Scotland

⅄ Journal 13 (1989) Inglis, Jim *The Organ in 19th Century Scotland.*
⅄ Journal 15 (1991) Buchan, Alan *The Hamiltons of Edinburgh, Part 1.*
Inglis, Jim *The Builders of Scotland's Organs - a Survey.*
Preece, Isobel Woods *"Cant Organe": a Lost Technique?*
⅄ Journal 21 *(1998)* Buchan, Alan *Early 19th Century Scottish Chamber Organs: Pipe Markings and Other Identifiers.*
⅄ Journal 24 (2000) Field, Christopher *A Musical Apparatus of Somewhat Complex and Intricate Mechanism.*
Kitchen, John *The Organs of St. Cecilia's Hall.*
Buchan, Alan *The 1843 Hill Organ of the Music Hall*
Welch, David *Some Developments in Church Music in NE Scotland.*
Carnill, Yvonne *In Search of Grandfather: T.W. Lewis (& C.P. Scovell).*
Buchan, Alan *James Bruce of Edinburgh.*
⅄ Journal 39 (2015) Buchan, Alan *The Hamiltons of Edinburgh, Part 2.*


BIOS Reporters. In the early years of the 21st century, various informative articles by David Welch on aspects of 18th and early 19th century organ building in the east of Scotland appeared in the following issues:

July 2004 - Organ Building prior to 1820 in NE Scotland.
October 2004 - correspondence on this and drawing of Trinity, Pollokshields.
January 2005 - correspondence on Pollokshields.
April 2005 - More on Organs prior to 1820 and correspondence.
July 2006 - Two 18th Century Organs in NE Scotland.
January 2009 - Organ Building in Peterhead c.1800.
April 2009 - Notes on Montrose and other Episcopal strongholds.
July 2011 - More on Peterhead.

*The Scottish Organist.* This was a journal of the Scottish Federation of Organists and ran from 1988-96, when it was superseded by *SFO News.* Copies of issues between 1995 and 1998, which contain articles on Scottish organ history, can be obtained from the author on alanbuchan@btinternet.com for the cost of postage.

*Choir & Organ:* issues from December 2016 containing articles on Scottish House Organs by Chris Bragg and Matthew Hynes: Cluny Castle, Glencruitten House, Mount Stuart, Scone Palace, Manderston House and Fyvie Castle. The articles are called *Border Controls.*

As readers of this publication you may also be a valuable source of information about pipe organs you know in your own locality or other parts of Scotland. Please do not hesitate to inform us of inaccuracies or new information on **alanbuchan@btinternet.com**

# A LIST OF ORGAN BUILDERS AND ABBREVIATIONS

## 1) Organ Builders (and the dates when their businesses operated)

| | |
|---|---|
| A&S | Abbott & Smith, Leeds (1890-1975) |
| Aeo | Aeolian Organ Co., Farwood, New Jersey (1887-1985) |
| Ahr | Jurgen Ahrend, Leer, Germany (1955-present) |
| All | William Allen, London (1794-1835) |
| Ann | Charles Anneessens et fils, Menin, Belgium (1831-present) |
| Arn | Ralph Arnold, Orpington (1966-2000) |
| Aub | Bernard Aubertin, Courtefontaine, France (1978-present) |
| | |
| B&T | Beale & Thynne, London (1890-1902) |
| Bell | Frederick F. Bell, Edinburgh (1950-78) |
| Ben | George Benson, Manchester (1885-1921) |
| Bev | Henry Bevington, London (1794-1941) |
| Bew | Bewsher & Fleetwood, Liverpool (1821-43) |
| Bin | James Jepson Binns, Leeds (1881-1931) |
| BFH | Binns, Fitton & Haley (1931-54) |
| BinT | The J.J. Binns Tuning Company (1953-63) |
| Bis | J.C. Bishop, London (1807-present) |
| B&H | Blackett & Howden, latterly Howden & Kent, Newcastle (1893-1975) |
| Bri | Richard Bridge, London (1730-58) |
| B&F | Brindley & Foster, Sheffield (1870-1939) |
| Bris | William & James Bristowe, London/Montrose (1726-42) |
| Bro | Joseph W. Brook, Glasgow (1880-1954). See also S&B. |
| Brk | George Brooksby, Glasgow (1919-48) |
| Brow | F.H. Browne, Canterbury (1871-present) |
| Bru | James Bruce, Edinburgh (1807-50). See also MWo, WSm & SBru. |
| Brug | Hendrik ten Bruggencate, Northampton (1970s) |
| Bry | Henry Bryceson, London (1796-1910). See also BBE & BBM below. |
| BBE | Bryceson Brothers & Ellis, London (1878-82) |
| BBM | Bryceson Brothers & Morten, London (1874-77) |
| BBT | Bryceson Brothers & Taylor (1882-1910) |
| Bur | Walter J. Burton, Winchester (1883-1915) |
| But | Samuel Butterworth, Huddersfield (1875-97) |
| Byf | John Byfield(s), London (1724-99) |
| | |
| C&C | Casey & Cairney, Glasgow (1965-1970) |
| C&M | Casson & Miller, Stranraer/Perth (1886-87). See MilJ and Pos. |
| Cat | Arthur E. Catlin, Edinburgh (1910-25) |
| Cav | Aristide Cavaillé-Coll, Paris, France (1833-99) |
| ChrE | John Christie, Edinburgh & Glasgow (1826-84) |
| ChrN | John Christie, Norwich (1923-30). See N&B. |
| Chu | Nigel Church, Stamfordham (1972-1987) |
| Cle | Clementi & Co., London (1798-1832). See DavJ. |
| Col | Peter Collins, Melton Mowbray (1964-2017) |
| Com | John Compton, London (1902-57) |
| ConJ | James Conacher, Huddersfield (1879-1902) |
| ConP | Peter Conacher, Huddersfield (1854-present) |
| Cop | Matthew Copley, Surbiton (1970-2013) |
| Cou | Cousans & Sons, Lincoln (1878-1974) |
| Cra | J.B. Cramer, London (1871-78) |
| Cro | John Croall, Edinburgh (c. 1850-80) |
| Cum | Alexander Cumming, west of Scotland/London |

| Dal | Thomas Dallam & Son, London (c.1600-1700) |
|---|---|
| Dan | David Daniels, Dalbeattie & Ayr (fl. 1950s-1970s). See also Sol. |
| DavA | A.E. Davies, London & Northampton (fl. 1930-65) |
| DavJ | James & David Davis, London (1790-1822) |
| DavJT | John T. Davis, Newcastle (1848-85) |
| D&R | Degens & Rippin, London (1961-1964) |
| Dec | Gebroeders Decap, Antwerp, Belgium (1902-present) |
| Dek | A.S.J. Dekker, Goes, Holland (1937-66) |
| Dick | Christopher Dickens, Spofforth, Yorks (1977-1989) |
| Dob | George Dobie, Glasgow (1892-96) |
| Don | John Donaldson, York (1783-1807) |
| Dre | John Dresser, Birmingham (1873-83) |

| Ebr | Frederick W. Ebrall, Birmingham (1900-23) |
|---|---|
| Edm | Alexander F. Edmonstone, Forteviot & Perth (1983-2013) |
| Ell | Thomas Elliot, London (1790-1832) |
| Eng | George & G.P. England, London (1758-1816) |
| E&B | Evans & Barr, Belfast (1903-50) |
| Ewa | William Ewart, Edinburgh (1865-73) |

| Fai | William Faigher (fl. 1888) |
|---|---|
| Fer | Ferguson, Edinburgh (fl. 1911) |
| Fin | George & Thomas Fincham, London (1853-1921) |
| Fle | D.A. Flentrop, Zaandam, Netherlands (1903-present) |
| Fli | Flight, London (1772-1887). See also F&R. |
| F&R | Flight & Robson, London (1806-42) |
| F&A | Forster & Andrews, Hull (1843-1956) |
| For | Forth Pipe Organs, Newton Village/Rosyth (2002-present). See also R&D. |
| Fro | Th. Frobenius & Sons, Lyngby, Copenhagen (1909-present) |

| Gei | Frank Geiger, Glasgow (1963-67). See also Com. |
|---|---|
| Gern | August Gern, London (1866-1917) |
| Gle | William B. Gledhill, Edinburgh (1899-1926) |
| G&G | Goetze & Gwynn, Welbeck, Notts (1980-present) |
| Gol | Robert C. Goldsmith, Edinburgh (1972-2012) |
| GDB | Grant, Degens & Bradbeer (1965-79). See also D&R. |
| Gra | Donald Grant, London (1853-58) |
| Gray | Robert, William and John Gray, London (1750-1845) |
| G&D | Gray & Davison, London (1845-1973) |
| Gre | Samuel Green, London (1772-96) |
| G&S | Griffen & Stroud, Bath (1895-1940) |
| Gri | Griffiths & Cooper, Ryde (1988-present) |
| Gro | Henry Groves, Nottingham (1957-present) |

| HDa | David Hamilton, Edinburgh (1824-63) |
|---|---|
| HDT | D. & T. Hamilton (1864-90) |
| HCF | C. & F. Hamilton (1890-1939) |
| Hard | Hardy & Son, Stockport (1845-1905) |
| H&B | Harmer & Burfield, Glasgow (1884-87) |
| Har | Harrison & Harrison, Durham (1872-present) |
| Hars | Harston & Sons, Newark (1869-1912) |
| Hay | Ambrose W. Hayter & Son, Letchworth (1906-39) |
| Hele | Hele & Co., Plymouth (1865-2002) |
| Hew | Thomas & Henry Hewins, Stratford (1856-1936) |
| Hill | William Hill & Son, London (1832-1916) |

| HNB | Wm. Hill & Son & Norman & Beard Ltd (1916-97) |
|---|---|
| Hils | H. Hilsdon Ltd., Glasgow (1911-76) |
| Hol | George M. Holdich, London (1841-94) |
| Holl | Henry Holland, London (1783-1827) |
| Holt | Frederick Holt, Edinburgh (1863-75) |
| HWm | William Holt, Leeds (1838-83) |
| H-J | Robert Hope-Jones, Birkenhead (1889-1903) |
| Hos | T.J. Hoskins, Ystrad (1933-36) |
| Hra | Gregor Hradetzky, Krems, Austria (1960-84) |
| Hume | David O. F. Hume, Glasgow (1910-48). See also SmRi. |
| Hun | Alfred Hunter, London (1856-1937) |
| Hyp | Andrew Hyphner, Llanelli |

| IngE | Eustace Ingram, sen., London & Hereford (1867-1900) |
|---|---|
| IGD | Eustace Ingram, Gray & Davison, London (1900-1902) |
| IHJ | Eustace Ingram, Hope-Jones, London (1902-1904) |
| IngEu | Eustace Ingram, jn., Hereford & London (1904-41) |
| Ing | Arthur E. Ingram, Edinburgh (1894-1956) |
| Ingl | Robert Inglis, Glasgow (1948-58) |

| Jar | Jardine & Co., Manchester (1846-1970) |
|---|---|
| Jhn | E.J. Johnson, Cambridge (1963-present) |
| Job | M. C. Jobborn, Wittenhall, Staffordshire (1912-16) |
| Joh | John Johnston, Edinburgh (fl. 1763-77) |
| JoH | Henry Jones, London (1853-1934) |
| JoG | H.G. Jones, Kippford (c. 1980-2008). See also Sol. |
| JoJ | James Jones, London (1772-83) |
| JoK | Kenneth Jones, Bray, Ireland (1978-present) |
| JoT | Thomas S. Jones, London (1854-1936) |
| JoW | William Jones, London (1806-38) |
| Jor | Abraham S. Jordan, London (1712-56) |

| Kea | Albert Keates, Sheffield (1885-1938) |
|---|---|
| Kel | Edward Kellie, Edinburgh (fl. 1620s) |
| King | Herbert King, Edinburgh (1890-1911) |
| Kin | Kingsgate Davidson, London (1925-66) |
| Kir | Alfred Kirkland, London (1874-1923) |
| KK | Karen Kitchen, Kelso/Auchterarder (2010-14) |
| K&B | Kirtley & Blossom, Glasgow (1912-53). See also Mir, Brk and HNB. |
| Koe | Helmut Kögler, St. Florian, Austria (1972-present) |

| Lam | Lammermuir Pipe Organs, Oldhamstocks (1983-present) |
|---|---|
| Law | Ernest Lawton, Aberdeen (1898-1947) |
| L&B | Laycock & Bannister, Keighley (1842-1983) |
| LTC | T.C. Lewis, London (1861-98) |
| Lew | Lewis & Co., London (1884-1919) |
| LTW | T.W. Lewis, Bristol (1908-40). See also S&L. |
| Lib | John Lightbown & Son, Whitley Bay (1970s-present) |
| Lig | James Lightoller, North Berwick (1993-present) |
| Lin | John and Henry C. Lincoln, London (1790-1848) |
| Llo | Charles Lloyd, Nottingham (1859-1930) |
| Loos | John Loosemore, Exeter (1635-74) |
| Loo | David Loosley, Stirling (1974-present) |

| | |
|---|---|
| McDA | Alexander Macdonald, Edinburgh (1890-98). See also HDT. |
| McDM | Michael and Andrew Macdonald, Glasgow (1975-present) |
| Mac | James A. Mackenzie, Glasgow (1960-2014) |
| Mag | T.W. Magahy, Cork (1875-1956) |
| Man | N.P. Mander and Mander Organs, London (1946-present) |
| Mel | David Melville, Leith (fl.1557-8) |
| MilJ | John R. Miller, Perth & Dundee (1886-1941) |
| MilP | Paul Miller, Bonnybridge (1998-present). See also HNB. |
| Mir | Robert, John & Alex (J.&A.), Alex N. & Adam Mirrlees, Glasgow (1812-1948) |
| Mon | Alfred Monk, London (1862-1926) |
| Moo | Stephen Moore, London (fl. 1790s) |
| M&S | Morgan & Smith, Brighton (1895-1949) |
| Mor | Theophile Mortier, Antwerp, Belgium (1906-48) |
| MWo | Muir Wood & Co. (Andrew Wood), Edinburgh (1798-1818). See also Bru. |
| | |
| Nel | H.J. Nelson, Durham (1880-1967) |
| NicF | James and F. C. Nicholson, Newcastle (1844-1919) |
| Nic | Nicholson & Co., Worcester/Malvern (1841-present) |
| N&N | Nicholson & Newbegin, Newcastle (1897-1920) |
| Nob | John Nobes, Stonehaven/Johnshaven (2002-present). See also R&D. |
| N&B | Norman & Beard, Norwich (1868-1916). See also HNB. |
| Not | Alphonse Noterman, London (1898-1995) |
| | |
| Ohr | Ohrmann & Nutt, London & Manchester (c. 1790-1804). See also Sne. |
| Osm | George Osmond, Taunton (1894-1993) |
| | |
| Pal | John Palmer, Greenock |
| Par | Thomas Parker, London (1764-87) |
| Pen | Thomas Pendlebury, Leigh/Cleveleys (1897-1988) |
| Pil | William Pilcher, London (1826-63) |
| Por | Joshua Porritt, Leicester (1867-1965) |
| Pos | Positive Organ Company, London (1886-1941) |
| Post | Robert Postill, York (1825-82) |
| Pri | Principal Pipe Organs, York (1986 -present) |
| Pul | Roger Pulham, Woodbridge (1970-present) |
| | |
| Rbt | Frank Roberts, Dundee (1875-89) |
| Ree | J.E. Reeve, London (1925-41) |
| Renn | Donald B. Rennie, Cults (amateur) (fl. 1980s) |
| Ren | John (sen & jnr.) and D.B. Renton, Edinburgh (1845-95) |
| Res | Rest Cartwright, London (1897-1961) |
| Ric | W.E. Richardson, Manchester (1857-1935) |
| Rie | Rieger, Schwarzach, Austria (1845-present) |
| Rob | Joseph & Thomas Joseph Robson, London (1806-76). See F&R and Fli. |
| Ros | Edward Rostrand, London (fl. 1764) |
| Rot | Frederick Rothwell, London (1887-1960) |
| R&D | Rushworth (& Dreaper), Liverpool & Edinburgh (1910-2002) |
| Rust | John Rayment Rust, Chelmsford (1845-1914) |
| | |
| San | Sandtner Orgelbau, Dillingen, Germany (1935-present) |
| Sau | Wilhelm Sauer, Frankfurt-an-der-Oder, Germany (1857-present) |
| Sav | Victor Saville, Thackthwaite (1983-present) |
| Sch | Merklin-Schütze, Brussels, Belgium & Paris, France (1853-70) |
| Scot | Scott Bros & Co., Dundee (1882-93) |

| | |
|---|---|
| Sco | Charles P. Scovell, Edinburgh (1908-40) |
| S&L | Scovell & Lewis, Edinburgh (1904-09). See also LTW. |
| Sim | H.C. Sims & Co., Southampton & Ryde (1866-1905) |
| Six | George Sixsmith, Ashton-under-Lyne (1955-present) |
| SBr | Small Bruce & Co., Edinburgh (1829-39). See also Bru. |
| SmB | "Father" Bernard Smith/Schmidt, London (1667-1708) |
| Sme | Charles A. Smethurst, Manchester (1950-80) |
| SmRi | Richard Smith, Glasgow (1888-1926) |
| SmRo | Ronald L. Smith, Edinburgh & Cleish (1968-1999) |
| Sne | John Snetzler, London (c. 1740-85) |
| Sol | Solway Organs, Dalbeattie (c. 1960-1980). See also JoG and Dan. |
| Spe | Speechly, London (c1870-1950s). See also IngE. |
| S&B | Spring & Brook, Glasgow (1879-80). See Bro. |
| Sta | David Stark, Nenthorn (1995-present) |
| Str | John Stringer & Co, Hanley (1869-96) |
| Swe | William Sweetland, Bath (1847-1902) |
| | |
| Tay | Stephen Taylor & Son, Leicester (1866-1965) |
| Tel | W. Telford & Son, Dublin (1830-c1950) |
| Thu | Charles Thurnam & Sons, Carlisle (1910-31) |
| Tic | Kenneth Tickell, Northampton (1984-present) |
| Tow | William Townsend, Edinburgh (1844-87) |
| Tru | J & A Trustam, Bedford (1836-1910) |
| | |
| Vin | H.S. Vincent, Sunderland (1880-1990s) |
| Vow | W.G. Vowles, Bristol (1858-1958). Post 1958, see Wal. |
| | |
| Wad | E. Wadsworth, Manchester & Aberdeen (1861-1946). See also War. |
| Wal | J.W. Walker, Ruislip/Brandon (1827-1976-present) |
| WRH | R.H. Walker, Chesham (1953-72) |
| Walc | E.F. Walcker, Ludwigsburg, Germany (1781-present) |
| Ward | John Ward, York (1814-55) |
| War | John Wardle, Aberdeen (1927-1940). See Wad for 1877-1926 work. |
| Wat | Conacher & Watson, Perth, then Allan Watson, Dundee (1896-1950) |
| Watt | Andrew Watt & Sons, Glasgow (1898-1965) |
| WaJ | James Watt, Glasgow (fl. 1762-76) |
| Wel | Henry Wellby & Sons, Edinburgh (1890-1942) |
| Well | David Wells, Liverpool (1981-present) |
| W-K | Wells-Kennedy Partnership, Lisburn (1966-present) |
| Welt | Michael Welte, Freiburg, Germany (1850-1932) |
| Whi | C & J Whiteley, Chester & Chislehurst (1869-1998) |
| Wilk | Wilkinson & Sons, Kendal (1829-1968) |
| Wil | Henry Willis & Sons, London/Petersfield/Liverpool (1847-present) |
| W&L | Willis & Lewis, London (1919-25). See Wil and Lew. |
| WiB | Basil Wilson, Lanton, nr. Hawick (1965-90) |
| Wis | Joseph Wishart, Aberdeen (c1840-76) |
| WSm | Wood Small & Co. (Andrew Wood), Edinburgh (1818-29) |
| WoW | Wood Wordsworth, Leeds (1920-81) |
| WoE | Peter Wood, Thaxted (1981-97) |
| WoP | Peter & Mark Wood, Harrogate (1981-present) |
| WoH | Philip & David Wood, Huddersfield (1966-present) |
| W&M | Wordsworth (& Maskell) (1866-1920). See also WoW and WoP. |
| Wur | Wurlitzer Cinema Organs, North Tonawanda, New York State (1910-1950s) |
| Yal | Alfred G. Yallop, London (1935-41) |
| You | Alexander Young, Manchester (1872-1927) |

# 2) Other Abbreviations

| | |
|---|---|
| **B** | Baptist |
| **C** | Congregational |
| **E** | Episcopal |
| **F** | Free Church of Scotland |
| **M** | Methodist |
| **RC** | Roman Catholic |
| (blank) | Church of Scotland |
| **UF** | United Free |
| **UP** | United Presbyterian |
| **URC** | United Reformed Church |

| | |
|---|---|
| blg | building |
| c | approximately |
| ch | church |
| cld | closed |
| cong | congregation |
| dem | demolished |
| dest | destroyed |
| dism | dismantled |
| encl | enclosed |
| ex | extended from (no of ranks) |
| fr | from |
| ind | independent |
| inst | installed |
| nr | near |
| o | cleaned, overhauled, restored or significant repair work |
| pd | pedals |
| ppd | pedal pull-downs |
| pf | prepared for |
| pt | part |
| r | work involving rebuilding or alteration |
| rem | removed |
| Res | residence of |
| scr | scrapped |
| sep | separate |
| ss | speaking stop(s) |
| temp | temporary |
| unencl | unenclosed |

| | |
|---|---|
| 1/5 | 1 manual, no pedal, 5 speaking stops |
| 1+pd/5 | 1 manual and pedals, 5 speaking stops |
| 2/22 | 2 manuals and pedal and 22 speaking stops |
| ( | organ no longer exists, or at least not in this location |
| Gt | Great manual and pipework |
| Sw | Swell manual and pipework |
| Ch | Choir manual and pipework |

# Scottish Federation of Organists Listing of Organs

**A-listed**  An organ which remains as originally built in all respects, tonally and mechanically. Only very minor alterations allowed.

**B-listed**  An organ which has been altered in some respects, but which is considered representative of its period.

**C-listed**  An organ which contains pipework of reputable origin or quality, but whose action, structure and console arrangements are not original or significant.

# GAZETTEER OF ORGANS

The organs are arranged alphabetically by location. Only locations which have had pipe organs are listed; those which have only had harmoniums, reed organs, or electronics are not included. In most cases, the current or final name of a church is given, even if the church was known by a different name at the time when the organ existed. However, when an organ was discarded before a building assumed a secular function, then the previous name of the building has generally been retained. Cross references are often given, to make it easier for users to find particular buildings. Many of the churches have changed names several times due to the unions of congregations. Former names or denominations of buildings are inserted in brackets immediately after the name of the location, and before the address. Where there are several older names, these are cited in reverse chronological order. Later functions of the buildings are sometimes given in brackets *after* the address and closure date. Within the four major cities (Edinburgh, Glasgow, Aberdeen and Dundee) subsequent locations of organs refer to locations within the city concerned, unless otherwise stated.

**Aberchirder West UF** (UP) Aberchirder cld 1906 (for former Parish Church see Marnoch)
   ⅄  (1903 Walc 1/

**Aberchirder St. Marnan's E**
   ⅄  (1853 organ
   ⅄  1876 G&D 1/3 no pd o1899 Wad,
     o1913 Wad

**Abercorn** nr Queensferry
   ⅄  (pre-1800 Anon 1/ fr local Res and r1893-98 Ing 2/10, rem 1999 Gol, post-2005 to Holland by de Feenstra

**16) The Anonymous 18th century organ which stood in Abercorn Church until 1999**

44

## ABERDEEN

**Adams & Stevenson** 35 Duthie's Court, Guestrow
  ⅄  (organ 1/5 for sale 22x1833

**Albion & St. Paul's C** (High UF/F cld 1935/West F pre-1867) west pt of "Triple Kirks", Schoolhill cld 1966
  ⅄  (1950 ConP 2/17 using 2ss fr Wis at St. Paul's C 1ss rem to St. Andrew's Cathedral E c1966, remainder rem 1968 to Craigiebuckler by Wal

**All Saints E** Smithfield Road (later St. John's for the Deaf)
  ⅄  (1820s WSm 2/9 from Forglen House nr Turriff to here 1936 & r Law, rem 1972 by David Murray to St. Machar's

**Astoria Cinema** cld 1967
  ⅄  (1934 Com 3/76 ex 8 o1947, rem 1967 to Powis School by Robert Leys

**Beechgrove** (UF) Beechgrove Avenue cld 2005
  ⅄  (1902 A&S 2/26 r1954 Wal 2/49 ex, o1965, o1996 Wal, to Melhus, Norway 2010

**Belmont Street C** - see St. Nicholas C

**Bethany House** Hardgate
  ⅄  (c1860 ConP 2/8 o1908 Wad, o1921 Wad, dism following water damage c1980 by Norman Marr

**Bieldside** - see Bieldside (outwith Aberdeen)

**Blackfriars C** Blackfriars Street cld 1886 (later pt of Robert Gordon's College)
  ⅄  (1876 F&A 2/15 +3pf rem 1886 to Skene Street C by Wad

**Blind Asylum** - see Royal Blind Asylum

**Bon Accord F** (Bon Accord St. Paul's/UF/F cld 1976) Rosemount Viaduct cld 2016
  ⅄  1923 Law 2/16 + 2pf r1966 R&D 2/17 + 2pf , used outwith services, redundant 2016

**Booth, John & Sons** 140 Union Street
  ⅄  (chamber organ 1/2 for sale ix1877

**Bridge of Don -** see Bridge of Don (outwith Aberdeen)

**Bucksburn** - see Bucksburn (outwith Aberdeen)

**Capitol Theatre** 431 Union Street
  ⅄  1933 Com 3/60 ex8 + traps disabled 2003, rem 2013 to store **A-listed**

**Carden Place -** see Melville, Melville Carden Place (Carden Place UP) and St. Mary's E

**Causewayend** - see St. Stephen's

**Concert Hall** Concert Close, Huxter Row sold 1783 (became saleroom)
  ⅄  (1752 Sne 1/5 (organ of Aberdeen Music Society) rem 1783 to Concert Hall, Queen Street, rem 1800 by Andrew Thomson of Banchory, rem 1807 to Marischal College Library, rem 1838 to ch, for sale 1859 at Wishart, Joseph, organ builder

**ABERDEEN (Cont.)**

**Convent of the Sacred Heart** Queens Cross
 ⅄ (ConP 1/

**Convents** - see also Nazareth House Chapel, St. Margaret of Antioch Convent E and St. Mary's Cathedral RC

**Cowdray Hall and Art Gallery** Schoolhill
 ⅄ (1889 Wad (3 hires for previous blg)
 ⅄ 1925 Bin 3/33 o1961 R&D **A-listed**
 ⅄ 18th C Anon 1/ r1790, 1964 to M. Thomas, Berks, r1976 Bowen, Northampton, 1981 in Palais Lascaris, Nice, to England 1986, to Aberdeen 1987 & r Edm 1/4

**Craigiebuckler** Springfield Road
 ⅄ (1883 ConP 2/14 o1890 Wad, o1898 Wad, r1934 Law, rem 1968
 ⅄ 1950 ConP 2/17 using 2ss fr St. Paul's C 1ss to St. Andrew's Cathedral E c1966, fr Albion & St. Paul's C to here 1968 & r Wal 2/25, o1999 **C-listed**

**Crematorium** Kaimhill cld 1978
 ⅄ (c1900 Pos 1/9 fr elsewhere post-1935 rem 1955 to St. Margaret of Antioch Convent E
 ⅄ (1955 R&D 2/26 ex4 rem Loo to storage at Stirling

**Crown Terrace B**
 ⅄ 1896 Wad 2/9 o1908 Wad, o1930 Law, fr Trinity, Marischal St & r1932 Law 2/9, r1968 Wal 2/9 (2ss fr Craigiebuckler), relocated in blg 2010 Nob, disused

**Crown Terrace M**
 ⅄ (1903 A&S 2/17 r1912 Law 2/19, r1986 SmRo 2/, rem to Riga 2003
 ⅄ (Cav 2/11 fr a French convent to Lymington Church 1903, to Sandwich M, to here 1910, to here storage in hall here 1966 by Tom Robbins & Duncan Johnstone, scr

**Davie, James Musicseller** Union Street
 ⅄ (assortment of organs 1815
 ⅄ (organ 1/6 & barrel organ 4ss for sale 1817
 ⅄ (organ 1/4 for sale 1819 & 1821

**Denburn** (Gilcomston St. Colm's/Gilcomston) Summer Street cld 2006 (now Hebron Hall)
 ⅄ (1897 B&F 2/17 r1910 Law, rem 1958
 ⅄ (1893 Wad 3/ fr North & Trinity & r1958-65 HNB 3/30, r Tarquin Wiggins & Norman Marr c1971-1995 3/34, scr 2011

**Devanha House** - see Res of Henderson

**East & Belmont** (UF/East UF/F) east pt of "Triple Kirks", Schoolhill cld 1973 (for East Parish Kirk see St. Nicholas Uniting)
 ⅄ (1901 Lew 3/27 dest fire
 ⅄ (1903 Lew 3/27 r1950 R&D 3/28, scr 1976

**Elim Tabernacle** - see Trinity

**Elm Hill Asylum** (later Royal Cornhill Hospital)
 ⅄ (1898 Wad rem 1908 Wad

**Emslie's Saleroom** 19 Market Street
Λ (organ 1/4 for sale 1855

**Exhibition** - see Kittybrewster

**Ferryhill North** (Ferryhill) Ferryhill Road cld 1990
Λ (1877 ConP 2/17 o1956 R&D, damaged by fire 1993 & scr

**Ferryhill** (Ferryhill South/UF/F) Rotunda Place
Λ (1903 B&F 2/19 r1921 Wad 2/19, r1968 R&D, disused 1992, scr 1994

**Free M** Dee Street
Λ (organ extant 1902-5

**Gallowgate** (UF/F) cld 1950
Λ (c1900 Law rem 1943 Law (bombed)

**Gerrard Street B** (John Knox Gerrard Street/John Knox's UF/F cld 1987)
Λ (1904 Wal 2/13 r1921 after fire Wal 2/13, dest 1988

**Gilcomston** (Gilcomston South/UF/F cld 2013) Union Street (now Independent)
Λ 1901 Bin 2/18 o1959 R&D, o1979 R&D, o2005 MilP **A-listed**

**Gilcomston** - see also Denburn

**Gilcomston Park B** 49 Gilcomston Park (later Cornerstone Church then Aberdeen City Church)
Λ (1898 Wad 2/11 fr Meldrum & Bourtie 1953, r1972 2/13, rem 1990 to Bannockburn Allan & r Loo 2/13

**Girls High School** 18-20 Albyn Place
Λ (1910 Wad 2/17 r1914 Wad, o1920 Wad, r1923 Wad +ss, dest fire 1935

**Grammar School** Skene Street West
Λ 1930 Law 2/13 o1952 Ing, r1965 in new hall R&D 2/15, disused 1994

**Greyfriars John Knox** (Greyfriars) Broad Street cld 2004
Λ (1903 Wil 2/16 +3ss 1906 Wil, o2000 Wil, rem 2009 to St. Joan of Arc RC, Farnham, Surrey by Wil

**High Hilton** (fr Aberdeen High 1936) Hilton Drive
Λ (1907 MilJ 2/11 to here 1937 fr Balgavies House, nr Forfar & r Law 2/12
Λ 1972 Wal ex fr Melville Carden Place 1994 & r Loo + 1s fr Kings College 2004

**High UF** - see Albion & St. Paul's C

**Hilton UF** - see Woodside North

**High School for Girls** - see Girls High School

**Holburn Central** (Holburn) Holburn Street cld 2007 (now Jesus House Church, Pentecostal)
Λ 1886 Har 2/19 o1891 Wad, r1925 Law 2/21, r1974 Gol, r1980s Gol 2/25 ex

47

**ABERDEEN (Cont.)**

**Holburn West** (UF/F) Great Western Road
⚸   1922 A&S 2/12 + 5pf (added later) r1964 R&D 2/17 + 1 pf, r1974 Man 2/18 + 3 pf with much new material, console moved 2009 Edm **B-listed**

**John Knox Gerrard Street** - see Gerrard Street B

**John Knox** (John Knox's (Mounthooly)/John Knox) cld 1996
⚸   (1903 Law 2/9 r1912 Law 2/12, rem 1975 to Cowdenbeath Cairns
⚸   (1876 F&A 2/15+3 pf fr Blackfriars C to Skene Street C & r1886 Wad 2/18, o1915 Wad, to here 1975 & r1978 R&D 2/21, rem to St. Mary's E, Carden Place & r1998 Edm

**John Street C** cld c1900 (Zion Chapel, now Mither Tap Pub)
⚸   (1877 F&A o1891 Wad

**King Street** (King Street UF/St. Andrew's UF/Commerce Street UF/F) cld 1968 (later King's Community Church, then Arts Centre)
⚸   (1905 Law 2/7 to here 1922 fr Res of James Lorimer & r Law, rem 1968 to South of St. Nicholas' Kincorth

**King's College** High Street
⚸   (pre-1505 organ rem c1580s, case rem 1642
⚸   (c1705 organ for E cong pt perhaps rem to St. Paul's E , o1745 Alex Chrystal
⚸   (1891 N&B 2+1pf/15 +9pf o1895 N&B, 1899 + 9ss by N&B, r1912 Hils 3/24
⚸   (1959 Har 2/15 to here fr Westminster Abbey (temp), o1971 Har, o1992 Har, o1997 Har, rem 2004 to Ballater St. Kentigern's E & r2008 Edm (Trumpet to High Hilton)
⚸   2004 Aub 3/27

**Kittybrewster P & J Northern Industries Exhibition (Olympia)**
⚸   (1932 Law 2/17 rem 1932 to Edinburgh St. Mary's Cathedral RC by Law

**Langstane** (West of St. Andrew/West UF/F) Union Street cld 1999 (now casino and bar)
⚸   1898 B&F 2/22 o1903 Wad following rat damage, o1921 Law, r1922 HNB 3/29, 1950s new console, r1968 HNB 3/35, disused but retained in divided blg

**Larg, P. : Music Salon** (agents for the Casson Positive)
⚸   (1898 Pos demonstration of this and other small organs

**Mannofield** Craigton Road/Countesswells Road
⚸   (1882 Wad 2/18 o1893 Wad
⚸   (1895 Wad 3/31 r1921 Wad 3/32, o1933 Law, scr 1967
⚸   1969 Wal 2/32 ex9

**Mannofield E** Kenfield cld 1894 (to Bieldside St. Devenick's E)
⚸   (organ o1887 Wad, o1893 Wad, rem 1894

**Mannofield** - see also St. Francis of Assisi RC

**Marischal College Library**
⚸   (1752 Sne 1/5 fr Concert Hall 1807, hired to Choral Society 1838, to Song School 1872

**Marischal College Mitchell Hall** Broad Street
- ⚜ (1895 H-J 3/22  o1912 Law, o1949 Wil, r1950 R&D 3/27, scr 1972, 1ss to Denburn
- ⚜ 1970 WRH 1/5 **C-listed**
- ⚜ 1972 WRH 2/19 **A-listed**

**Marr, J. Music Seller** 179 Union Street (later Marr Wood & Co.)
- ⚜ (chamber organs for sale 1838
- ⚜ (1900 Law 1+pd/5  on display c1900, rem to Gamrie
- ⚜ (1875 BBM 4m console for Fort Augustus Abbey on display here 1937

**Masonic Temple** St. John's Place
- ⚜ (c1850 Wish 1/
- ⚜ (1911 Pos 1/10  sold
- ⚜ 1913 Wad 2/9 +4pf  o1959 R&D

**Mastrick** Greenfern Road
- ⚜ (1892 Wad 2/11  o1909 Wad, fr Fraserburgh St. Andrew's 1961 & r R&D 2/11, scr 1990

**Mastrick C** (now MS centre)
- ⚜ (c1964 Sol 1/5 ex 2, scr

**Mastrick** - see also St. Clement's E

**Mechanics Institute** Market Street (now hotel)
- ⚜ (1879 Wad 2/11  rem 1885-86

**Melville Carden Place** (Carden Place/UF/UP) Carden Place cld 1989
- ⚜ (1882 Wad 2/19  r1921 Wad 2/23, scr 1972
- ⚜ (1972 Wal  rem to High Hilton 1994

**Melville** (UF) Carden Place/Skene Street cld 1962
- ⚜ (1921 Wad 2/17  scr 1962

**Midstocket** (St. Ninian's) Midstocket Road
- ⚜ 1906 Walc 2/25  o1959 R&D, r1965 Wal 2/33 **B-listed**

**Mitchell Hall** - see Marischal College

**Mormon Tabernacle** North Anderson Drive
- ⚜ (1965 DavA 2/23 (pt electronic)

**Music Hall** Union Street
- ⚜ 1854 Wil  to here 1859 & r Wil 3/34, o1886 Wad, r1889 Wil 3/35, fire damage 1896, r1939 Wil/Law 3/48, o1957 Wal, o1989 Nic **B-listed**

**Music Society -** see Concert Hall

**Nazareth House Chapel RC** Claremont Street
- ⚜ (1874 ConJ 1/5  o1917-20 Wad, rem 1991 to St. John the Baptist RC, Ellon & r Edm

**North & Trinity** (North of St. Nicholas) King Street cld 1954 (for North UF see Queen Street)
- ⚜ (1893 Wad 3/30 (first Wad with pneumatic action)  rem 1958 to Denburn

**ABERDEEN (Cont.)**

**Northfield** Byron Crescent
⚓ 1933 Ing 2/9 to here 1964 by R&D from Fairnilee House, Yair, nr Selkirk **A-listed**

**Powis** Powis Place cld 1988
⚓ (1901 Law 2/16 rem 1969 Wal to storage in St. Mary's E, then to farmhouse near Auchnagatt, not extant

**Powis School**
⚓ (1934 Com 3/76 ex8 fr Astoria Cinema 1967 by Robert Leys, dest fire 1982

**Provost Ross's House** Shiprow
⚓ (chamber organ extant 1960s, rem

**Queen's Cross** (UF/F) Albyn Place
⚓ 1889 Wil 2+1pf/20 r1917 Har, r1956 to gallery R&D 2/29, console moved downstairs 1981, o1986 R&D, r2014 Lib 2/30 **C-listed**

**Queen Street** (North of St. Andrew/North/UF/F) Queen Street cld 2017
⚓ 1913 MilJ 2/21 fr Dundee Chapelshade 1945 Law, o1963 Wil, r1989 Edm 2/25

<u>**Residences**</u> (mostly tuned by Wad)

Adams, W:
⚓ (pre-1891 organ rem 1906 Wad

Anderson, Alex of Bourtie - see Bourtie (outwith Aberdeen)

Anderson, Mr., perfumer:
⚓ (organ 1/8 fr London, extant 1795-76 lent to St. Andrew's Cathedral E

Anderson, J:
⚓ (1888 Wad 1/

Beattie, Dr. James:
⚓ (1788 organ by Laing & J. H. Beattie (son), fr Peterhead Res of Dr. Laing to here 1788, but pt of organ to Song School

Cowper, Mrs, Viewfield House, Springfield Road, Craigiebuckler:
⚓ (1887 Wad

Dawson Mr:
⚓ (1894 Wad 1/ o1910 Wad

Duthie, N. Shipbuilding Yard:
⚓ (1874 Hill (est.) 2/

Foote, Rev. James, Golden Square
⚓ (chamber organ extant 1840s

Gullett, A, 2 Fountainhall Road:
⚓ (1814 All 1/6 fr Banchory Res c1946, rem 1988 to Ballater, Res of Dr. Stanley Ewen

Hamilton:
>  (pre-1885 organ

Henderson, Mrs. Devanha House:
>  (pre-1885 organ

Hopley, Ian:
>  1960 ConP 2/21  fr Chapel End M, Nuneaton 2006, to here 2009

Innes, Major - see Banchory Res of Innes, Raemoir

Jamieson. Queens Road:
>  (pre-1892 organ

Keith:
>  (pre-1888 organ

Ledingham, John:
>  (1897 organ for Queen Victoria's Diamond Jubilee  afterwards to a room at Westminster
   Abbey, to here, rem 1930s to Cults by R&D

Lorimer, James, shoemaker, 55 King's Gate:
>  (1905 Law 2/7 rem 1922 to Aberdeen King Street

Macbeth, James, 181 Union Street (musical instrument maker):
>  (1888 Wad 1/

McIntosh, Mr:
>  (1888 Wad 1/

McKennons:
>  (pre-1902 organ

Mandie, Mr:
>  (pre-1907 organ

Marr, Norman G., 63 Devonshire Road:
>  (various ss & pts fr Bethany House, Mitchell Hall, Rutherford, Forfar East & Old, Huntly
   Strathbogie 1960s to 2015

Miller, Bruce:
>  (pre-1907 organ

Murray, David:
>  (c1800 Anon 1/5  fr Letterfourie House 1965 to Cults Res of Davidson and then to here
   1970 (temp housed in Edmonstone Piano Shop, Rosemount Viaduct), rem 1981 to
   Burrelton Res of David Murray

Nichol, Francis Hay, Clark's Court, King's Gate:
>  (1842 Hill 2/12 no pd

51

**ABERDEEN (Cont.)**

Ogilvie, A:
⚓ (pre-1885 organ

Reid, James, surgeon, 36 Constitution Street:
⚓ (1833 German organ for sale 1834, to here, rem to Huntly Masonic Hall (St. John's RC) 1834

Reid:
⚓ (pre-1889 organ o1889-98 Wad

Res of Doctor:
⚓ (1888 James Graham to Carnoustie Res of Graham post-1892, post-1925 to here, rem to Nairn St. Mary's RC

Ross:
⚓ (pre-1899 organ o1899 Wad

Simpson, Archibald:
⚓ (organ 1/6 sold by Wishart 1866

Smith, G. Wellington Place:
⚓ (1873 Hill o1894 Wad 2/

Thompson:
⚓ (Wad chamber organ

Walker, C.L. 111 Crown Street:
⚓ (1876 Sch 1/6 for sale

Wells, Mr:
⚓ pre-1896 organ

Whiteley, J. Bedford Row:
⚓ (c1715 organ 1/5 r in new case 1800s, to here, to Perth Res of Edmonstone & r1985 Edm

Wilson, A.G., King's Gate:
⚓ (1928 Law 2/13 rem 1960s to Inverness St. Mary's RC

**Robert Gordon's College** Schoolhill
⚓ (c1778 Gre or Sne fr Aberdeen Trinity Qualified Chapel to here 1806 by Gillet & Massie, o1830 SBr, r1885 Wad + ss

**Rosemount** Caroline Place cld 1990
⚓ (1886 Wad 2/19 o1893 Wad, r1901 Law, r1912 N&B 2/23, o1919 Law, some pipes 1995 to Rubislaw

**Rosemount** (Rutherford/UF/F) Rosemount Place cld 2006
⚓ (1901 Law 3/28 r1952 Wil 2/22, o1964 Wil, scr 1984 some pipes to Aberdeen Denburn by Norman Marr

**Royal Blind Asylum** 50 Huntly Street
  ⅄  (1844 Wis chamber organ erected 1895 Wad  rem 1950 M. Thomas

**Royal Cornhill Hospital** - see Elm Hill Asylum

**Rubislaw** Queens Cross
  ⅄  (1875 Cra  r1879 G&D, o Wad, rem 1890 to Aberdeen St. Clement's West
  ⅄  1890-99 Wil 2/22 , o1905 Wad, r1926 Wil 3/30 + 10pf, o1937 Wil, r1952 Wil 3/38, r1968
     Wal 3/40, r1977 Gol 3/39, o1982 R&D, r1995 Edm 3/42 (1ss fr St. John's E) **B-listed**

**Rudolf Steiner School** Camphill
  ⅄  1978 Col 1/3  fr Redbourn 1978

**Rutherford** - see Rosemount

**Ruthrieston South** - see South Holburn

**Ruthrieston West** (UF/F) Broomhill Road
  ⅄  (1896 organ
  ⅄  (1926 Law 2/21  o1958 R&D, scr 1975

**Sacred Heart Torry RC** Grampian Road
  ⅄  1842 Wis/Mir 1+pd/7  to present blg
     post-1910, o2014 MilP **A-listed**

**17) The 1842 organ in the
Sacred Heart RC Church, Torry**

**St. Andrew's Cathedral E** King Street
  ⅄  (organ 1/8  borrowed fr Res of Anderson 1795
  ⅄  (c1795 Gre 2/8  fr London 1795, o1809 JoW, o1813 JoW, fr former St. Andrew's Chapel,
     Longacre 1817, survived fire 1817, rem MWo
  ⅄  (organ 1/8 (GG compass) fr Hawick Res of Prof Dove Wilson to here 1903, rem 1911 to
     Aberdeen St. Marks Mission E by Wad
  ⅄  (1857 Sch 1+pd/5  to here, after storage at Ellon (temp) fr Forgue St. Margaret's E 1970,
     rem 1971 to Aberdeen St. George's Tillydrone by Philip Wright
  ⅄  1818 MWo 2/c14  o1847 HDa, r1871 Bry 3/20, 1872 + 1ss, 1880 to chamber & r1885
     3/22 +1pf by BBT, o1905 Wad, r1917 HNB 3/28, o1940 HNB, 1ss fr Albion St. Paul's
     c1966, r1970 R&D 3/30, r1978 R&D 3/35, r1985 HNB 3/36 +1pf, o2015-16 MilP **C-
listed**

**ABERDEEN (Cont.)**

**St. Andrew's** - see also Langstane

**St. Clement's** (St. Clement's East/St. Clement's) St. Clement's Street cld 1987
⚒ (1875 F&A 2/17 o1917 Wad, damaged & scr

**St. Clement's E** Regent Quay (ex-Prince Regent Street 1928, cong to Mastrick 1960)
⚒ (1904 Law
⚒ (Innes pre-1891 fr Banchory Res of Major Innes, Raemoir, to here 1928 & r War

**St. Clement's West** (UF/F) Castle Terrace cld 1963
⚒ (1875 Cra r1879 G&D, o Wad, fr Rubislaw 1890
⚒ 1903 Law 2/17 r1932 Law 2/17, damaged & rem 1973, 1ss to Denburn

**St. Columba's** - see Bridge of Don (outwith Aberdeen)

**St. Devenick's** - see Bieldside (outwith Aberdeen)

**St. Fittick's** - see Aberdeen Torry

**St. Francis of Assisi RC** Deeside Drive
⚒ 1897 Wad 2/10 fr Folla Rule St. George's E, Rothienorman & r1982 Edm 1/8, resited & r c2000 Edm 1/8

**St. George's in the West** John Street cld 1969
⚒ (1889 Wad 2/17 +1pf r1902 Wad 2/18, scr 1970

**St. George's Tillydrone** (Tillydrone-Hayton) Hayton Road
⚒ 1857 Sch 1+pd/5 fr Forgue St. Margaret's E to storage at Ellon, then to St. Andrew's Cathedral E 1970 (temp), to here 1971 by Philip Wright 1/5 recased and pd rem, redundant 2017 **C-listed**

**St. James the Less E** Union Street
⚒ 1884 Wad 2/14 +1pf to here fr former ch in Crown Street c1888, r1906 Wad 2/16, o1909 Wad, o1916 Wad, r1928 to south of chancel War 2/22, o1974 R&D **A-listed**

**St. John the Evangelist E** Golden Square
⚒ (c1809 MWo 1/6 r WSm 2/9 for sale 1829-32
⚒ (1832 HDa rem c1850 to new ch

**St. John the Evangelist E** St. John's Place/Crown Terrace
⚒ (1832 HDa fr former ch in Golden Square c1850
⚒ (1881 Wad 2/16 r1885 Wad 2/19, r c1927 Ing 2/21, o1979 HNB, damaged by water, rem 1982 (1ss to Rubislaw), facade extant

**St. John's UF** (UP) Woodside cld 1925 (now offices)
⚒ (1900 Pos extant 1909

**St. Joseph's RC** Tanfield Walk, Woodside
⚒ (organ extant 1891-99
⚒ (Pos 1/5 o1961 R&D, rem to Pluscarden Abbey RC

**St. Machar's** The Chanonry
- ⊥ (1518 organ extant
- ⊥ (c1820s WSm 2/9 fr Forglen House nr Turriff, to All Saints E 1936 & r Law, to here 1972 by David Murray, to Schagen Doopsgezinde Kerk 1989-90, o1992-2000 Hoevers/Oranje/Schroevers/Verloop, to Monnickendam Grote Kerk. See page 17.
- ⊥ 1891 Wil 2+1pf/24+9pf 9 ss added 1897-99 Wil, o1910 Wil, r1928 R&D 3/39 (moved), o1945 R&D, r1956 R&D 3/41, r1973 Man 3/46 +10pf, o1991 Edm, o2002 Edm **B-listed**

**St. Margaret of Scotland E** 106 Gallowgate
- ⊥ (1885 organ rem 1903 Wad
- ⊥ 1909 Wad 2/12 o1917-18 Wad, o1936 War, r Nob

**St. Margaret of Antioch Convent E** 17 The Spital cld 2006
- ⊥ (1886 Wad 1/ rem 1955 to Birmingham
- ⊥ c1900 Pos 1/9 fr Aberdeen Crematorium 1955 R&D, derelict

**St. Margaret's School -** see Girls High School

**St. Mark's** (South/UF/F) Rosemount Viaduct
- ⊥ 1900 Wil 2+1pf/22 +6pf r1904 after fire Wil 2+1pf/22+6pf, r1970 R&D 2 +1pf/ , r1990s **C-listed**

**St. Mark's Mission E** Magdala Place cld 1957 dem 1980
- ⊥ (organ 1/8 (GG compass) fr Hawick Res of Prof Dove Wilson 1903 to Aberdeen St. Andrew's Cathedral, to here 1911 Wad

**18) The early 19th century Scottish-made organ in St. Mark's Mission**
From John Clark *Aberdeen in Old Picture Postcards* (2001)

**St. Mary's E** Carden Place ("Tartan Kirk")
- ⊥ (1865 G&D 2/ fr Kent o1865 Wis, r1882 Wad 2/17, o1889 Wad
- ⊥ (1896 A &S 2/18 o1916 Law, bombed 1943 & rem Law, r1952 HNB 2/22, rem 1999
- ⊥ 1876 F&A 2/15+3pf fr Blackfriars C to Skene Street C 1886 & r Wad 2/18, o1915 Wad, to John Knox 1975 & r R&D 2/21, to here 1997 & r1998 Edm with new action **C-listed**
- ⊥ 1778 Gre 1/5 fr Westhall Manor, Oyne 1946 & r Law 1+pd/6, o1984 Edm 1/5 **A-listed**

**ABERDEEN (Cont.)**

**St. Mary's Cathedral RC** Huntly Street
  ⋏  (1875 ConP 1/ (for "St. Mary's Convent")
  ⋏  1887 ConJ 3/27 o1927 Law, r1978 Loo 3/27, r1984/1986 Edm 3/27, r1994 Edm 3/30
    **B-listed**

**St. Nicholas Uniting** (St. Nicholas) Union Street
  ⋏  (1437 earliest organ recorded in Scotland
  ⋏  (1485 two organs extant 1521, dismantled 1574-96, pt extant late 18th C and 1982
West Kirk:
  ⋏  1880 Wil 2/20 r1905 Law, r1927 Wil 3/31, r1972 Wal, r1991-93 Edm, o2013 MilP
    **C-listed**
Transept (Oil Chapel):
  ⋏  1825 Bew 1/6 fr Res nr Ballintuim, Perthshire to here & o1991 Edm, rarely used
    **A-listed**
East Kirk cld 1980:
  ⋏  (1887 Wad 2/23 r1902 Law 3+1pf/29+6 pf, o1922 HNB
  ⋏  1936 Com 3/70 four divisions ex12 console disconnected 2009-14, redundant 2016
    **A-listed**
Crypt:
  ⋏  (1797 All 1/6 to here 1900, rem 1960s by dealer

**19) The 1797 William Allen organ in the crypt of St. Nicholas, Aberdeen**
From the archives of the Kirk of St. Nicholas

**St. Nicholas C** (Belmont Street C) Belmont Street, re-opened 1967 cld 1995
  ⋏  (1877 F&A 2/16 r1907 Wad 2/
  ⋏  (chamber organ 2/10 for sale 26i1884
  ⋏  (1911 Wad 2/ using older material r1936 ConP 2/24, rem 1996 to Edinburgh Leith Res
    of Gardiner

**St. Nicholas Union Grove** (St. Nicholas UF/UP) Holburn Street cld 1973 (now flats)
  ⋏  (1901 B&F 2/ r1937 HNB 2/21, scr 1976

**St. Ninian's** - see Midstocket

**St. Ninian's E** 696 King Street, Seaton
  ⋏  (1888 Wad 1/ r1912 Law, r1920 Com 2/14, to here 1936-37 by George Blacklock from
    Stonehaven Res of Dr. J.G. Mackintosh & r Rev. Ian Begg, scr 1967

**St. Paul's** (UF/UP) Rosemount Viaduct cld 1962 (now flats)

⊥   (1906 Cou 2/16  o1919 Wad, o1947 Law/Ing, scr 1964

**St. Paul's C** St. Paul Street

⊥   (1856 Wis 2/15 no pd  o1904 Wad, r1912-13 Wad, 2ss rem to Albion & St. Paul's 1950

**St. Paul's E** Loch Street cld 1966

⊥   (1722 Thomas Hollister  completed 1727 Bris 1/10, r1783 Don 2/8 no pd, o1780s & 1798
      Moo, o1798 Don, r1818 All, fr former ch in Gallowgate to here & r1867, r1881 in chancel
      Wad 2/19, o1887 Wad, o1896 Wad +ss, o c1920s Lawrance, o1940 War, dispersed 1983

⊥   (1818 Ell  to here c1880, extant 1965, rem by dealer

**20) The 1722/1727 organ in St. Paul's Episcopal Chapel, Gallowgate, photographed in 1866
just before the chapel was demolished.**
**Reproduced with the permission of Historic Environment Scotland (Sarah Dutch) SC 1579699
and the Aberdeen Diocese of the Scottish Episcopal Church.**

**ABERDEEN (Cont.)**

**St. Peter's E** 191 Victoria Road, Torry cld 1970s
⊿ (1898 Wad
⊿ (1903 Wad 2/13+3pf o1917 Wad, o1950, r1965 R&D 2/14, scr 1970s

**St. Peter's RC** Justice Street
⊿ (c1800-15 Mathison fr Tynet RC 1814 & r Mathison, returned 1815 to Tynet
⊿ (1815 F&R o1895 Wad
⊿ 1927 Law 2/10 o2014 MilP **B-listed**

**St. Stephen's** (Causewayend/UF/F) Powis Place
⊿ 1905 N&B 2/14 damaged 1943, r1954 Hils, o1997 HNB

**Scandinavian Church (Sjomans Kyrkan)** Castle Terrace
⊿ (1840s Ren 1/4 to here 1948, rem 1970 to Stonehaven Res of Charles Davidson

**21) The Renton organ from the 1840s which stood in the Scandinavian Church until 1960. It has recently been restored in Essex.**
Photograph by Charles Davidson

**Skene Street C** Skene Street
⊿ (1876 F&A 2/15+3pf fr Blackfriars C 1886 & r Wad 2/18, o1915 Wad, rem 1975 to John Knox by R&D

**Song School** 46 Union Street cld c1890
⊿ (1752 Sne bureau organ 1/5 fr Concert Hall to Marischal College Library 1807, to here by 1872
⊿ (pre-1876 Wis (pt fr 1788 organ at Peterhead Res of Dr. Wm. Laing) valued 1893 Wad, rem 1898 to Portlethen by Law

**South** Belmont Street cld 1955 (for South UF see St. Mark's)
  ⅄ (1901 Law 2/17 +1pf r1921 Wil, rem 1955

**South Holburn** (Ruthrieston South/Ruthrieston) Holburn Street
  ⅄ (1902 Pos 2/22 three divisions rem pre-1966

**South of St. Nicholas Kincorth** (Kincorth) Kincorth Circle
  ⅄ (1905 Law 2/7 fr Res of James Lorimer to King Street 1922, to here 1968 Wal, scr 1985

**Tonic Solfa Institute**
  ⅄ (organ extant 1887

**Torry** (UF/F) Victoria Road cld 1991
  ⅄ (1947 Com 2/18 ex4 to Torry St. Fittick's c1991

**Torry St. Fittick's** (St. Fittick's) Walker Road
  ⅄ 1947 Com 2/18 ex4 fr Torry c1991 by R&D, o2005 McDM and resited **A-listed**

**Torry UF** Grampian Road
  ⅄ 1950 organ 2/11

**Torry** - see also Sacred Heart RC and St. Peter's E

**Trinity** (UF/F/Theatre) Crown Street cld 1981
  ⅄ (1892 Hill 2/17 o1892 Wad, r1930 Law 2/21, o1964 Wal, scr 1981

**Trinity** Marischal Street cld 1929 (became Elim Tabernacle)
  ⅄ (1896 Wad 2/9 o1908 Wad, o1930 Law, rem 1932 to Aberdeen Crown Terrace B & r Law 2/9

**Trinity C** Shiprow cld 1984 (now museum)
  ⅄ (1899 Pos 1/
  ⅄ (1904 Law 2/21 console to be communion table, scr

**Trinity Qualified Chapel** The Green, later Netherkirkgate, off George Street
  ⅄ (c1778 Gre or Sne rem 1799 to Netherkirkgate blg, to Robert Gordon's College 1806

**Triple Kirks** - see Albion & St. Paul's C and East & Belmont

**Union Grove B**
  ⅄ (1903 Walc 1/3 o1917 Wad, rem

**Unitarian** Skene Street blg cld 1987 (now Kingdom Hall)
  ⅄ (1886 Wad 1/ fr elsewhere
  ⅄ (1906 Wad 2/17 o1912 +1ss, scr c1990

**University** - see King's College & Marischal College

**West** - see St. Nicholas Uniting, Langstane and Albion St. Paul's

**Wilson, Andrew, Bookseller** 43 Castle Street
  ⅄ (chamber organ 1/6 for sale 1859

**Airdrie Flowerhill** - see Airdrie Cairnlea above

**Airdrie Graham Street** (UF/F) cld 1954
⅄ (1900 Pos

**Airdrie Graham Street B**
⅄ 1906 A&S 2/15 r1939 A&S, o1960 A&S

**Airdrie High** (UF/F) North Bridge Street
⅄ 1915 Bin 2/17 r1980s 2/17, r2006

**Airdrie New Monkland** Condorrat Road, Glenmavis
⅄ 1909 Bin 2/14 o2009 MilP

**Airdrie New Wellwynd** (West) Wellwynd
⅄ 1909 Bin 3/32 o1998 R&D, o2017 Wil **A-listed**

**Airdrie Res of Dr. John Burnett**
⅄ 2003 Lam 1+pd/2

**Airdrie St. Margaret's RC** 96 Hallcraig Street
⅄ (1872 ConP rem

**Airdrie St. Paul's & St. John's E** (St. Paul's) Springwells Avenue
⅄ 1911 B&F 2/8 o1965 Wal, o1998 R&D **A-listed**

**Airdrie Wellwynd** (UF/UP) Wellwynd cld 1995
⅄ (1888 F&A 2/19 r1973 R&D, o1978 R&D, redundant 1995, rem by 2009

**Airlie** (latterly pt of Isla Parishes) cld 2013
⅄ 1884 B&F 1+pd/5 r1893, o1971 Wal (Loo)

**Alexandria** (North/UF/F) Lomond Road, Balloch
⅄ (1901 Ing 2/22 fr Greenock Sir Michael Street 1949 to Bro workshop, to former ch here 1953 & r Bro 2/22 by 1955, to new ch 1965 & r Wil 2/22, disused, most rem

**Alexandria Bridge Street** (UF/UP) cld 1987 dest by fire 2000
⅄ (1922 Ing 2/20 vandalised, dest

**Alexandria C** (Ind)
⅄ 1864 ConP extant 1960

**Alexandria Our Lady & St. Mark RC** Ferry Loan
⅄ (1860 Mir supplied by De Monti, Glasgow, replaced by harmonium
⅄ 1882 Har (est. only)

**Alexandria St. Andrew's** (Old) Mitchell Way cld 1994
⅄ (1911 N&B 2/ o1919 HNB, o1927 HNB, o1973 Wil, to Vierhiovenkerk, Delft 1990s

**Alexandria St. Mungo's E** Main Street
⅄ 1880s Llo 1+pd/8 fr Matlock Bath M, to here 1970s & o1989 Mac **A-listed**

**Alford Grampian Transport Museum**
⊥ 1923 Mortier (Antwerp) dance organ (automaton) r1946 Decap (Antwerp), fr France to
St. Alban's Organ Museum, rem 1967 to Rothiemay Res & o, to here 1983

**Alford St. Andrew's E** Donside |Road
⊥ (1913 Law 2/9 scr 1993

**Allanton** nr Shotts
⊥ ( Walc 1/ extant 1950s

**Alloa Chalmers** (UF/West F) cld 1970
⊥ (1925 A&S 2/18 rem to Alloa North 1970s

**Alloa Ludgate** (West/UF/UP) Bedford Place
1904 Lew 3/28 o1955 HNB, o1973 R&D **A-listed**

22) The 1904 Lewis organ in Alloa Ludgate (formerly West)
Photograph by Andrew Caskie, reproduced with permission of Alloa Ludgate Church

**Alloa Moncrieff UF** (Townhead UP) Drysdale Street
⊥ 1884 LTC 2/17 o1913 Lew, r1988 Loo

**Alloa North** (St. Andrew's) Mar Place/Ludgate cld 2009
⊥ (Ing 1/ rem c1970 to Glasgow (location not known)
⊥ 1925 A&S 2/18 fr Alloa Chalmers 1970s, disused 1994, redundant 1995

**Alloa Res of A.P. Forrester-Paton** Inglewood Lodge
⊥ (1897 N&B 3/18 r1947 3/28, rem post 1950 to St. John the Divine, Bulwell & r HNB

**Alloa Res of James B. Hunter**
⊥ (organ extant 1884-88

63

**Alloa St. John the Evangelist E** Broad Street (see also Alloa St. Mungo's RC)
⅄    (1869-72 Nic 2/ o1888 F&A, r1908 HCF 2/20, o1960 R&D, dest 1999 except Lorimer case

**Alloa St. Mungo's** Bedford Place
⅄    1904 Walc 3/38 rem to west end & r1964 Watt 3/41, disconnected 1996

23)  **The 1904 Walcker organ in St. Mungo's, Alloa, at the time of its installation.**
Photograph supplied by Walcker Orgelbau

**Alloa St. Mungo's RC** (first blg E pre-1869) Mar Street
⅄    (c1850s Mir 2+ppd/  to previous blg 1876, r Law 1+ppd/ , rem 1961 to Glasgow Wallacewell
⅄    1961 Watt 2/22 ex3 in new blg

**Alloa Town Hall**
⅄    (1888 F&A 3/36  r1902 Lcw, o1909 Lew, rem 1960s

**Alloway**
- ⅄ (1873 F&A 2/17  r1909 N&B 2/17, o1928 HNB, r1969 Dan 2/31 ex, rem by 1990

**Alness** cld 1929
- ⅄ (1909 Law 1/7  rem to Alness (UF/F)

**Alness** (UF/F)
- ⅄ 1909 Law 1/7

**Alness** - see also Rosskeen

**Altyre House** near Forres
- ⅄ (1799 Don  o1830s HDa, to Fortrose St. Andrew's Episcopal 1915 & r Law

**Altyre Mission**
- ⅄ organ extant 1914

**Alva** (Eadie/UF/Alva UP) Stirling Street
- ⅄ 1893 F&A 2/17  fr Millport West to here 1948 & r HNB 2/17, moved in building 1989 R&D

**Alva St. Serf's** (Alva) cld 1981
- ⅄ (1895 F&A 2/20  r1906 F&A, o1927 F&A, rem 1982 to Glasgow Holy Cross RC by McDM

**Alves** (South/UF/F)
- ⅄ 1902 Walc 1/3

**Alyth** (High) Kirk Brae
- ⅄ (1900 Walc 2/21  dest fire 1977, some pipes to Glenalmond Trinity College 1978
- ⅄ 1978 Loo 3/40  with pipes by Har from Blairgowrie Hill & Dysart Barony, r2005 For

**Alyth St. Ninian's E** St. Ninian's Road
- ⅄ (1882 Wad 2/11  rem 1954
- ⅄ 1909 MilJ 2/10 from Meigle St. Margaret's E 1954 & r R&D **C-listed**

**Ancrum** - see Monteviot

**Annan Erskine** (UF/Annan UP) cld 1974
- ⅄ (1907 Bin 2/14 o1913 Bin, o1959 Bin, rem 1977 to Stones M, Ripponden, Yorks

**Annan Greenknowe** (Greenknowe) cld 1930
- ⅄ (1914 You 2/11  extant 1929

**Annan Old** Church Street
- ⅄ (1913 Ing  o1980s R&D

**Annan St. Andrew's** (St. Andrew's Greenknowe Erskine/St. Andrew's Greenknowe/St. Andrew's UF/F) Bank Street
- ⅄ 1900 Vin 2/  o1959 R&D, o2000 R&D console moved

**Annan St. John the Evangelist E** St. John's Road
- ⅄ (c1890s Pos 2/5 no pd rem 1931 to Gretna All Saints E by Thu

**Annan URC** (C) Station Road
- ⅄ 1903 Wad 2/14 +1pf o1939 War, o1959 Jar, r1999 2/15

**Anstruther** (Easter/St. Adrian's) School Green (see also Cellardyke)
- ⅄ 1908 Tay 2/15 o1973 R&D **A-listed**

**Anstruther B** cld 2000s
- ⅄ Walc 1/6

**Anstruther Chalmers Memorial** (UF/UP) Backdykes cld 1973
- ⅄ (1891 Wad 2/15 r1935 G&D 2/18, o1965 Wil, rem 1983 to North Berwick St. Baldred's E by Gol

**Anwoth** cld 2001
- ⅄ 1924/1935 Pos 1/4 o R&D, rem to Gatehouse St. Mary's E 2002 by McDM

**Aquhorties RC College** nr Inverurie cld 1829
- ⅄ (1824 organ by Bishop James Kyle

**Arbirlot**
- ⅄ 1874 Har 1/4 r1903 Har 2/10, o1960 Har **A-listed**

**Arbroath Abbey** (see also Arbroath Old & Abbey)
- ⅄ (a "large and beautiful organ" extant 1517

**Arbroath B** Springfield Terrace
- ⅄ (1870 organ 1/8

**Arbroath C** (Old Secession Church cld 1958) Keptie Street cld
- ⅄ (c1820 WSm 1+Sw/7 to Edinburgh Kirk Memorial C post-1903, gift of Mr. Hunter, 1946 to here, rem to Carlops 1968

**Arbroath Erskine** (UF/UP) Commerce Street cld 1959 (became Old Parish hall)
- ⅄ (1894 B&F 2/20

**Arbroath Inverbrothock** James Street cld 1977 (later B, then New Life Church) See also Arbroath St. Andrew's
- ⅄ (1868 Ren rem to Arbroath West (St. Margaret's) 1882
- ⅄ (1882 Str 2/18 scr 1970s

**Arbroath Knox's** (UF/F) Howard Street
- ⅄ 1895 ConP 2/18 to here 1948 from Brechin West & r Bro, o1994 SmRo 2/18 **A-listed**

**Arbroath Ladyloan** (Ladyloan High/UF/F) Mount Zion Brae cld 1973 (became church youth centre) dem 1991
- ⅄ (1925 Bro scr 1986

**Arbroath Ladyloan St. Columba's** (St. Columba's/Princes Street UF/UP) cld 1990
- ⅄ (organ 2/ to here 1951

**Arbroath Old** Kirk Square cld 1990
  ⚓ (1881 ConP 2/19 dest fire 1892
  ⚓ (1896 B&F 2+1pf/24+6pf r1922 Law 3/28, r Wil, pd ss to Carnoustie 1999, pt to Dundee St. Luke's E, case survives

**Arbroath Old & Abbey** (Abbey) West Abbey Street
  ⚓ (c1885 ConP 2/15 r1928 Ing 2/15, o1960 R&D, scr 2004, 1928 case survives

**Arbroath Public Hall** - see Arbroath Webster Theatre

**Arbroath Qualified Chapel E**  - see Arbroath UF & St. Mary's E

**Arbroath Res of D.T. Christie**
  ⚓ (1874 Har 1/ (ests.)

**Arbroath St. Andrew's** (Hopemount/Inverbrothock UF/F) Hamilton Green
  ⚓ (1901 Wad 2/20 scr 2001, case extant

**Arbroath St. John's M** Ponderlaw Street
  ⚓ 1902 Law 2/12 to here 1946 fr Edzell South by Bro, o R&D **B-listed**

**Arbroath St. Margaret's** - see Arbroath West

**Arbroath St. Mary's E** Ponderlaw Street/Springfield Terrace
  ⚓ (c1760 Sne 1/8 fr meeting place 1791 to Qualified Chapel E
  ⚓ (1814 organ in former St. Mary's Chapel E, High Street (later Arbroath UF cld 1924 & 2014) to here 1854, rem 1871
  ⚓ 1871 F&A 2/22 o1895/1901 Wad, o1916 Wad, o1922 F&A, r B&H 2/22, r c1972 Sol, disused 1980s

**Arbroath St. Thomas of Canterbury RC** Dishtownland Street
  ⚓ c1850s Post 1/8 r1868 with pd 2/10, to here by 1887 Wal, o1940s moved to gallery, o2001 Edm **A-listed**

**Arbroath St. Vigean's** Kirkstyle
  ⚓ 1875 Har 2/18 +1pf r1920s Bro 1ss changed, o1978 Har **B-listed**

**Arbroath UF** (High Street UF/F cld 1924/St. Mary's E to 1854/Qualified E) High Street cld 2014
  ⚓ (1814 organ rem 1854 to St. Mary's E, Ponderlaw Street, rem 1871

**Arbroath Webster Theatre** (Arbroath Town Hall/Public Hall)
  ⚓ (1874/1882 F&A 3/31 o1893 F&A, rem 1950s

**Arbroath West** (St. Margaret's) Keptie Street
  ⚓ (1868 Ren fr Arbroath Inverbrothock 1882, rem to Glasgow St. Luke F & r1898 MilJ
  ⚓ 1897 Bin 2/20 o Law, o1955 R&D, o2004 Lib **A-listed**

**Arbuthnott** (St. Ternan's)
  ⚓ 1890 Wad 1+pd/7 o1908 Wad, o1999 Edm **A-listed**

**Arbuthnott Manse**
  ⚼  (c1900 John Riddoch (amateur) 1/3 rem to Stonehaven Res c1909

**Ardgowan House St. Michael & All Angels Private Chapel E** nr Inverkip
  ⚼  (1856 Fli
  ⚼  (1886 Wil 2/16 rem 1921 to Port Glasgow St. Mary the Virgin E by Mir

**Ardmay** - see Arrochar

**Ardoch** Perthshire
  ⚼  1904 MilJ 1/10 fr Monzie South 1949

**Ardoe House Res of A. Ogston** Banchory-Devenick (fr 1947 hotel)
  ⚼  (organ o1887 Wad, o1894 Wad

**Ardrossan & Saltcoats: Kirkgate** - see Saltcoats New Trinity

**Ardrossan Barony St. John's** (Barony/New) Arran Place cld 2014
  ⚼  1889 Wad 2/22 o1902 Ing, r1937 BFH 2/22, 1947 blower moved Watt, o1951 BFH console moved

**Ardrossan C** Glasgow Street
  ⚼  (1872 Andrew Leckie (amateur) 2/9
  ⚼  (1899 Ing 2/7 rem 1961
  ⚼  1901 Bin 2/27 fr Edinburgh Morningside High 1962 R&D & the SCWS, Beith

**Ardrossan Church of the Nazarene** (Ardrossan Park/UF/UP blg cld 1959, rem to Dalry Road) Glasgow Street
  ⚼  (1860s F&A 2/14 to here 1900 SmRi, rem c1959

**Ardrossan St. Andrew's E** South Beach
  ⚼  (1875 John McKay (organist here, amateur) 2/13
  ⚼  (1896 Ing 2/11
  ⚼  (1896 F&A 2/19 fr Glasgow Kinning Park by amateur & r, case extant 2014

**Ardrossan St. John's** (UF/F) cld 1987
  ⚼  (1897 B&F 2/13 o1922 B&F, r1927 Bin 2/15, o1959 BinT 2/16

**Ardrossan St. Peter in Chains RC**
  ⚼  1967 Wal 2/30 ex7 o1983 McDM

**Ardwell** Wigtownshire - see Stoneykirk Ardwell

**Arisaig St. Mary's RC**
  ⚼  c1866 G&D 1/6 r Law

**Armadale East** (UF/F) cld 1973
  ⚼  (1903 Walc 1/

**Arnsheen Barrhill** (Arnsheen) Barrhill cld 2007
  ⚼  (1890 B&F 1/5 r1953 Watt, scr

**Arpafeelie St. John the Evangelist E** Kessock,Tore
⋏ (1890 Wad 1/ rem before 1972

**Arran** - see Lamlash and Brodick

**Arrochar**
⋏ c1860 Scottish chamber organ 1/5 inst BFH

**Arrochar Ardmay House Hotel** proprietor R. Cordner
⋏ Hill 2/20 to here c1939 fr Lochwinnoch location by Gardner/Watt, o c1960s Mac with 1ss fr Coodham House, extant c1999

**Ashkirk**
⋏ 1983 WiB 2/11 ex3

**Athlestaneford**
⋏ 1936 Com 2/13 to here 2000 from Kingussie St. Andrew's & r Gol

**Auchenblae (West Mearns)** - see Fordoun

**Auchenhalrig** - see Tynet

**Auchencairn & Rerrick** (now the Bengairn Parishes)
⋏ (organ 1/ rem
⋏ 1956 Sol 1/5 ex1 replaced/r1979 1/6+p

**Auchincruive House Res of R. Oswald** (now West of Scotland College of Agriculture) St. Quivox, Ayrshire
⋏ (1875 Hill 3/15 rem 1922 to Kilwinning Erskine

**Auchindoun RC** nr Dufftown (ruined, then restored as house c2000)
⋏ (1818 MWo

**Auchinhalrig -** see Tynet

**Auchinleck** (Barony)
⋏ (1897 IngE dest by fire 1939
⋏ 1939 HNB 2/13 o1970s HNB, r2014 MilP 2/13

**Auchterarder** (Barony/Auchterarder) High Street
⋏ 1905 MilJ r1928 HNB 2/14, console moved 1950s, o1985 HNB, r2004 Edm 2/14

**Auchterarder** - see also Millearn House

**Auchterarder St. Andrew's & West** (St. Andrew's/UF/F) High Street cld 1983
⋏ (1920 A&S 2/15 scr

**Auchterarder St. Kessog's E** St. Kessog's Place
⋏ 1935 Ing 2/13 o1995 Edm **A-listed**

**Auchterarder St. Margaret's Hall** at Collearn Castle (Res of McKintosh) dem 1927
⋏ (1877 Hill 2/ rem 1884 to Edinburgh Mansfield Traquair Centre & r ConJ

**Auchterarder Stanley's Antiques**
- (c1850 HDa 2/8 later 1/6  fr Fettercairn House to Cambuslang St. Charles RC, to here 1999 McDM, rem to Japan
- (1913 B&H 2/17  o1973 Mac, fr Glasgow Dennistoun B 1999, in store, rem

**Auchterarder West** (UF/South UF/UP) High Street cld 1954
- (1915 Bin 2/14

**Auchterderran Kinglassie** (Auchterderran St. Fothad's/Auchterderran) Woodend Road
- 1907 Ing  moved in blg 1929 Ing, o1987 R&D

**Auchtergaven** Cairneyhill Road, Bankfoot blg cld 2004 (dest fire)
- (1906 N&B 2/14  r1989 Edm 2/14

**Auchterless** Aberdeenshire
- 1904 Wad 2/15  o1915 Wad, o1994 SmRo **A-listed**

**Auchtermuchty** (Old) Croft, Fife
- 1913 Ing 2/12

**Auchtermuchty St. Serf's E** (pt of National Archives)
- (1903 Pos 1/

**Auchtertool**
- 1886 C&M 2/10  o2004 Edm **A-listed**

**Auldearn** nr Nairn
- 1899 Pos 1/7  o1993 Edm **A-listed**

**24) The Casson Positive organ in Auldearn Church**

70

**Aviemore** - see Rothiemurcus

**Avoch** Braehead
   ⅄   1908 MilJ 1/6 divided keyboard, no pd **B-listed**

**Avoch C** High Street
   ⅄   (1902 Pos 1/
   ⅄   1906 F&A 2/15 fr Tain Town Hall 1944 by Law, o2000 R&D **A-listed**

**25) The Forster & Andrews organ in Avoch Congregational Church originally in Tain Parish Church, which became Tain Town Hall**

71

**Avonbridge** (UF/UP) West Lothian
⁜ small organ 1/4 builder unknown

**Ayr** Fort Street (north end)
⁜ (c1459/60 Thomas Broun o1537, o1550 by a monk, abandoned 1559

**Ayr Auld (St. John the Baptist)** Blackfriars Walk
⁜ (1878 Hun 3/25 r1902 N&B, o1923 HNB, rem 1940s
⁜ (1901 N&B 3/31 o1923 HNB, to here 1951 from Ayr Cathcart, Fort Street, scr 1974 Wal
⁜ 1952 Wal 3/50 (with Wal material from 1880s) to here fr Eastbourne St. Mary the Virgin
   1971 & r1974 Wal 2/28

**Ayr Castlehill** Castlehill Road
⁜ 1964 R&D 2/20 ex4 o2000s

**Ayr Cathcart** (UF/UP) Cathcart Street blg cld 1951
⁜ (organ 1/ to here 1886
⁜ (1899 B&H 2/ rem 1951 to Ayr Cathcart, Fort Street & r Watt 2/27

**Ayr Cathcart** (Auld New Kirk Mission 1810-1951) Fort Street cld 1981
⁜ (1874 ConP 2/22 rem 1901 to Glasgow Springburn North by Mir
⁜ (1901 N&B 3/31 o1923 HNB 3/31, rem 1951 to Ayr Auld
⁜ (1899 B&H 2/ fr Cathcart Street blg to here 1951 & r Watt 2/27 in N&B case with reed
   unit, scr 1984 WoP and John Wilson, console to Stranraer Trinity

**Ayr Darlington New** (Darlington Place/UF/UP) Main Street cld 1981
⁜ (1898 B&F 2/23 r1970 Hils 2/25, rem 1985 to Inch & r John Wilson 2/26

**Ayr Gaumont Theatre** 113 High Street dem 1968
⁜ (1927-29 Jar 3/67 +17 traps ex10 rem 1962 Hils

**Ayr Good Shepherd Cathedral RC** cld 2000 dem
⁜ (1903 Wad 3/24 +2pf r pre-1921 3/26, o1961 Mac, fr Glasgow St. Peter's E 1964 &
   r Hils 3/25

**Ayr Holy Trinity E** Fullarton Street
⁜ (1850 Mir small organ fr Glasgow St. John's E 1867 (in previous blg here)
⁜ (1888 Lewis 3/24 dest fire 1937
⁜ (1937 Com 3/58 ex rem 1973 to Ulster, but case survives

**Ayr Lochside -** see Ayr St. Columba's Lochside

**Ayr New (or Auld New) -** see Ayr Cathcart, Fort Street

**Ayr Newton on Ayr M**
⁜ Vin 2/

**Ayr Newton on Ayr Old** cld 1962 (see also Ayr St. James)
⁜ (1910 Vin 3/26 with piston in pulpit for minister to reduce organist's volume rem Hils
   1965 for use at Ayr Newton Wallacetown

**Ayr Newton Wallacetown** (Newton on Ayr/ Newton on Ayr New/UF/F) Main Street
⁜ 1924 HNB 2/16 r1965 Hils 3/35

**Ayr Old** - see Ayr Auld and Ayr Cathcart

**Ayr Playhouse Theatre** Boswell Park
⚐ (c1932 Hils

**Ayr Res of Butler**
⚐ 1874 Hill 3/ (est. only)

**Ayr Res of Murdock**
⚐ 1925 HNB

**Ayr St. Andrew's** (UF/F) Park Circus
⚐ (1901 B&F r Ing 2/16, rem 1978, case extant

**Ayr St. Columba's** (Trinity UF/UP) Midton Road
⚐ 1904 Bin 3/26 r1962 BinT 3/35, r1985 Har 3/36, r2005 Har 3/38, o2015 1ss changed
⚐ Har 1/3 fr University of Reading 2012

**Ayr St. Columba's: Lochside** Lochside Road/Murray Street
⚐ (1902 F&A 1/7 moved in blg 1957, fr Prestwick South c1985, rem

**Ayr St. James's** Prestwick Road, Newton-on-Ayr
⚐ (1925 Hils 2/14 scr, except case

**Ayr St. Leonard's** St. Leonard's Road
⚐ 1887 Har 2/27 r1910 Vin 3/30, r1961 Hils, r1992 Nic 2/31

**Ayr St. Margaret's RC** John Street (Cathedral fr 2007)
⚐ (1868 organ
⚐ (1900 Hard 2/13 o2000 MilP, scr 2011

**Ayr St. Quivox** - see Auchincruive House

**Ayr Sandgate** (West UF/F) Sandgate cld 1981 (now pub)
⚐ (1896 F&A 2/22 scr 1986, some pipes to Peebles Old

**Ayr Sang Schule** cld
⚐ (1538 organ

**Ayr Town Hall**
⚐ (1881 LTC 3/ o1883 LTC, dest by fire 1897
⚐ 1904 Lew 3/27 o2007 McDM, o2012 Har **A-listed**

**Ayr Wallacetown** (Wallacetown North) John Street cld 2010
⚐ (1903 Ing 2/

**Ayr Wallacetown C**
⚐ Walc 1/

**Ayr** - see also Heads of Ayr

**Ayton**
⚐ 1894 F&A 2/22 o1997 Lig **A-listed**

**Balanreich** - see Ballater Res of Stanley Ewen

**Balerno** (UF/UP)
⋏ (c1850 HDa r1870s HDT 1/10, o1922 & 1925 HCF, to here 1975 from Edinburgh Napier University, Craighouse by ESO volunteers, rem to Forteviot & o1992 Edm

**Balerno St. Mungo's E**
⋏ (1900 organ rem c1940

**Balfron** (North)
⋏ Har 2/ to Balfron 1951, inst here & r R&D 2/9

**Balgavies House** (Res of Miss Lumsden) nr Forfar
⋏ (1907 MilJ 2/11 rem 1937 to Aberdeen High Hilton & r Law 2/12

**Ballachulish St. John's E** (see also Onich)
⋏ 1879 Wad 2/9 **A-listed**

**26) The Wadsworth organ in St. John's, Ballachulish,
one of several churches endowed by Bishop Chinnery-Haldane**

74

**Ballantrae**
⊥    c1900 JoT 1/4  to here c1920s

**Ballater** - see Glenmuick

**Ballater North** (UF/F) Braemar Road cld 1938
⊥    (1900 Pos 1/5
⊥    (c1914 Sau 2/13  rem to Uphall South c1940

**Ballater Res of Dr. Stanley Ewen, Balanreich**
⊥    1814 All 1/6  fr Banchory Res c1946 to Aberdeen Res of Archibald Gullett, 2
      Fountainhall Road, rem 1988 by Edm and inst here by Edm & Ewen, r Loo by 2008

**Ballater St. Kentigern's E** (St. Saviour's E) Braemar Road
⊥    (1907 Walc 2/7  scr
⊥    1959 Har 2/15  fr Westminster Abbey (temp) to Aberdeen University King's College
      Chapel 1959, o1971 Har, o1992 Har, o1997 Har, rem 2004 & r2008 Edm here with Walc
      material fr old organ **B-listed**

**Ballater St. Nathalan RC** Golf Road
⊥    c1840s Fli 1/5  fr elsewhere to here **A-listed**

**Ballingry** - see Benarty St. Serf's

**Ballintuim Res of Miss Constable** Perthshire
⊥    (1825 Bew 1/6  fr elsewhere to here 1855, rem 1991 to Aberdeen St. Nicholas Uniting &
      o Edm

**Ballintuim Woodhill House Chapel RC**
⊥    (organ  extant 1855

**Balloch** - see Alexandria (North)

**Ballochmyle Res of Mrs. Crookston** Ayrshire
⊥    (c1920 HNB  rem 1926 to London by HNB

**Balmaghie** nr Kirkcudbright cld 2015
⊥    c1900 Pos 1/5  fr Tongland 1989 by amateur

**Balruddery Res of J. Martin White** nr Dundee
⊥    (1883 F&A 2/14  dest by fire
⊥    (c1890 Casson/Thynne 4/42 (derived)  r1894 H-J/MilJ 3/30, dest with house 1970s

**Banchory-Devenick**
⊥    1902 Pos 2/  moved in blg 1930

**Banchory-Devenick**  - see also Ardoe

**Banchory Res** (see also Blackhall Castle)
⊥    (1814 All 1/6  rem c1946 to Aberdeen Res of A. Gullett

**Banchory Res of Mr. Cuncliffe, Mavisbank**
⊥    (organ  o1895 Wad

**Banchory Res of A.G. Innes, Raemoir**
⊥    (Innes pre-1891  extant 1904-16, rem 1928 to Aberdeen St. Clement's E

**Banchory Res of Miss Barbara Ramsay**
ㅅ (1896 organ moved 1906, extant 1911

**Banchory St. Ternan's E** High Street
ㅅ (organ c1850 rem c1870
ㅅ 1904 Wad 2/13 o R&D, o1995 Wil **A-listed**

**Banchory Ternan East** (Banchory-Ternan) Station Road
ㅅ (cabinet organ to here fr London 1878, rem to ch hall
ㅅ 1887 Wad 2/17+1pf o1902 Wad +1ss, o1921 Wad, r1930-32 War 2/19 and moved, o Wil, r2008 Edm 2/17 **B-listed**

**Banchory Ternan West** (South UF/F) High Street
ㅅ 1924 Ing 2/12 r1985 Edm 2/14, o2015 McDM 2/12

**Banff** (St. Mary's)
ㅅ 1892 ConP 2/21 o1921 Wad, r1929 Hils 2/22, o1970s Edm 1ss changed, o1988 McDM, o2009 McDM

**Banff Millseat C**
ㅅ (organ rem 1900

**Banff Our Lady of Mount Carmel RC** (present blg 1870)
ㅅ (pre-1806 MWo to here 1820 fr Macduff by WSm, rem 1829 to Portsoy Church of the Annunciation RC

**Banff Res of Reburn, George**
ㅅ (organ for sale 1868 per Wishart, Aberdeen

**Banff Res of Mr. E.B. Thomson, Inverichney**
ㅅ (1902 Walc 1/5

**Banff St. Andrew's E**
ㅅ (pre-1730 organ 2/ r1733, o1736 & 1741, dest 1746 by Cumberland's army
ㅅ (1759 Jordan o1776 Shand, to new chapel 1833, sold to F&A 1871
ㅅ 1871 F&A 2/14 moved 1919, r1922 Watt, o Hils, disued in 1980s

**Banff Trinity and Alvah** (Trinity/High UF/F) cld 1994
ㅅ (1913 Wad 2/18 o1971 Hils, o R&D, o Loo, for sale 1995, rem 2003

**Bangour Hospital Church**
ㅅ 1925 Jar to here 1930 & r Jar 3/23 +3pf, o1937 Jar, o1940 Jar, o1964 ConP +3ss

**Bangour Village Hospital Recreation Hall**
ㅅ (1931 Chr 2/60+26 traps ex9 fr Carlisle Lonsdale ABC Cinema 1972 by STOPS & SmRo, rem 1980 to Ripon Res of B. Smallwood, thence to Germany

**Bankfoot** - see Auchtergaven

**Bannockburn Allan** Main Street/New Road
ㅅ (organ fr Stirling Marykirk to here 1938, rem 1959
ㅅ 1898 Wad 2/11 fr Meldrum & Bourtie to Aberdeen Gilcomston Park B 1953, r1972 2/13, to here 1990 & r Loo 2/13

**Bannockburn Our Lady & St. Ninian's RC** Quakerfield
⅄ c1930 Ing 1/7 r c1980 Edm, o Loo, disused

**Bargeddie** nr Glasgow
⅄ 1876 Wil 2/13 r1938-44 G&D 2/18 , r1963 Wil 2/20, o2007

**Barr** Ayrshire
⅄ (organ extant 1956 rem by 2000

**Barrhead Arthurlie** (UF/Barrhead UP) blg cld 1967 (ch now called Barrhead St. Andrew's)
⅄ (Walc 2/ r1926 Ing 2/16, scr

**Barrhead Bourock** (Barrhead) Main Street
⅄ (1900 A&S 2/19 r1956 Watt 2/
⅄ 1984 Jhn 2/17

**Barrhead C** Arthurlie Street
⅄ (1881 Mir case, soundboards, reservoirs survive

**Barrhead M** Cross Arthurlie Street
⅄ (Ebr 2/ to Barrhead Westbourne 1920 by Watt, to here c1931, scr

**Barrhead Res of Gordon Frier** - see Glasgow entry

**Barrhead Res of Hugh Millar**
⅄ (1885 ConP

**Barrhead St. John's RC** Darnley Road/Aurs Road
⅄ (organ damaged by fire
⅄ 1961 R&D 2/22 ex4 o2004 McDM

**Barrhead South & Levern** (South/UF/F) Main Street cld 2013
⅄ 1903 Watt r1937 HNB 2/

**Barrhead Westbourne** (UF) cld 1931
⅄ ( Ebr inst 1920 Watt 2/ , rem c1931 to Barrhead M

**Barrhill** - see Arnsheen Barrhill

**Barry** (East/UF/F)
⅄ 1902 Law 2/9 fr Barry West post-1955 R&D

**Barry West** (Barry) cld 1955
⅄ (1902 Law 2/9 rem to Barry (East) post-1955 & r R&D

**Barthol Chapel**
⅄ (Pos 1/4 o c1971 Gol
⅄ c1845 Ren fr Boharm Mulben 1976 & r Gol 1/5, o2004 Aub **C-listed**

**Bathgate Boghall**
⅄ 1964 R&D 1+pd/10 ex2

**Bathgate EU URC** (C) Marjoribanks Street
⅄ 1922 Bin 2/14

**Bathgate High**
⚲  1899 Bis 2/23  o1978 SmRo 2/23 (console moved), o Wil

**Bathgate St. David's** cld 2007
⚲  (1863 HDa 2/22 +4pf  r1894 King 2/22, o1914 Ing, fr Edinburgh Augustine C 1930 & r Ing 2/24, r c1965 R&D, redundant 2009, rem

**Bathgate St. John's**
⚲  1927 HNB 2/15  o1976 Loo, o2001 Lig, o2002 Lib

**Bearsden All Saints E** Drymen Road/Glenburn Road
⚲  (1926 Watt 2/10  o R&D
⚲  (1972 Chu 1/5  to Fotheringay 1996 (temp), then to Stoke Doyle St. Rumbald's 2000
⚲  c1914 Sau 2/13  fr Ballater North to Uphall South c1940, to here 1995 & r Ian McNaught & congregation 2/13

**Bearsden Cross** (South/UF/New Kilpatrick UP) Drymen Road at Ledcameroch Road
⚲  (1878 F&A 2/8+1pf  moved within church 1882
⚲  (1900 B&F 2/21  dest 1941
⚲  1906 Lew 2/16  fr Glasgow Eglinton Street UF 1921 to Glasgow Eglinton Elgin by Brk, to here 1953 & r HNB, o1982 R&D 2/16, r2012 Har 2/22
⚲  (c1960 Cou 1/5 with one older ss  fr Kilbrandon & Seil 2012 by Matthew Hynes (temp), dest 2012

**Bearsden New Kilpatrick** Manse Road
⚲  (1878 Hun 2/14
⚲  1909 N&B 2/19  r1974 R&D 2/23, o2005 For 2/25
⚲  c1870 Ewa 1/7  o1900, fr Polkemmet House to Longridge 1960s R&D, o1994 McDM, fr Longridge 2005 to here & o Matthew Hynes

**Bearsden North** (UF/F) Drymen Road/Thorn Road cld 2006
⚲  1902 Bin 2/21  o1981 HNB, extant 2016

**Bearsden Res of Ninian Glen, Auchendrane** Roman Road
⚲  (1910 N&B 2/

**Bearsden Res of J. W. Macfarlane**
⚲  (1884 Wil 2/10  rem 1921 to Glasgow St. Cuthbert's & Queen's Cross & r Watt 2/10

**Bearsden St. Peter's College RC** cld 1966
⚲  (organ  rem c1966 to Cardross St. Peter's College RC by Hils

**Beauly** - see Kilmorack and Eskadale

**Beauly Beaufort Castle Res of Ann Gloag** (Res of Lord Lovat)
⚲  1911 N&B 2/8  o Law, o R&D

**Beauly St. Mary's RC**
⚲  1937 Law 2/9  r1938 Law

**Bedrule** (under Ruberslaw fr 2003)
⚲  1912 N&B 2/8 to here 1926 by Ing **A-listed**

**Beith C** Bellman's Close
⊥   (Walc 1/7 to here 1929 & r Watt 1/5 no pd, scr 1980

**Beith** (High/Beith)
⊥   1886 Har 3/30 disused 2012 **A-listed**

**27) The all-mechanical three manual Harrison organ in Beith Parish Church**

**Beith Trinity** (UF/Hamilfield UF/Beith F) cld 2011
⊥   (1905 N&B Norvic in former church, dest by fire 1917
⊥   (1937 HNB 2/12 o1997 McDM, o2005 McDM

79

**Belhaven** Dunbar
  ⊥   1908 F&A 2/11  o1960s R&D **B-listed**

**Belhaven The Manor House** Dunbar
  ⊥   (1850 Tow 5ss barrel organ  rem 1967 to Edinburgh Huntly House Museum

**Belhaven** - see also Glasgow

**Belhelvie** Aberdeenshire
  ⊥   1904 Walc 1+pd/7  r Loo 2/ ex4, disused 2016

**Bellie** The Square, Fochabers
  ⊥   (1887 ConJ 2/10  r Ing, o1998, scr 2006

**Bellshill Central** (Macdonald Memorial/East UF/Bellshill F) Main Street
  ⊥   1924-31 Hils 2/17  o1961 R&D, o2006 McDM, o2015 McDM

**Bellshill Mossend Holy Family RC** Calder Road/Hope Street
  ⊥   (c1870s organ 2/  to here fr elsewhere, rem 1966
  ⊥   1966 C&C 2/21 ex5  o1981

**Bellshill Mossend M** (Primitive M/Burke Memorial) cld (now Orange Hall)
  ⊥   (1905 F&A 1/7

**Bellshill Sacred Heart RC** Cross Gates
  ⊥   (1978 Brug 1/3 (temp)  completed 1984 and rem to Glasgow Unitarian, Berkeley Street by Mac
  ⊥   1980 Brug 2/9

**Bellshill St. Andrew's UF** (Bellshill St. Andrew's/Bellshill West UF/Bellshill UP) Main Street/North Road
  ⊥   (1892 F&A 2/17  o1904 F&A, dest by fire 1942
  ⊥   1921 Watt 2/19  to here 1963 fr Greenock Elim Pentecostal (Greenbank/UF/UP) by  Watt, o c2010 For, now disused

**Bellshill West** (Bellshill) Main Street
  ⊥   (1886 Bro 2/18  r1905 N&B 2/20, o1918 HNB, scr 1970, material dispersed, case extant

**Benarty St. Serf's** (Ballingry)
  ⊥   (1966 Wil 1 +pd/3 +5pf  scr 2005

**Bervie** King Street, Inverbervie
  ⊥   1904 Law 2/18  o1948, o1973 R&D, o1985 R&D +1ss, o2003 Nob **A-listed**

**Bieldside St. Devenick's E** North Deeside Road/Baillieswells Road
  ⊥   1910 Wad 2/13 +2pf  r HNB 2/15 **B-listed**

**Biggar** (St. Mary's) Kirkstyle
  ⊥   (ref to organ in 1545
  ⊥   1889 ConP 2/  in north transept  r1935 Sco 2/21 into chamber, r c1965 Wal, r1995 Edm 2/21

**Biggar Gillespie** (UF/UP) High Street cld 1946/1953
⚲   (1908 Sco  rem 1952 to Musselburgh St. Andrew's High

**Biggar Gillespie-Moat Park** (Moat Park UF/UP) Kirkstyle cld 1976
⚲   (1910 Lew 2/10  rem 1980 to Menstrie & r Loo (2ss changed)

**Birkhill House Res of Lord Dundee** Fife
⚲   c1860 Tow 1+pd/4  o1995 Edm **A-listed**

**Birnam St. Mary's E** Perth Road
⚲   (1863 Lew
⚲   1874 F&A 2/10  r1908 MilJ 2/12 (moved), r1994 Edm 2/12 (1ss changed) **B-listed**

**Birnam -** see also Dunkeld

**Birnie** Moray
⚲   1970 Wal 1/4

**Bishopbriggs Kenmure** (UF/Bishopbriggs UP) Viewfield Road
⚲   1911 Lew 2/18  fr Glasgow Buccleuch (Garnethill) 1946 Wil, disused, 3ss used at
    Bearsden Cross 2012

**Bishopbriggs St. James the Less E** (cong fr Springburn) Hilton Road
⚲   1964 Wal 2/18 ex3  fr Clydebank St. Columba's E 1996 Mac

**Bishopbriggs Springfield Cambridge** (Springfield/UF/F) Springfield Road
⚲   (Walc 1/3  fr Res of Rev. Primrose 1924 to former blg, now hall

**Bishopbriggs -** see also Cadder

**Bishopton** (Erskine/Old Erskine)
⚲   (c1850 Bev 2/9  fr Paisley Woodside House 1896 & r Mir 2/9 (1ss changed), o1975 Mac,
    innards rem 2015 McDM
⚲   1956 Wal 1/11 ex4  fr Edinburgh St. Cuthbert's (temp) to Oban Christ Church Dunollie
    1957, to here 2014 by McDM, inst in old case

**Bishopton Convent of the Sisters of the Good Shepherd** (Bishopton House) now Good Shepherd
Centre
⚲   (c1905 Rutt 2/  fr Glasgow Res to Paisley Orr Square, to here 1960

**Bishopton Rossland** (Erskine UF/F) cld 1971
⚲   (1902 Watt 2/11  rem Hugh Ross 1993 to storage, to Gereformeerde Kerk, Lutten, the
    Netherlands & r1997 Feenstra/Bogaard 2/12

**Blackburn** (UF/F) Aberdeenshire cld 1932
⚲   (1902 Pos 1/

**Blackford** Perthshire
⚲   1898 Ing 2/  o HNB, vandalised & o2017

**Blackhall Castle** nr Banchory
⚲   (organ  pre-1944

**Blackridge Res of Robert Leys**
⊥  (1927 ChrN 3/ ex5 fr Stratford Empire Theatre, Essex to Stirling Res of Arthur Nicol 1971, to here 1985, to Hornstrup, Anton Stormlund Forsamlingshus, Denmark 2001

**Blackwood St. John's RC** Carlisle Road
⊥  1883 Dre 1+ppd/4 o1981 McDM

**Blair Atholl** Perthshire
⊥  1910 MilJ 2/10 o2009 Loo, o2010 Edm

**Blair Castle** Perthshire
⊥  (organs extant 1764 & 1769 o1832 F&R, o1865 Vietor
⊥  1630 "I.L." 1/5 positive-regal to here 1857 **A-listed**

**Blair Atholl St. Adamnan's Kilmaveonaig E**
⊥  c1800 Anon 1/5 fr Letterfourie House nr Buckie (temp at Buckie St. Peter's RC) 1965 to Cults Res of Charles Davidson, 1970 to Aberdeen Res of David Murray, rem 1981 to Burrelton Res of David Murray, rem c1990 to Forteviot Workshop of A.F. Edmonstone, installed here 1999 by Edm

28) Left: The 1902 Watt organ from Bishopton Rossland, now at Lutten in the Netherlands
29) Right: The Anon Scottish organ in Blair Atholl Episcopal Church

**Blair Drummond Res of Mrs Drummond**
  ⅄  (1875 Hill

**Blairgowrie** - see also Marlee

**Blairgowrie** (St. Andrew's/UF/F) James Street
  ⅄  1907 N&B 2/18  r1989 Edm 2/23

**Blairgowrie The Hill** (Blairgowrie) Kirk Wynd cld 1976
  ⅄  (1873 ConP 2/17 with pipes from 1869  o1896 Wad, rem by 1913
  ⅄  (1913 Har 2/14  pt to Alyth 1978, pt to Edinburgh Morningside 1980

**Blairgowrie Public Hall** Brown Street
  ⅄  (1869 ConP 2/20  rem 1915 to Blairgowrie Riverside M

**Blairgowrie Riverside M** Boat Brae cld 2014
  ⅄  (1869 ConP 2/20  fr Blairgowrie Public Hall 1915 & r Kea 2/20, r Hils, rem 2015 to Seville Parroquia de Santiago, St. James, Alcala de Guadiara

**Blairgowrie St. Mary's** cld 1968
  ⅄  (1902 Walc 1+pd/6  r1926 Wat 2/10

**Blairgowrie St. Mary's South** (South/UF/F) Reform Street cld 2002
  ⅄  1924 Hils 2/16  o1986 McDM, redundant 2002

**Blairgowrie St. Stephen's RC** John Street
  ⅄  (1846 organ  extant1856
  ⅄  (1906 organ  r1952, rem

**Blairquhan Castle** Straiton, Ayrshire sold 2015
  ⅄  WSm barrel organ 5ss
  ⅄  other barrel organ, extant 2003

**Blairs College** Kincardineshire
  ⅄  (1835 Wis with material by Fli  o1891-5 Wad, rem 1902 to Dingwall St. Lawrence RC
  ⅄  1903 Law 3/32  r1939 Law 3/32, r1965 HNB 3/32, o2002 MilP

**Blanefield** - see Strathblane

**Blantyre Livingstone Memorial** (UF/Blantyre UP) Glasgow Road
  ⅄  1907 Watt  r1956 Watt 2/ , o1988 McDM 2/8

**Blantyre Old** (High Blantyre, Blantyre) Hamilton Road
  ⅄  1825 Ward 1/8  r 2/13 Bro at Farnley Hill M, fr Leeds 1893 by Bro, r1914, r1920 Bro 2/12, o c1975 Hils 2/11 +3pf, disused

**Blantyre St. Andrew's** (Stonefield & Burleigh/Stonefield) Church Street blg dest by fire 1979 and replaced
  ⅄  (1871 ConP 3/31  o1920 Mir, fr Hamilton Victoria Hall 1949 & r Hils, o1957 Watt, discarded 1981, one mixture to Glasgow Dennistoun New
  ⅄  (1846 HDa 1/6  r1857, fr St. Andrews St. Andrew's E to St. Andrews B 1869, to St. Andrews C pre-1920, to Milngavie St. Joseph's RC 1978, to Glasgow Newlands St. Peter's College 1979, to here 1982 & r McDM 1/8 with new case

**Blantyre St. Joseph's RC** Glasgow Road
ᴧ (c1877 Bis fr exhibition rem 1966
ᴧ 1967 C&C 2/21 ex6 o1982 MMcD

**Boarhills Falside Smiddy Res of Dr. Keith Birkenshaw** Fife
ᴧ Wal 2/

**Boddam** nr Peterhead
ᴧ 1937 organ

**Boghall** - see Bathgate

**Boharm** Banffshire cld 1946/74
ᴧ (1899 Law 2/12 rem to Boharm Mulben 1976 without case

**Boharm** (Boharm: Mulben/Boharm UF/F) Banffshire cld by 2002
ᴧ (c1845 Ren to here early 20th century, rem 1975 to Barthol Chapel
ᴧ (1899 Law 2/12 fr Boharm 1976 by Philip Wright, o1979 R&D, rem by Loo to storage at Pluscarden

**Bo'ness Craigmailen UF** (UP) Braehead
ᴧ 1896 B&F 2/22

**Bo'ness Old** Panbrae Road
ᴧ (1876 Har 2/13 fr former ch 1886, o1929 Har, r1933 Sco 2/21, o1961 Wil, dismantled 1990s.

**Bo'ness St. Andrew's** (UF/F) Grange Terrace
ᴧ 1926 Ing r1973 R&D 2/19, disused 1995

**Bo'ness St. Catharine's E** Cadzow Crescent
ᴧ (chamber organ in former church installed 1891 fr Mrs. Marshall of Richmond
ᴧ 1903 MilJ 1/7 fr Dalgety 1983 Loo, o2017 Loo

**Bo'ness** - see also Carriden

**Bonhill** (Old)
ᴧ (1882 Har 2/11 r1936 BFH 2/21, o1961 Watt, o1982 McDM, scr 1989

**Bonhill North** (UF/UP) cld 1975
ᴧ (Com 2/ rem R&D

**Bonnybridge St. Helen's** (Bonnybridge) High Street
ᴧ 1956 Com 2/ "Augmentum"

**Bonnyrigg** (Cockpen UF/F) Midlothian
ᴧ (1903 Vin 2/15 o1904, o1960 Wil, o1992 R&D, scr 1999

**Borthwick** Midlothian cld 2018
ᴧ 1893 F&A 2/14 o1986 R&D **A-listed**

**30) The 1893 Forster & Andrews organ in Borthwick Parish Church**

85

**Bothwell** (St. Bride's)
- ⚥ (c1880s Bro rem pre-1933 by Hils
- ⚥ (1890 F&A 2/17 o1900 F&A, r1933 Hils 2/22, r1981 McDM with pt fr Bothwell Kirkfield & Wooddean, disused, console rem

**Bothwell Kirkfield & Wooddean** (Kirkfield//UF/F) cld 1976
- ⚥ (1890 ConP rem to Glasgow Merrylea 1915
- ⚥ (1914 Ing 2/24 (3 divs) scr 1976, pt to Bothwell

**Bothwell St. Bride's RC and Poor Clare Monastery**
- ⚥ 1958 Wal 2/10 +8pf o1975 McDM, fr Glasgow Christian Scientist 1 to here 1989 McDM, completed SmRo

**Bothwell Wooddean** (UF/UP) cld 1941
- ⚥ (1912 Watt 2/11 rem 1946 to Hamilton Gilmour & Whitehill by Watt

**Bourock** - see Barrhead

**Bourtie Res of Alex Anderson** nr Inverurie
- ⚥ (organs made pre-1799

**Bow of Fife** (Monimail UF/F) cld 1944/1980
- ⚥ (1913 N&B 2/12 rem 1983 to Cupar Old & St. Michael of Tarvit & r Loo

**Bowden**
- ⚥ 1912 Ing 2/13 +2pf o1950s HNB, o1969 R&D, o2007 Sta 2/14, o Lig **B-listed**

**Bowden Village Hall**
- ⚥ (1902 organ

**Boyndie** (St. Brandon's) Banffshire cld 1948/1994
- ⚥ (organ o1891/1900 Wad
- ⚥ 1910 Wad 2/9 redundant 1996

**Boyndie House Res of Ogilvie-Forbes** (chapel)
- ⚥ (c1850 amateur 1/5 r1876 Wis, 1897 to Fraserburgh Our Lady Star of the Sea RC & o Wad

**Braco** - see Ardoch

**Braemar Castle** (Res of Stanley Bond)
- ⚥ (c1860 anon 2/8 rem 1935 to Braemar St. Margaret's E

**Braemar St. Andrew's RC** Auchendryne Square
- ⚥ (organ o1890 Wad
- ⚥ 1903 Wil 2/11 +1pf r1901 Law 2/12, o1994 Wil **B-listed**

**Braemar St. Margaret's E** Castleton Terrace cld 2001
- ⚥ (c1860 anon 2/8 to here 1935 fr Braemar Castle, rem 1960 to Aberlady by R&D

**Braes of Rannoch** Bridge of Gaur
  ↓  (1908 organ  rem 1990
  ↓  1935 Rot 2/7  o1978 R&D, fr Urquhart 1991 & r Loo 2/7

**Braidwood House** near Carluke (now care home)
  ↓  1930 Ing 2/15

**Brechin B** (West & St. Columba's/St. Columba's/East UF/F cld 1974) Panmure Street/Southesk Street cld 1992 for sale 2011
  ↓  (1896 B&H 2/15  o1959 R&D, extant 1996

**Brechin Cathedral** Church Lane
  ↓  1878 ConP 3/32 +2pf  in east gallery  o1890 Wad, o1894 Scot, o1895 MilJ, r1901 MilJ 3/34 in west gallery, o1913 Law, r1930 Law 3/28 in new cases, r1953 R&D, r1968-69 R&D 3/36, +2ss post-1971, r2006 Lib 3/38 (3ss changed) **B-listed**

**Brechin City Road UF** (UP) cld 1914
  ↓  (1883 Wad 2/  r1894 Wad moved within blg +1ss

**Brechin East** cld 1937 (for East F see Brechin B)
  ↓  (1905 Bis  r1907 B&H 2/17

**Brechin Gardner Memorial** (Southesk/Gardner Memorial West & St. Columba's/Gardner Memorial) Southesk Street/Damacre Road
  ↓  1903 Bin 2/13 disused 2005 **C-listed**

**Brechin Holy Trinity RC**
  ↓  organ extant 1840s

**Brechin Maison Dieu** (UF/UP) Witchden Road cld 1990
  ↓  Com  derelict

**Brechin Res of R.W. Orr**
  ↓  (1924 Law  completed later

**Brechin St. Andrew's E** Argyle Street/St. Andrew Street
  ↓  1842 Bru  to present church 1888 & o Wad, r1920s HNB 2/11, o1985 HNB, disused **C-listed**

**Brechin St. Ninian's RC** (UF/Bank Street UF/UP cld 1963) Bank Street
  ↓  (1955 Com  rem

**Brechin West & St. Columba's** - see Brechin B

**Brechin West** (UF/F) cld 1948
  ↓  (1895 ConP 2/18  rem 1948 to Arbroath Knox's & r Bro

**Bridge of Allan Chalmers** (UF/F) Henderson Street cld 2003
  ↓  (1897 B&F 2/17  r1951 R&D 2/20, o1973 R&D, r1980 Loo 2/32

**Bridge of Allan** (Holy Trinity/St. Andrew's) Keir Street
  ↓  1884 LTC 2/22  r1904 A&S 3/30, o2002 Edm, disused **B-listed**

**Bridge of Allan** - see also Lecropt

**Bridge of Allan Res of C.E. Allum**
⊥ (pre-1895 ConP

**Bridge of Allan St. Saviour's E** Keir Street
⊥ (1872 F&A 1/9 o1960 R&D, o1990s R&D, scr

**Bridge of Allan Trinity** (UF/UP) cld 1942
⊥ (1903 Lew 2/13 rem 1946 to Dundee Stobswell (Park) by Sco

**Bridge of Don St. Columba's** (shared church) Aberdeen
⊥ (c1840 Bis 1/8 fr West Wemyss 1983 & r Edm, rem 2008 to Yorkshire school

**Bridge of Earn** - see Dunbarney

**Bridge of Weir Freeland** (UF/F) Main Street
⊥ 1913 Sco 2/10 o1978 R&D

**Bridge of Weir Quarrier's Home Mount Zion Church** cld 2002
⊥ (1899 Walc 2/25 r1961 HNB 2/28, o1982 HNB, rem 2007

**31) The 1899 Walcker organ in Mount Zion Church, Bridge of Weir**

**Bridge of Weir Ranfurly** (UF/UP) cld 1968
 ⚔  (1906 Bin 2/

**Bridge of Weir St. Machar's Ranfurly** Kilbarchan Road
 ⚔  1901 Bro 2/15 (mechanical) o1958 Watt, console rem 1972, rest extant

**Bridgend St. Columba's E** Islay
 ⚔  1935 Com 2/12  r1982 G. Harrison 2/20 ex3, fr Millport Cathedral of the Isles c2002

**Brightons** (Polmont South/Polmont UF/F)
 ⚔  Watt 2/16  to here fr Glasgow & r1950 Watt 2/16, r1970s SmRo 2/17, o c2005 Loo

**32) The Watt organ at Brightons Church**

**Brodick** (St. Bride's/Brodick UF) Glencloy Road
 ⚔  1931 Watt 2/8  o1984 G. Harrison

**Broom** Newton Mearns
 ⚔  1975 Wal  2/ ex4  r1979 Corkhill

**Brora** - see Clyne

**Broughton, Glenholm & Kilbucho** (Broughton) Peeblesshire
 ⚔  (1920 Hils 2/7  scr 2003

**Broughty Ferry** - see under Dundee

**Broxburn** (St. Andrew's/St. John's/East UF/UP))
 ⚔  (1923 Ing 2/12  r c1953 Ing 2/12, dest fire 1966

**Broxburn SS John Cantius & Nicholas RC**
 ⚔  1887 Har 2/8  fr Kirkcaldy Res of John Blyth 1892 Har, o c1925-30, 1949 to west gallery,
     o1975 R&D

**Broxburn St. Nicholas UF Cont.** (St. Nicholas cld 1964)
 ⚔  Ing 2/

**Broxburn West** (UF/F) cld 1975
⚓ (1903 Watt 1/7 no pd

**Buchanan** nr Balmaha
⚓ (1878 Ric 2/7 no pd

**Buckhaven & Wemyss** (Buckhaven/St. David's/UF/UP)
⚓ 1952 R&D 2/30 ex4

**Buckhaven & Wemyss** - see also East Wemyss and West Wemyss

**Buckie All Saints E** Cluny Square
⚓ 1872 Bev 1+ppd/6 fr Cluny Castle, Aberdeenshire 1877 F&A, o1920 Wad, o1980 McDM **A-listed**

**Buckie B** Cluny Place
⚓ (1913 Walc 1/ o1917 Wad

**Buckie High School**
⚓ (1928 War 2/11 fr Buckie West 1971 by pupils & Mr. Fraser & r Wal 2/17, dest

**Buckie** - see also Letterfourie House

**Buckie M** North Pringle Street
⚓ Nel 2/15 to here 1953

**Buckie North** (Buckie) Cluny Square
⚓ (1899 Pos o1917 Wad
⚓ 1898 B&F 3/ r L&B 3/ , fr Keighley M 1953 Nel, r1957 Nel, o1968 Wal 3/26, o1989 Edm, r Gol, r McDM, r Loo 3/25

**Buckie St. Peter's RC** St. Andrew Square
⚓ (1824 WSm to here 1842 from Dufftown St. Mary's RC by Bru
⚓ (1867 ConP 2/16 r ConP, r1912 Law 2/21, o R&D, o1994 Lig, rem 2000, some pipes to Motherwell
⚓ (c1780s 1/5 fr Letterfourie House (temp) pre-1960, rem 1960 to Cults Res of I. & Charles Davidson
⚓ (1888 James Graham 2/c8 to Carnoustie Res of Graham c1892, rem post-1925 to Aberdeen Doctor's Res, rem to Nairn St. Mary's RC, c1965 to Pluscarden Abbey by monks, r1976-77 Loo, rem 2000 to here Loo (temp), scr 2000, some pipes to Motherwell
⚓ 1875 BBM 4/65 fr London, The Hall, Primrose Hill, Regents Park, Res of N.J. Holmes to Albert Palace, Battersea, to Fort Augustus 1894, in store until 1917, r by the brothers in Abbey 3/30, r1937 Law 4/73, r1979 R&D 3/37, fr Fort Augustus Abbey to here & r2000 R&D 3/38

**Buckie South & West** (Buckie South/UF/Buckie F) High Street/East Cathcart Street
⚓ 1901 Wad 2/11 r1928 Wad 2/11, 1983 Loo 2/13

**Buckie West** (UF/UP) Cluny Square cld 1970
⚓ (1928 War 2/11 rem 1971 to Buckie High School by Wal

**Bucksburn St. Machar's E** Oldmeldrum Road
⟂    1902 Wad 2/13  o1980s R&D, o2005 Edm **A-listed**

**Bucksburn** - see also Stoneywood

**Bucksburn Stoneywood** (Bucksburn/Newhills UF/F) Oldmeldrum Road
⟂    (1900 Pos  o1919 Wad
⟂    (1924 Law 2/12  disused 1995

**Bucksburn Stoneywood Res**
⟂    c1890 Wad

**Budge Bank House** - see Halkirk

**Buittle** Kirkcudbrightshire cld 2010
⟂    1904 N&B 1/4 no pd  o1912 K&B

**Burghead** (UF/UP)
⟂    (c1900 Walc 1/5  scr 2015 (woodworm)

**Burntisland** (St. Columba's) East Leven Street
⟂    1909 Cou 2/20  r1937 Cou 2/21, o & moved 1967, o c1987 Loo, o1998 SmRo

**Burntisland Erskine UF** (UP) Kinghorn Road
⟂    1922 Hils 2/16  r1984 Loo 2/19 with pts from Johnstone St. Paul's 1989

**Burntisland Res of W.R. Thomas & J.J.K. Rhodes**
⟂    (barrel organ by Flight & Kelly 4ss

**Burntisland St. Andrew's** (Couper UF/F) cld 1977
⟂    (1901 G&D 2/15 +1pf  rem to Dunfermline Queen Anne High School 1977-1981 & completed Loo

**Burntisland St. Serf's E**
⟂    (1905 Walc 1/  to here 1930s, o1999 by American organ builder, scr 2007
⟂    1901 Wad 2/10  moved in ch 1915-17 & 1ss changed Wad,  fr Lochgelly St. Andrew's 2007 & r Edm 2/10

**Burrelton Res of David Murray**
⟂    (c1800 Anon 1/5  fr Letterfourie House 1965 to Cults Res of Charles Davidson, then to Aberdeen Res of David Murray 1970, to here 1981, rem c1990 to Forteviot Workshop of Edm

**Busby** (West/UF)
⟂    (1913 Watt 2/  r1985 R&D, rem 1992 except case

**Busby** (Res of Alexander Ovenstone)
⟂    (1883 ConJ 3/11  disused 1937, rem 2009 Budgen & Hynes to Milborne Port, English Organ School, Dorset

**Bute** - see Rothesay, Mount Stuart and Port Bannatyne

**Butlins** - see Heads of Ayr

**Cadder** Cadder Road, Bishopbriggs
ǂ (1874 Hun 2/18 fr Glasgow St. Paul's E 1888 & inst 1908 Watt 2/18, scr 1956
ǂ 1915 N&B 2/16 o1929 HNB, fr Dumbarton High Street 1956 & r Watt 2/15 with 1ss fr
Hun org, o1990s R&D after water damage

**Cadder South Hall** Bishopbriggs
ǂ (c1900 N&B 1/5 rem 1922 to Edinburgh St. Bride's

**Caddonfoot** nr Galashiels
ǂ 1933 Ing 2/11 r2007-2012 Sta 2/15

**Cadzow** - see Hamilton

**Cairnie-Glass** (Cairnie) nr Huntly cld 1994
ǂ 1902 Wad 2/

**Cairnryan** - see Lochryan

**Calder, Kirk of** Midcalder
ǂ 1888 ConJ 2/16 o1986 R&D **A-listed**

**Calder** - see also Coatbridge Calder

**Calderbank**
ǂ 1909 A&S 2/9 fr Dunblane Leighton 1955 & r Wil 2/9, o1987 McDM, r2005 Wil

**Caldercruix & Longriggend** (Caldercruix Steeple)
ǂ (1913 Watt 1/7 c1930 fr Caldercruix Ind, o2004 McDM, scr
ǂ 1968 Wal 2/17 ex3 fr Paisley Abbey to Paisley School Wynd C 1969 Wal, o1982 McDM,
rem to Paisley Oakshaw Trinity 2003 by McDM, to here 2004 McDM

**Caldercruix Ind** (West UF/F) cld 1939 now Ind
ǂ (1913 Watt 1/7 rem c1939 to Caldercruix & Longriggend

**Calderhead** - see Shotts

**Caldwell** Uplawmoor, Renfrewshire
ǂ 1903 Ing 2/10 disused

**Callander** (St. Bride's/Callander UF/F) South Church Street
ǂ 1900 A&S 2/24

**Callander St. Andrew's E** Leny Road
ǂ 1886 C&M 2/8 +6pf r1898 A&S 2/10 +4pf, disused

**Callander St. Kessog's** (Callander) Ancaster Square cld 1985
ǂ (1901 Wil 3/20 r1911 Vin 3/20, r post-1940 Ing 3/25, rem 1987 to Forfar St. Margaret's
by Australian amateurs

**Callart House** North Ballachulish
ǂ (c1902 Welte Orchestrion disused from 1948, sold by auction 2000

**Cally House** Gatehouse of Fleet (later hotel)
⚲ (1877 Ren 2/10 rem 1936 to Sorbie

**Calton Moor** - see Poltalloch House

**Cambo House** East Fife
⚲ (1883 F&A 2/11 rem to Kingsbarns 1953
⚲ (1886 HDT 2/11

**Cambray College** (i.e. Cumbrae) - see Millport

**Cambuslang B** Greenlees Road
⚲ 1901 Walc 1+pd/7 o1984 Wil

**Cambuslang** (Old/Cambuslang) Cairns Road cld 2011, for sale 2016
⚲ (1896 A&S 2/19 r1922 ConP in chamber, r1969 ConP 2/23, console moved 1999 McDM, pt rem c2014

**Cambuslang Rosebank & West** (Rosebank UF/F) Main Street at Bridge Street blg cld 1966
⚲ (1899 Walc 2/24

**Cambuslang St. Bride's RC** Greenlees Road
⚲ 1977 Brug 1+pd/5

**Cambuslang St. Cadoc's RC** Wellside Drive
⚲ (Walc 1/5 to here 1962 Watt, o1977 McDM, rem 1994
⚲ new organ

**Cambuslang St. Charles RC** Newton Farm Road
⚲ (c1850 HDa 1/8 o1884 War, fr Fettercairn House 1979 & r McDM 1/6, rem 1997 to Stanley's Antiques, Auchterarder, then via English/Irish dealer to Japan

**Cambuslang St. Columba's E** Newton Farm Road cld 1985
⚲ (1909 SmRi 2/ in original blg cld 1927

**Cambuslang St. Paul's** (UF/UP) Bushyhill Street cld 1987 dem
⚲ (1913 Ing 2/ rem 1987

**Cambuslang Trinity St. Paul's** (Trinity/UF/Cambuslang UP) Glasgow Road at Beech Avenue cld 2008
⚲ (1900 Walc 2/23 +1ss Mir, o1948 HNB, r1968 ConP 3/31, o1992 HNB, scr to dealer 2011

**Cambuslang West** Glasgow Road at Somervell Street cld 1955 sold 1965
⚲ (1888 Bro 2/12 fr Glasgow Kelvingrove International Exhibition 1888 by Bro, o1899 Bro, o1907 Bro, o1909 Mir, rem 1914 by Vin, then to Glasgow Renfield Free Church Mission
⚲ (1915 Vin 2/21 + 2pf added later o1944 Mir, rem 1961 to Larkhall Chalmers & r BinT

**Cambusnethan** - see Wishaw

**Campbeltown Highland** New Quay Street
⚲    1954 Har 2/11  disused, console dismantled 2000s

**Campbeltown Lochend UF Cont.** (F) Lochend Street cld
⚲    (1922 Har 2/11  rem 1986 to England

**Campbeltown Lorne Street** (UF/F) cld 1990 (Heritage Centre)
⚲    (1880 LTC 2/16 +1pf  fr Glasgow Lansdowne 1911 to Glasgow workshop of SmRi, to
here 1920 &  inst SmRi 2/18, r1967 Hils 2/21, scr

**Campbeltown Lorne & Lowland** (Lowland/Longrow/UF/UP) Longrow
⚲    (1895 B&F 2/22  o c1910 B&F, r1927 B&F 2/27, r1967 Hils 2/27, disused 2004, case
survives

**Campbeltown Lowland** (Castlehill) Main Street cld 1971 (flats)
⚲    (1878 ConP  r1927 ConP 2/17, rem pre-1971

**Campbeltown Res**
⚲    (c1886 Bro 2/9  rem 1891 to Campbeltown St. Kiaran's E

**Campbeltown St. Kiaran's E** Argyll Street
⚲    (organ extant 1852 in previous blg (UP)
⚲    c1886 Bro 2/9  fr Campbeltown Res to here 1891, o1973 Har, disused

**Campsie High** (Campsie) Lennoxtown cld 1978 dest fire 1980s
⚲    (organ 1/  fr Edinburgh C ch 1901 by Ing
⚲    (1908 N&B 2/  o1923

**Campsie** (Trinity/West/UF/UP) Lennoxtown blg replaced.1988
⚲    (1908 LTC 2/14  o1969 Mac, scr

**Canna, Res of John Lorne Campbell**
⚲    c1800 John Maule barrel organ, 3ss

**Cannich** - see Marydale

**Canonbie: United** (Canonbie)
⚲    (c1900s Walc 1/  rem c1972
⚲    1972 W.R.C. Lang & friends 2/21 + traps, pts fr Newbattle, Co. Durham

**33) The unusual case design of the Lang organ at Canonbie**

**Caputh** Perthshire
⚤   c1830 SBr  fr Delvine House 1909 & r1914 MilJ 2/12, o1950s Wil, o1998 Edm

**Carberry Tower Res of Lady Elphinstone** nr Musselburgh (later Church retreat)
⚤   Chapel: 1960s Wal 1+pd/  ex2
⚤   Library: 1864 Hill 2/  r1899 HCF 2/10, r1914 HCF 2/10

**Carbisdale Castle** (SYHA, Res of Salvesen to 1944, Res of Countess of Sutherland to 1933)
⚤   (c1917 B&F 2/7  rem 1950 to Dingwall Castle Street

**Cardross** (Old) dest 1945
⚤   (1913 Hils 2/14

**Cardross** (Burns/UF/F) Station Road
⚤   1958 Wil 2/14 inst 1963

**Cardross St. Peter's College RC** cld 1980
⚤   (organ  fr Bearsden St. Peter's College RC c1966 & r Hils, scr

**Carfin Hall** nr Mossend
⚤   (1887 Bro  saloon organ

**Carlops**
⚤   c1820 WSm 1+Sw/7  to Edinburgh Kirk Memorial C post-1903, gift of Mr. Hunter, rem 1946 to Arbroath C, to here 1968, o2008 Edm **A-listed**

**Carluke Kirkton** (UF/UP) Station Road
⚤   1937 HNB 2/11  o1961 BinT, water damaged 2015, o2016 MilJ

**Carluke Res of T Forsyth** (see also Braidwood House for Res nr Carluke)
⚤   (1934 Com 3/  ex5 + traps  fr London Astoria Purley, to East Kilbride Civic Centre 1976, to here late 1970s, rem 1982 to Spalding, Res of C. Booth

**Carluke St. Andrew's** (Carluke) St. Andrew's Court
⚤   1903 Wil 2/15  o2010 For & after water damage 2015 **A-listed**

**Carluke St. John's** (UF/F) Hamilton Street/Park Street
⚤   (1908 or 1911 organ
⚤   1932 Bro  console moved 1949, moved & r1979 SmRo

**Carluke URC** Carnwath Road
⚤   organ  fr Res inst Hils 3/

**Carmunnock**
⚤   (1893 Wad 2/11  fr Glasgow St. Michael's Mission fr St. George's (St. Peter's E), Burnside Street to here 1948 & r BFH, rem

**Carmyllie** (East/Carmyllie) Angus
⚤   1912 MilJ 2/  fr Dundee St. Roque's Chapel 1953 & r R&D 2/11, o1996 Lib

**Carnbee** Fife
⚤   (1873 Ren

95

**Carnoustie** (Old) Dundee Street
⅄ 1902 Vin 3/25 (using older German pipes) o1971 R&D, r1989 Lib 3/30, r1999 Lib 3/32 with pd flues from Arbroath Old, pt of pd to Colliston

**Carnoustie Erskine** (UF/UP) Dundee Street cld 1932 (now bar)
⅄ (1906 Wad 2/13 +3pf to Invergowrie 1934 by Bro (purchased by auction 1932)

**Carnoustie Holy Rood E** Maule Street
⅄ 1904 MilJ 2/12 o1957 Hils, r1970 HNB 2/12, o2002 MilP **B-listed**

**Carnoustie Panbride** (Newton Panbride/UF/F) Arbroath Road
⅄ (1902 Law 2/12 rem c1960

**Carnoustie Residence of James Graham, Balbride**
⅄ (1888 James Graham (amateur) rem post-1925 to Aberdeen Res of doctor

**Carnoustie St. Anne's RC** Thomas Street
⅄ 1965 Wal 2/18 ex fr Dundee St. Teresa's RC 2008

**Carnoustie St. Stephen's** (UF/F) cld 1969
⅄ (1903 MilJ 2/17 scr

**Carnwath Walker Memorial** (UF/F) cld 1938 (ch hall)
⅄ 1913 Watt

**Carriden** Bo'ness
⅄ 1925 B&H fr Glasgow John Knox & Tradeston 1943 & r Sco/Wil 2/15, r1977 Gol, r1985 Gol 2/17, r1994 Gol 2/24, currently disused

**Carsphairn**
⅄ 1922 Pos 1/4 to here 1931, no case

**Carstairs**
⅄ 1921 Hils r1989 McDM 2/9 (2ss by Mirrlees)

**Carstairs House Res of R. Monteith**
⅄ 1859 G&D 1/

**Castle Douglas** (St. Ringan's/Queen Street UF/Macmillan F) Queen Street
⅄ (Vin 2/
⅄ 1903 IHJ fr Castle Douglas St. George's UF 1930 & r Ing 2/19, r1960s, o1994 Sav, r1997 Sav

**Castle Douglas St. Andrew's** Marle Street/Lochside Road cld 1989 (later theatre)
⅄ (1904 Lew 2/14 r1965 Sol 2/ , rem 1993 to Greystokes, Cumbria by Sav

**Castle Douglas St. George's UF** (F) cld 1923
⅄ (1903 IHJ rem 1930 to Castle Douglas (St. Ringan's) & r Ing

**Castle Douglas St. John the Evangelist RC** Abercromby Road cld 2007
⅄ (1868 F&A 2/11 o1976 R&D, rem 2010 to Clifford St. Edward, King & Confessor, West Yorkshire & r Skrabl 2/12

**Castle Douglas St. Ninian's E** St. Andrew Street
⼂ (1874 organ
⼂ 1889 Har (est only)
⼂ 1984 WoP 2/9 using Lewis pipes

**Castle Fraser** nr Kcmnay
⼂ (1816 Ell 2+ppd/11 rem 1938 to Kemnay St. Anne's E by Law

**Castle Grant** - see Grantown-on-Spey

**Castlehill** - see Ayr and Forres

**Castle Kennedy** - see Inch

**Castleton** - see Newcastleton

**Catrine** (High)
⼂ 1883 Har 2/14 **A-listed**

**Cellardyke** Toll Road, Anstruther
⼂ 1906 Ing 2/20 **A-listed**

**Cellardyke B**
⼂ (1903 Walc 1/

**Ceres**
⼂ (1919 organ disused, rem

**Challoch** - see Newton Stewart

**Channelkirk** nr Oxton
⼂ c1900 N&B 1/5 fr Cadder South Hall to Edinburgh St. Bride's 1922, to Edinburgh St. Martin's 1958, to here 2012 & r Sta 1/5

**Chapel of Garioch** Aberdeenshire
⼂ 1923 E&B 2/13 **A-listed**

**Chirnside** Berwickshire
⼂ 1880 ConP 1+pd/7

**Chryston** (Chryston East) nr Glasgow
⼂ (1903 Har 2/19 scr

**Chryston West** (UF/F) cld 1950
⼂ (1901 Watt 2/ rem 1951 to Prestonpans Grange

**Clackmannan** (St. Andrew's-on-the-Hill/Clackmannan) Port Street
⼂ (1926 Ing 2/14 disused 1993

**Clackmannan Erskine** (UF/UP) Kirk Wynd cld 1932
⼂ (1904 Watt 1/4 r later

**Clarkston** - see Greenbank

**Clarkston St. Aidan's E**
⅄ (ConP to here 1960 & r ConP, r1969 C&C 2/26, organ rem to house c2002 by amateur, case survives

**Clashmore Public Hall** nr Dornoch
⅄ (organ gifted by Carnegie

**Cleish** Kinross-shire
⅄ 1927 E&B 2/16 o1960 R&D, o1976 SmRo, fr Edinburgh Lockhart Memorial to Edinburgh St. Giles 1990, 1992 to here & r SmRo 2/ (new action)

**Cleland** Lanarkshire
⅄ 1905 Watt 2/ fr Glasgow Partick Highland Gaelic F post-1945

**Clola** - see Deer

**Closeburn** Dumfriesshire
⅄ 1887 Wil 2/11 r1938 Wil 2/14, o later

**Cluny** (North) Aberdeenshire
⅄ 1911 Vin 2/8 o2012 Edm

**Cluny Castle** Aberdeenshire
Chapel:
⅄ (1872 Bev 1+ppd/6 rem 1877 to Buckie All Saints E
⅄ (1877 F&A 2/10 damaged by fire 1926
⅄ 1928 Wad using material fr old organ rem 1993 to Cluny South (temp) by David McGinnigle, returned 2000s Nob
Stairwell:
⅄ 1873 F&A 2/11 (3 ss divided) **A-listed**

**Cluny South** (Linton House Chapel/West UF/Free) Sauchen cld 1933, sold 2010 with organ
⅄ (1903 Law 1+pd/6 o 2010 Edm, sold 2012 on e-bay

**Clydebank Abbotsford -** see Clydebank Waterfront

**Clydebank Faifley** (Hardgate) Faifley Road, Duntocher
⅄ 1966 Wal 2/18 ex4 o1982 McDM

**Clydebank Kilbowie St. Andrew's** (Kilbowie) Kilbowie Road
⅄ (1904 Bro rem 1951
⅄ (1955 BinT 2/27 fr Glasgow St. Mark's Lancefield 1968 by C&C, scr 1984

**Clydebank Morison Memorial URC** Glasgow Road
⅄ (1910 Bro 2/14 dest by fire
⅄ 1912 Bro 2/14 o1961 Mac

**Clydebank Our Holy Redeemer RC** Simon Street/Glasgow Road
⅄ (Walc 1/ rem 1954 quarried/scr
⅄ (1955 Watt 2/22 ex5 r1958 Watt 2/22 ex5, rem, some ss to Clydebank Town Hall
⅄ (1900 Pos 1/ fr Kilsyth Anderson to Res of Tom Logue, Glasgow c1970, to here 1984, rem 1993
⅄ 1867 Mir 2/16 o1980 Mac, fr Glasgow St. Joseph's RC 1985 to storage in Glasgow St. Columba of Iona RC Maryhill, to here 1996 & inst 1997 McDM **A-listed**

**Clydebank Radnor Park** (UF/UP) Radnor Street
⟂    (organ r Hils, dest by fire WW2

**Clydebank St. Columba's E** Glasgow Road cld 1996
⟂    (Pos 1/ rem 1964 to Mac workshop, parts used
⟂    (1964 Wal 2/18 ex3 rem to Bishopbriggs St. James the Less E 1996 Mac

**Clydebank St. James'** Dumbarton Road cld 1974
⟂    (1879 Dre 2/23
⟂    (1921 Bin 2/23 rem to new ch at Clydebank Waterfront & r1980 WWo 2/25

**Clydebank St. Mary's RC** Chapel Road, Duntocher
⟂    (1902 Bro
⟂    1848 Bev 1/6 fr Castle Donnington, Derbyshire 1979 & o McDM, disused

**34) The Bevington organ at St. Mary's, Duntocher, originally in Castle Donnington, Derbyshire.** Photograph by Michael Macdonald

**Clydebank Town Hall** Dumbarton Road

⚓ (1939 Wur 3/107 ex13 fr Stockport Ritz Cinema to storage 1960s, to here 1994, o1994-
99 Ian Macnaught and SCOT team, rem 2006 to storage, to Glasgow Pollokshaws Burgh
Hall 2008

**Clydebank Union** (UF/UP) Dumbarton Road cld 1976

⚓ (1907 N&B 2/18

**Clydebank Waterfront** (Abbotsford/West/UF/F) Abbotsford Road

⚓ 1921 Bin to here fr Clydebank St. James & r1980 WWo

**Clynder Res of Dr. Andrew Baxter**

⚓ (1998 Lam 2+pd/7+1pf fr Gartocharn Res 2000, rem 2012 to Merchant Taylor's School,
Herts & r 2/8

**Clyne** Brora, Sutherland

⚓ 1920 Law 2/7 o1979 Edm

**Coalsnaughton** (UF/UP) cld 1994

⚓ (c1905 Pos 1/6 fr Norfolk & inst Watt, redundant 1995, rem to Glasgow, scr

**Coatbridge Blairhill Dundyvan** (Blairhill UF/UP) Blairhill Street

⚓ 1931 Ing 2/12 o2005 McDM, disused 2006

**Coatbridge C** Buchanan Street/Bank Street blg cld

⚓ (1851 Bev fr Glasgow Athenaeum Assembly Rooms 1853 to Glasgow Dundas St C, to
here 1899 & r Watt

⚓ (Wil/Har r1911 Watt 2/ with new console, to here c1945 fr Paisley area & r Watt 2/12 in
Bev case, scr 1976

**Coatbridge Calder** (Garturk) Calder Street

⚓ 1870 Wil 2/15 o1964 Wil, o1987 Wil **B-listed**

**Coatbridge Clifton** (Coats) Jackson Street cld 2008 (now Ind)

⚓ (1875 Wil 2/17 r1972 R&D 2/18 following fire damage, o1999 Edm, rem to Coatbridge
St. Patrick's RC 2010 McDM

**Coatbridge Coatdyke** (Cliftonhill/Coatdyke UF/UP) East Muiryhall Street/East Stewart Street cld
1993

⚓ (1912 A&S 2/10 r1978 McDM 2/13, rem 1994 to Port Glasgow St. John the Baptist RC
by McDM

**Coatbridge Coatdyke** - see also Coatbridge Holy Trinity

**Coatbridge Dunbeth** (UF/UP) Weir Street cld 1993

⚓ (1899 B&F 2/23 r1955 Wil 2/23 rem c1975

**Coatbridge Dundyvan** Dundyvan Street/Henderson Street cld 1974 damaged fire 2007

⚓ (1913 Vin 3/25 rem

**Coatbridge Holy Trinity & All Saints RC** East Muiryhall Street/Quarry Street (Trinity/Coatdyke
Parish cld 1973)

⚓ 1913 Vin 3/28 o1937 Wil, o1982 G. Harrison, r1990 SmRo 3/

**Coatbridge Maxwell** (East UF/F) Weir Street cld 1993
⊥   (c1900 Walc 1/5  engine to Scone New 1924

**Coatbridge Middle** (Middle UF/F) Church Street blg cld 1951
⊥   (Walc 1/

**Coatbridge Middle** (West UF/Langloan/Drumpelier UF) Bank Street
⊥   c1908 Walc 1+pd/

**Coatbridge New St. Andrew's** (St. Andrew's/Gartsherrie) Church Street/Baird Street
⊥   1870 Wil 2/15 +1pf  o1902 Wil, r1937 Watt 2/20 +1pf, o2010 Mac

**Coatbridge Old Monkland** Woodside Street
⊥   1907 Har 2/14  disused 2007 water damage

**Coatbridge St. Augustine's RC** Dundyvan Road/Buchanan Street
⊥   (1871 F&A 3/31 (4 depts)  r1887 F&A, fr Kilmarnock Corn Exchange c1906 Watt, r
      c1920 Watt 2/ , r1985 Edinburgh Cinema Organ Club per Larry Maguire
⊥   1934 HNB/K&B 2/11  using pt of case of Gern fr Paisley Woodside House, fr Glasgow
      Gordon Park to here & r c1990 SmRo using existing F&A case/console

**Coatbridge St. John the Evangelist E** St. John Street cld 1992
⊥   (1726 organ  r1781, fr Douglas Support 1844 & r Bru & Joseph Baker, pt rem 1867 to
      Lanark Christ Church E
⊥   (1866 Mir  fr Glasgow Polytechnic Exhibition 1867 & r Joseph Baker with pipes added
      from organ above, moved to chamber 1871, r1897 Bro, sold 1916 to Watt
⊥   (1859 Hol 2/21 fr London St. Paul's, Herne Hill to here 1914 Bro, r Watt 2/27, o Hils, o &
      resited 1963 Mac, rem 1993 WoP

**Coatbridge St. Mary's RC** Hozier Street, Whifflet
⊥   (Bru  organ extant 1878 in former blg
⊥   Wil 2/  fr Res to Watt workshop & inst 1955 Watt

**Coatbridge St. Patrick's RC** St. John Street
⊥   (Mir  moved within former ch 1866
⊥   (c1870 ConP 3/15  fr Res in Wales 1907 Watt, o1953 Watt & moved in blg, r1978 McDM
      3/15, o2006 McDM, rem 2009 to Germany by Dutch builder
⊥   1875 Wil 2/18  r1972 R&D 2/18, o1999 Edm, fr Coatbridge Clifton 2009 & r McDM
      2/17

**Coatbridge St. Thomas M** cld c1968
⊥   (1874 ConP 2/  scr c1970

**Coatbridge Summerlee Heritage Centre**
⊥   1937 Com 3/102 ex7  fr Liverpool Mayfair Cinema 1987 to East Kilbride Civic Centre, to
      here 1992, o2010-14 For

**Coatbridge Town Hall**
⊥   (1895 Wil 4/42 +1pf  1ss added later, r1954 Wil 4/43 +6pf, dest fire 1967

**Coatbridge Trinity** (Coatdyke Parish) cld 1973 - see Coatbridge Holy Trinity & All Saints RC

**Cockburnspath** - see Dunglass

**Cockenzie & Port Seton Old**
⅄  (1814 Cle/DavJ 2/13 no pd  inst & o1816 MWo 2/ , converted to equal temperament by HDa 1828, o1831 HDa, r pre-1894 Tow 2+pd /14, fr Edinburgh St. George's E 1933 & r Sco 2/14, dismantled 1963
⅄  (1965 Sol 2/21 ex 3  using some pipework from old organ, rem 1988
⅄  1925 MilJ 2/12  fr Dundee Rattray Street B 1988 & r SmRo 2/12, r2011 Pri **B-listed**

**35) The 1814 James Davis organ at Cockenzie Old c. 1960.** Photograph by Bob Hooker

**Cockpen & Carrington**
⅄  1888 Wad 2/14 +2pf  2ss added later,  r post-1975 Nic 2/16 **B-listed**

**Coldingham** (Priory)
⅄  1908 Bin 2/14  fr Coldingham St. Andrew's 1955 R&D, r2014 Sta 2/16

**Coldingham St. Andrew's** (UF/UP) cld 1940/1952
⅄  (1908 Bin 2/14  to Coldingham 1955 & r R&D

102

**Coldstream** (Old) High Street
- 1877 ConP 2/16  to here 1902 fr Glasgow Blackfriars, r1935 B&H 2/20, o1980 Chu, disused 1993, operational 2010

**Coldstream Community Centre** (St. Cuthbert's/West/UF/UP cld 1963) High Street
- (1894 Har 2/8  rem 1906 to Bedlington Primitive M
- (1909 Har 2/15 in new blg  rem to Monifieth South 1998 by LIb

**Coldstream Rodger Memorial** (UF/F) Victoria Street cld 1950
- (1882 Bev 1+pd/7  o1937 Har, rem 1951 to Leitholm

**Coldstream St. Mary's & All Souls** E
- 1890 HCF 1+pd/6  fr The Hirsel Chapel E 1897 & r Ing 2/12, o1985

**Coldstream The Hirsel Chapel** E
- (1890 HCF 1+pd/6 rem to Coldstream St. Mary's & All Saints 1897 & r Ing
- (Gern 2/  r1902 Ing 2/14, rem 1958 by R&D

**Collearn** - see Auchterarder St. Margaret's Hall

**Collessie F** - see Ladybank

**Colliston** Angus
- c1865 HDT 1/7 +1pf (some pipes G&D)  to here c1895 & r MilJ, r1999 Lib 1+pd/9 (pd ss fr Carnoustie) **B-listed**

**Colliston** Kirkcudbright - see Dalbeattie

**Colmonell**
- 1908 N&B 2/19  o1924 HNB, o2004 For **A-listed**

**Colmonell UF** (F)
- (1904 N&B Norvic  rem 1968 by C&C (some pipework to Old Luce)

**Coltness House Res of Walter Houldsworth** nr Wishaw
- (1881 LTC 2/13 (all encl)  rem c1951 to Motherwell B by BFH
- (1906 Bev 1/

**Coltness** - see also Newmains Coltness Memorial

**Colvend**
- 1915 Brow 1+pd/5  o1977 HNB, extant 2000

**Comrie** (St. Kessog's/West UF/F) Burrell Street
- (1906 Lew 2/14  fr London Exhibition to Kilmacolm St. Columba's, to here 1959 by HNB, scr following heat damage 2012

**Comrie St. Margaret's RC** Drummond Street
- organ

**Condorrat** - see Cumbernauld Condorrat

**Conon Bridge** - see Ferintosh

**Coodham House Res of Sir W. Houldsworth** Ayrshire
⅄   (1873 Hill 3/25 +2pf  r1874 Hill, r1909 Hill 3/32, in chapel, dest
⅄   (1868 Hill 3/21  fr Norbury Booth's Hall, Cheshire 1898, in billiard room, rem 1961 Mac
     for use at Glasgow Lochwood

**36) The Hill organ in the chapel at Coodham**

**Cookney** Kincardine cld 1982
⅄   1903 Pos 1/5  extant 1982

**Corehouse** nr Lanark
⅄   organ extant

**Corgaff** cld 1996/2006
⅄   (1902 Pos 1/  extant 1997

**Cornhill** - see Ordquhill, Aberdeenshire (1870s HDT organ at Cornhill, Northumberland)

**Corrie** Arran
⅄   c1960 Sol 1/5 ex2 encl

**Corsock** (Corsock Murray-Dunlop/UF/F)
⅄   (organ extant by 1934  o1948 Hils
⅄   (organ  to here 1950 Hils, extant 1987, disused by 2007

104

**Coulter Mains** nr Biggar
- (1762 WaJ 1/4 fr Glasgow Res of James Watt to Malt's Lodging, College 1776, 1815 to Glasgow Res of Archibald McLellan, 78 Miller Street & o McLellan & Steven + 1ss, rem to Mugdock Castle, Milngavie, sold 1854 to A.G. Adam of Denovan, to here 1863 & o 1864 Ren, rem 1918 to Giffnock Res of George A. Macfarlane

**Coupar Angus Abbey** Queen Street
- 1892 Wad 2/19 o1909 Wad, o1957 R&D, o2006 Lib **A-listed**

**Coupar Angus St. Anne's E** (St. Mary's E) Forfar Road
- (1848 organ
- (1871 Holt
- 1887 Har 2/13 r1998 Edm 2/13 2ss changed **B-listed**

**Cove St. Mary's E** Loirston Road, Kincardine (for Cove, Dunbartonshire see Craigrownie)
- (pre-1886 Wad

**Cowdenbeath Cairns** (UF/UP) cld 1998
- (1903 Law 2/9 r1912 Law 2/12, fr Aberdeen John Knox Mounthooly & r1975 R&D, rem 1999 to Lauder & r2003 Sta

**Cowie & Plean** (Cowie UF) nr Stirling blg cld 2017
- 1905 Pos

**Cowie & Plean** (Plean)
- 1910 Walc 1/ to here 1939

**Cowie Episcopal School** Kincardine
- (c1830s SBr 1/5 fr Stonehaven St. James the Great to Cowie House 1877, to here pre-1894

**Cowie House Res of Major W.D. Innes** Kincardine
- (c1830s SBr 1/5 fr Stonehaven St. James the Great to here 1877, rem to Cowie Episcopal School pre-1894

**Coylton** Ayrshire
- (1906 N&B 2/10 scr 2000s, case survives

**Craig** - see Montrose South & Ferryden

**Craigforth House -** see Stirling

**Craigiehall** nr Dalmeny
- (organ for sale 1734

**Craigneuk** - see Wishaw

**Craigrownie** (Cove & Kilcreggan: Craigrownie) Church Road
- (1887 Bro 2/13
- 1910 Bin 2/17

**Craigrownie Cove & Kilcreggan: Lindowan** (Kilcreggan UF/UP) Rosneath Road cld 1952 then hall, for sale 1999
- (1894 IngE 2/18 r1924 HNB 2/17

**Crail** (St. Mary's) Marketgait
- ⊥ (organ extant 1517
- ⊥ 1893 Har 3/27 r1926 Har 3/28, fr Kirkcaldy Res of John Blyth 1936 & r Sco 3/29, o1959 Wil, o1990s For

**Crail Res**
- ⊥ (1889 ConP 2/11 r1924, fr Glasgow Cardonald 1955 to Loanhead East, rem c1980 to Fa'side Castle, Wallyford, later to store in Kirkcaldy Res, later to here

**Crail St. David's** (North UF/F) St. Andrews Road cld 1954
- ⊥ (c1900 Pos/MilJ 1+pd/6 divided keyboard rem 1954 to Denbeath

**Cranstoun, Crichton & Ford** (Cranstoun) Midlothian
- ⊥ c1920s Ric 2/10 fr Moffat Well Road Centre (Warriston) 1936 by Ing 2/10

**Crathes Castle**
- ⊥ (organ extant 1754-62

**Crathie**
- ⊥ 1895 Wil 2/11 +2pf r1911 Vin 3/16, r1932 Law 3/16, o1961 R&D, o1974 R&D, disused 1997

**Craufurdland Castle** nr Kilmarnock
- ⊥ (c1850 Bru/Ren 1/4 rem 1890 to chapel of Myres Castle, Fife, moved 1921 to drawing room at Myres

**Crawford** cld 1994
- ⊥ (1960s Sol 1/+pd

**Crawfordjohn** cld 1986 (now museum)
- ⊥ (1912 Hils 2/8 o1980 Gol, disused, redundant 1992

**Creetown** - see Kirkmabreck

**Crichton** cld 1992 (now run by Crichton Collegiate Church Trust)
- ⊥ 1899 Bro 2/9 +1pf o1973 R&D, o2002 Lam, o2012 Wil 2/10 **A-listed**

**Crichton Manse** (Res of Peter Ferguson-Smyth)
- ⊥ (1792 Hugh Russell fr Humbie Stobshiel 1991, rem 2005
- ⊥ (1987-89 Lam 1/5 fr Humbie Stobshiel 1991, rem 2005, to Rosslyn Chapel, then Edinburgh Mayfield Salisbury 2010 Lam
- ⊥ (18th C South German fr Amsterdam to Humbie Stobshiel 1991, rem 2005

**Crichton Memorial Hospital Chapel** - see Dumfries

**Crieff** (St. Andrew's & St. Michael's/St. Michael's) Strathearn Terrace
- ⊥ (1867 Ren in previous blg
- ⊥ 1882 F&A 2/22 o1898 F&A, r1906 SmRi 2/26, r1963 Hils 2/27, o1978, o1990s R&D, o2007 For

**Crieff B** King Street/Addison Terrace
- ⊥ (c1900s N&B 1/ extant 1960s

**Crieff C**
- ⚜ 1900 Bro 2/9

**Crieff Hydro**
- ⚜ (Pos 1/ rem 1900
- ⚜ 1900 IngE 2/12 o c1985 HNB **A-listed**

**Crieff Res of J. Bennett McNeill**
- ⚜ (1742 Sne 1/6 to here c1975 fr Edinburgh Res, 3 Ravelston Ct, returned to Edinburgh Res 1978

**Crieff St. Andrew's** (North UF/UP) Church Street cld 1989 (now St. Andrew's Hall)
- ⚜ 1905 N&B 2/13 o c1933 Hils, for disposal 2013 **A-listed**

**Crieff St. Columba's E** Perth Road
- ⚜ (small organ
- ⚜ (1878 Bis 2/12 o1886 Wad, o1891 Bis, r1902 Bis 2/17, r1980s SmRo, scr 1985

**Crieff St. Fillan's RC** Chapel Road
- ⚜ 1845 Ren 1/8 no pd fr Murthly Castle RC Chapel 1871 & r Ren 1/8 with new case front, o1968-70 Watt, o1985 McDM, o2003 McDM

**Crieff St. Margaret's College**
- ⚜ (1853 Bev 1/6 rem 1863 to Pitfour Castle, Glencarse, Perthshire

**Crieff South & Monzievaird** (South/UF/F) Commissioner Street cld 1997
- ⚜ 1899 A&S 2/19 r1951 in west gallery R&D 2/28, redundant 1997

**Crimond**
- ⚜ 1905 ConP 2/10 o1984 Edm 2/10

**Cromarty** (West/Stewart Memorial/UF/F)
- ⚜ (1926 Watt dest by fire 1932
- ⚜ 1933 Ing 2+pd/ disused fr c2010

**Cromlix House Chapel Property of Andrew Murray** (Hotel) Perthshire
- ⚜ c1903 MilJ 2/14 o R&D, disused

**Crossford** Lanarkshire
- ⚜ 1938 Ing 2/10 completed 1950s Wil, o1989 McDM

**Crosshouse** Ayrshire
- ⚜ 1901 F&A 2/16 o1922 F&A + trem, o1977 Mac 1ss fr Glasgow Abbotsford Chalmers, console resited **A-listed**

**Cruden** Aberdeenshire
- ⚜ 1903 Wad 2/14 o2008 Edm **A-listed**

**Cruden St. James the Less E**
- ⚜ (organ fr Italy, rem by 1843
- ⚜ 1849 Rust 2/12 moved from gallery to chamber by 1876, o1898 Wad, o1918 Wad, o1928 Wad, o1984 Gordon Harrison and rem back to gallery, o2011 Edm **A-listed**

**Culcreuch Castle Hotel** nr Fintry
⅄ (1810 Edinburgh-made organ 1/5 to and from Fintry 1815, extant 2001, rem

**Cullen and Deskford** (Cullen Auld)
⅄ (16th century organ
⅄ (c1903 Walc 1/
⅄ 1914 N&B 2/9 o1917 Law

**Cullen House**
⅄ (1766 Byf 1/6 to here 1957 fr Grantown-on-Spey Castle Grant, rem 1975 to Finchcocks Musical Museum, Kent, sold to France 2016, to Alan Rubin collection

**Cullen St. Mary's E** (UF/UP cld 1905) Station Road/Reidhaven Street cld 1960s (now store)
⅄ (organ

**Cullen Seafield** (UF/F) cld 1946 Seafield Street (now antiques store)
⅄ (1900 Pos 1/ casework added 1904, o1911 Law, extant 1960s

**Culross Abbey**
⅄ 1909 N&B 2/13 o1990s Loo

**Culross Res of Lord Colville**
⅄ (organ extant 1728

**Culross St. Serf's Private Chapel E** Dunimarle Castle
⅄ (1874 HDT 1/6 mostly dest by vandalism, pipes rem Hugh Ross c1985

**Culsalmond & Rayne** (Rayne)
⅄ 1910 Law 1+pd/7 fr Kintore UF 1929, o Edm, o2016

37) The 1910 Lawton organ at Rayne, originally built for Kintore UF Church
for £185. Photograph by R.B. McCartney

108

**Culter** - see Peterculter

**Cults** (Cults West/Cults) North Deeside Road, Aberdeenshire
- ⚱ (1902 Walc 1/
- ⚱ 1897 organ at Queen Victoria's Diamond Jubilee, to room at Westminster Abbey, rem to Aberdeen Res of John Ledingham, to here 1931 & R&D 2/8, 1ss changed 2006

**Cults East** (UF/F) Aberdeenshire cld 2004 (now Outreach Centre)
- ⚱ (1926 Wad 2/14 +2pf dest fire 1941
- ⚱ (Hay & Rennie 1/6 installed c1980, rem to Drumlithie St. John's E

**Cults Res of Charles Davidson**
- ⚱ (c1800 Anon 1/5 fr Letterfourie House to here by Ian Davidson 1965, rem 1970 to Aberdeen Res of David Murray/Edm piano shop

**Culzean Castle** Ayrshire
- ⚱ 1790s Broderip & Wilkinson barrel organ 8ss

**Cumbernauld Abronhill**
- ⚱ 1970 Vin 2/23 ex 3 o1989 McDM

**Cumbernauld Condorrat**
- ⚱ c1890 Kir 1/6 fr Longriggend & o1975 Mac, o2014 Mac **A-listed**

**Cumbernauld Holy Name E** Flaming Road
- ⚱ (organ pt 1884 ConJ fr Glasgow Christ Church E c1980 by Burke, unplayable, scr

**Cumbernauld Kildrum** Clouden Road
- ⚱ 1962 Wil 1+pd/8 ex2

**Cumbernauld Res of Joseph Cairney**
- ⚱ c1810 Cle barrel organ 4ss + 2 traps fr Portnacroish Res 1978, o McDM, to here 1980s

**Cumbernauld Sacred Heart RC** Kyle Road
- ⚱ 1906 N&B 2/ o1925 HNB, fr Paisley Abbey Close to here c1968 C&C & r 2/ ex

**Cumbrae** - see Millport

**Cuminestown St. Luke's E** nr Turriff
- ⚱ (1878 organ new organ chamber 1903, organ relocated 1906 by Wad

**Cuminestown** - see also Monquhitter

**Cumnock** - see under "Old Cumnock" or "New Cumnock"

**Cupar B** Provost Wynd
- ⚱ (1936 organ

**Cupar B** (Bonnygate/UF/UP cld 1972) Bonnygate
- ⚱ 1929 HNB

**Cupar Boston** (UF/UP) West Port cld 1918
- ⚱ (1896 Dob (Watt) 2/9 rem 1918 to Glasgow Yoker

**Cupar Old & St. Michael of Tarvit** Kirkgate
   ⊥   (1892 B&F 2/15  o1957 R&D, scr by Loo after fire 1983
   ⊥   1913 N&B 2/12  fr Bow of Fife 1983 & r Loo 2/22

**Cupar St. James the Great E** St. Catherine Street
   ⊥   1875 HDT 1+pd/9  r1897 MilJ 2/12, r1990 Edm 2/12 (2ss changed), o2002 Edm, o2011 MilP **B-listed**

**Cupar St. John's and Dairsie United** (St. John's UF/F) Bonnygate
   ⊥   (1903 Walc 2/20  r1982 Loo 3/45 pt ex, o1990s R&D, rem 2010

**Cupar St. Michael's** West Port cld 1938/1951
   ⊥   (1866 Holt 2/13

**Cupar** - see also Rankeillor House

**Dailly** (St. Machar's)
   ⊥   1921 HNB 2/13  o1985 HNB **B-listed**

**Dailly St. Columba's** (UF/F) cld 1937
   ⊥   (1901 Kir

**Dalbeattie & Kirkgunzeon** (Dalbeattie/Craignair) Craignair Street
   ⊥   1897 F&A 2/19  o1972 , o JoG

**Dalbeattie B** (Park/UF/Colliston UF cld 1987) Mill Street blg cld 2006
   ⊥   1924 Bin 2/  for sale c2004

**Dalbeattie Christ Church E** Blair Street
   ⊥   (Walc 1/  rem 1960
   ⊥   (1902 Wad 1+pd/8  fr Tillymorgan St. Thomas E 1961 & r as new organ by Sol and rector, rem 2013 to Cumbria Res

**Dalgety** blg cld
   ⊥   (1903 MilJ 1/7  rem 1983 to Bo'ness St. Catharine's E by Loo

**Dalkeith Buccleuch** (West) cld 1990
   ⊥   (1906 Bin 2/24  rem to Dalkeith St. Nicholas Buccleuch 1991 R&D

**Dalkeith Buccleuch Street** (UF/UP) cld 1955
   ⊥   (1898 Vin 2/

**Dalkeith St. David's RC**
   ⊥   (1854 HDa  moved within church 1869, rem later
   ⊥   1869 HDT 2/13 + 1pf  o1909 HCF, o1963 R&D, o1983 Gol **A-listed**

**Dalkeith St. John's UF** (Dalkeith F) Buccleuch Street cld 1911
   ⊥   (1902 IHJ 2/15  rem 1911 & r1912 in Dalkeith St. John's & King's Park

**Dalkeith St. John's & King's Park** (King's Park UF/UP)
   ⊥   1902 IHJ 2/15  fr Dalkeith St. John's UF & r1912 Ing, r1964 R&D 2/17, r SmRo (1ss changed)

**Dalkeith St. Mary's E**
- ⅄   1845 HDa 3/22  r HDT 3/23, r1891 HCF 3/23 (1ss changed), o1974 R&D, o1994 R&D, o1997 R&D **B-listed**

**38) The 1845 Hamilton organ in St. Mary's Episcopal Church, Dalkeith.**
Photograph by Campbell Harper

**Dalkeith St. Nicholas Buccleuch** (St. Nicholas/Dalkeith)
- ⅄   (1884 F&A 2/16 +2pf 2ss added later, r1906 2/20, rem 1964
- ⅄   1906 Bin 2/24  fr Dalkeith Buccleuch 1991 R&D, re-erected 1997 R&D **A-listed**
- ⅄   1820s WSm 1/9 +Sw fr Beeslack House, Penicuik pre-1974 to Edinburgh Res of J & S Barnes, to here 2007 & o2007 Lam **A-listed**

**Dalmahoy St. Mary's E**
- ⅄   c1830 HDa 1/  to here pre-1880 & r HDT, r1902 HCF 2/14 with new facade in chancel chamber, r1979 SmRo 2/14, o1992 W-K, r2009 Wil 2/16 **C-listed**

**Dalmellington** (Kirk o' the Covenant)
- ⅄   1914 Vin 2/14

**Dalmeny** nr South Queensferry, Edinburgh
- ⅄   1984 Lam 1+ppd/5

**Dalmeny** - see also Craigiehall

**Dalmuir Our Lady of Loretto RC** (Dalmuir Old cld 1976) cld 2007 dem
- ⅄   (1912 N&B 2/16  damaged WW2, o1984 McDM **B-listed**

**Dalreoch** - see Dumbarton

**Dalry** Kirkcudbrightshire
- ⅄   c1900s Pos  extant 1976

**Dalry Biggart Memorial Hall** Ayrshire
⋏ (c1840 chamber organ 2/ extant 1960s, rem

**Dalry St. Andrew's & West** (St. Andrew's UF/F) Ayrshire cld 1962
⋏ (1904 Law 2/

**Dalry St. Margaret's** The Cross, Ayrshire
⋏ (1889 ConP 3/ dest by fire 1951
⋏ 1899 B&H 3/32 o1903-09 SmRi, r1914 Ing 3/35, o1928 Ing, o1942 Ing, fr Glasgow St. Matthew's Highlanders' Memorial 1953 HNB 3/35, o1999 MilP

**Dalry St. Palladius RC** Aitken Street, Ayrshire
⋏ 1850s Mir extant 1873

**Dalry West** Ayrshire cld 1946
⋏ (1924 E&B extant early 1960s

**Dalry** - see also under Edinburgh

**Dalrymple** (Old)
⋏ 1906 S&L 2/10

**Dankeith Castle** Ayrshire
⋏ pre-1910 Bin chamber organ 2/

**Darvel** (Central) Hastings Square
⋏ 1908 F&A 2/16 **A-listed**

**Darvel Irvine Bank & Easton Memorial** (Easton Memorial UF/F) West Main Street cld 1992
⋏ (1910 Watt 2/ disused 1938

**Daviot** (St. Colm's) Aberdeenshire
⋏ 1912 Law 1/7 no pd o1976 Loo

**Deanston House Res of Sir John Muir** Perthshire (now nursing home)
⋏ (c1897 ConP

**Dean Castle** - see under Kilmarnock

**Deer** Aberdeenshire (See also New Deer)
⋏ 1898 Wil 2/11 +3pf added later, r1900 Wad, o1977 R&D **A-listed**

**Deer Clola** (Clola UF/F) cld 1975
⋏ (1904 Cou 1/6

**Deer St. Drostan's E**
⋏ (1850s London-made organ to here post-1851, for sale 1877
⋏ 1878 Por 2/10 enlarged 1896 Wad 2/11 **A-listed**

**Deer Stuartfield** (Old Deer UF/F) cld 1953
⚒ (1900 Wad 2/11  o1930 James Mcbeth, Aberdeen, extant 1953

**Deer Stuartfield C** cld 1900
⚒ c1878 organ, extant 1892

**Delvine House** Perthshire
⚒ (c1830 SBr  rem to Caputh 1909 & r1914 MilJ

**Denbeath** nr Buckhaven cld 2004
⚒ c1900 Pos/MilJ 1+pd/6  fr Crail St. David's 1954

**Denholm** (UF/F) (under Ruberslaw fr 2003)
⚒ 1976-77 WiB 2/20 ex4 using pipes from Hawick B

**Denny** (Old) Duke Street/Glasgow Road
⚒ 1906 SmRi 2/20  r1997 Gol, o1999 Lig

**Denny Broompark** (UF/UP) Church Walk cld 1963
⚒ (1903 B&H 2/  organ chamber added 1910

**Denny Dunipace** (Dunipace North/Dunipace/UF/F)
⚒ pre-1920 Pos

**Dennyloanhead** (UF/UP) Denny Road/Bonnybridge Road cld 1991
⚒ (1860 ConP 2/10  post-1920 to Falkirk Salon Theatre, to here 1932 & r 2/10 by Ing,
o1964 R&D, rem to Dunblane St. Blane's 1991 & o SmRo

**Denovan House Res of J.G. Adam** nr Falkirk
⚒ (c1762 WaJ 1/4  fr Glasgow Res of James Watt to Glasgow Malt's Lodging, College
1776, 1815 to Andrew McLellan, 78 Miller Street, Glasgow, o McLellan & Steven + 1ss,
rem to Mugdock Castle, Milngavie, to here 1854, rem 1863 to Coulter Mains,
Lanarkshire

**Deskford** (St. John's) Banffshire cld 2004
⚒ (1904 Law  extant 2015

**Devanha House** - see Aberdeen, Res of Henderson

**Dingwall Castle Street** (UF/F)
⚒ (c1917 B&F 2/7  fr Carbisdale Castle 1950, to here 1952 & r HNB 2/18, dest 1990
⚒ 1895 F&A 2/13  o1921 F&A, r c1972 Gol 2/23, fr North Berwick Blackadder 1990 & r
1991 McDM 2/19

**Dingwall St. James the Great E** Castle Street
⚒ (1852 chamber organ  dest by fire 1871
⚒ (1872 Bev 2/8  o1892 Wad  pt for sale 1907
⚒ 1908 Sco 2/10 using Bev case and some pipework  r1931 HNB 2/10

**Dingwall St. Lawrence RC** Castle Street
⚒ (organ inst 1892 Wad
⚒ (1835 Wis with material by Fli  o1891-95 Wad, to here 1902 fr Blairs College by Wad

**Dirleton**
⚓ 1900 Ing 2/10 +2pf **A-listed**

**Dollar** (St. Columba's/Dollar) Bridge Street
⚓ 1926 R&D 2/16

**Dollar Res of John Collyer**
⚓ (small organ rem 1912

**Dollar St. James E**
⚓ (organ facade only inst rem by 1955

**Dornoch Cathedral**
⚓ 1893 IngE 2/19 r1908 G&D (resited) 2/19, o1979 R&D, r1980 Nic 2/22

**Dornoch St. Finbarr's E**
⚓ Bev 1/4

**Dornoch** - see also Skibo Castle

**Douglas Castle** Lanarkshire (dem 1938)
⚓ (Gern 2/ extant 1900, rem 1938 R&D

**Douglas St. Bride's**
⚓ 1930 Nel 2/12 r1964 R&D, o1983 McDM

**Douglas Support** Coatbridge
⚓ (1726 organ r1781, rem 1844 to Coatbridge St. John the Evangelist E & r Bru & Baker

**Douglas Water & Rigside** cld 2014
⚓ (N&B Norvic r here Watt 1/5, dest c1982

**Doune St. Modoc's E** George Street, Doune (see Kilmadock for other churches in Doune)
⚓ 1878 Bev 1/7 r1951 Bell, o2001 Lib, o R&D

**Dowally** Perthshire cld 2017
⚓ 1900 Pos 1/6 fr Dunkeld Cathedral 1908 **A-listed**

**Drainie St. Geraldine's** - see Lossiemouth

**Dreghorn C** cld 2002
⚓ (1904 Wad 2/10 dest 2002

**Dreghorn: Perceton & Dreghorn** (UF/F) cld 1993 ch rem to Japan 1996
⚓ (1899 F&A 2/ redundant 1996, scr

**Dreghorn Res**
⚓ (organ rem 1934 to Kilmarnock Martyrs & r Watt

**Dreghorn & Springside** (Dreghorn & Pearston Old)
⚓ 1913 Ing 2/

**Drumblade** (North) Huntly cld 2016 (photograph on page 20)
  ⚭   1901 Wad 1/6 no pd  redundant 2017

**Drumchapel -** within Glasgow

**Drumlithie St. John's E**
  ⚭   (post-1863 org  o1898 Wad, extant 1904
  ⚭   Hay & Rennie 1/6  inst c1980 at Cults East to here c2004

**Drumlithie -** see also Arbuthnott Manse

**Drummond Castle** nr Muthill/Crieff
  ⚭   (barrel organ  fr Muthill St. James E 1856
  ⚭   (organ  rem 1856 to Muthill St. James E

**Drumoak** Aberdeenshire
  ⚭   c1960 Sol 1/c6  rem 2018

**Dryburgh Tweed Horizon Centre** (Strathclyde Residential School 1973 to 1993/St. Columba's College, White Fathers Monastery cld 1963)
  ⚭   (1883 Gern 2/11  fr Monteviot House 1958 & o R&D, rem 1994 to Edinburgh Stockbridge by Lig

**Drymen**
  ⚭   1966 R&D 1+pd/10 ex2

**Duff House** Banffshire
  ⚭   (chamber organ extant 1799

**Dufftown -** see Mortlach and Auchindoun

**Dufftown St. Mary's RC** Fife Street
  ⚭   (1824 WSM  rem 1842 to Buckie St. Peter's RC
  ⚭   (1842 Bru 1/9
  ⚭   c1870s ConP 2/8 disused **A-listed**

**Dufftown St. Michael's E** Conval Street
  ⚭   c1900s amateur 1/5  fr Res elsewhere  o1981 Edm

**Duffus**
  ⚭   1913 Law 1/10  r1985 Edm

**Dumbarton Dalreoch** Cardross Road cld 1984
  ⚭   (1922 W&L 2/12  dest 1985

**Dumbarton High** (UF/F) High Street cld 1972
  ⚭   (1903 Lew 3/30  rem 1980 to Dumbarton St. Michael RC by McDM

**Dumbarton High Street** (UF/UP) cld 1956
  ⚭   (1915 N&B 2/16  o1929 HNB, rem to Cadder 1956

**Dumbarton Knoxland** Knoxland Square cld 1984
  ⚭   (1913 N&N  r1966 Hils 2/27, dest

**Dumbarton M** Dumbarton Avenue
⊥ organ extant 1878

**Dumbarton North** (UF/F) cld 1972
⊥ 1903 Walc 1+pd/6

**Dumbarton Notre Dame Convent RC** Clerkhill
⊥ (1936 Wal 2/18 ex o1984 McDM, dest

**Dumbarton Riverside** (Old) High Street
⊥ (organ extant 1527 in blg on same site
⊥ (1886 Wil 3/24 r1939 Wal 3/27, o1958 Wal, r1980 Gol 3/ , disused 1987, rem 1993

**Dumbarton St. Augustine's E** High Street
⊥ 1880 S&B 2/16 r c1910s Bro, disused, usable **A-listed**

**Dumbarton St. Michael's RC** Cardross Road, Dalreoch
⊥ 1903 Lew 2/30 fr Dumbarton High 1980 & r1981 McDM 2/26, o2009 McDM

**Dumbarton St. Patrick's RC** Strathleven Place
⊥ (post-1830 Mir in previous blg
⊥ 1886 F&A 2/ fr Glasgow East Campbell Street UF 1928 & r Watt, r1973 Wil 2/26

**Dumbarton West** (Bridgend UF/UP) West Bridgend
⊥ 1875 ConP fr previous blg & r1899 ConP 2/17, r1948 HNB, r1998 McDM 2/17

**Dumfries Academy** Academy Street
⊥ 1951 R&D 2/31 ex7 o1961 R&D, disused, returned to use 2010s

**Dumfries Buccleuch Street** (UF/UP) cld 1945 (later hall, then independent ch)
⊥ (1902 N&B 2/13 o pre-1925 Hils, rem 1948 to Dumfries Troqueer

**Dumfries Crichton Memorial Hospital Chapel**
⊥ 1903 Lew 2/21 o1991 Har **A-listed**
⊥ 1979 WiB 1/7 ex2

**Dumfries C** Irving Street
⊥ organ r1958 R&D

**Dumfries Greyfriars** - see Dumfries St. Bride's Anglican

**Dumfries Holywood** - see Holywood (outwith Dumfries)

**Dumfries, Jardine, William, joiner**
⊥ (Har 2/7 for sale viii1930

**Dumfries Loreburn UF cont** (UF/UP)
⊥ (1890 organ extant 1911
⊥ 1923 Cat 2/16

**Dumfries M** cld c1982
⊥ (Hun 2/13 o1899 N&B, rem c1982 to Carlisle M

**Dumfries Maxwelltown Laurieknowe** (Maxwelltown) cld 1976
- ⅄   1904 Ing 2/14

**Dumfries Maxwelltown West** (UF/F) Laurieknowe/School Lane
- ⅄   (1887 You 2/18 to here fr Kilmarnock West High 1897 & o N&B, o1899 N&B, r1948 HNB, rem 2012

**Dumfries Northwest** (Lochside) Lochside Road
- ⅄   1966 HNB 1+pd/6

**Dumfries Res of Mr. Hattersley**
- ⅄   1926 Wur 2/ ex5 fr New York Jamestown Majestic, 1932 to London Film-o-phone Studio, Marylebone Road, 1933 to West Hampstead Decca Studio, 1946 to Grantham Marco Club, 1967 to High Wycombe Organ Centre, 1972 to Kings Lynn Reliance Garage, c1980 to Res in Middlesborough, 1987 to here

**Dumfries St. Andrew's Cathedral RC** English Street
- ⅄   (1831 SBr to St. Paul's, West Marsh, Grimsby 1899 & r Cou, then to Tattershall Collegiate Church, Lincolnshire 1968 & r Cou retaining Bruce case
- ⅄   (1897 Cou fr Lincoln Cathedral (temp) & r1898 Cou 2/24, dest fire 1961
- ⅄   1964 R&D 2/20 ex4

**Dumfries St. Bride's Anglican** (Independent) (Greyfriars cld 2004, sold 2008)
- ⅄   (1873 Rob 2/17 moved 1875, r1891 Ing, o1902 N&B
- ⅄   1921 Ing 3/30 using old pipework, disused 1996, case extant

**Dumfries St. George's** (UF/F) George Street
- ⅄   (1898 B&H 2/ rem 1966

**Dumfries St. John the Evangelist E** Newall Terrace
- ⅄   (1807 MWo to new chapel 1817 (St. Mary's, Castle Street), to new church 1868
- ⅄   (1872 Hill 2/14 r1889 F&A 3/21, r1903 Wad 3/24
- ⅄   1938 Har 3/26 using old pipework r1969 Har 3/35, r2008 Har 3/37

**Dumfries St. Joseph's College RC** Craigs Road
- ⅄   c1925 organ r1936 Bro 2/16 +2pf, r1972 Sol 2/16 +2pf

**Dumfries St. Mary's-Greyfriars** (St. Mary's) St. Mary's Street
- ⅄   1884 Har 2/21 r1891/1896 Har in chancel 2/21, r1917 Bin 3/26 + 3pf, o1974 R&D

**Dumfries St. Michael's & South** (St. Michael's) St. Michael Street
- ⅄   1890 Wil 2/15+1pf additions 1892 Wil, r1933 Wil 2/25, o1973 Wil, o2001-5 Wil, 1ss changed 2012

**Dumfries South & Townhead** (South/UF/F) Shakespeare Street/Nith Place cld 1983
- ⅄   (1923 A&S 2/13 pipework rem 1985 to Greenock St. Patrick's RC McDM

**Dumfries Townhead** (UF/UP) Lovers Walk/Academy Street cld 1951
- ⅄   (1923 Watt 2/17 rem 1953 to Kirkconnel & r Watt

**Dumfries Troqueer** (Laurieknowe Troqueer/Troqueer) Troqueer Road
- ⅄   (1890 F&A 2/17 enclosed .r1932 HNB
- ⅄   1902 N&B fr Dumfries Buccleuch Street 1948, r1954 HNB, o1979 R&D

**Dunbar** (Old) Queens Road  (see also Belhaven)
  ⊥   (1901 F&A 3/28  o1960 R&D, r1965 R&D 3/28, r c1977 Gol 3/35, dest fire 1987

**Dunbar Abbey** (UF/F) High Street cld 1966
  ⊥   (1950s Com 2/18 ex3  rem 1972 to Whitekirk

**Dunbar Erskine UF** (UP) Larner Street cld 1917
  ⊥   (c1900s N&B 1/

**Dunbar M** Victoria Street cld 2017
  ⊥   c1894 B&H 2/11 **A-listed**

**Dunbar St. Anne's E** Westgate
  ⊥   1896 Wil 2/13 **A-listed**

**Dunbarney and Forgandenny** (Dunbarney) Manse Road, Bridge of Earn, Perthshire
  ⊥   1929 MilJ 2/12   r 2/12

**Dunbarton** - see Dumbarton

**Dunblane Cathedral**
  ⊥   (1873 HDT 2/19  rem 1893 to London St. Simon's Rockley Road by IngE & r as 3/27
       with existing Bevington organ
  ⊥   (1893 IngE 2/27 (Anderson case)  r1907 IngE 3/39, r1914 IngE 3+1pf/39 (Lorimer case),
       r1915 IngE 4/45, r1936 IngE 4/48, r1957 HNB 4/56, rem 1989
  ⊥   1990 Fle 3/41  o2013 Fle

39) Dunblane Cathedral: the 1873 Hamilton organ in the Choir, the 1893 Ingram with its case
by Sir Rowand Anderson and the 1914 case  by Sir Robert Lorimer, later redesigned to
incorporate the Flentrop organ in 1990.
Reproduced with kind permission of Dunblane Cathedral

**Dunblane Holmehill Res of J. Templeton**
⚲ (c1910s A&S 2/9

**Dunblane Leighton** (UF/UP) cld 1952
⚲ (1909 A&S 2/9 rem 1955 to Calderbank & r Wil 2/9

**Dunblane Queen Victoria School**
⚲ c1890 IngE 2/ o1960 R&D, r1980 HNB 3/22

**Dunblane St. Blane's** (East/UF/F)
⚲ (1907 Ing 2/9 disused 1977, rem 1980 to Eddleston & r Gol 2/10
⚲ 1860 ConP 2/10 post-1920 to Falkirk Salon Theatre & r Ing 2/10, rem 1932 to Dennyloanhead, o1964 R&D, to here SmRo & o1991

**Dunblane The Holy Family RC** (St. John & St. Blane)
⚲ 1883 A&S (Abbott) 2/7 no pd r Wal, to here 1936 fr Glasgow Pollok House & r Wal

**Dunblane St. Mary's E**
⚲ 1845 Wood/Ren r1888 Bis (organ moved), r1899 Bis (moved again), o1910 Ing, r1936 BFH 2/13, o1958 R&D, o1994 Gol, o2000 R&D **C-listed**

**DUNDEE**

**Albert Institute** - see McManus Galleries

**Albert Square** (UF/F) Meadowside/Chapel Street cld 1955
⚲ (1906 N&B 1/ o1924 HNB

**Balgay** (Balgay St. Thomas/Balgay/St. Thomas Chapel of Ease) 200 Lochee Road
⚲ (c1830s chamber organ 2/ fr Res of Christie 1906 by Lind, rem 1924 to Murroes
⚲ (1924 Wat rem 1960s

**Barnhill St. Margaret's** 10 Invermark Terrace
⚲ (1932 Hay 1+pd/ to here 1932 & r Wat, rem 1974 to Edinburgh Richmond Craigmillar by Douglas Galbraith

**Baxter Park** (UF/F) Arbroath Road/Baxter Park Terrace cld 1981 (later Free Presbyterian) cld c1992
⚲ (1930 MilJ 2/ pt rem to Westerkirk & r2005 JoG 2/10 including Walc pipes

**Belmont House** 15 Perth Road
⚲ (1909 Wat 2/12 rem 1932 to Monifieth Holy Trinity E
⚲ (1914 organ

**Blackscroft Mission** - see St. Roque's Chapel E

**Bonnethill** (UF/F) Hilltown cld 1978
⚲ (1932 MilJ 2/14 o1952 Hils

**Broughty Ferry Brook Street C** 87 Brook Street cld 2005
⚲ 1864 ConP 2/15 +2pf to here 1864 from Dundee Exchange Rooms, r1890 to east end ConP 2/17, console rem **B-listed**

**Broughty Ferry New Kirk** (East UF/F) 370 Queen Street
⚲ 1894/1900 G&D 2/19 r1939 G&D, r1970 Wal, r1986 SmR console moved **B-listed**

**Broughty Ferry Panmure Villa, Res of Thomas Smieton**
  ⅄  (1875 Nicholson of Bradford 3/16

**Broughty Ferry Queen Street** (UF/UP) Queen Street/Camphill Road cld 1953
  ⅄  (1876 Str 2/  r1910 Wat 2/18

**Broughty Ferry St. Aidan's** 440 Brook Street cld 2005
  ⅄  (1875 F&A 2/16  o1893 F&A, r MilJ, r Parry, o2001 Edm, dispersed post-2005

**Broughty Ferry St. James'** (Beach) 5 Fort Street
  ⅄  1909 Sco 2/13  fr Monifieth St. Rule's 1969 & r1970 by Neil Pattie, r2006

**Broughty Ferry St. Luke's & Queen Street** (St. Luke's/UF/F) 5 West Queen Street
  ⅄  1894 G&D 2/19  to here 1895 G&D 2/23, r1957, r1983 Six, o1991 Six

**Broughty Ferry St. Mary's E** Queen Street
  ⅄  (1858 Bev
  ⅄  1887-92 B&F 2/17, o1896 Wad, r1916 Hils 2/19, o1930 Hils, o1950, r1982 Wal 2/22, r2015 Nic

**40) The Brindley organ of St. Mary's, Broughty Ferry soon after it was opened**

120

**Broughty Ferry St. Stephen's & West** (St. Stephen's) 96 Dundee Road
  ♦ (1880 Str 3/29  r1958 Hils, rem 1969, reeds to Forfar Lowson Memorial

**Broughty Ferry West** (UF/F) cld 1962
  ♦ (1890 Wil 2/20  sold c1963

**Caird Hall** High Street
  ♦ 1923 Har 3/50  o1991 Har **A-listed**

**Castle Street C** cld 1949
  ♦ (1895 MilJ 2/18 +2pf  r1904 2/20

**Catholic Apostolic** Meadow Place cld 1867
  ♦ (post-1842 organ  rem to new church 1867 - see St. Mary Magdalene E

**Central B** Ward Road
  ♦ (1865 Holt 2/  r with new console, extant 2000, later scr except case

**Chapelshade** off Barrack Road cld 1940
  ♦ (1913 MilJ 2/21  rem 1945 to Aberdeen Queen Street by Law

**Clepington** - see Coldside and also St. James

**Coldside** (Clepington) Isla Street/Main Street
  ♦ (1904 Walc 1+pd/8  rem c1960
  ♦ 1856 F&A 3/28 +1pf  1858 +1ss, r1872/74 F&A 3/33, fr Glasgow Claremont 1899 to Glasgow Wellpark & r SmRi 3/c38, to here 1953 Watt, r1957 Hils 3/33, o1999 SmRo

**Corn Exchange** - see Kinnaird Hall & Exchange Rooms

**Craigiebank** Greendykes Road/Craigie Avenue blg cld 2013
  ♦ (1882 Spe 3/  r1903 Rot 3/30, fr Stoke Newington Rectory Road C 1948 & r1949 Rot 3/29, o1977 R&D, rem 2014 by A. Giacobazzi to RC Mission in Kazakhstan

**Crematorium** Macalpine Road
  ♦ (1936 organ  rem
  ♦ 1954 Wil 2/13  r1998 R&D 2/13

**Downfield Mains** (Downfield South/Downfield UF/UP) Haldane Terrace
  ♦ (1875 Rbt 1+pd/7  fr Tay Square to hall here 1885 by HDT, rem to ch 1889
  ♦ 1910 MilJ 2/10  r1969 Hils 2/11, o Six

**Downfield** - see also St. Luke's E

**Dudhope** (UF/F) 113 Lochee Road cld 1955
  ♦ (1900 Pos 1/

**Dundee St. Mary's** (East) east pt of city ch, Nethergate (other pts Old & St. Paul's & Steeple)
  ♦ (organ extant 1470
  ♦ 1865-66 F&A 3/35 +1pf  r1893 F&A 3/35 +1pf, r1908 MilJ 3/36, r1939 Rot 3/46, r1969 Wal 3/46, r1987 Wal 3/44, disused 2017

**English E Chapel** - see Qualified West Chapel E

**Exchange Rooms** Castle Street/Exchange Street
- ⅄ (1864 ConP 2/15 +2pf rem 1864 to Broughty Ferry Brook Street C

**Fairmuir** 329 Clepington Road cld 2011
- ⅄ (c1890 Wad 2/11 erected 1910 MilJ, r c1990 R&D 1ss changed

**Freemasons Lodge**
- ⅄ organ proposed 1764, and in 1864, organist in post 1918

**Gaumont Theatre** 25 Cowgate (now nightclub)
- ⅄ (1928 Wur 2/21 + traps ex6 scr 1960 Bell

**Gilfillan Memorial Independent** (pt of Congregational Federation) 24 Whitehall Crescent
- ⅄ (1882 Scot 2/ rem
- ⅄ (1850 Hill 3/23 fr Liverpool School for the Blind 1894 & r H-J/MilJ 4/29 +2pf, o1895 Wad, r1906 N&B 4/48 +1pf, r1924 Hils 4/47, r1951 Hils, r1970s Parry (organist) 4/47, abandoned 1989, console removed

**High -** see St. David's High

**High School** (Panmure Trinity C cld 1984) Bell Street
- ⅄ (1906 MilJ 2/17 rem 1990

**Hilltown** (UF/F) cld 1970 (for Hilltown see also St. Mary Our Lady of Victories & St. Salvador's)
- ⅄ (1916 MilJ

**Kinnaird Hall Picture House** (Kinnaird Hall/Corn Exchange) Bank Street (dest 1966 fire)
- ⅄ (1865 F&A 4/47 +2pf o1883 F&A, o1902 F&A, r1908 N&B 4/48 , r1922 Wat 3/33 + 2 traps, scr c1950

**Lindsay Street C** cld 1923
- ⅄ (1858 G&D 1/10 for sale 1882
- ⅄ (1882 Bis 2/12 fr Brighton Health Congress per Methuen Simpson, rem c1885 to Unitarian Williamson Memorial

**Lochee** (Lochee West/UF/UP) 191 High Street, Lochee
- ⅄ 1890 Hill 3/25 o1935 MilJ + Trem, o1980 R&D **A-listed**

**Lochee East** (UF/F) 140 High Street cld 1959
- ⅄ (1900 MilJ 2/10

**Lochee Old & St. Luke's** (Lochee Old/East St. Ninian's/St. Ninian's/Lochee) Bright Street/Methven Street cld 2006
- ⅄ (1884 F&A 3/22 exported 2007 to the Netherlands, in storage Nijsse, Rotterdam

**Lochee St. Luke's** 136 High Street cld 1985
- ⅄ (1883 Wad 2/16 r1897 Wad, o1910 Wad, o1936 Hils, o1965 Mac, rem to St. Luke's E, Downfield 1988 by Andrew McHutchison

**Lochee -** see also Dudhope, St. Mary's RC and St. Margaret's E

**41) Three organs in Lochee: Lochee West (Hill 1890), Lochee Old (Forster & Andrews 1884) and St. Mary of the Immaculate Conception RC (originally Butterworth 1880)**


**Logie** 15 Scott Street cld 1982
    ⅄  (1904 MilJ 2/18

**Logie & St. John's (Cross)** (St. John's (Cross)) Shaftesbury Road
    ⅄  1878 F&A 2/14 fr former church in South Tay Street 1925 & r Wat 3/32, r1967 Wil, disused 1990

**McCheyne Memorial** - see St. Peter's McCheyne

**McManus Galleries** (Albert Institute) Albert Square
    ⅄  (1877 Str for Fine Art Exhibition 1877, rem

**Mains** Old Glamis Road blg cld 1994, cld 2011
    ⅄  (Ing 2/ to here post 1933 r Hils rem 1970s

**Maryfield Victoria Street** (Maryfield) 9 Morgan Street/Baldovan Terrace cld 1976
    ⅄  (1890 Scot 2/20 o1936 Wat, rem, 2ss reused Andrew McHutchison at St. Luke's E

**DUNDEE (Cont.)**

**Meadowside** (Albert Square & St. George's/St. George's/St. Andrew's & Chapelshade UF/St. Andrew's/UF/F) 32 Meadowside cld 1981
⼈ (1901 MilJ 1/5 r Edm, sold 1982

**Meadowside St. Paul's** (St. Paul's/UF/F) 114 Nethergate
⼈ 1902 Walc 3/30 r1973 R&D 2/29

**Menzieshill** Charleston Drive
⼈ 1962 Wil "Junior Development" disused 2014

**Methven Simpson Music Sellers** 122 Nethergate later 22 Reform Street
⼈ (organ 1/4 for sale 1859
⼈ (1875 F&A
⼈ (1903 Walc 1/7
⼈ (organ to Dundee St. James' c1929
⼈ (other small organs in transit

**Miller, John R., organbuilder** Dens Road (works), 7-11 Caldrum Street (Lindsay Street)
⼈ (chamber organ 2/10 for sale vi1929
⼈ (many other organs being built, in transit or under repair

**Morison C** (Evangelical Union) Guthrie Street cld 1968 (Downfield Musical Society)
⼈ (c1830s SBr 1/7 for sale fr Res 1861, rem to Edinburgh Res of Dr. McArthur, Beachcroft, Trinity by 1883, rem to Kirkcaldy West End C 1898 & r King 1+pd/8, to here 1920 & r MilJ, rem 1928 to Aberfeldy C
⼈ (1876 HDT 2/12 to here 1928 fr Dundee School Wynd UF

**Ogilvie** - see Stobswell

**Old St. Paul's & St. David's and Wishart Memorial** (Old St. Paul's & St. David's/Old St. Paul's/St. Paul's South) middle pt of city ch, Nethergate cld 1978
⼈ (1891 Scot 3/21 +5pf o1922 Wad, r1935 Wat/Rot 2/23
⼈ (1898 MilJ 2/20 to here 1947 fr St. David's & r Rot with new console, scr

**Panmure C** - see High School

**Park** - see Stobswell

**Plaza** Hilltown
⼈ (1928 organ rem 1929 to another church

**Princes Street C** cld 1957
⼈ (1906 MilJ 2/14 (organ gallery 1859) o1951

**Qualified West Chapel E** High Street cld 1829
⼈ (1757 Bri inst Shunnyman o1780 Williamson, r1784 Fournier + Sw, fr previous chapel at Seagate 1785, o1795 James Logan, o1798 Moo, o1809 Letts, o1812 MWo, o1820 P. Mancor

**Rattray Street B** cld
⼈ (1925 MilJ 2/ rem to Cockenzie Old 1988 & r SmRo

**Residences** - see also Balruddery (outwith Dundee) and Taypark House

Aimer, G., Union Place, Magdalen Yard:
⼈ (barrel organ for sale 1859

Brown, Henry, 45 High Street:
⼈ (chamber organ 1/4 for sale i1852

Brown, James, Broughty Ferry:
⼈ (barrel organ for sale 1859

Mr. Christie, 28 Dura Street
⼈ (1830s chamber organ (Gt with pipes, Sw harmonium reeds) rem to Balgay 1906

Dundee, Earl of - see Birkhill, North Fife

Galloway, David, 11 Fort Street:
⼈ 1915 Bin 2/10

Hill, Wilson:
⼈ 1845 Hill 2/10 (est. only)

Hinchliffe, James, 93 Nethergate (studio):
⼈ 1899 J.B. Clarke/Bin/ConP 3/8 r here by ConP & Hinchliffe

Jolson, S:
⼈ 1867 Hill (est. only)

Macdonald, John, teacher of dancing:
⼈ (chamber organ for sale 28ix1789

Methuen, W:
⼈ 1858 G&D 1/4

Miller, Rev. Wm.:
⼈ (Wal fr Devon to here c1960s rem 1973 to Monikie by Michael Miller

Nagel, Mr:
⼈ 1864 Hill 3/38 (est. only)

Smeeton, Thos., Panmure Villa:
⼈ 1875 Nic 3/16

White, A:
⼈ organ o1899 N&B

White, J. Martin - see Balruddery, Angus

Wilson, Mr:
⼈ 1845 Hill barrel and finger 2/10 (est. only)

**Roseangle Ryehill** (Roseangle) - see Dundee West

**DUNDEE (Cont.)**

**Ryehill** (UF/UP) 79 Perth Road/Mid Wynd cld 1980
⚰ (1880 Hill 2/15  r1926 Wat, rem, sold to Gerald Baker, London

**St. Andrew's** 2 King Street
⚰ 1921 HNB 2/16  o1950s, r1994 Edm 2/21

**St. Andrew's Cathedral RC** Nethergate
⚰ (1830 organ  to new blg 1836, rem 1864 by F&A to school
⚰ (1864 F&A 2/19  r1869 F&A 3/23, r1928 MilJ 2/21, rem

**St. Clement's** - see Steeple

**St. Cuthbert's** (Willison & Bell Street/Bell Street UF) Bell St/Constitiution Road cld 1940
⚰ (1904 Law 2/20  fr Willison UF 1928, rem to Edinburgh Lochend 1941 by Law

**St. David's** North Tay Street cld 1947
⚰ (1898 MilJ 2/20  rem to Old St. Paul's & St. David's 1947 by Rot

**St. David's High** (High/UF/F) 119a Kinghorne Road
⚰ 1904 Wad 2/14  o1909/1912 Wad, console moved 1954, r1964 R&D 2/14, r1996 Lib 2/15

**St. David's North** (St. David's in the West/UF) 273 Strathmore Avenue (later pt of St. David's High) cld 2014
⚰ 1899 Bin 2/21  fr Edinburgh Wester Coates 1973 & r1975 by SmRo

**St. Enoch's** (F) Nethergate cld 1963
⚰ (1882 B&F 2/23

**St. Francis Friary RC** Tullidelph Road cld
⚰ 1954 Watt 2/  ex  fr Glasgow Macgregor Street C c1958 & r Watt

**St. James'** (North Clepington/Clepington UF/James UP) Arklay Street cld 1988
⚰ (organ to here c1929 fr Methven Simpson
⚰ (1897 MilJ 2/19 +2pf  fr Lasswade Old post-1950 & r Rot 2/c30

**St. John's** - see Logie & St. John's (Cross), and West

**St. John the Baptist E** Albert Street
⚰ (1905 Vin 2/13  o1910 N&B/Hils
⚰ c1860 Bev 1/6 to here 1982 by Six, r2005 Edm 1/6

**St. Joseph's RC** Wilkie's Lane/Blackness Road
⚰ (1880 But 2/10 +2pf  to be added soon after
⚰ 1901 Walc 2/22  r c1930 MilJ, r1986 McDM, o1994 SmRo

**St. Luke's E** Baldovan Road, Downfield (see Lochee for St. Luke's Parish)
⚰ (1842 2/10  fr Forfar St. John the Evangelist E 1908, to Monifieth Holy Trinity E, to here 1932, scr 1965 some pipes to Unitarian Williamson Memorial
⚰ 1883 Wad 2/16  r1897 Wad, o1910 Wad, o1936 Hils, o1965 Mac, fr Lochee St. Luke's 1988 Andrew McHutchison & r 3/29 with other pts

**St. Margaret's** - see Barnhill St. Margaret's

**St. Margaret's E** 17 Ancrum Road, Lochee
- ⊥ (1902 MilJ 2/15
- ⊥ 1866 organ 1+pd/8  r MilJ, to here 1972 fr St. Mary's Convent E, r1979 WWo 1/8

**St. Mark's** 158 Perth Road/Greenfield Place cld 1968 (now Gate Independent Church)
- ⊥ (1880 Str 3/29  r1915 MilJ 3/29, extant 1984, rem c1990 to Lancashire, case remains

**St. Martin's E** Derby Street
- ⊥ c1860 Bev 1/ to here 1970s WWo +2ss

**St. Mary's** Nethergate - see alphabetically under "Dundee" above

**St. Mary & Modwena Chapel E** King Street cld 1960s
- ⊥ (1864 Ren 1/3

**St. Mary's Convent E** Adelaide Place cld
- ⊥ (1866 1+pd/8  r MilJ, rem 1972 to St. Margaret's Lochee E by amateur

**St. Mary Magdalene's E** Blinshall Street cld 1952 (Rock Climbing Centre)
- ⊥ (1812 MWo  to here 1853 fr St. Paul's E temp by Ren, rem to St. Paul's Cathedral E
- ⊥ (1879 Har 2/21 +1pf  o1928 MilJ, r1946, rem 1956 Wil to Bournemouth Moortown Holy Trinity

**St. Mary Magdalene's E** (Catholic Apostolic cld 1947) Constitution Road/Dudhope Crescent
- ⊥ (organ post 1842  fr Catholic Apostolic, Meadow Place 1867 & r 2/11, rem 1874
- ⊥ 1874 ConP 3/22 +4pf  r1937 Rot 3/27, r1986 Nic 3/30 (Rot console to Reid Collection now at St. Cecilia's Hall, Edinburgh University)

**St. Mary of the Immaculate Conception RC** 41 High Street, Lochee
- ⊥ 1880 But 2/13  r c1900 Scot 2/17, r c1953 Watt after fire, disused

**St. Mary Our Lady of Victories RC** 36 Forebank Road, Hilltown
- ⊥ 1861 Boothe of Leeds 2/25  r1914-16 Law 3/32,  r c1950s, r1980 Gol, r2004 Cop

**St. Matthew's** 78 Broughty Ferry Road cld 1981
- ⊥ (1901 Law 2/15

**St. Patrick's RC** Arthurstone Terrace
- ⊥ 1897 B&H 2/17  r c1952 Watt 2/

**St. Paul's E** Castle Street cld 1853 (see also Qualified Chapel)
- ⊥ (1812 MWo 2/  rem 1853 via St. Mary Magdalene's E to St. Paul's Cathedral & r Ren

**St. Paul's Cathedral E** Castlehill
- ⊥ (1812 MWo 2/  fr St. Paul's E 1853-55 by Ren, for sale 5v1865, rem 1865 to Montrose URC by Ren
- ⊥ 1865 Hill 3/25  r1894 Wad 3/29, o1902 Wad, o1922 Wad, r1936 Rot 3/36, o1957 R&D, r1975 HNB 3/40

**St. Paul's** - see also Meadowside St. Paul's and Old St.Paul's

**DUNDEE (Cont.)**

**St. Peter's F** (St. Peter's/UF/F cld 1982) Perth Road/St. Peter Street
ㅅ (1913 MilJ 2/20 scr 2010

**St. Peter's McCheyne** (McCheyne Memorial/UF/F) 328 Perth Road/Shepherd's Loan cld 1999
ㅅ 1899 MilJ 2/19 o1937 Ing, r1996 Lib, some pipes to storage in West Church

**St. Roque's Chapel E** 26 Foundry Lane
ㅅ (1912 MilJ 2/ rem 1953 to Carmyllie

**St. Salvador's E** Church Street, Hilltown
ㅅ 1882 W&M 2/22 +1pf o1932 Rot, o1974 R&D, o1997 Har 2/23 **A-listed**

**42) The 1882 Wordsworth & Maskell organ in the splendour of Bodley's interior
at St. Salvador's, Hilltown, Dundee**

**St. Teresa RC** Graham Street cld 2005
⅄ (1965 Wal 2/18 ex rem 2008 to Carnoustie St. Anne's RC

**St. Vincent de Paul RC** Pitkerro Drive cld 2012
⅄ organ tuned Wal

**School Wynd UF** (UP) Lindsay Street cld 1926
⅄ (1876 HDT 2/12 rem 1928 to Morison C

**Steeple** (St. Clement's) west pt of city ch, Nethergate
⅄ 1912 Wat/ConP 2/26 r1964 Wil 2/27 ex, moved to gallery, o Edm, o R&D

**Stobswell** (Ogilvie UF/F) 170 Albert Street/Dura Street
⅄ (1898 Vin 2/19 rem (twin organ cases on wall)

**Stobswell** (Park UF/UP) Morgan Street/Park Avenue cld 1976/1985
⅄ (1903 Lew 2/13 to here 1946 fr Bridge of Allan Trinity by Sco, extant 1976, rem post 1990

**Strathmartine** (Downfield Strathmartine/Mains & Strathmartine UF/F) 513 Strathmartine Road
⅄ 1914 MilJ r1987 SmRo +ss

**Taypark House** (Res of William Robertson)
⅄ (chamber organ for sale 14v1881

**Tay Square** (UF/UP) cld 1952
⅄ (1875 Rbt 1+pd/7 rem 1885 to Downfield Mains (hall) by HDT
⅄ (1885 Scot 2/20 +2pf o1923 Wat, rem 1954 to Monquhitter

**Trinity** (Wallacetown) 73 Crescent Street
⅄ (1892 B&F 2/16 dest fire 1955
⅄ 1955 R&D 2/30 ex7 r2010 For 2/15

**Trinity C** Victoria Road/Crescent Street cld 1968 (later Victoria Road Evangelical cld 1984) dem 2004
⅄ (1892 Scot 2/15 r R&D

**Unitarian Williamson Memorial** Constitution Road cld 1969
⅄ (1882 Bis 2/12 fr Brighton Health Congress to Dundee Lindsay Street C 1882, to here c1885

**Unitarian Williamson Memorial** Dudhope Street
⅄ pt of organ from St. Luke's E & r1965 by Rev. Wm Miller 1+pd/ ex 2 , disused 1994, console rem

**University Chaplaincy** Cross Row, off Nethergate
⅄ 1978 Col 2/7 o2000s Edm

**Victoria Street** (UF/UP) Brown Constable Street/Victoria Street cld 1965
⅄ (1906 N&B 2/21

**Wallacetown** - see Trinity

**Ward Chapel C** Constitution Road
   &#8613;    1865 Holt 2/19 in west gallery  r1880-81 in apse gallery HDT 3/29, r1886, r1901 MilJ
        3/29, r1906, r1912, r1929 MilJ, r1955-58 R&D 3/29, o1972 R&D

**Wesleyan M** Ward Road (later Mission Nightclub)
   &#8613;    1884 Scot 2/17 +3pf  extant 1998

**West** (Roseangle Ryehill/Roseangle/St. John's UF/F) 130 Perth Road
   &#8613;    1896 HCF 3/25  r1910 N&B, r1924 Hils 3/29, r1968 Hils to gallery

**Whitfield** Haddington Avenue
   &#8613;    1971 R&D 2/  ex

**Willison UF** (F) Barrack Street cld 1928
   &#8613;    (1904 Law 2/20  rem 1928 to St. Cuthbert's

**Wishart Memorial** (UF/Wishart UP) 61 King Street cld 1975 (now Wishart Centre)
   &#8613;    (1925 MilJ 2/14  o1963 R&D

\* \* \* \* \* \* \* \* \* \* \* \* \* \* \* \* \* \* \* \* \* \* \* \* \*

**Dundonald** (St. Giles) Ayrshire
   &#8613;    (1865 HDT 2/10 no pd  rem c1906 to Falkirk Erskine Hall
   &#8613;    1906 N&B 2/16  o Har

**Dundrennan** - see Rerrick

**Duneaton** - see Crawfordjohn

**Dunecht House St. John's Chapel E** (Lady Cowdray's Chapel) Aberdeenshire
   &#8613;    (c1900 Ing  r1910 Bin, rem 1930 to Echt
   &#8613;    (1928 Bin 3/32  rem to Sledmere House, E. Yorkshire 1947 & r Bin 3/41 (4 divisions),
        r1984 Pri 3/51 (4 divisions)

**Dunfermline Abbey** St. Margaret Street
   &#8613;    (organ extant pre-1505  dest 1560
   &#8613;    1882 F&A 2/28  r1911 Sco 4/44, r1966 Wal 3/52, r1980-86 Loo 3/53, o For
   &#8613;    (organ 2/10 (temp)  rem 1911 by Sco, to Edinburgh McCrie Roxburgh 1917
   &#8613;    (1902 MilJ 2/8  fr Forgan 1983 to Stonehaven Dunnottar by Loo, to here 1984 by Loo
        (temp), rem, then 1991 to Stirling St. Mary's RC & r Loo
   &#8613;    (1985 Lam 1 +pd/7 (temp in nave 1985)  rem 1985 to Altrincham St. Vincent's RC,
        Cheshire and 1986 to Edinburgh Stockbridge by Lam
   &#8613;    (c1980s Loo 2/  ex3 (temp for 1985 festival, also used in Abbey Hall)

**Dunfermline C** - Canmore Street C see Dunfermline URC; Bath Street C see North C

**Dunfermline Chalmers Street-Headwell** (UF/UP) cld 1942 (Masonic Lodge until 1950)
   &#8613;    (1912 Bro 2/10  rem 1943 to Inverkeithing St. Peter's by Ing

**Dunfermline Gillespie Memorial** (Gillespie UP) Chapel Street cld
   &#8613;    1908 Cou  disused

**Dunfermline Holy Trinity E** East Port
- ⊥ (1842 Bru fr Dunfermline North C (Trinity E) 1891, rem c1895
- ⊥ 1895 HCF 2/18 o1915 HCF, o1952 Wil, o1995 R&D, o2012 For, o2017 For **B-listed**

**43) The 1895 Hamilton organ in Holy Trinity, Dunfermline, with case designed by Sir Rowand Anderson**

**Dunfermline North** Golfdrum Street (see also Dunfermline St. John's for North UF)
- ⊥ (1902 Walc 2/18 console removed, case extant

**Dunfermline North C** Pilmuir Street, formerly Bath Street (Bath Street C/EU/Trinity E cld 1891) cld 1974
- ⊥ (1842 Bru rem 1891 to Dunfermline Holy Trinity E
- ⊥ (1903 Bin 2/20 o1962 R&D, extant 1984

131

**Dunfermline Queen Anne High School**
  ⊥  1901 G&D 2/16 +1pf  fr Burntisland St. Andrew's 1977-1981 & completed later Loo, rem to new school & o2003 For

**Dunfermline Res of Henry Bardner**
  ⊥  (organ (Gothic front)  for sale 16ii1833

**Dunfermline Res of Sir John Ross**
  ⊥  1877 Lew 2/  (est. only)

**Dunfermline St. Andrew's** Chapel Street/Queen Anne Street cld 1974
  ⊥  (1902 Walc 2/16

**Dunfermline St. Andrew's Erskine** (Erskine/Queen Anne Street UF/UP) Pilmuir Street/Queen Anne Street  blg disused, cong moved
  ⊥  1899 Ing 3/  o1970s R&D 2/16, struck by lightning 1999

**Dunfermline St. Andrew's South** (UF/F) St. Margaret Street cld 1951 (cong to St. Ninian's)
  ⊥  (1914 MilJ 2/

**Dunfermline St. John's** (North UF/F) Bruce Street cld 1958
  ⊥  (1910 Sco 2/

**Dunfermline St. Leonard's** Brucefield Avenue
  ⊥  1910 Bin 2/21  o1960 Wil **B-listed**

**Dunfermline St. Margaret's** (UF/UP) East Port  blg cld 1974, cong moved to Touch
  ⊥  (1904 Bin 2/15  pt rem 1981 to Largo & r Loo 2/25

**Dunfermline St. Margaret's** Abel Place, Touch
  ⊥  1974 Wal 2/  ex

**Dunfermline St. Margaret's Hall** St. Margaret's Street
  ⊥  (1878 LTC 3/26  dest by fire 1961

**Dunfermline St. Margaret's RC** East Port
  ⊥  1872 Hol 1+pd/6  fr Houghton, Hunts to Saltby St. Peter's & o1985 Martin Renshaw, to here & r1987 Loo

**Dunfermline St. Ninian's** Whitelaw Road/Allan Crescent
  ⊥  1966 Wal 2/  ex 5  rem to new blg 1995 by R&D

**Dunfermline St. Paul's** (St. Columba's/UF/Abbey F) Canmore Street blg dest 1976
  ⊥  (1909 Lew 2/  scr 1976

**Dunfermline Townhill & Kingseat** (Townhill UF/F) Main Street
  ⊥  1908 Walc 1/  disused

**Dunfermline URC** (Canmore Street C) Canmore Street
  ⊥  (1859 Bev
  ⊥  1903 MilJ  r1974 Gol, r1980 Loo 2/17, r2004 Loo 2/19

**Dunfermline Viewfield B** East Port/Viewfield Terrace
  ⊥  (1912 Bro 2/22  r1970s Gol, scr 2007 Gol

**Dunfermline West B** Chalmers Street/Dewar Street
   ⚲  (1905 Bro  rem

**Dungavel Immigration Centre** (Prison/NCB Centre/POW/Res & Chapel for Duke of Hamilton) nr Strathaven
   ⚲  1912 B&F 2/7  disused 1992

**Dunglass** (Cockburnspath)
   ⚲  (c1830 SBr 1/4  to Eyemouth Old post-1870, r1903 HCF 1/6 to here pre-1954, rem to storage, to Eyemouth Masonic Lodge 1957

**Dunglass Collegiate Church** cld 1560
   ⚲  (organ extant 1481

**Dunimarle** - see Culross

**Dunipace** - see Denny

**Dunkeld** - see also Birnam and Dowally

**Dunkeld**
  **1) Cathedral**
    ⚲  (organ ref in 1514
    ⚲  (1900 Pos 1/6  rem to Dowally 1908
    ⚲  1908 Bev 2/12  r1975 Gol, r1982 Loo, r1988 Edm 2/16

  **2) Little Dunkeld** School Lane, Birnam
    ⚲  (1935 A&S 2/  scr 1992

**Dunkeld East** (UF/F) cld 1931 (antiques shop)
   ⚲  (1901 Pos  inst Bro

**Dunmore St. Andrew's E** nr Falkirk cld, dem
   ⚲  (1850 Bev  rem c1900
   ⚲  (c1900 Pos  inst by Graham of Edinburgh

**Dunning St. Serf's** cld 1972
   ⚲  (1934 Com 3/ ex6  fr Paisley Regal ABC 1958 & r

**Dunnottar** - see Stonehaven

**Dunoon High Kirk** (Old & St. Cuthbert's/Old/High/Dunoon) Kirk Square
   ⚲  (1895 Ing 2/16  r1957 R&D 2/20, scr 1991

**Dunoon Holy Trinity E** Kilbride Road
   ⚲  (1850 Rob
   ⚲  (1882 Har  r1967 L&B, dest c1970

**Dunoon St. Andrew's Mission Hall E** Alfred Street
   ⚲  (1903 B&H

**Dunoon St. Cuthbert's** (UF/Argyll UP) cld 1982
   ⚲  (1903 Bis 2/  o1958 R&D

**Dunoon St. John's** (UF/F) Argyll Street
  ⊥   1895 Bro 2/22  r1921 Ing 3/33, r1948 Com 3/34, o1966 R&D, o1990s R&D, o2004 For

**Dunrossness** Shetland
  ⊥   1913 organ

**Duns** Church Square
  ⊥   (1865 ConP 2/20  dest by fire 1879
  ⊥   1881 ConP 2/21  r1912 ConP 2/21, r1970 R&D, o1993 SmRo, o2003 Sta **B-listed**

**Duns Boston** (Boston UF/F) Station Road/Boston Court cld 1953 (later used as B ch)
  ⊥   (1911 ConP 2/10  rem 1956 to Olney Cowper Memorial, Bucks, later scr

**Duns Castle**
  ⊥   (1854 G&D 1/5  finger and barrel, rem to Duns Christ Church E

**Duns Christ Church E** Teindhill Green
  ⊥   (1854 G&D 1/5  fr Duns Castle
  ⊥   1876 organ inst 1878 Har 2/16  moved & r1927 Har 2/16

**Duns** - see also Marchmont and Manderston

**Duns South** (South UF/UP) Currie Street cld 1976
  ⊥   (HDT 1/8  fr St. Abbs The Mount 1907 HCF & r 2/11 no pd (with harmonium reeds)

**Dunscore East** (UF/F) disused
  ⊥   (1909 Vin  fr Dunscore Renwick post-1918, rem to Dunscore post-1940

**Dunscore** (Old)
  ⊥   (1909 Vin  fr Dunscore Renwick to Dunscore East post-1918, to here post-1940

**Dunscore Renwick UF** (UF/UP) cld 1918
  ⊥   (1909 Vin  rem to Dunscore East post 1918

**Duntocher** - see Clydebank

**Dupplin Castle** (Res of Lord Kinnoull) nr Perth
  ⊥   (1866 F&A 2/20  rem 1914 to Methven

**Durie House Res of Gibson** nr Leven
  ⊥   (organ for sale 1ii1786

**Durisdeer** Dumfriesshire
  ⊥   1967 Sol 1/3 ex1

**Duror St. Adamnan's E** Appin
  ⊥   c1700 SmB 1/7  r Sne, r c1783 Don, case by Thomas Parker, fr location on east coast,
       post-1817 to Fort William Rosse Chapel E & r 1/10, to here 1881 BBE/Wardle & r 1/6, o
       Wad, o1978 McDM, o & new blower 1990 McDM

**Duror South Cuil Res of D. Kerr Jamieson**
  ⊥   1820s WSm barrel organ 4ss  to here 2009 fr Mac workshop Glasgow Berkeley Street
       (stored in neighbour's, the Macleod Music Salon)

**44) Left: The Father Smith organ at Duror in its original position**
**45) Right: The case of the Wood Small barrel organ stored at Duror**

**Durris** Aberdeenshire
⅄   1903 Law 2/9

**Dysart St. Clair** (St. Serf's UF/F) West Port
⅄   (organ to here post-1948
⅄   1926 Wil 2/11 (encl) fr Res of J. McCoard, Kilcreggan in 1945 to Edinburgh Kirk
      Memorial C by Ing, o1956 Ing, r1971 SmRo 2/11, to here 1977 by SmRo

**Dysart Barony** (Dysart) Townhead/Normand Road cld 1972 (later hall)
⅄   (1890 Har 2/24 r1919 Ing 3/30, pt to Dysart St. Clair, rem to Alyth 1978 Loo

**Eaglesham** (Old & Carsewell)
⅄   1884 Wil 2/10 fr Bearsden Res of J.W. Macfarlane to Glasgow St. Cuthbert's & Queen's
      Cross & r1921 Watt, to here & r1979 Mac 2/10

**Eaglesham Res of Dr. Roger Jacob**
⅄   1994 Hyp 2/9 for sale 1995

**Earlston**
⅄   1892 B&F 2/9 **A-listed**

**Earlston St. John's** (Earlston UF/UP) cld 1946
⅄   (1905 Pos 1/5

135

**Eastfield Res of Joseph Cairney** West Lothian - see Cumbernauld

**East Kilbride Civic Centre**
  ⚓ (1934 Com 3/ +traps ex5 fr London Astoria, Purley 1976, rem 1979 to Carluke Res of T. Forsyth
  ⚓ 1926 Wur 2/53 +17 traps ex10 fr Embassy Theatre, Baltimore to Edinburgh Odeon Cinema 1930, to Kirkcaldy Res of T. K. Lockhart 1964, to here 1979, r1984 with parts from 1930 Hils 3/76 + 27 traps ex11 fr Paisley Picture House.
  ⚓ (1937 Com 3/102 ex7 fr Liverpool Mayfair Cinema to here 1987, rem 1992 to Coatbridge Summerlee Heritage Centre.

**East Kilbride Claremont** High Common Road
  ⚓ 1966 Wal 2/18 ex3 o1983 McDM

**East Kilbride Old** Montgomery Street
  ⚓ (1929 Bro 2/14 ind pallet chests rem post 1987

**East Kilbride West** (UF/UP/R) West Mains Road
  ⚓ 1920 Watt 2/ r1960 BinT 2/11

**East Kilbride Westwood** Belmont Drive
  ⚓ 1964 R&D 1+p/10 ex2 re-erected in present building 1992

**East Linton** - see Prestonkirk

**East Mainland** - see Holm, Orkney

**East Wemyss St. George's** (UF/F) Fife cld 2008
  ⚓ (B&F to here post-1937 rem c1955

**East Wemyss St. Mary by the Sea** Fife (Wemyss) cld 1976
  ⚓ (1903 B&F r1913 B&F 2/13, r McDM

**Eastwood** - see Glasgow

**Ecclefechan** - see Hoddom

**Eccles** Roxburgh
  ⚓ 1907 N&B Norvic 1/7

**Ecclesmachan St.Machan's** West Lothian
  ⚓ c1875 ConJ 1+pd/7 o1994 R&D **A-listed**

**Ecclesmachan Res of the Rev. Henry Liston**
  ⚓ (c1818 F&R 1+Sw/ enharmonic organ

**Echt** Aberdeenshire
  ⚓ (c1900 Ing r1910 Bin, to here 1930 fr Dunecht St. John's E, o1977 R&D, disused 1979, facade survives

**Eddleston** nr Peebles (see also Portmore House)
  ⚓ 1907 Ing 2/9 fr Dunblane St. Blane's 1980 & r Gol 2/10

**EDINBURGH** Note: several churches in Leith are listed under "Leith" in the Edinburgh lists below. The same applies to Portobello and Corstorphine.

**Abbey** Cadzow Place cld 1975 (see also Holyrood Abbey)
- ⚲ (1877 ConP 2/15  r1899 Wel 2/16, o1963 R&D 2/16, scr 1979

**Academy, The Edinburgh** Henderson Row
- ⚲ 1913 Lew 2/13  r1962 Com 2/26, r1978 Gol 2/29

**Acorn Centre** - see Leith M

**Albany Street C** Albany Street/24a Broughton Street cld 1968 (later Church of Nazarene cld)
- ⚲ (1841 Hill 2/13 with barrel mechanism  r1842 Bru 2/30, possibly fr Millearn House, Perthshire to here c1867 & r Ren, o1868, rem 1875 to Dalry URC
- ⚲ (1875 HDT 2/17 +1pf   1ss changed later, rem c1968, pt to Res of Angus Sibley

**Alexander's Coach Works** Canongate
- ⚲ (barrel organ for sale 23iii1761

**Alison House (Edinburgh University Music Dept)** (Music Faculty/Ironmongery Factory & Showroom) 12 Nicolson Square
- ⚲ 1950 Har 1+pd/6 (separate pipes for flats and sharps) fr Ampleforth Abbey to Reid Concert Hall 1951, to here 1976 by Har **A-listed**
- ⚲ 1984 W-K 2/4

**All Saints E** - see St. Michael's & All Saints E

**Argyle Place** (UF/UP) Chalmers Crescent cld 1974
- ⚲ (1911 Ing 2/24 (4 Gt ss encl) o1956 R&D, o1970 SmRo, 1974 damaged by fire & rem, pt to St. Catherine's Argyle 1980

**Assembly Hall** Castlehill
- ⚲ 1935 HNB 2/29  disconnected 1993, o1998 R&D with new action **B-listed**

**Assembly Rooms & Music Hall** George Street
- ⚲ (1775 Sne 1/9  fr St. Cecilia's Hall to Assembly Rooms 1802, rem 1835 to St. John the Evangelist E (incorporated in large organ)
- ⚲ (c1750 Eng (temp) fr Exeter to here by 1817, rem 1818 to St. John's E
- ⚲ (1830 HDa incl trumpet  extant 1841
- ⚲ (1838 Plessing of Baden automatic organ demonstration (temp)
- ⚲ (1843 Hill 3/37 in Music Hall  o1844 Hill, tuning altered 1851 Hill, r1879 Hill, rem 1912
  **Photograph on page 156**

**Astoria Cinema** Manse Road, Corstorphine cld 1974
- ⚲ (1929 Ing 2/24 +14 traps ex4 encl   1935 console moved, o1970 by organist, rem 1976, 1985 console to St. Albans Musical Museum, organ rem by Charles Davidson,  sold 2014 to Corstorphine Trust

**Augustine URC** (C/Augustine Bristo C/Augustine C) George IV Bridge
- ⚲ (1863 HDa 2/22 +pf in west gallery  r1894 King 2/22, o1914 Ing, rem 1929 to Bathgate St. David's & r Ing
- ⚲ (1929 Ing 2/24 (4 Gt ss in box)  o1942 Ing, o1969 R&D, rem 1994, case extant

**EDINBURGH (Cont.)**

**Barclay Viewforth** (Barclay/Barclay Bruntsfield/Barclay/UF/F) Barclay Place
⊥   1898 H-J 3/15   r1899 IHJ, 1902 +6ss by Lew, r1906 Lew 3/34, o1939 Wil, o1958 R&D, r1969 Hils 3/41 with new console, console moved 1998 R&D, 1ss changed 2008 by For

**Baron Smith's Qualified Chapel** E Blackfriars Wynd cld 1818, sold 1823
⊥   (1736 organ rem 1736
⊥   (1784 Sne rem 1815 by MWo, pt used elsewhere

**Barony & St. James's Place** (Barony/St. Mary's UF/F) Albany Street cld 1956
⊥   (1906 Ing 2/23   r pre-1921 Ing 3/29, rem 1956

**Barr, J.G. (auctioneer)** 76 Queen Street
⊥   (barrel organ auctioned 17ii1842

**Belford** (St. Cuthbert's UF/Dean UF/F) Douglas Gardens cld 1970
⊥   (1898 B&H

**Bellevue Chapel** (German Church disused 1914, cld) Rodney Street
⊥   (1880 Walc 2/10   rem 1929 to Warriston Crematorium

**Belmont House** Corstorphine (blg replaced 1828)
⊥   (chamber organ 1/10   for sale 10iv1788

**Beverley Cinema** (Blue Halls cld 1954) cld 1959 West Port/Lauriston Street
⊥   (1930 Ing 2/   ex6 scr c1960

**Blackhall St. Columba's** Queensferry Road
⊥   (1865 HDT 2/20   r1882 B&F 3/29, fr Greyfriars Old 1932 by Ing, r1935 Ing 3/29 with new console, r1947 Ing 3/30, o1961 R&D, r1974 Gol 3/35 with new console, o1990 SmRo
⊥   2006 Edm 2/28 using 9ss from old organ

**Bonnington** - see Leith Bonnington and Res of Crawfurd (Redbraes)

**Boroughmuir School** (St. Oswald's/St. Mark's cld 1957) Montpelier Park
⊥   (1900 M&S 2/   r1911 Ing 3/34, scr 1988

**Braid** - see Morningside Braid

**Bremner's Music Shop**
⊥   (Sne 1/6   for sale 22vii1767

**Brighton Street EU** (Relief Chapel to 1846) Brighton Street off Lothian Street cld 1900s
⊥   (1856 Ren rem 1871 by Ren
⊥   (1871 Holt 2/   incl Trumpet scr 1910

**Bristo B** Queensferry Road/Buckingham Terrace
⊥   1888 HDT 2/19   r1907 Bin 2/ , fr St. James's Place 1935 Wel, r Sco 2/20, o1950s Wil

**Bristo** - see also Pollock, Seventh Day & Augustine URC

**Broughton McDonald** (Broughton Place/UF/UP) Broughton Place cld 1991
- ⅄ (1890 Wil 2/22 r1907 N&B 3/33 +1pf, r1953 Com 3/34 (new console), o1962 Com, rem 1993 to R&D Liverpool where stored, pt to Auckland St. Matthew's by Wil 2011

**Broughton St. Mary's** (St. Mary's) Bellevue Crescent
- ⅄ 1882 LTC 2/14 +3pf +3ss c1893 SmRi, o1897 Ing, r1902 IHJ 2/17, o1985 R&D, o2002 R&D/For , o2012 by For after ceiling damage **A-listed**
- ⅄ (c1850s Ren 1/8 to Fortrose & r1914 Cat 1/8, to Scourie Res 1986, to Leithen Lodge 1987, case only to here 1999, rem 2002 to Stow Manse (see also Leithen Lodge)

**Broughton St. Mary's Church Centre** (Broughton Place Church Hall) 7 East Broughton Place cld 2005
- ⅄ (c1890 "Scudamore" Har 1+ppd/3 fr Edinburgh Res of Raoul Kunz to Res of W.E. Smith, rem to Water of Leith Mission E 1903 by HCF, rem 1976 & r later by Hugh Ross and friends to St. David of Scotland E, o1984 Sir Ronald Johnson, rem 1995 to here by Alan Buchan, rem 2005 to Heriot & o Sta
- ⅄ (1830s SBr barrel organ 3ss fr Hawick Res of M. Webb post-1958 to Burnley Res of W. Blakey, rem post-1992 to London Botany Bay, Enfield, Middlesex by George Crutchley & o1990s, to here 1999, rem 2000 to Mid Calder Res of Buchan

**Bruce, James & Co. (Workshop 1815-43)** (Small Bruce & Co./Wood Small & Co./Muir Wood & Co.) Amphion Place, Low Calton (North Back of Canongate) See also Muir Wood & Co. and Wood & Co.
- ⅄ (3 organs for sale fr former Muir Wood workshop 1815
- ⅄ (1817 MWo 3+ppd/21 on display iv1817, rem xi1817 to Glasgow St. Andrew's RC
- ⅄ (c1700 SmB 2/10 no pd fr Charlotte Chapel 1819 to storage here, rem 1828 to Peebles for St. Peter's E
- ⅄ (c1819 MWo 3/19 on display, possibly to Gateshead St. Mary's E
- ⅄ (c1795 Gre 2/8 fr London 1795 to Aberdeen St. Andrew's E, o1809 JoW, o1813 JoW to new blg 1817, probably to here 1817
- ⅄ (chamber organs 1/7 and 1/4 on display 9i1819
- ⅄ (1825 WSm 3+ppd/19 on display vi1825, rem to Glasgow St. Mary's E
- ⅄ (second hand organ 1/6 & chamber organ 1/5 for sale iii1826
- ⅄ (second hand chamber organ for sale 1829
- ⅄ (1832 SBr 2/21 no pd on display , rem 1833 to Derry Long Tower RC, Ireland
- ⅄ (1834 SBr organ for convent damaged by fire x1834
- ⅄ (1836 SBr large and powerful organ on display
- ⅄ (c1830 SBr 2+pd/11 for sale 14i1837 fr Res
At 1839 Sequestration:
- ⅄ (three chamber organs, 1/2, 1/4 & 1/6; four barrel organs; two bird organs and one machine organ to be sold (still available at shop, 101 George Street, 1840, when some sold to Wood & Co.)
- ⅄ (1840 SBr 2/24 organ on display 15viii1840, rem 1840 to Dublin St. Peter's RC.
- ⅄ (1713 Cuvillié/Hollister fr Dublin St. Peter's RC to here 1840, inst in St. Mark's Unitarian 1842
At 1841 Sequestration:
- ⅄ (one small church organ, one church organ and one large organ (for Mr. Mould, North Bridge) to be sold
- ⅄ (1841 Bru 1/10 + Sw on display, for sale
At 1843 Sequestration:
- ⅄ (two chamber organs 1/3 and 1/6, church organ 1/7 +Sw being built
- ⅄ (small barrel organ

**EDINBURGH (Cont.)**

**Bruce, William, Saleroom** 27 North Bridge, later 2 Register Place, then at 24 Waterloo Place
 ⊥ (organ 1/5 for sale 13ii1804
 ⊥ (organ 1/6 for sale 2ix1815 and 1816
 ⊥ (organ 1/3 for sale 15vii1820
 ⊥ (barrel organ for sale 1iii1821
 ⊥ (Res organ for sale 5v1821
 ⊥ (chamber organ for sale 8iii1824

**Bruntsfield Evangelical** (Bruntsfield/UF/UP/Viewforth UP cld 1967) Westhall
Gardens/Leamington Terrace
 ⊥ (1902 N&B 2/20 +1pf (1ss added later), o1958 R&D, disused 1995, rem (building
 divided horizontally)

**Buccleuch** Chapel Street cld 1969 (later storeroom for University, fr 2015 Greek Orthodox)
 ⊥ (1899 IGD 2/19 pt rem 1974 SmRo, console & action on e-bay 2015

**Burdiehouse -** see Kaimes Lockhart Memorial

**Caledonian Bazaar** Wemyss Place
 ⊥ (grand organ extant 1834
 ⊥ (1832 HDa barrel organ 6ss for sale here 1835

**Canongate** Canongate, Royal Mile (see also Holyrood Abbey)
 ⊥ (1871 ConP 2/ fr Musselburgh Inveresk St. Michael's 1894, rem 1956
 ⊥ (1910 N&B 2/21 + solo division & barrel mechanism fr Rankeillor House, nr
 Springfield, Fife 1960 by HNB, barrel mechanism rem, rem 1990
 ⊥ c1850s Mir 1/5 chamber organ repaired Robert Thomson (Yorks), o Bro, fr Perth to
 Fettes College 1930s, to here c1964 on loan, o1991 Lam **A-listed**
 ⊥ 1998 Fro 2/20 o2018 WoH

**Capitol Cinema** Manderston Street cld 1961 (now Mecca Bingo)
 ⊥ (1928 Ing 2/47 + 14 traps ex8 rem 1968 to ch in Fife

**Cargilfield School** Gamekeepers Road
 ⊥ 1911 N&B 2/11 to new chapel 1921, o1923 HNB, o2009 For

**Carrick Knowe** Saughton Road North
 ⊥ 1973 SmRo 2/13 using Ing material from Nicolson Street

**Catholic Apostolic Church** 22 Broughton Street blg cld 1876 (later St. Oran's cld 1948)
 ⊥ (pre-1870 Wal 2/ to here post-1858, rem 1876 to Mansfield Traquair by HDT

**Catholic Apostolic Church -** see also Mansfield Traquair Centre

**Central B** (Methodist Central Hall cld 2010) Earl Grey Street
 ⊥ 1904 Vin 3/40 r1930 Sco 3/33, r1958 Wal 3/48, r1970 SmRo 3/48, r1974 SmRo 3/52 (3ss
 fr Leith Kirkgate), 1979 1ss changed by SmRo, 1989 new console SmRo

**Chalmers** (Chalmers Territorial UF/West Port F) West Port cld 1958
 ⊥ (1901 IGD 3/32 rem to storage in Hereford, 1973 console & some pipes to Belmont
 Abbey RC, Hereford

140

**Chalmers Lauriston** (Lauriston/UF/UP) Lauriston Place cld 1980
   ⅄  (1889 ConP 3/30 +1ss (pd) 1905, r1909 Sco 3/31, r1924 Sco 3/30 + new console & to chamber, o1954 Ing, rem 1981 or later

**Chaplaincy Centre (Edinburgh University)** (New North/UF/F cld 1941) Forrest Road cld 1976
   ⅄  (1904 Hill 2/22  r1905 Hill 2/25, dest by fire 1932
   ⅄  (1932 HNB 2/27  r1961 HNB 3/27, rem 1978 to George Watson's College

**Charlotte Chapel B** (Rose Street E cld 1818) 204 West Rose Street (new blg 1908)
   ⅄  (c1700 SmB 2/10 no pd  to here 1797, for sale 26i1818, rem 1819 to Bruce, James & Co. by WSm
   ⅄  (1929 B&H 2/13 +1pf  scr 1973, facade rem 2017

**Charlotte Chapel B** (St. George's West/St. George's UF//F cld 2010) Shandwick Place
   ⅄  1897 LTC 2/23  r1907 N&B 2/26, o1919 HNB, r1930 R&D 3/34 +1pf, o1948 R&D, 1955 console moved, r1981 R&D 3/32, o2005 For, console moved 2015 For
   ⅄  (chamber organ extant in hall 1893-99

**Christ Church Morningside E** Morningside Road, Holy Corner
   ⅄  1878 ConP 2/19  o1886, r1892 & 1902 HCF 2/22, r1921 HCF 2/22, r1929 Sco, r1971 SmRo 2/32, 1ss later rem,  r1993 R&D 2/31

**Christ Church Trinity E** 118 Trinity Road cld 1980
   ⅄  (1876 JoH 1/
   ⅄  (1882 Bev  rem to Constantinople Pera EU by Ing 1897
   ⅄  (1889 LTC 2/16  fr Res of Earl of Aberdeen, 27 Grosvenor Street, London to storage 1891, to here 1897 by IngE 2/16, o1961 Wil, r1968 SmRo 2/20 +7pf with pt fr Leith Bonnington, rem 1982 to St. Vincent's E

**Christian Scientist** (First Church/Second Church) 9 Young Street
   ⅄  1978 Man 2/8 (no Sw)  2004 + doors to Pos, r2006 W-K 2/8 (4ss changed)

**Christian Scientist** - see also Union Advertising Agency

**Churchhill Theatre** - see Morningside High

**City of Edinburgh M** (Nicolson Square M) Nicolson Square
   ⅄  1864 F&A 2/18 +1pf  r1890 King 2/19, r1911 Ing 2/22 +1pf, r1976 Gol 2/23 with material fr Queen's Hall, o1994 Lig, o2000 Lig, disused

**Cluny** - see Morningside

**Coburg Street UP** - see Leith St. Ninian's Coburg Street

**Colinton** (St. Cuthbert's) Dell Road
   ⅄  1908 N&B 2/18  r1928 R&D 2/20 to west gallery, o1962, r1974-76 SmRo 2/34, o1987 SmRo, o1998 SmRo, o2007 For, r2016 For 2/25

**Colinton** - see also St. Cuthbert's E

**EDINBURGH (Cont.)**

**College** (College Street UF/South College Street UP) South College Street cld 1960 (later used by Edinburgh University)
    ⅄   (1874 Holt 3/22 (first UP organ in Edinburgh) r1885 Har, r1910 Ing 3/24 +2pf

**Colt Bridge House** Murrayfield - see under Residences

**Concert Hall** Playhouse Close, Canongate cld 1767
    ⅄   (1753 organ rem 1762
    ⅄   ( Thornbuckle of London chamber organ for sale 20iv1774

**Constitution Street C** Constitution Street cld 1964
    ⅄   (c1910 Sco 1/5 fr Res of A. J. Reid to here 1926 Sco, rem 1964 to Saughton Mains C

**Convent** at end of Links (for other convents see St. David's, Gillis College, St. Catherine's, and Napier University Craiglockhart Chapel)
    ⅄   (1834 SBr damaged by fire in workshop, Amphion Place

**Corri & Sutherland Music Shop** (Corri & Co./Corri & Dussek) 37 North Bridge cld 1815
    ⅄   (organs for sale 1786
    ⅄   (chamber organ for sale 4xi1790
    ⅄   (chamber organ for sale 1/8 26ix1795
    ⅄   (large and small barrel organs for sale 11xi1796
    ⅄   (organ for sale 27vii1797
    ⅄   (organ1/4 and two bird organs for sale 16iv1798 & 6iv1799
    ⅄   (barrel organ 5ss by Holland for sale 1799
    ⅄   (barrel organ by Jones for sale 5viii1799
    ⅄   (organ 1/5 for sale 13xii1800
    ⅄   (church and chamber organs for sale 1811

**Corstorphine Craigsbank** Craigs Crescent
    ⅄   1965 Wal 2/18 ex3 encl

**Corstorphine Old** Kirk Loan
    ⅄   (1888 ConP 2/12 rem 1905 to Inverleith St. Serf's
    ⅄   1905 HCF 2/16 o1948 Com 2/17, r1961 Com 2/19 (new console), r1973 SmRo 2/21, r2005 For 2/21 (new console)

**Corstorphine St. Anne's** Kaimes Road/St. John's Road
    ⅄   1922 Ing 2/23 o1950 & 1975, r1997 SmRo 2/27 (some pipes fr Mayfield), o2006 MilP
    **B-listed**

**Corstorphine St. Ninian's** (UF/F) St. John's Road/St. Ninian's Road
    ⅄   1902 Walc 2/13 r1913 HCF & rem to transept 2/16, r1934 Ing, resited & r1957 R&D 2/20, o1975 R&D, o2007 For

**Corstorphine UF** Glebe Terrace
    ⅄   1901 Pos 1/6 fr Freuchie UF, Fife 1967, o2003 Edm

**Corstorphine** - see also Astoria Cinema, Belmont House, St. John's RC & St. Thomas E

**Cowgate Chapel** - see St. Patrick's RC

**46) Left: The 1905 C. & F. Hamilton organ in Corstorphine Old Parish Church with
case designed by George Henderson and console by Compton**
Reproduced with kind permission of Corstorphine Old Parish Church
**47) Right: The 1892 organ by Herbert King which stood in Dalry Congregational Church
until 2005. The organ contains older pipes by Bruce**

**Craig House** - see Napier University Craighouse

**Craigentinny St. Christopher's** Craigentinny Road/Avenue cld 2016
⅄   1900 Ing 2/24 r1956 in chamber, damaged by fire 1968, fr St. Catherine's Argyle to here
    1969 & r SmRo 2/22, o1988 SmRo

**Craiglockhart** Craiglockhart Avenue
⅄   (1906 Law 2/16 in north aisle scr 1962
⅄   1962 R&D 2/15 +2pf (using material fr old organ) in west gallery o1974 R&D, 1978
    +2ss R&D, +1ss 1993 R&D, disused 2016, console rem

**Craigmillar Park** (Mayfield South/Mayfield)
⅄   1892 B&F 2/19 o1909 Sco, r1929 Ing 3/28, o1957 R&D (console moved), r1963 R&D
    3/28, r1969 R&D 3/33, o2008 Lig, r2014 Lig 3/34

**Craigmillar Park** (UF/F) - see St. Margaret's School

**Craigmillar** - see Richmond Craigmillar

**Craigsbank** - see Corstorphine Craigsbank

143

**EDINBURGH (Cont.)**

**Cramond** Cramond Glebe Road
⚒ (1912 N&B 2/14  o1974 R&D, o1977 R&D (water damage), o1990 R&D after water damage with 2ss changed, scr 1998

**Dalglish & Forrest Saleroom** 59 Castle Street - see Lauriston Lodge & Res of Bowman

**Dalmeny Street** - see Leith Dalmeny Street

**Dalry URC** (C ) Caledonian Road cld 2005
⚒ (1841 Hill 2/13 with barrel mechanism  r1842 Bru 2/30, possibly fr Millearn House, Perthshire to Albany Street C & r1867 Ren, rem to here 1875 by Millar +1ss, r1892 King 2/13, rem to storage at Stow Manse 2005

**Davidson** (UF/Eyre Place UP) Eyre Place/Crescent cld 1945
⚒ (1928 Ing 2/13 +6pf (added later)  rem 1946 to Inverness St. Columba's High, inst 1953

**Davidson's Mains** (UF/Cramond UF/F) Quality Street
⚒ (1968 Vin 2/23 ex3 encl  console moved, rem 1999

**Dean** Dean Path/Ravelston Terrace cld 2016
⚒ 1903 HCF 2/19  o2007 Nic **A-listed**

**Dean -** see also Belford and Res of Muir

**Dowell's Saleroom** 97 George Street
⚒ (Gothic barrel organ 5 ss for sale 12iv1845
⚒ (chamber organs 1/2 and 1/11  for sale 25iii1848

**Dublin Street B** Dublin Street cld 1987
⚒ (1864 Ren 1+pd/11  r1880 B&F 3/   pt fr temp organ at St. John's E, rem 1898
⚒ (1898 B&F 2/21  c1905 to east end, r1957 Bell 2/21, rem 1987

**Duddingston** Old Church Lane
⚒ (1879 Ren 2/11  rem 1889
⚒ (1881 You 2/15  fr Res to here 1889, r1921 2/22, scr 1968

**Duke Street URC** (C/EU) Duke Street, Leith blg cld 2005 and replaced
⚒ (c1712 1/5  fr Old St. Paul's E 1716 to unknown location, to former EU chapel in Storries Alley/St. Andrew Street, Leith 1854, rem 1867 (sold to Andrew Jupp, Edinburgh)
⚒ 1867 ConP 2/18  r1930 Ing 2/21, o1960 Wil, r1977 Gol 2/25, r2008 in new blg by Robin Gardiner, organist, with console fr Linlithgow St. Michael's

**Dunedin Consort (portable organ)**
⚒ 1999 Lam 1/3  housed in Res

**Edinburgh Academy** - see Academy

**Episcopal Training Colleges -** see St. Andrew's Hall, Normal Practising School and St. Mary's Music School

**Exhibitions -** see
Meadows (1886)
Meggetland (1890)
Saughton Park (1908)

**Fairmilehead** Frogston Road West
- ⅄ (French organ fr Oxford University Music School to London, to here 1949 by Wil 2/13, rem 1969
- ⅄ 1991 Lam 2/16 in gallery  r2006 Lam 2/17 in chancel (new case)

**Fettes College** Carrington Road
- ⅄ 1873 HDT 2/  r1900 Vin 2/19, r1928 R&D 3/30, moved fr chapel to hall 1953 R&D, o1959 R&D
- ⅄ (c1850s Mir 1/5  repaired R. Thomson (Yorks), o Bro, fr Perth to here 1930s, rem c1964 to Canongate

**First Church of Christ Scientist -** see Christian Scientist and also Union Advertising Agency

**Forth Pipe Organs -** see Newton Village and Rosyth (outwith Edinburgh)

**Fortune's Room** Register Street
- ⅄ (1812 M. Haddock of Cork  "Androides" organ exhibited

**Fountainhall Road** (UF/UP/Mayfield UP) Fountainhall Road cld 1958
- ⅄ (1897 IngE 2/27  r1906 S&L 3/22, o1928, rem 1962 (5ss  to Mayfield Salisbury)

**Freemasons' Hall** 96 George Street
- ⅄ (1859 HDa  in gallery of previous blg  extant 1889
- ⅄ 1913 B&F 3/32  o1936, o2010 For **A-listed**

**Galbraith J.M.** (Gow & Galbraith 57 Princes Street) 31 St Andrew Square/2 Hanover Street cld 1829
- ⅄ (organ 1/6 for sale 28iv1827, 23vii1827, 15iii1828 & 19i1829
- ⅄ (barrel organ 4ss  auctioned at 2 Hanover Street 22v1834

**Gaumont Cinema** (Rutland) Torphichen Street cld 1963
- ⅄ (1930 Ing 3/  +14 traps ex11  rem 1958, traps to Lancashire Res

**George Watson's College** Colinton Road
- ⅄ 1932 HNB 2/27  r1961 HNB 3/27, fr University Chaplaincy Centre, dism 1978, to here 1982 & r 3/27 by staff & pupils with pipes fr Glasgow St. Kenneth's, o1988 R&D

**Georgian House** 7 Charlotte Square
- ⅄ c1810 Gow & Shepherd 4ss barrel organ  fr Res of Mr. Dixon, 6 North East Circus Place 1975 **A-listed**

**German Church -** see Bellevue Chapel

**Gillis Centre RC** (Gillis College/St. Margaret's Convent) Whitehouse Loan
- ⅄ (1829 WSm 2/9  fr Holy Trinity 1835
- ⅄ (1893 G&D 2/7  fr Res of J.S. Sturrock to here 1894, o1900 G&D, o1956 Wal, disused 1994, rem 2009 to storage at Newton Village workshop of For, scr 2015

**EDINBURGH (Cont.)**

**Gilmerton** (pt of Tron Kirk: Gilmerton & Moredun) Ravenscroft Street
⅄　(1959 Vin 2/23 ex3 encl scr 2009

**Good Shepherd Convent RC** Woodhall Road cld 1980
⅄　( Hos 2/11 fr Convent of the Good Shepherd RC, Bristol 1945-48 by R&D, rem 1980

**Good Shepherd E, Church of the** 13 Murrayfield Avenue
⅄　1884 B&F 3/19 fr Res of Finlay B. Anderson, C.A. 1904 & inst 1905 S&L, o1908 &
　　1911 Sco 3/19, o1914 Ing, o1935 G&D, r1949 R&D 3/18, r1967 Wil 3/29 +4pf

**Gorgie Dalry Stenhouse** (Gorgie Dalry/Gorgie/Cairns Memorial/UF/Gorgie UP) 190 Gorgie Road
⅄　(1875 HDT 2/16 fr Palmerston Place 1902 by N&B, r c1920 Ing 2/20, o1951 R&D 2/21,
　　disused 1988, scr 2006

**Gorgie F** - see North Merchiston

**Gow & Shepherd Music Shop** 16 Princes Street (see also Galbraith)
⅄　(organ 1/5 for sale 18vi1807

**Grange -** see St. Catherine's Argyle, Salisbury and Marchmont St. Giles

**Granton** Boswall Parkway
⅄　(1829 organ 1/ (no pd) fr St. James E, Broughton Street to former ch here 1896 & r Ing
　　2/11
⅄　1936 R&D 2/32 ex4 encl o1962 R&D **A-listed**

**Granton House** West Shore Road
⅄　( HDT 2/7 rem 1907 to Leven St. Margaret's E

**Greenbank** (UF/UP) Braidburn Terrace
⅄　1927 Ing 2/23 r1972 SmRo 2/30, r1978 SmRo 2/32, r1992 SmRo 2/32, o2011 MilP

**Greenside** Royal Terrace
⅄　(1885 Har 2/13 fr Co. Durham 1886 by DavJT, rem 1933 to St. Margaret's, Pleasance
⅄　1933 Ing 2/21 using old case and other pts o1965 Wil, o1993 R&D

**Greyfriars** (Greyfriars Tolbooth & Highland/Greyfriars/Greyfriars Old & New) Greyfriars Place,
Candlemaker Row
Old Greyfriars (East):
⅄　(1865 HDT 2/20 r1882 B&F 3/29, rem 1932 to Blackhall St. Columba's
New Greyfriars (West):
⅄　(1866 HDT 3/36 r1872 F&A, fr Glasgow Park to here 1889 by HDT, o1901 HCF, r1938
　　G&D in unified blg 3/37, o1960 Hils, scr 1989
Greyfriars:
⅄　1990 Col 3/49 using material fr 13ss fr Greyfriars New by HDT, + 1ss 1993, 1997 1ss
　　replaced, o1999 & 2003 Col, o2009 Clevedon
⅄　c1850 HDa 2/8 no pd fr Res of Dr. R.A. Goodsir to Royal Arch Hall 1907, rem 1957 to
　　Rudolph Steiner School & r by Ronald Johnson & George Ward (1ss changed), to here
　　1970 & o Hils **B-listed**

**48) The 1865 Hamilton organ in
Old Greyfriars after its enlargement of 1882**

**Guthrie Memorial** (UF/F) Easter Road cld 1962
⚐ (1924 E&B 2/

**Hamilton, G. (bookseller)** 34 Nicolson Street
⚐ (pre-1825 small organ for sale 19iii1825

**Hamilton, John (music seller)** 24 North Bridge
⚐ (chamber organ 1/6 for sale 17iv1806

**Hamilton, David (organbuilder)** (Hamilton & Murray) 63 North Bridge, rem 1824 to 3 Hanover Street, rem 1828 to 30 St. Andrew Square (fr 1838 Hamilton & Müller)
⚐ (1824 HDa 1/6 + Sw (also barrel organs) on display at North Bridge and later at 24 Waterloo Place saleroom
⚐ (1825 Holl 1/4 for sale vii1825
⚐ (1827 HDa 1/5 for sale 19iv1827
⚐ (chamber organ 1/4 fr Res, re-cased 1827 for sale 17v1827 & 13xii1828
⚐ (chamber organ 1/6 for sale 19vii1827
⚐ (second hand finger organ for sale 1831
⚐ (1831 HDa 3/20 on display 1831-32, still for sale 1846
⚐ (1832 HDa barrel organ 6ss auctioned in Caledonian Bazaar, Wemyss Place 1835

**Hamilton & Müller** 116 George Street cld 1888
⚐ (1839 HDa large chamber organ for Res of gentleman
⚐ (organs for sale 11iv1844 after death of partner J.M. Müller
⚐ (1854 HDa 2/ organ for Germany on display
⚐ (1860 HDa 2/ organ for Cilgerran Church, Cardigan
⚐ (1867 HDT 2+ppd/15 for Res of gentleman
⚐ (1868 HDT three chamber organs on sale 1868
⚐ (1827 WSm o1840 Wood/Bru, o1851 Tow, o1859 & 1864 Ren, o1867 Tow, to here 1875 fr Old St. Paul's E, returned & r1880 HDT
⚐ (1870 Holt 2/9 fr here 1882 to Ashby St. Ledger's, Northamptonshire by HDT, r1971 Bowen 2/9

147

**EDINBURGH (Cont.)**

**Hay & Son** North Bridge
⊥ (chamber organ for sale 16ii1795

**Haymarket** (UF/UP) Dalry Road cld 1960
⊥ (organ 2/10 acquired 1911 by Sco, to McCrie Roxburgh 1917 by Sco, to here & r1921 Sco

**High** (UF/F) Mound Place cld 1935 (now Edinburgh University Divinity Faculty)
⊥ (1897 Vin 2/ rem 1935 to Stenhouse St. Aidan's
⊥ (1903 Cou 1/5 on display 22v1903 in ch hall

**High Kirk of Edinburgh** - see St. Giles' Cathedral

**Highland** (St. Columba's/UF/F) Cambridge Street cld 1956
⊥ (1924 organ

**Highland Tolbooth St. John's** (Tolbooth St. John's/Tolbooth) Castlehill cld 1981
⊥ (1902 IHJ 2/16 +5pf 5ss added later, rem 1980s

**Hillside** (Lady Glenorchy's North/Lady Glenorchy's UF/F) Greenside Place cld 1978
⊥ (1902 Bin 2/21 o1956 R&D, vandalised, rem 1986-89

**Holy Cross E** Quality Street, Davidson's Mains
⊥ (1897 H-J 1/ rem 1903
⊥ (1903 HCF 1+pd/7 o1905, fr former ch 1913 HCF
⊥ (1983 Gol 2/24 ex8 using material fr HCF organ scr 1993 by SmRo

**Holyrood Abbey, Chapel Royal & Abbey Church** Abbey Strand cld 1560/1690
⊥ (1497 regal in West lodgings (portable)
⊥ (1537 organ used for funeral of Queen Madeleine
⊥ (1541 pair of organis plus organ loft in Chapel Royal
⊥ (1557 organis for Chapel Royal rem 1562
⊥ (1616 Dallam 2/ no pd for Chapel Royal broken up 1638, rem 1649
⊥ (1633 organes (exact location not clear)
⊥ (organis extant in Abbey Church 1638-43
⊥ (1687 organ dest 1688

**Holyrood Abbey** (UF/Abbeyhill UF/UP) Dalziel Place
⊥ (1902 Walc 2/15 r1913 HCF 2/15, o1959 R&D, console moved 1968, r1981 SmRo 2/17 and new console, dism 2002 R&D due to blg work, scr 2006

**Holyrood garden near palace**
⊥ (organ used for recitals by Pescatore 1753

**Holyrood Palace** (Halyrudehouse) Queen's Park
⊥ (1631 organ in chamber

**Holy Spirit E** - see St. Matthew's E

**Holy Trinity** (Lady Glenorchy's South/Lady Glenorchy's/Roxburgh F to 1847/Roxburgh Place Independent/Relief) Roxburgh Place cld 1969
   ⅄  (1829 WSm 1/9 for sale xii1833/iv1835/i1837, rem to Gillis Centre (St. Margaret's Convent)
   ⅄  (1896 F&A 2/ r1914 F&A 3/23 in new blg

**Holy Trinity** - see also Trinity College

**Holy Trinity E** Dean Bridge cld 1951 (later electricity sub-station, then re-opened)
   ⅄  (1838 HDa 3/17 r1865 Holt 3/17, r1872 HDT, rem 1911
   ⅄  1912 Lew 2/17 rem 1949 to Stirling Viewfield Erskine

**Hope Park** (UF/UP) Hope Park Terrace cld 1940
   ⅄  (1893 B&F 3/26 r1910 Sco 2/ , rem 1941 to Hawick St. Margaret's & Wilton South

**Hope Park** - see also Queen's Hall

**Hope Park & Buccleuch C** Hope Park Terrace cld 1979
   ⅄  (1908 Ing 2/16 scr 1984

**Hopetoun** (St. James) McDonald Road cld 1974
   ⅄  (1902 Walc 2/17 r1959 Bell 2/21 (2ss rem to St. Columba's-by-the-Castle E), rem 1974 Bell to storage at Queensferry St. Mary's E, then scr

**Huntly House Museum** Canongate (now Museum of Edinburgh)
   ⅄  1850 Tow 5ss barrel organ fr Manor House, Belhaven c1967, disused **A-listed**

**Inverleith** (St. James UF/F) Inverleith Gardens, Ferry Road cld 2011 (now Edinburgh Tabernacle - Pentecostal)
   ⅄  (1900 Wal 2/14 dest by fire 1929
   ⅄  (1929 Wil 2/22 to here fr Liverpool factory 1931 by Wil, o1959 Wil, r1969 Wal 2/28, 1978 2ss changed by Gol, o1986 Gol, 1991 +1ss, o2006 R&D, rem 2014 to Valencia

**Inverleith St. Serf's** (Leith St. Serf's) Clark Road/Ferry Road
   ⅄  (1888 ConP 2/12 fr Corstorphine Old 1905 & r HCF 2/12, rem 1930 to Leith St. Thomas
   ⅄  1931 R&D 3/29 o1949 R&D, o2009 Pri, r2014 Pri 3/29 (new action and chests)
   ⅄  (organ lent by Pri 2014 rem

**Jameson's Bookshop/Lodgings** nr Old Post Office, Parliament Square
   ⅄  (organ 1/6 + barrels for sale 25xii1784 & 30viii1785

**John Ker Memorial** (UF/UP) Polwarth Gardens cld 1981
   ⅄  (1902 Kir 2/22 scr 1984, pt to SmRo

**John's Coffee House** - see Res of Seton

**Junction Road** - see Leith St. Thomas' Junction Road

**Juniper Green** (Juniper Green St. Andrew's/UF/F) Lanark Road
   ⅄  1914 Hils 2/18 gas engine r1978 SmRo 2/24 with new console (pt fr Juniper Green St. Margaret's)

**EDINBURGH (Cont.)**

**Juniper Green St. Margaret's** (Juniper Green) Lanark Road cld 1974
⊥ ( Ing 2/16 to here 1906 by You  rem 1954
⊥ (1906 F&A 2/22  fr Glasgow Plantation Cornwall Street 1954 & r R&D 2/23, rem 1978, pt to Juniper Green

**Kaimes Lockhart Memorial** (Burdiehouse) Gracemount Drive blg dem 2010
⊥ (1961 Wal 1+pd/4  rem 2010 to Norham Res, Northumberland

**King's Church** - see Viewforth

**King's Hall** (Edinburgh City Fellowship/St. Paul's Newington/Newington East/Newington UF/F cld 1984) South Clerk Street
⊥ (1902 HCF 2/24  r1908 HCF 2/26, o1951, rem 1987, case extant

**Kirk Memorial C** (Abbey Mount EU) Montgomery Street cld 1979
⊥ (c1820 WSm 1/7 + Sw  to here post 1903, gift of Mr. Hunter, rem 1946 to Arbroath C
⊥ (1926 Wil 2/11 (encl)  fr Res of James McCoard, Kilcreggan 1945 by Ing, o1956 Wil, r1969 SmRo 2/11, rem 1977 to Dysart St. Clair by SmRo

**Kirk o'Field** (Charteris-Pleasance/Charteris Memorial) Pleasance cld 2013
⊥ (1976 SmRo 1+pd/9 using early 20th century material  +2ss 1984 SmRo, rem 2016 to St. Margaret's & St. Leonard's Catholic Church of Pius X by For

**Lady Glenorchy's** - see Holy Trinity and Hillside

**Lady Yester's** Infirmary Street cld 1938 (used by Edinburgh University)
⊥ (1888 Wad 2/19  r1924 Ing

**Launie's Sale Room** - see Ros's Music Shop

**Lauriston Lodge** East Lauriston Lane
⊥ (Gothic chamber organ with 6 barrels  for sale by Dalglish & Forrest 10iii1838

**Lauriston** - see Chalmers Lauriston

**Leith Bonnington** (UF/UP) Summerside Street cld 1968
⊥ (1880 You 2/17  r1911 You 3/23, r1929 Sco 3/  (resited), r1961 ConP 2/25 console to east end, rem 1968, pt to Christ Church Trinity E

**Leith Dalmeny Street** (UF/UP) Dalmeny Street cld 1950/1964 (now Ukranian RC)
⊥ (1929 Watt 2/15  rem 1963 to St. Nicholas' Sighthill

**Leith Ebenezer UF (continuing)** (UF/UP) Great Junction Street blg cld 1979
⊥ ( Vin 2/11  to here 1945, rem by 1979

**Leith F** (Thomas Elder Memorial/UF/F) Casselbank Street
⊥ (1901 IGD 2/20  rem to Leith St. John's West 1909

**Leith Kirkgate** (UF/UP) Henderson Street cld 1973
⊥ (1902 F&A 2/19  fr Peebles St. Andrew's UF 1922 by Sco 2/19, scr 1974, 2ss to Central B

**Leith M** (Methodist Central Hall) Junction Place, Leith cld 2012
(now YMCA Acorn Centre)
- ⚶ 1880 Walc 2/10 fr German Church to Warriston Crematorium 1929 & r Ing, to here 1945 & r Sco 2/12, r1987 SmRo 2/15

**Leith North** (North Leith & Bonnington/North Leith) Madeira Street
- ⚶ 1880 Wad 3/28 o1895 Wad, r1920 Ing 3/35 with new console, r1950 R&D 3/37 in gallery, r1959 Hils 3/37, o1980 WoW

**Leith St. Andrew's** (Leith Claremont/South UF/F) Easter Road/Lochend Road
- ⚶ (1902 B&F 2/21 rem 1970

**Leith St. Andrew's Place** (Leith St. Andrew's/St. Andrew's Place UF/UP) Academy Street/St. Andrew's Place cld 1973 (now Hindu)
- ⚶ (1899 B&F 2/22 o1960 R&D, scr 1967
- ⚶ (1905 ConP fr Greenock Gaelic 1967, rem c1976 to storage at Newcraighall, then rem

**Leith St. John's** (St. John's East/St. John's) Constitution Street cld 1956
- ⚶ (pre-1870 Wal 2/ fr first Catholic Apostolic, Broughton Street to Mansfield Traquair 1876, o1879 HDT, to here 1884 & r HDT 2/14, r1930 Watt, r Ing, rem to St. Bride's 1957

**Leith St. John's West** (UF/F) Queen Charlotte Street cld 1954
- ⚶ (1901 IGD 2/20 fr Leith F 1909 & r Ing 2/20

**Leith St. Ninian's Coburg Street** (Leith Harper Memorial/North Leith Coburg Street UF/North Leith UP) Coburg Street cld 1962
- ⚶ (1879 HDT 2/ r1899 HCF 2/21, r1907 HCF 2/24, rem 1962

**Leith St. Ninian's Ferry Road** (Leith St. Nicholas/North Leith UF/F) Ferry Road cld 1982
- ⚶ (1898 Hill 3/28 o1923 Wel, o1951 R&D, rem 1983 to Aldershot St. Andrew's Garrison & r1984 Har 3/31 (4ss changed)

**49) The 1897 Hill organ at Leith St. Ninian's Ferry Road prior to its removal to Aldershot.**
Photograph by Hugh Ross

**EDINBURGH (Cont.)**

**Leith St. Paul's** Lorne Street cld 1999 (bought by World Conquerors Christian Centre, but ch blg disused)
⊥ (1880 1+pd/ fr St. Margaret's E 1893 by HCF, rem 1902 by Hirst Mellor, Kirkcaldy
⊥ 1903 B&F 2/20 o1929 HCF, o1958 HNB, r1981-84 Gol 2/37 ex, o1997, derelict

**Leith St. Serf's** - see Inverleith St. Serf's

**Leith St. Thomas'** Mill Lane/Sheriff Brae cld 1975 (Sikh Temple)
⊥ (1888 ConP 2/12 fr Corstorphine Old to Inverleith St. Serf's 1905 & r HCF, to here 1930 by Ing, o1950 Ing 2/12, rem 1962

**Leith St. Thomas's Junction Road** (Junction Road/UF/UP) Great Junction Street cld 2009 (now Moslem)
⊥ (1903 Bin 2/23 o1922-24 Gle, o1936 R&D, o1953 R&D console moved, o1972 R&D, o1998 Lig, rem 2010 to London St. Stephen's, Rochester Row, Westminster & r Gri 2/24

**50) The 1903 Binns in St. Thomas' Junction Road Church in 1995, and in its new home at St. Stephen 's, Rochester Row, London in 2012**

**Leith South** Kirkgate, Leith
⊥ 1887 B&F 3/29 +1pf 1921 +2ss, o1932, r1964 ConP 3/35, r1972 R&D 3/40 with new console

**Leith Wardie** (UF/UP) Primrose Bank Road
⊥ (1893 B&F 2/14 r1905 HCF 2/16, r1935 R&D 2/14, r1960 R&D 2/15, o1990s R&D, scr 2002

152

**Leith -** see also Constitution Street C, Duke Street URC, St. James the Less E, St. Mary Star of the Sea RC and Scandinavian Lutheran

**Lesage (print & frame maker)** 21 Hanover Street
   ⅄  (barrel organ for sale 10xii1840

**Leven Lodge** west end of Meadows
   ⅄  (large organ for sale 26v1783
   ⅄  (organ for sale 28iii1796

**Liberton** Kirkgate, Liberton
   ⅄  (1930 Ing 2/15 o1958 Wil, o1963 Wil, pt rem 1973 to Motherwell South Dalziel by SmRo, facade pipes rem 1979 to Fife

**Liberton Northfield** (Northfield/Liberton UF/F) Gilmerton Road
   ⅄  1903 Ignatius Wroczina 2/13 using material by Walc **B-listed**

**Location (unknown)**
   ⅄  (1778 Don

**Lochend** (UF) Sleigh Drive cld 1994
   ⅄  (1904 Law 2/20 fr Dundee Willison UF to Dundee St. Cuthbert's 1928, to here 1941 & r Law 2/20, o1971 SmRo, scr 1995 by Lig

**Lockhart Memorial** (St. Mungo's) Albion Road cld 1987
   ⅄  (1927 E&B 2/16 o1960 R&D, o1976 SmRo, rem 1990 to St. Giles' (temp) by SmRo

**Lodge Canongate Kilwinning** St. John Street
   ⅄  1757 Sne 1/6 o1828 HDa, o1906 HCF, r1912 HCF 1/8, o1928 HCF, o1956 Ing, o1975 R&D **A-listed**

**Lodge Roman Eagle** Johnston Terrace
   ⅄  1819 Ell 1/4 fr Res of Bro. D.M. Hamilton to previous Lodge in Melville Place, to here 1927, disused mid-1960s, reservoir and some metal pipes missing

**Lodge St. David** Canongate (later at Lawnmarket)
   ⅄  (organ presented in 1744

**Logan, James, Music Shop** Parliament Square
   ⅄  (1786 James Logan 1/6 for sale 17vii1786

**London Road** (UF/UP) London Road/Easter Road cld 2017
   ⅄  (1903 HCF 2/23 damaged by fire 1962 & rem by 1965

**Lothian Road** (UF/UP) Lothian Road cld 1976
   ⅄  (1905 N&B 2/22 o1916 +1ss N&B, o1960 Wil, scr 1978 by Bell

**McCrie Roxburgh UF** (McCrie Roxburgh F/McCrie F) Davie Street/West Richmond Street cld 1920 (now ind ch)
   ⅄  (organ 2/10 to here 1917 by Sco, rem 1921 to Haymarket by Sco

**McDonald Road** (UF/UP) McDonald Road cld 1974
   ⅄  (1911 Sco 2/20 +3pf o1958 R&D, o1964 R&D, scr 1976

**EDINBURGH (Cont.)**

**McEwan Hall** Teviot Place
- 1897 H-J 4/46  r1953 Wil 4/62, o1980 R&D, 3 reeds replaced fr St. Giles' Cathedral 1991 by R&D, r2010-14 For 4/62

**Mackintosh, Watchmaker** Grassmarket
- (SBr barrel organ 4ss  sold 1959 to F.F. Hill of Godalming, Surrey

**McVittie's Wedding Parlour** South Charlotte Street cld
- (1936 Wil 2/13 lent 1939-40 to St. Giles', rem 1945 to Warriston Crematorium

**Mansfield Traquair Centre** (brick store cld 1997/Reformed B cld 1988/Catholic Apostolic Church cld 1958) Mansfield Place/East London Street
- (pre-1870 Wal 2/  fr first Catholic Apostolic, Broughton Street to here 1876 & r HDT, o1879 HDT, rem 1884 to Leith St. John's by HDT
- (1877 Hill  fr Auchterarder St. Margaret's Hall 1884 & r ConJ 2/11, o1886 Wel, r1888-91 Wel +ss, 1892 rem fr west end to south gallery by Wel, o1901 Wel, o1904 Wel, r1907 Ing 3/40 +2pf, o1934 G&D, pipes rem 1976 by SmRo, case extant

**Marchmont St. Giles'** (Grange/Robertson Memorial) Kilgraston Road
- 1884 B&F 2/18 +1pf  o1913 Ing, r1923 Ing 2/22 to chamber with new action, o1946 Wilk, r1963 Man 2/24 with new console & action, o1988 R&D reversed console, o2003 R&D/For

**Marshall Street B** Marshall Street/Nicolson Square
- (c1860 Cro 2/10 no pd (Hill pipes)  r c1880 HDT 2+pd/10, fr Res of Croall, 21 Broughton Street to here 1916 & r HCF 2/11, rem 1945 to Lasswade St. Leonard's E

**Martin Hall** - see New College

**Mayfield Salisbury** (Mayfield/Mayfield & Fountainhall/Mayfield North/Mayfield UF/F) Mayfield Road
- (1895 Vin 2/23  r1910 Cat 2/24, r1932 Ing 2/24 to chamber with new console, r1962 Hils 3/34 incl 5ss fr Fountainhall Road, r1970 R&D 3/34 after fire, to gallery with new console, scr 1996 by SmRo (2ss to Corstorphine St. Anne's)
- 1987-89 Lam 1/5  fr Humbie Stobshiel House Res of Peter Ferguson-Smyth to Crichton Manse 1991, rem 2005, then to Rosslyn Chapel, rem to here 2010 by Lam as chancel organ

**Mayfield** - see also Craigmillar Park and Fountainhall Road

**Meadows, Edinburgh International Exhibition 1886**
- (1886 Bis 4/40  rem 1886 & r1887 for Manchester Exhibition by Bis

**Meadows** - see also Leven Lodge

**Meggetland, Edinburgh International Exhibition of Industry, Science & Art 1890**
- (1890 IngE 3/33  rem, pts used elsewhere
- (1890 Har 1/3  rem to St. Matthew's E

**Merchiston Castle School** Colinton Road
- 1933 Ing 2+1pf/22 +5pf  r1957 R&D 3/38, o1973 R&D, r1987 R&D 3/39, r1997 R&D 3/38, o2009 For

154

**Methodist Central Halls** - see Central B and Leith M

**Methven Simpson** 83 Princes Street cld 1960s
⊥ (1901 Walc 1/5 + another two in 1902 + two in 1903 + one in 1908 (Dulsannels)

**Moray Knox** (UF/Knox's UF/F) High Street/Cranston Street cld 1930
⊥ (1902 Walc 2/10 fr Moray UF 1910 & r Ing 2/14, rem 1939 to Montrose South & Ferryden by Ing

**Moray UF** (F/Canongate Central F) Holyrood Road cld 1910
⊥ (1902 Walc 2/10 rem to Moray Knox 1910 & r Ing 2/14

**Morningside** (Cluny/St. Matthew's) Cluny Gardens/Braid Road
⊥ 1901 Wil 2/14 (3/28 pf) r1929 R&D 3/32, o1962 R&D, o1978 R&D, r1980 R&D 3/36 (incl Tuba fr Fort Augustus Abbey), r2004 Har 3/33

**Morningside** - see also Christ Church E, Napier University (Morningside Parish), North Morningside, Royal Edinburgh Hospital and South Morningside

**Morningside Braid** (Braid/UF/UP) Nile Grove cld 2003
⊥ (1898 B&H 2/24 console moved 1920s, r1951 Com 2/31 with new console, o1982 SmRo, r1991 SmRo +1ss fr Napier University Morningside Church, console rem 2004, facade only survives

**Morningside High** (UF/F) Morningside Road at Churchhill cld 1960 (Churchhill Theatre)
⊥ (1901 Bin 2/27 rem 1962 to Ardrossan C

**Morningside United** (C/Athenaeum/North Morningside UF/UP) Chamberlain Road, Holy Corner
⊥ (1904 Cou 2/12 r1929 in new blg
⊥ 1955 R&D 2/24 using pipework fr Cou organ o1994 SmRo

**Mortonhall Crematorium** Howdenhall Road
⊥ 1967 Har 2/9 o2017 Har

**Mould, Engraver** North Bridge - see Bruce workshop 1841

**Muir, James, Auctioneer**
⊥ (two chamber organs for sale 1798

**Muir Wood & Co. (Shop)** 16 George Street, rem 1801 to 7-13 Leith Street (workshop to Amphion Place 1815 - see also Bruce, James & Co. and Wood & Co.)
⊥ (organs for sale 17xi1797 and 1798
⊥ (chamber organ 1/4 fr Res for sale at Leith Street 6vii1801
⊥ (1784 Sne 1/6 fr Baron Smith's Chapel for sale 2ix1815 plus two chamber organs

**Muirhouse** - see Old Kirk & Muirhouse

**Murrayfield** Abinger Gardens
⊥ (You 2/15 fr Res of Smith Clark, Drumsheugh Gardens to Res at 8 Fettes Row 1914, to here 1920, rem 1936
⊥ 1889 Bro 2/20 o1892, r1925 Ing 3/28, fr Stirling Holy Rude & r1936 HNB, o1952 Ing, r1962 R&D 3/41 with new console, o1983 R&D, o2006 For

**EDINBURGH (Cont.)**

**Museums** - see Huntly House (Museum of Edinburgh), National Museum & St. Cecilia's Hall

**Music Academy** 4 Queen Street
  ⅄  (church or chamber organ  for sale 4ix1834

**Music Hall** - see Assembly Rooms & Music Hall

**51) The 1843 Hill organ in the Music Hall, with the Edinburgh Choral Union,
shortly before the organ was removed in 1912**

**Napier University Craiglockhart Chapel** (Convent of Sacred Heart) Colinton Road
  ⅄  1935 Com 2/11 ex2  disused c2005

**Napier University Morningside Church** (Morningside cld 1990) Morningside Road/Newbattle
Terrace (for sale 2017)
  ⅄  (1875 ConP 3/31  r1888 LTC to chamber, rem to London
  ⅄  1921 W&L (Lew) 2/26 +1pf  using some ConP material  r1978 Nic 2/26 (3ss changed),
     o1988, 1ss to Morningside Braid 1991 by SmRo, cable disconnected 2000s

**Napier University Craighouse** (Royal Edinburgh Hospital Thomas Houston Clinic/Craig House)
Craighouse Road
  ⅄  (c1850 HDa 1/10  r1870s HDT, o1922 & 1925 HCF, rem 1975 to Balerno by ESO
  ⅄  (1980 W-K 2/2  fr Edinburgh Res of Philip Sawyer to here 1992, rem 2000 to Stockport
     Res of Andrew Dean

**National Museum of Scotland** (Royal Scottish Museum) Chambers Street
  ⅄  (1833 HDa pneumatic lever  to BAAS, Birmingham 1839 and returned, passed to HDT
     1864, to HCF 1890, to here 1934, rem later to Reid Collection, Edinburgh University then
     to St. Cecilia's Hall 1967

**National Museum of Scotland Depository** Commercial Street, 2015 to West Granton Road
  ⅄  1850s Ren barrel organ 4ss  fr Inverness Res, sold at Philips 1993 to Hugh Ross, Leithen
     Lodge, sold 1994 to National Museum of Scotland

**New College (Martin Hall)** North Bank Street
- ⚓ (organ by amateur rem 1937 to Newtonmore St. Andrew's
- ⚓ (1939 Com 2/11 ex2 encl rem 2011
- ⚓ 1975 San 1+pd/6 to here 2011 fr Standingstone Farm, East Lothian by Lam

**Newhaven** (Newhaven-on-Forth) Craighall Road blg cld 1990s
- ⚓ (1883 ConP 2/10 r1936 G&D 2/14 +2pf in west gallery, o1955 Hils, o1981 SmRo console moved, disconnected 1996

**Newhaven St. Andrew's** (Newhaven UF/F) Pier Place cld 1974
- ⚓ (1896 IngE 3/27 + carillon scr 1981

**New North** - see Chaplaincy Centre

**Newington** - see Queen's Hall, King's Hall & Salisbury

**New Restalrig** - see Willowbrae

**Nicolson Square M** - see City of Edinburgh M

**Nicolson Street** (UF/UP) Nicolson Street cld 1969
- ⚓ (1912 Ing 2/24 r1933 Ing after fire into chamber, rem 1973, pt to Carrick Knowe

**Normal Practising School E** Orwell Place cld (fr St. Andrew's Hall, later Orwell School)
- ⚓ (organ extant 1898
- ⚓ (1905 N&B 1+pd/6

**North Leith** - see Leith North, Leith St. Ninian's Ferry Road & St. Ninian's Coburg Street

**North Merchiston** (Gorgie UF/F) Slateford Road cld 1986
- ⚓ (1870s organ fr London to here 1897 & r Ing 2/9, r1921 HCF, rem c1956 to Glasgow St. Maria Goretti RC by Watt

**North Morningside** (UF/Morningside UP) Chamberlain Road cld 1981 (Liddell Centre)
- ⚓ (1881 BBE 2/25 r1899 Ing, r1931 R&D 2/27, r1969 R&D 2/29, o1977 R&D, most rem 1984 to Perth St. Leonard's-in-the-Fields & r Loo

**Oddfellows Hall** 14 Forrest Road
- ⚓ (1903 Pos 1/6 (amongst other Pos organs) rem 1903 to Smailholm

**Odeon Cinema** (New Victoria) South Clerk Street cld 2003
- ⚓ (1926 Wur 2/53 +17 traps ex10 fr Baltimore Embassy Theatre 1930, rem 1964 to Res of T.K. Lockhart, Kirkcaldy

**Old College Music Classroom** College Street
- ⚓ (1846 HDa 4/5 no pd +16 barrels, 1ss + pipes fr G&D o1856 HDa, rem 1859 to Reid Concert Hall & later incorporated into Hill organ

**Old Kirk** Pennywell Road cld 2014
- ⚓ 1972 Vin 1/6 ex2 redundant 2014

**Old Kirk & Muirhouse** (Muirhouse/St. Andrew's Muirhouse) Pennywell Gardens
- ⚓ 1964 Wil 2/10 +1pf (unenclosed) o1991 Wil

**EDINBURGH (Cont.)**

**Old St. Paul's E** (St. Paul's to 1884) Jeffrey Street/Carrubbers Close
   ⅄  (1712 organ 1/5 (no pd) rem elsewhere 1716, to Duke Street URC, Leith 1854
   ⅄  (organ fr Res of Dr. Charles Webster to here 1782 & o James Logan, o1802 Richard
      Livingston, o1807/1811/1815 MWo, o1824 ChrE, organ sold to Mrs. Phillips, organist
      1827
   ⅄  (1827 WSm o1840 Wood/Bru, o1851 Tow, o1859 & 1864 Ren, o1867 Tow, stored 1875-
      1880 (temp) & returned & r HDT, for sale 1887, sold 1893
   ⅄  1888 Wil 2/14 +3pf, + 3ss 1904 Wil, o1921 W&L, r1936 Wil 2/15 +3pf, o1948 Wil,
      r1961 Wil 2/23, r1969 Wil 2/26, r1977 Nic 2/31 with new console, o2000 Nic

**Palace Cinema** 15 Princes Street cld 1953
   ⅄  (1929 Hils 2/58 +17 traps ex8 rem 1953 to store in Hilsdon workshop, 4 Dorset Street,
      Glasgow, rem 1975, pt scr, pt 1979 to Edinburgh Playhouse, pt in 1985 to Edinburgh Res
      of Gordon Lucas & Larry Maguire

**Palmerston Place** (UF/UP) Palmerston Place
   ⅄  (1875 HDT 2/16 rem 1902 to Gorgie Dalry Stenhouse by N&B
   ⅄  (1902 N&B 2/22 +2pf 2ss added later, o1920 Sco, r1962 Wil 3/40, rem 1990
   ⅄  1992 W-K 2/29 using 9ss fr previous organ

**Parliament House** Parliament Square/High Street
   ⅄  (1794 Gre r1810 All to here 1815 by All from London Covent Garden Theatre for
      Edinburgh Festival & returned
   ⅄  (1814 MWo 2/9 no pd lent from St. Mary's RC Cathedral 1819 & 1824 for Edinburgh
      Festival, moved and returned by WSm

**52) Parliament Hall during the 1819 Edinburgh Festival showing the (rear of) the 1814 Muir Wood organ transported specially from St. Mary's RC Cathedral for the Festival week.**
The painting by James Skene is reproduced with the kind permission of Capital Collections, Edinburgh City Library

**Paterson & Sons** (Paterson & Roy) 27 George Street
- ⋏ (MWo chamber organ for sale 1832
- ⋏ (pre-1841 organ for sale 27ii1841
- ⋏ (1903-11 N&B fourteen Norvic organs supplied here, six to Glasgow branch

**Penson & Robertson -** see Robertson

**Peter, Alexander, warehouse** Advocate's Close
- ⋏ (chamber organ for sale 6xii1757

**Picture House** 56 Princes Street cld 1951
- ⋏ (1925 Wur 2/50 ex8 inst by Sco rem 1938 to Granada Cinema, Kingston upon Thames

**Pilrig St. Paul's** (Pilrig & Dalmeny Street/Pilrig/UF/F) Pilrig Street/Leith Walk
- ⋏ 1903 F&A 2/18 o1920s, o1963 R&D console moved, o1988 R&D **B-listed**

**Pius X Catholic -** see St. Margaret's & St. Leonard's

**Playhouse Theatre** (Playhouse Cinema/Theatre) Greenside Place
- ⋏ (1929 Hils 3/35 +19 traps disused 1948, o1970, +1ss 1971, r1974 3/57 +28 traps ex (4ss fr Neath Empire Cinema, Wales), 1979 + pt from Edinburgh Palace Cinema, 1981 console fr Paisley Picture House & r 3/96 ex +21 traps by STOPS, 1985 disused and additions rem to Edinburgh Res of Gordon Lucas & Larry Maguire, rem 1995 to Greenlaw New Palace Centre

**Pleasance -** see Willis, Henry & Sons

**Pollock Hall** (Bristo UF/UP cld 1937) Easter Croft, Potterow cld 1960s
- ⋏ (1905 F&A 2/23 rem 1967 to Loanhead

**Polwarth** (Candlish/UF) Polwarth Terrace/Harrison Road
- ⋏ 1903 F&A 2/24 r1974 Gol 2/24, r1984 SmRo 2/24

**Portobello B** (Cinema cld 1919/Town Hall cld 1912) 189 Portobello High Street
- ⋏ (organ extant 1922 rem by 1959

**Portobello Lodge** Figgate Street (Tower Street)
- ⋏ (Kir 2/ reed instrument r1920 HCF with 5ss of pipes & pd, r Watt, fr Res of Rev, Robert C. Strang to Res of Harry Willis c1925, rem c1968 to here, facade only survives

**Portobello Old** (Old & Windsor Place/Old) Marlborough Street cld 2014
- ⋏ 1872 ConP 2/14 r after fire 1895 by Wel, r Sco, r1920 Ing 2/23, o1930s Ing, o1955 R&D, r1975 SmRo 2/23 (with material fr Portobello Windsor Place), r1984 Wil 2/23

**Portobello Regent Street** (UF/UP) Regent Street cld 1952
- ⋏ 1868 ConP 3/27 fr Johnstone Public Hall pre-1925 to Res of Rev. Robert C. Strang & r Watt 2/ , to here 1925 by Ing

**Portobello & Joppa** (Portobello St. Philip's Joppa UF/F) Abercorn Terrace/Brunstane Road North
- ⋏ (1907 Bur 2/27 o1925, rem 1962 pt to Kelso St. Andrew's E

**EDINBURGH (Cont.)**

**Portobello St. James'** Rosefield Place cld 2014
⊥   1934 R&D 2/31 ex4 encl redundant 2014 **B-listed**

**Portobello URC** (C) Marlborough Street cld 2009
⊥   (c1910 Sco 1/5 fr Res of A. J. Reid to Constitution Street C, Leith 1926 by Sco, rem to Saughton Mains C 1964 by Wil, to here 1969 Wil

**Portobello Windsor Place** (UF/UP) Windsor Place/Portobello High Street cld 1974
⊥   (1911 N&B 2/20 rem 1975, pt to Portobello Old

**Portobello** - see also St. John's the Evangelist RC, St. Mark's E & St. Martin's

**Prestonfield** Cameron Toll cld 1974
⊥   (1902 IHJ 2/14 o1968 R&D, rem 1976 to West Calder High School

**Priestfield** (Rosehall/UF/UP) Dalkeith Road
⊥   1880 ConP 2/16 r1901 Bin 2/18, 1980 console moved by SmRo, disused and console rem 1991

**Pringle, George (wareroom)** 227 High Street
⊥   (barrel organ 4ss for sale vi1825

**Purdie, Robert Music Shop** 70 Princes Street
⊥   (chamber organ 1/6 +Sw for sale 24xi1821

**Queen Street** (UF/F/St. Luke's F) Queen Street cld 1947/1960
⊥   (1904 F&A 2/24 rem 1958 to St. David's Viewforth

**Queen's Hall** (Newington & St. Leonard's/Newington/Hope Park cld 1976) South Clerk Street
⊥   (1873 F&A 2/25 r1908 Ing, rem c1976 Gol, some pipes to City of Edinburgh M
⊥   (c1810 Gray 1/10 fr Costessy Hall, nr Norwich to church in Costessy 1924, to workshop of Dick & o Dick 1970, to here 1979, rem 1991 to English Organ School, Milborne Port, Dorset

**Redbraes** Bonnington - see Res of Crawfurd

**Regent Picture House** Abbeymount cld 1970
⊥   (1930 Com 2/ ex6 scr 1956 Wil

**Reid Concert Hall** (Reid Music School) Teviot Place (Park Place)
⊥   (1846 HDa 4/5 no pd +16 barrels (1ss fr G&D) o1856 HDa, fr Old College 1859, rem 1869 (1ss inst in organ below)
⊥   (1861 Hill 4/36 + 4pf r1867-69 F&A 4/47, 1ss changed Hill 1870, +1ss & case added 1874 Wel, +4ss Hill 1880, console moved 1885, 2ss changed Wel 1887 4/54, r1907 Hill 4/53, dism 1941, rem 1945-47 by Sco & Har
⊥   (1950 Har 1+pd/6 (separate pipes for flats and sharps) fr Ampleforth Abbey 1951, rem to Alison House 1976
⊥   1978 Ahr 2/21 o2012 Ahr
⊥   Various items in Reid Collection - rem 2013 to storage, then in 2017 to St. Cecilia's Hall - see entry under St. Cecilia's Hall

**Reid Memorial** West Savile Terrace
⊼   1932 R&D 3/36 (with Solo div)  o1948 R&D +1ss, o1964, o1998 R&D (action altered) 3/37 **A-listed**

**Renton, John, organbuilder** 4-6 North Bank Street
⊼   (1846 Ren 1/8  on display  rem to chapel in north
⊼   (1894 chamber organ with five barrels  for sale, property of late John Renton jnr.

<u>Residences</u> (anonymous residence organs are on page 165)

Anderson, Finlay Blair C.A., 24 St. Andrew Square:
⊼   (1884 B&F  rem 1904 to Church of the Good Shepherd E & r1905 S&L

Anderson, George, 4 Albyn Place:
⊼   ( Sne 1/5  for sale 8vii1826
⊼   ( Mastermann barrel organ for sale 8vii1826

Anderson, R.B., Lynedoch Place
⊼   (B&F

Backhouse, Peter E., 40 Palmerston Place:
⊼   1983 W-K 2/2

Barclay, Captain Andrew, 27 Brighton Place:
⊼   (chamber organ 1/6 in antique case  rem 1844

Barnes, John & Sheila, 3 East Castle Road:
⊼   (1820s WSm 1/9 +Sw  fr Beeslack House, Penicuik pre-1974, rem 2007 to Dalkeith St. Nicholas Buccleuch
⊼   (1830s SBr  demonstration chest, rem 2007 by Christopher Gray, Melton Mowbray

Bell, Mrs, 3 George's Place, Leith Walk:
⊼   (small organ for sale 18iii1847

Binny, Mrs., St. Anne's Yards:
⊼   (chamber organ for sale 14iv1787

Bowman, Charles, 57 Princes Street:
⊼   (large MWo organ for sale 2iv1818
⊼   (c1820 WSm 2/11  for sale 17v1824 (per Dalglish & Forrest)

Boyd, Mr, 1 Norton Place:
⊼   (Gothic chamber organ 1/4  fr Res to here for sale 7viii1845

Christie, Adam, retired teacher, 5 Wharton Place, Lauriston:
⊼   (1791 JoJ 1/5  fr St. Peter's E, o1825, for sale iii1826

Clare, John A., 72 Northumberland Street, rem to Gullane 1985:
⊼   (1861 Tru 1/4  o c1950 R&D, fr London Barnet Hospital to Res 1960s, to here 1972, rem 1985 to Gullane Res
⊼   (c1890 amateur 1/3 (paper pipes)  fr West Wickham, Kent to Edinburgh Res of Sir Ronald Johnson c1950, to here c1973, rem 1985 to Gullane Res

**EDINBURGH (Cont.)** Residences

Clark, Smith - see Smith-Clark

Clark, Stephen, organist St. Paul's, Cowgate:
⊥  (1775 Sne/JoJ 1/7  sold, rem to Res of Mrs. General Scott 1775

Craig, Tom & Claire, Colinton:
⊥  (early 19<sup>th</sup> century organ 1/3, fr Argyll ch to Loanhead Res of Craig, lent to Portnacrois Holy Cross E 1973 and returned

Crawfurd, Sir Hugh, Redbraes, Bonnington:
⊥  (pre-1789 Pilnes chamber organ for sale 14ix1789

Croall, John, 21 Broughton Street:
⊥  (c1860 Cro 2/10 no pd (Hill pipes)  r c1880 HDT + pd 2/11, rem to Marshall Street B 1916 & r HCF 2/16

Cruickshank, John:
⊥  (Law  chamber organ

Davidson, Charles, 23 Eglinton Crescent:
⊥  pts of organs at different times - see Fenton Barns, Stonehaven, Rosyth & Haddington

Dixon, Mr, 6 North East Circus Place:
⊥  (c1810 Gow & Shepherd 4ss barrel organ  rem to Georgian House 1975

Douglas, Baillie, Merchiston Avenue:
⊥  (Sco 2/

Gardiner, Robin, organist Duke Street URC:
⊥  1911 Wad 2/  r1936 ConP 2/24, fr Aberdeen St. Nicholas C 1996, in store

Goodsir, Dr. R.A:
⊥  (c1850 HDa 2/8 no pd  rem 1907 to Royal Arch Hall

Hamilton, Bro. D.M.:
⊥  (1819 Ell 1/4  rem pre-1927 to Lodge Roman Eagle

Hamilton, Frederick, 24 Shandwick Place:
⊥  (organ  rem 1942, bequeathed to W.C.S. Heathcote, 11 Clarence Street

Hart, Michael:
⊥  (c1799 DavJ barrel organ  1ss  rem to Glasgow Res of Gordon Frier

Hay Mr., Coates Crescent:
⊥  (Cle barrel and finger organ 16ss for sale 9v1818

Heathcote, William C.S., 11 Clarence Street
⊥  (organ  fr Res of Frederick Hamilton 1942

Henderson, Mr.:
⊥  (1846 Hill 1/ (Est.)

Innes, Gilbert of Stow, 24 St. Andrew Square in 1801:
    ⚓   (1775 Sne/JoJ 1/7 fr Res of Mrs. General Scott 1795

Johnson, Sir Ronald, 14 Eglinton Crescent:
    ⚓   (c1890 amateur 1/3 (paper pipes) fr West Wickham, Kent to former Res at 6 Morningside Park c1950, to here 1965, rem c1973 to Res of John Clare, 72 Northumberland Street
    ⚓   (1751 Sne 1/4 fr prayer room, Fulneck Moravian Church, Leeds in 1890 to Richmond, Res of Mr. A.F. Mordaunt-Smith, Surrey, to former Johnson Res at 6 Morningside Park in 1947, to here 1965 & r Man 1/4, rem 1996 to St. Cecilia's Hall

Johnstone, James, Straiton:
    ⚓   (barrel organ for sale 2iv1842

King, J:
    ⚓   (1881 Har rem pre-1965

Kitchen, Dr. John P: 34 Spottiswoode Road, rem 2011 to 27 Minto Street:
    ⚓   (1988 Lam 2/2 to here fr North London Res of Rhidian Jones 1993 & returned 2003
    ⚓   2003 Lam 2+ppd/4

Kunz, Raoul de Drew, organist Christ Church E, Morningside:
    ⚓   (1890 "Scudamore" Har 1+ppd/3 rem 1895 to Res of W.E. Smith

Lee, Osmond, St. Alban's Road:
    ⚓   (Kir 1/5 no pd bought by Andrew Wood, Edinburgh & rem 1905 to Elie St. Michael's E & r HCF

Livie, James:
    ⚓   (organ altered HNB 1921

Lucas, Gordon and Maguire, Larry:
    ⚓   (1929 Hils 2/58 +17 traps ex8 fr Edinburgh Palace Cinema 1953 to store in Hils workshop, 4 Dorset Street, Glasgow, 1975 pt to store in Edinburgh Playhouse, pt to here & r 2/26, r c1985 STOPS 4/50 ex12 + 1 trap, incl additions fr Edinburgh Playhouse, rem 1991 to Greenlaw New Palace Centre

McAllister, Anne, Portobello:
    ⚓   (1985 Lam 2+ppd/2 rem to Linlithgow Res of Philip Sawyer and Anne McAllister 1988

McArthur, Dr., Beachcroft, Trinity:
    ⚓   (c1830s SBr 1/7 for sale fr Res 1861, to here by 1883, rem 1898 to Kirkcaldy West End C & r King 1+pd/8

McConochie, A.G., 18 Atholl Crescent:
    ⚓   (1881 Hill 2/ chamber organ (Est)

McKeith, Charles:
    ⚓   (1854 Hill 2/ (Est)

McKenzie, Sir G.:
    ⚓   (organ extant 1842 (Hill Est)

**EDINBURGH (Cont.)** Residences

McNeill, J. Bennett, 13 Stirling Road, rem late 1960s to 3 Ravelston Court:
⊥ (1742 Sne 1/6 found in parents' attic, to here, rem 1970s to Crieff Res and returned 1978, rem 1993 to Ripon, Res of Alan Cuckston

McPherson, John and/or Thomas, Bells Wynd:
⊥ (pre-1750 Sne 1/5 rem 1750 to St. Cecilia's Hall, returned c1762

Macpherson, Normand, watchmaker, below the Cross:
⊥ (chamber organ for sale 15ii1772

Maxwell, Bishop Robert:
⊥ (ane payr of brokin organis in oratory 1540

Montgomery, R.:
⊥ (chamber organ to here by G&D 1839

Muir, William Campbell, 74 Great King Street - see Inistrynich, Argyll

Muir, Sir William, Dean Park House, Queensferry Road:
⊥ (c1880s Bev to here 1885, rem 1905

Murray Alex & Mary, 1 Gordon Road:
⊥ (1975 WiB 2/24 ex3 fr older material (no Sw) 1977 +1ss (half rank), rem 2017 to Gattonside Res of J. & E. Wilson

Nasmith, Michael W.S., Luckenbooths:
⊥ (chamber organ for sale 16iii1778 & 20ii1779

O'Donnell E., 52 Hanover Street:
⊥ (organ 1/6 for sale 1854

Parsons, Antony, Hammerman's Land, Cowgate:
⊥ (cabinet organ for sale 1715

Paterson, J.W.:
⊥ (1851 Hill barrel & finger organ (Est)

Phillips, Mrs, organist Old St. Paul's
⊥ (organ fr Res of Dr. Charles Webster to Old St. Paul's E 1782 & o James Logan, o1802 Richard Livingston, o1807/1811/1815 MWo, o1824 ChrE, to here 1827

Powley, Dr. Thomas, Morocco's Close, Canongate:
⊥ (organ 1/7 for sale 3vii1775 & 17vii1775

Raldson, Thomas:
⊥ (1860 Ren r1875 ConP 2/12, rem to Res of Miss A. Souter

Reid, Archibald .J., 6 Denham Green Avenue:
⊥ (c1910 Sco 1/5 rem 1926 to Constitution Street C, Leith by Sco

Residences (Anon):
- ⚹ (c1860 Mir 1/4  rem to Kinneff
- ⚹ c1820 WSm barrel organ 5ss  fr Argyll Res & o2011 Edm
- ⚹ (c1830 SBr 2+pd/11  for sale 14i1837
- ⚹ (1901 Walc 1/5
- ⚹ cinema organ  r c1970 with organ fr Woolwich Granada  fr Carlisle Res to here 1990 and combined with organ fr Workington Ritz (1938 Wur fr Minnesota)
- ⚹ (chamber organ  rem 1920 to Girvan Chalmers by Sco

Res at 2 Hanover Street:
- ⚹ (chamber organ 1/6  for sale

Res at 4 Park Street:
- ⚹ (organ auctioned 4xi1843

Res at 12 Atholl Crescent:
- ⚹ (chamber organ with Sw for sale 4v1834

Res at 14 Maryfield Place:
- ⚹ (organ 1/4 for sale 8iii1834

Res at 23 Abercromby Place:
- ⚹ (chamber organ extant 9vi1832

Res at 31 Dundas Street:
- ⚹ (finger organ for sale 8v1819

Res at 33 East Claremont Street:
- ⚹ (chamber organ for sale 16iii1836

Res at 34 Blair Street:
- ⚹ (chamber organ with barrels  for sale 15vi1837

Res at 35 Royal Terrace:
- ⚹ (chamber organ for sale 6iv1837

Res at 120 Lauriston Place:
- ⚹ (finger organ for sale 15v1830

Res at Colt Bridge, Murrayfield:
- ⚹ (organ 1/6 for sale 13iii1830

Res in Cowgate:
- ⚹ (organ  rem 1715

Res at Fountainbridge:
- ⚹ (organ for sale 17ix1760

Res at Lauriston Lodge, East Lauriston Lane:
- ⚹ (finger and barrel organ for sale 10iii1838

Res on Old Post Office Stairs, Parliament Square:
- ⚹ (barrel organ 6ss for sale 30vii1785

**EDINBURGH (Cont.)** Residences

Res in Potterrow:
  ⅄  (chamber organ for sale 13ii1760

Res at Wester Dalry House:
  ⅄  (organ for sale 15v1830

Ritchie, George, WS, 1 Inverleith Terrace:
  ⅄  (Bru 2/10 no pd  for sale 12i1844

Robertson, Miss Edith, 34 Rosebank Cottages:
  ⅄  (c1860 Cro 1/4  rem to St. Mary's Cathedral E 1970 & r SmRo

Ross, Hugh L.E., 19 Mayfield Gardens:
  ⅄  (1888 Fai 1/  r1896 2/9, fr Res to St. Andrew's Newcraighall E 1904 by Ing, o1950s, to
      here 1982, rem with other organ pts 1989 to Scourie and/or Leithen Lodge

Sawyer, Philip J. 143 Warrender Park Road:
  ⅄  (1980 W-K 2/2  fr former Res at 19 South Trinity Road to here 1982, rem 1992 to Napier
      University Craighouse Campus

Sawyer, Philip J. & McAllister, Anne, 18 West Savile Gardens:
  ⅄  (2002 Lam 2/3  rem 2006 to Cambridgeshire Res
  ⅄  2008 Lam 2/6

Scott, Mrs. General Scott:
  ⅄  (1775 Sne/JoJ 1/7  fr Res of Stephen Clarke to here 1775, for sale 1795, rem to Edinburgh
      Res of Gilbert Innes of Stow

Seton, Mr. of Touch, Fortune's Close
  ⅄  (1771 Joseph Hollman 1/8  to here fr Touch, nr Stirling 1787, for sale 26i1797 at John's
      Coffee House

Shairp, Thomas (RBS), Broughtonloan:
  ⅄  (chamber organ for sale 22iv1786

Shearer, Mr. M, West Bow:
  ⅄  (organ clock 2ss for sale 3iii1788

Sibley, Angus:
  ⅄  (1974 by Sibley  pt fr Albany Street C, unfinished, rem c1976 to England

Smith, W.E.:
  ⅄  (c1890 "Scudamore" 1+ppd/3  fr Res of Kunz 1895  rem 1903 to Water of Leith Mission
      E

Smith-Clark, Mr., Drumsheugh Gardens, rem to "The Goulds" 8 Fettes Row 1914:
  ⅄  (You 2/15  rem 1920 to Murrayfield

Souter, Miss Anne Bower Carnegy, Trinity House, Trinity Road:
  ⅄  (c1860 Ren  r1875 ConP 2/12, fr Res of Thomas Raldson to here, rem 1909 to St. Philip's
      E by HCF

Spalding, Mrs, Post Office, Warriston Crescent:
    ⅄   (organ 1/ +Sw for sale 25iv1829

Stair, Lady:
    ⅄   (pre-1760 organ 1/5  for sale 1760

Stewart, Miss, Learmonth Terrace:
    ⅄   (1881 Wil 2/  rem 1904 to Elgin Res of A.M. Gregory by HCF

Strang, Rev. Robert C., 3 Montebello, Portobello:
    ⅄   (1868 ConP 3/27  fr Johnstone Public Hall pre-1925 and r Watt 2/ , rem to Portobello Regent Street 1925 by Ing.
    ⅄   (Kir 2/  reed instrument  r1920 HCF with 5ss of pipes & pd, r Watt, rem c1925 to Res of Mr. Harry Willis

Sturrock, J.S:
    ⅄   (1893 G&D 2/7  rem 1894 to Gillis Centre RC

Sutherland, Miss, 41 Great King Street:
    ⅄   (c1830s organ  to here fr other Res, for sale 6ii1845

Symes, Mr., New Street:
    ⅄   (barrel organ for sale 12iii1791

Tipple, Colin J., 73 Great King Street:
    ⅄   (1983 W-K 2/2 (no Sw)  rem 2006 to Yeovil Res of Simon Clarkson, Somerset

Trail, Mr., 90 George Street:
    ⅄   (organ for sale 1853

Watson, Miss, Oswald Road:
    ⅄   (1893 G&D 2/

Willis, Harry, Brighton Place:
    ⅄   (Kir 2/  reed instrument  r1920 HCF with 5ss of pipes & pd, r Watt, fr Res of the Rev. Robert C. Strang c1925, rem c1968 to Portobello Lodge

Wood, Christopher J. 28 Tylers Acre Road:
    ⅄   (1982 W-K 1+pd/3  rem 1988 to St. Albans Res of Wood

Wood, D., Portobello:
    ⅄   (1905 You 2/9

**Restalrig -** see St. Margaret's and also Willowbrae

**Richmond Court Chapel (Independent)** (B cld c1825) North Richmond Street cld 1846
    ⅄   (organ and chapel for sale 16iv1846

**Richmond Craigmillar** Wauchope Road
    ⅄   (1932 Hay 1+pd/  to Dundee Barnhill St. Margaret's 1932 & r Wat, to here 1974 by Douglas Galbraith 1+pd/5, rem 1977 to Strathkinness

**EDINBURGH (Cont.)**

**Robertson's Music Salon** (Penson & Robertson) 39/47 Princes Street
ᴧ   (Gothic chamber organ 2/10  for sale 1819
ᴧ   (pre-1828 chamber organ  fr Res for sale 15xi1828 & 29i1829
ᴧ   (ch or chamber organ for sale 8ix1834 - see Music Academy
ᴧ   (organ  for sale 9i1836 at 150 gns
ᴧ   (organ with Swell  for sale 25v1837 at 300 gns

**Rochhead, Andrew, & Sons** 4 Greenside Place cld 1818
ᴧ   (chamber organs for sale 29viii1808
ᴧ   (chamber organ 1/6  for sale 21xi1811 & ii1813

**Roseburn** - see Wester Coates

**Rosehall** - see Priestfield

**Ros's Music Shop** Carrubber's Close
ᴧ   (chamber organ with 3 barrels for sale 17viii1785 at Launie's Sale Room

**Roxburgh Place** - see Holy Trinity and St. Peter's

**Royal Arch Hall** (Lodge Dramatic & Arts of Edinburgh/remaining property of St. Luke's Lodge)
76 Queen Street
ᴧ   (c1850 HDa 2/8 no pd  fr Edinburgh Res of Dr. R.A. Goodsir 1907, rem 1957 to Rudolf
    Steiner School

**Royal Bank of Scotland** - see Res of Innes

**Royal Blind Asylum & School** Craigmillar Park
ᴧ   (1876 HDT 3/22 (incl pt fr St. Paul's & St. George's E)  r Sco 3/24, rem c1962
ᴧ   (German organ 1/  in store here 1950s, rem 1962

**Royal Edinburgh Hospital Chapel** (West House) Morningside Terrace
ᴧ   (1902 G&D 2/

**Royal Edinburgh Hospital Thomas Houston Clinic** - see Napier University Craighouse

**Royal Exchange** High Street
ᴧ   (two barrel organs for sale 25vii1774

**Royal High School** Regent Road, rem 1968 to East Barnton Avenue
ᴧ   1898 IngE 2/18  fr St. Paul's to here 1947 & r Ing 2/20, rem 1967, to new school 1968 & r
    R&D 2/22

**Royal Infirmary Chapel** Lauriston Place cld 2003
ᴧ   (1879 ConJ 1+pd/6  1954 + blower, o1979 R&D, rem 2005 Sta to storage at Nenthorn
    workshop

**Royal Victoria Hospital Chapel** Craigleith Road
ᴧ   (1907 Sco 2/7  scr 1981

**Rudolf Steiner School** Colinton Road
  ⅄  (c1850 HDa 2/8 no pd  fr Edinburgh Res of Dr. R.A. Goodsir 1907, rem 1957 to here & r Ronald Johnson & George  Ward (1ss changed), rem 1970 to Greyfriars

**Rushworth & Dreaper** (Ingram & Co. cld 1956) Balcarres Street rem c1990 to Newton Village
  ⅄  (various organs in transit and under repair

**Rutland Cinema -** see Gaumont Cinema

**Sacred Heart RC** Lauriston Street (for Sacred Heart Convent see under Napier University)
  ⅄  (1867 HDT 2/23 (east end)  r1893 HCF 3/29 +1pf,  o1899 HCF, scr 1964 by R&D
  ⅄  (1905 Not 2/14 (sacristy)  rem 1927 to St. Francis RC
  ⅄  1907 S&L 2/24 (west gallery)  fr West Coates 1964 & r R&D (retaining 1874 HDT facade fr West Coates), r1974 R&D
  ⅄  1971 Har 2/24 (east gallery)  o1979 Har, fr Perth St. John's E & r2013-15 by For

**53) The 1907 Scovell & Lewis organ in the Church of the Sacred Heart, Lauriston, which retains the 1874 facade with design attributed to David Bryce, found also in the chamber organs of John Croall**

**St. Aidan's** Stenhouse Drive cld 1993
  ⅄  (organ r1951 Bell
  ⅄  (1889 Kir 2/12  r1901 Kir 2/13, o1925, o1936 G&D, o1950s, fr Galashiels St. John's 1969 & r SmRo 2/13 + 1pf, rem 1995 Lig (pt of case to Stockbridge)

**St. Aidan's and St. Andrew's E** (St. Aidan's) Hay Drive cld 1996
  ⅄  (N&B 1/

**St. Andrew's Drumsheugh** (St. Andrew's UF/F) Drumsheugh Gardens cld 1955
  ⅄  (1894 Vin 2/22

**St. Andrew's E** Holyrood Road cld 1950
  ⅄  (Cro 1/5 to here 1857 (gift of St. Paul's & St. George's) rem 1868 to Scandinavian Lutheran, Leith
  ⅄  (1868 Ren  r1875 HDT +2ss, rem 1907
  ⅄  (1907 Ing 2/15  rem 1951, to St. Martin's E 1952

**EDINBURGH (Cont.)**

**St. Andrew's Hall** Leith Wynd (Episcopal Training School, later Normal Practising School)
    ♫ (organ presented 1853 rem c1875

**St. Andrew's Newcraighall E** Newcraighall Road cld 1981
    ♫ (1889 Fai 1/ r1896 2/9, to here fr Res 1904 by Ing, o1950s, rem 1982 to Res of Hugh Ross

**St. Andrew's Qualified Chapel E** (Playhouse Theatre cld 1737) Carrubber's Close cld 1774 (later Relief/Old Licht/Unitarian 1814-23/RC Mission/Irvingites/Jacobin Club/Celebrated Cathedral of the Prince of Darkness (Atheist Club)/Arab & Bohemian Mission cld 1872)
    ♫ (1747 Sne 1/7 rem 1775 to Glasgow St. Andrew's by the Green E

**St. Andrew's & St. George's West** (St. Andrew's & St. George's/St. Andrew's) George Street
    ♫ (1880 ConP 3/30 +2pf 2ss added later, o1904 N&B, r1967 R&D 2/26, rem 1984
    ♫ 1984 W-K 2/18 pt fr old organ r2014 W-K 2/20

**St. Andrew Square Cinema** Clyde Street cld 1952
    ♫ (1924 Ing 3/28 ex8 + chimes rem 1939 to Stirling St. Ninian's Old

**St. Anne's Oratory RC** 9 Randolph Place cld c2005
    ♫ (attrib HDa/HDT 1/6 rem 1964

**St. Barnabas E** Simpson's Court, Greenside Row cld 1950
    ♫ (1886 Har 1+pd/4 scr 1951

**St. Bernard's Davidson** (St. Bernard's South/UF/F) Henderson Row/West Silvermills Lane cld 1980
    ♫ (1923 Sco 2/11 rem 1981 to storage in St. Stephen's Centre by Hugh Ross, scr 1983

**St. Bernard's** - see Stockbridge

**St. Bride's** Orwell Terrace cld 1973
    ♫ (chamber organ 1/5 no pd extant 1911, for sale 1923
    ♫ (c1900 N&B 1/5 fr Cadder South Hall, nr Glasgow, to here 1923, o1934 Ing, rem to St. Martin's, Magdalene Drive 1958
    ♫ (pre-1870 Wal 2/ fr first Catholic Apostolic, Broughton Street to Mansfield Traquair 1876 by HDT, o1879 HDT, to Leith St. John's 1884 & r HDT 2/14, r1930 Watt, r Ing, to here 1957 & r R&D 2/16, rem to Willowbrae (New Restalrig) 1974

**St. Catherine's Argyle** (St. Catherine's in Grange/Grange UF/F) Grange Road (cld 1968, re-opened 1974)
    ♫ (1900 Ing 2/24 +1pf r1956 in chamber, rem 1969 to Craigentinny St. Christopher's & r SmRo
    ♫ 1980 SmRo 2/29 ex9 using material from Argyle Place

**St. Catherine's Convent RC** Lauriston Gardens
    ♫ 1858 Bev 1+pd/7 o1974 R&D **A-listed**

**St. Cecilia's Hall** (Dance Hall/School/Freemasons Hall/B meeting house/
St. Cecilia's Hall/St. Mary's Masonic Chapel **-** adjacent) Niddry Street/Cowgate
- (organ hired for St. Mary's Chapel  inst by Bri 1735  rem by 1750
- (organ fr John McPherson  inst in St. Mary's Chapel by Sne 1750, painted 1753, o1758 Joh, rem c1762 to Res of John McPherson
- (organ fr Craigforth House, Stirling Res of John Callender 1763 to new hall here by Joh rem by 1775
- (1775 Sne 1/9  rem 1802 to Assembly Rooms
- c1700 attrib SmB 1/3  fr Cherington (C of E), Gloucstershire, c1850s to Rectory of Rev. George, rem 1871 to storage, c1879 to Islington Church Missionary College Res of Rev. Andrew Frost, o1880 Wal, rem 1882 to Melthan Mills nr Huddersfield Res of C.L. Brook, rem to Fairlie Res of T.W. Hirst by 1930s, rem 1952 to Reid Concert Hall, o1952 Wil, rem to 46 George Square by Wil, rem 1964, to here 1967 **A-listed**
- c1800 Ohr 1/5  possibly in London Res of James Bartleman, 1930s to Ditchley House, Woodstock, Res of Nancy Lancaster (casework altered), to here & r1968 Man 1/5, o2016 **G&G  A-listed**
- c1760s attrib Par 1/4  r1894-97, to Res(s) of Verney family, damaged 1976 by fire, to store in Claydon brewhouse 1976, 1977 to Arundel  Res of Nicholas Plumley, o1984 Christopher Stevens, rem 1993 G&G & o1997, to Laigh Room here 1998 G&G, o2003 G&G after damage **A-listed**
- (1751 Sne 1/4  fr prayer room, Fulneck Moravian Chapel, Leeds to Richmond Res of  Mr. A.F. Mordaunt-Smith, Surrey, to former Res of Sir Ronald Johnson, 6 Morningside Park 1947 to later Res, 3 Eglinton Crescent 1965 & r Man 1/4, rem 1996 to here, sold 1999 to Canada
- 1833 HDa pneumatic lever with 1 pipe  demonstrated at BAAS, Birmingham 1839, fr HDa to HDT c1864, to HCF c1890, to National Museum of Scotland 1934, later to Reid Collection, Edinburgh University, to here 1967
- c1820 organ 1+pd/4  rem fr Cowan Bridge M, Cumbria 1981  to here 1984, not erected, in storage
- c1820s anon barrel organ  barrel with Scottish tunes
- c1840 Bev barrel organ, 3 ss  fr Reid Collection
- 1745/48 Crang/Sne Claviorganum  Sne pt replaced 1950s (history in collection guide)
- 1937 Rot console  fr Dundee St. Mary Magdalene E 1986

**St. Christopher's -** see Craigentinny

**St. Colm's** (Dalry Haymarket/Dalry/UF/F) Dalry Road blg cld 1989, ch cld 2011
- (1903 F&A 2/14  fr Haddington West 1933 & r Ing 2/18, scr 1989 SmRo, 1ss to St. Cuthbert's E

**St. Colm's College -** see Union Advertising Agency Ltd.

**St. Columba's Blackhall -** see Blackhall St. Columba's

**St. Columba's-by-the-Castle E** Johnston Terrace
- (1846 Ren (temp in schoolroom)
- (1847 Tow 2/10
- 1880 ConJ 2/14  o1924 Ing, r1928 Ing in gallery, o1932 & 1938 Bell, 1958 +1ss Bell, 2ss changed 1960 by Sir Ronald Johnson, r1965 Mac/Man 2/18, r1998 Lig in nave

**St. Columba's RC** Upper Gray Street, Newington
- (1880 ConJ 2/9  fr Peebles St. Joseph's RC 1889, o1949 R&D, o1984 R&D (1ss changed), rem 1997 to St. Andrews St. James RC
- 1997 Cop 2/22 +1pf  +1ss later, r2011 Cop 2/24

**St. Cuthbert's** King's Stables Road/Lothian Road
- ⚲ (1894 Hill  rem 1899
- ⚲ 1899 H-J 4/26  r1928 HNB 4/29, r1957 Wal 4/65 +17pf, r1998 Wal 4/67, o & r2002 4/68 Wal, o2003 + Cymbelstern
- ⚲ (1956 Wal 1/11 ex4 (temp)  rem 1957 to Oban Christ's Church Dunollie
- ⚲ (c1850 Rob 1+pd/7  (in ch hall, cld 1991) fr Stewarton Lainshaw House, Ayrshire to here post-1893, rem 1926, to Saughtonhall URC & r1930 HCF

**St. Cuthbert's E** Westgarth Avenue
- ⚲ 1909 Ing 2/10  o1931 Ing & moved to tower, o1961 R&D, r1972 SmRo 2/11, r1990 SmRo 2/20, disused 1998

**St. Cuthbert's UF** (F) Spittal Street cld 1911
- ⚲ (1889 2/  (first Free Church organ in Edinburgh) moved fr gallery by King, rem to St. David's Morrison Street 1911 & r King

**St. David's Lodge -** see Lodge St. David

**St. David of Scotland E** Boswall Parkway
- ⚲ (c1890 "Scudamore" Har 1+ppd/3  fr Edinburgh Res of R. Kunz to Res of W.E. Smith 1895, rem to Water of Leith Mission E 1903 by HCF, rem 1976 by Hugh Ross and friends, inst here later, o1984, rem 1995 to Broughton St. Mary's Church Centre

**St. David's Broomhouse** (Broomhouse) Broomhouse Crescent
- ⚲ 1963 R&D 1+pd/10 ex2

**St. David's Convent** 6 Salisbury Road cld by 2000
- ⚲ (1913 Law

**St. David's Morrison Street** (St. David's UF/F) Morrison Street cld 1961
- ⚲ (1889 2/  moved fr gallery to chancel at St.Cuthbert's UF & r King, to here 1911 & r King

**St. David's Viewforth** (St. David's) Viewforth cld 1973
- ⚲ (1904 F&A 2/24  fr Queen Street to here 1958 by R&D, rem 1976 to King's Church (Viewforth)

**St. Francis RC** (college cld by 1926/school cld 1902/St. Patrick's RC blg cld 1856) Lothian Street/Bristo Place cld 1987
- ⚲ (1835 SBr 2/15 + 18 note pd  o1841, rem to St. Patrick's RC, Cowgate  1856
- ⚲ (1905 Not 2/14  fr Sacred Heart RC 1927 by R.W. Pentland 2/13, rem c1964

**St. George's** Charlotte Square cld 1962 (later West Register House)
- ⚲ (1882 Wil 2/21  r1897 Wil 3/28, o1914 Wil, r1932 Wil 3/38, rem 1965 (pt stolen, pt to Stony Stratford St. Giles, Bucks & r1967-69 by Starmer Shaw)

**St. George's E** York Place cld 1932 (later casino)
- ⚲ (1793 Dav  o1810, rem 1814 MWo
- ⚲ (1814 Cle/DavJ 2/13  inst by MWo & o1816, converted to equal temperament 1826 by HDa, o1831 HDa, r pre-1894 2+pd/14, r pre-1894 Tow, rem 1933 to Cockenzie & Port Seton Old

**St. George's Episcopal School** Clyde Street
- ⚲ (organ installed 1853

**St. George's West -** see Charlotte Chapel B

**St. Giles' Cathedral** (High or East, West or Tolbooth, Old/St. Giles' Cathedral E/Great & East Kirks/High Kirk/St. Giles' Collegiate RC/St. Giles' RC) High Street/Parliament Square
- ⚲ (1468, 1494, 1536, 1552-60 organs extant, rem 1560
- ⚲ (1878 Har 2/21+5pf (in High Kirk, SE corner)
- ⚲ (1884 Har 3/32 using pipework fr previous organ r1885 Har 4/40, r1887 Har 4/c48, r1891 Ing 4/60, +1ss & case 1895, + carillon 1897 Ing, r1909 Ing 4/64 in south transept, o1936 Ing
- ⚲ (1936 Wil 2/13 (temp) fr McVittie's Wedding Parlour 1939 and returned 1940
- ⚲ (1940 Wil 4/74 with second console 2/17 in Moray Aisle 1948 1ss changed, 1960 1ss added, 1980 second console rem, o1982 Wil, scr 1990 R&D & Lam
- ⚲ (1927 E&B 2/16 (temp) o1960 R&D, o1976 SmRo, fr Lockhart Memorial 1990, rem 1992 to Cleish & r SmRo
- ⚲ 1992 Rie 3/57 plus Glocken

**St. James -** see Hopetoun and Inverleith

**St. James' E** Broughton Street/Broughton Place
- ⚲ (1829 organ 1/ no pd 1880 moved fr gallery to nave, sold 1885 & in 1896 rem to Granton

**St. James' E** (Christ Church-St. James/St. James) Inverleith Row, Goldenacre
- ⚲ (1896 B&F 3/18 +4pf r1898 B&F 3/24, r1967 Hils 3/28, scr 1984 SmRo, 1ss to St. Cuthbert's E
- ⚲ 1982 Chu 2/8 o Lam

**St. James the Less E** Yardheads, Leith/Quality Street (1770) united 1806 to new blg in Constitution Street, replaced 1864, pt blg cld 1978
- ⚲ (1755/1757 Sne 1/5 o1770, o1783 Don, rem 1805 by MWo
- ⚲ (1806 MWo 2/11 gilded 1826, o1840 HDa, 1ss replaced 1850 HDa, rem 1864 HDT to new chapel (temp), then used elsewhere
- ⚲ (1864 HDT 2/15 +1pf 1ss added later, r1890 LTC 2/19 +1pf, o1963 R&D 2/20, rem 1980 to Rosewell St. Matthew RC by John Anderson 2/18 +1pf (pd 16' ss rem)

**St. James' Place** (UF/UP) King Street/Cathedral Lane cld 1933 (later St. Mary's RC Hall cld 1978, later John Lewis store cld 2015)
- ⚲ (1888 HDT 2/19 r1907 Bin 2/ , rem to Bristo B, Buckingham Terrace 1935 by Wel

**St. John the Baptist RC** St. Ninian's Road, Corstorphine
- ⚲ 1964 Wal 2/28 ex5 (4 encl) o2010 Loo

**St. John's** Victoria Street cld 1939
- ⚲ (1890 Har 2/21 r1911 Ing

**St. John's Oxgangs** Oxgangs Road North cld 2013
- ⚲ (1972 SmRo 1/7 ext 3 rem 2017 by Charles Davidson

**EDINBURGH (Cont.)**

**St. John the Evangelist E** Princes Street
- ⊥ (c1750 Eng 2/12 fr Exeter to Assembly Rooms 1817, to west gallery here & r1818 MWo with new case, r1833 HDa +pd, r1835 HDa 3/20 using 1775 Sne fr Assembly Rooms as Ch division, r1863 HWm 3/33, r1880 B&F in side aisle 3/35, o1890 Har, organ rem by Ing
- ⊥ (1879 B&F (temp) rem 1880, material to Dublin Street B
- ⊥ 1900 Wil 3/31 (using some 1882 material) r1910 R&D 3/43 (4/50 pf), o1949 & 1962 R&D, r1974 Gol 3/52, o1993 Gol, r2003 Pri 3/38 +6pf, r2012 Pri 3/41 +4pf

**54) The George England organ at the west end of St. John's Episcopal Church, photographed by George Washington Wilson in 1870. The case was designed by William Burn and installed by Muir Wood & Co of Edinburgh.**
Reproduced with the permission of Aberdeen University Library

174

**St. John the Evangelist RC** (St. John's E cld 1834) Brighton Place, Portobello
- ⚑ (1826 WSm  extant 1834
- ⚑ (Scottish chamber organ  rem before 1935
- ⚑ 1924 A&S 2/15  fr Hawick St. Andrew's 1960 & r1961 R&D 2/18, r1976 Loo 2/19

**St. Kentigern's E** St. Peter's Place cld 1940
- ⚑ (organ sold 1941

**St. Leonard's** - see St. Margaret & St. Leonard's

**St. Luke's -** see True Jesus Church & Unitarian Chapel

**St. Margaret & St. Leonard's Catholic Church of Pius X** (URC cld 1992/Church of Christ/St. Leonard's cld 1932) St. Leonard's Street
- ⚑ (1879 F&A 2/13  dest by fire
- ⚑ 1880 F&A 2/13 +6pf  for sale 1933, but retained **A-listed**
- ⚑ 1976 SmRo 1/9 using early 20$^{th}$ century material, + 2ss 1984 by SmRo, fr Kirk o' Field 2016 by For

**St. Margaret's** off the Pleasance cld 1969
- ⚑ (1885 Har 2/13  to Greenside 1886  fr C. Durham by DavJT, to here 1933 by Sco, rem post-1969

**St. Margaret's** (Restalrig/Restalrig Collegiate RC) Restalrig Road South
- ⚑ (1515 organ
- ⚑ (1936 Com 2/11 ex2 encl  o1988, damaged slightly by fire 2000, rem 2002 by Sta to storage at Nenthorn nr Kelso

**St. Margaret's -** see also Gillis Centre (former convent) and Juniper Green

**St. Margaret's E** Easter Road
- ⚑ (1880 1+pd/  rem 1893 to Leith St. Paul's by HCF
- ⚑ 1893 IngE 2/10  o1940 Ing, r1945 Ing 2/11, o1995 Lig

**St. Margaret Mary RC** Boswall Parkway
- ⚑ (HDT or anon 1/7  to here c1940 by Sco, o1964, rem by 1980s

**St. Margaret's School** (Craigmillar Park/UF/F cld 1966) East Suffolk Road cld 2012
- ⚑ (1901 Bin 2/22 +1pf  o1930 R&D, o1952 R&D 2/22 +1pf, scr 1977

**St. Margaret's -** see Juniper Green

**St. Mark's E** St. Mark's Place, Portobello
- ⚑ (c1828 HDa  extant 1830/1845
- ⚑ (1872 HDT 2/15  1892 rem fr gallery to new chamber HCF, r1899 Ing 2/20, r1972 SmRo 2/20, o1990 R&D, o2004 For, scr 2010

**St. Mark's RC** Oxgangs Avenue
- ⚑ 1907 B&H 1+pd/5  fr St. Peter's RC 1969 by R&D

**St. Mark's Unitarian** Castle Terrace
 ⊿ (1823 WSm 1/ with barrels fr Unitarian Chapel, Young Street 1835 & r SBr 2/ , o1838 HDa, rem 1842
 ⊿ (1713 Cuvillié fr Dublin St. Peter's RC to Bruce Workshop 1840, to here 1842 & r Bru 2/12, o1854 Ren, r1869 Tow 2/15 with pd, r1881 HDT 2/16, organ rem fr case 1912
 ⊿ 1912 Ing 2/20 (4 Gt ss encl) in old case o1958 R&D, disused 2012 **A-listed**

**55) The organ in St. Mark's Unitarian Church with Classical case of 1713
by Jean Baptiste Cuvillié built for St. Peter's Church, Dublin.**
Photograph by Peter Backhouse, reproduced with the kind permission of
St. Mark's Unitarian Church

**St. Martin's** Magdalene Drive, Portobello blg cld 2013
 ⊿ (1900 N&B 1/5 fr Cadder South Hall, nr Glasgow, to Edinburgh St. Bride's 1922, to here 1958, to Channelkirk 2012 & r Sta 1/5

**St. Martin's E** Gorgie Road/Murieston Road blg cld 1981
 ⊿ (1889 Ren in former ch
 ⊿ (1870 Vow 3/23 fr Res of R.E. Curwen, Westerlee, St. Andrews to here 1900 by Ing, scr 1951
 ⊿ (1907 Ing 2/15 fr St. Andrew's E to here 1952 & r Bell 2/18, o Hils, r1971 SmRo 2/20, rem 1982 to St. Martin's E, Dalry Road

**St. Martin's E** (Gorgie B/Gorgie EU) Dalry Road/Murieston Crescent
⚓ 1907 Ing 2/15 fr St. Andrew's E to St. Martin's E, Gorgie Road 1952 & r Bell 2/18, o Hils, r1971 SmRo 2/20, to here 1982 & r Gol 2/20, o & 1ss changed 1990s Edm

**St. Mary's Cathedral E** Palmerston Place/Manor Place
⚓ (1878 Wil 2/12 rem 1879 by Wil, to Canterbury Cathedral and then Gloucester Cathedral 1885, to New Deer St. Kane's 1887
⚓ 1879 Wil 4/49 1897 new console by H-J (4/60 planned, incl west end div), o1901 N&B, o1906 S&L, o1922 Sco, r1931 Har 4/53 with new console, o1946 R&D, r1959 Har 4/54 +3pf, o1967 Har, r1979 Har 4/57 +3pf, r1995 Har 4/58, o2009 Har **B-listed**
⚓ c1860 Cro chamber organ 1/4 (using early 19th (c Edinburgh pipework) fr Res of Miss Edith Robertson, 34 Rosebank Cottages 1970 & o SmRo (1ss changed), o1985 Lam
⚓ 1973 Joh 1/5 bureau organ fr Glasgow Res of Gordon Frier 2012

**St. Mary's Cathedral E Song School**
⚓ 1887 Wil 2/6 +2pf 1930-31 resited in Cathedral (temp), r1942 R&D 2/8, o1963 Har, o1998 Edm, o2004 Edm **B-listed**

**St. Mary's Cathedral RC** (St. Mary's Chapel) Picardy Place
⚓ (1814 MWo 2/9 no pd lent to Parliament House in 1819, 1822 & 1824, moved within blg 1834 SBr, r1841-43 HDa 3/15 with pd, r1860 HDa 3/18 +1pf, moved to North gallery 1895 Ing, rem to storage 1927
⚓ (1932 Law 2/17 fr Aberdeen Exhibition, Kittybrewster 1932 r1962 R&D 2/17, rem 2008
⚓ 2007 Cop 3/63 with two consoles (pt fr Preston Town Hall 1882 Wilk 4/54 rem to store 1989)

**St. Mary's Chapel** Niddry Street - see St. Cecilia's Hall

**St. Mary's Music School** (Episcopal Theological College) Rosebery Crescent
⚓ 1936 R&D 2/19 ex4 (encl) o1957 R&D
⚓ 1998 Col 3/11 box organ fr Glasgow Res of Gordon Frier 2016

**St. Mary's** - see also Broughton St. Mary's and Barony St. James's Place

**St. Mary Star of the Sea RC** Constitution Street, Leith
⚓ (1854 Post r1858 Post, o1858 Tow, scr 1926 by Ing
⚓ 1897 B&F 2/19 fr Glasgow St. Matthew's 1926 by Ing, o R&D, r c1976 Gol 2/21 with different console

**St. Matthew's -** see Morningside

**St. Matthew's E** (Church of the Holy Spirit) Sunnybank Terrace, Abbeyhill cld 1944, dem 2015
⚓ (1890 Har 1/3 fr Meggetland Exhibition to previous blg in Taylor Place (later Abbeyhill M), lent 1892 to Barnoldswick M, Yorkshire, returned by 1896, facade fr Listowel Presentation Convent, Co. Kerry by HCF 1899, to new blg 1902 & r 1/5 HCF, o1924 Pentland, o1925 Orr, rem 1960 to Lullingstone St. Botolph's, Kent

**St. Michael's** Slateford Road
⚓ 1895 B&F 2+1pf/22 +18 pf r1911 B&F, o1959 R&D, r1974 Gol 2/23 new console, o1986 R&D

**EDINBURGH (Cont.)**

**St. Michael's & All Saints E** (All Saints) Brougham Street, Tollcross
⚲ (1867 Holt 2/11 +4pf rem 1893 to Logie Pert nr Montrose
⚲ (1893 G&D 3/18 1898 to chamber, r1950 Wil 3/21, scr 1970
⚲ (1986 Nic 1/3 fr Perth St. Ninian's Cathedral E 1997 (temp), returned 2000
⚲ 1870 F&A r1920 A&S 3/34, fr Scarborough Bar C to Scarborough Emmanuel URC (C), Manor Road 1966 & r WoW 2/33, to here 1992 & r WoP 2/33, r1998 Edm 2/34, o2009 Edm with mobile console

**St. Michael's E** (F) Hill Square cld 1966
⚲ (1895 B&H 2/11 scr

**St. Mungo's** - see Balerno (listed outwith Edinburgh) and also Lockhart Memorial (within Edinburgh)

**St. Nicholas' Sighthill** Calder Road
⚲ 1929 Watt 2/15 fr Leith Dalmeny Street 1963 & r Watt 2/15, r1990 SmRo

**St. Ninian's** - see under Leith and Corstorphine

**St. Ninian's & St. Triduana's RC** Marionville Road
⚲ (organ extant 1980

**St. Oran's** - see Catholic Apostolic

**St. Oswald's** (St. Mark's) - see Boroughmuir School

**St. Patrick's RC** (Cowgate UP/USC cld 1856/Cowgate Relief/St. Paul's E cld 1818) South Gray's Close, Cowgate
⚲ (1774 Sne 2/14 no pd o1783 Don, rem 1818 to St. Paul's & St. George's E by MWo
⚲ 1835 SBr 2/16 + 18 note pd fr St. Francis RC (St. Patrick's) to here 1856, r1864 Holt 2/15 + full pd (moved within blg 1867), r1900s 2/17, pipework of 3ss rem c1960s to storage but scr 1988, o1988 (amateur) **A-listed**.

56) The 1835 James Bruce organ in St. Patrick's

178

**St. Paul's** (UF/F) St. Leonard's Street cld 1942 (later Cygnet Theatre)
- ⚘ (1898 IngE 2/18  rem 1947 to Royal High School, Regent Road & r Ing

**St. Paul's & St. George's E** (St. Paul's E) York Place
- ⚘ 1774 Sne 2/14 no pd  o1783 Don, fr St. Patrick's (St. Paul's), Cowgate & r1818 & 1819 MWo 3/20, o1822 WSm, r1840 HDa +pd 3/22, r1870 HDT 3/40, o1881 HDT, r1892 by Bis fr west gallery to chancel, r1906 Har 3/44, o1925 Har, r1947 R&D 3/45, r1990 R&D 3/45 with mobile console, o2008-10 For

**St. Paul's E -** see St. Paul's & St. George's and St. Patrick's RC above

**St. Paul's Newington -** see King's Hall

**St. Paul's Qualified Chapel E** Skinner's Close cld 1774 (later Theatre/Old Licht/Henderson F & Rose Street Mission) dem
- ⚘ (1749 Sne 1/8  rem 1775 to Peterhead St. Peter's E by Joh

**St. Peter's E** Roxburgh Place, rem to Lutton Place 1865
- ⚘ (1791 JoJ 1/5  o1825, rem 1826 to Res of Adam Christie, organist
- ⚘ (1826 WSm
- ⚘ 1865 Holt 2/  o1891, r1913 Sco 3/40, r1959 R&D 3/42, 1986 1ss changed R&D, 1987 +2ss Gol, r2010 Pri 3/51
- ⚘ (organ 2/8 on loan fr Pri 2009-2010

**St. Peter's RC** Falcon Avenue
- ⚘ (1907 B&H 1+pd/5  rem 1969 to St. Mark's RC

**St. Philip's -** see also Portobello and Joppa

**St. Philip's E** Logie Green Road
- ⚘ c1860 Ren  r1875 ConP 2/11, fr Res of Thomas Raldson to Res of Miss A. Souter, Trinity House, to here 1909 by HCF, o1981 SmRo with 2ss changed **B-listed**

**St. Salvador's E** Saughton Mains Street
- ⚘ (organ 1+pd/4  to here c1949 from Sale, Cheshire, sold 1998 to antique dealer

**St. Serf's -** see Inverleith St. Serf's

**St. Stephen's Centre** (St. Stephen's cld 1992/2013) St. Vincent Street
- ⚘ 1880 Wil 3/31 +1pf  +1ss c1900, o1920 Wel, r1923 Sco 3/33, o1946 Wil, r1956 Wil in new upper sanctuary 3/33, o1980 Har 3/32, o1993 Lig, o2010 For following water damage **A-listed**
- ⚘ (1923 Sco 2/11  fr St. Bernard's Davidson 1981 to storage here, scr 1983
- ⚘ (1985 Lam 1+pd/7  fr Dunfermline Abbey nave to Altrincham St. Vincent's RC, then to Stockbridge (St. Bernard's) 1986, rem 1994 to storage here, rem to Lilliesleaf 1998 & r Sta

**St. Stephen's Comely Bank** (St.Stephen's UF/F) Comely Bank Road/East Fettes Avenue
- ⚘ 1902 Bin 2/23  o1961 Wil, o1983 R&D, o1994 McDM **B-listed**

**St. Teresa's RC** Niddrie Mains Road
- ⚘ 1961 Watt 2/19 ex3  disused 1996 (temp)

**EDINBURGH (Cont.)**

**St. Thomas English E** Rutland Square cld 1938 (now casino)
⟂ (1843 Bev 2/13 r1882 B&F 3/21, r1907 S&L 3/24, rem 1940 to St. Thomas E, Glasgow Road, except facade

**St. Thomas E** Glasgow Road, Corstorphine
⟂ 1843 Bev 2/13 r1882 B&F 3/23, r1907 S&L 3/24, to here fr St. Thomas English E & r 2/21, r1966 Wil 2/22 +2pf (new console)

**St. Vincent's E** St. Stephen Street
⟂ (1859 HDa 1/7
⟂ (1872 Tow 1/ r1897 B&H 2/11, o1971 R&D, scr 1982 by SmRo
⟂ 1889 LTC 2/16 fr Res of Earl of Aberdeen, 27 Grosvenor Street, London to Christ Church Trinity E 1897 by IngE 2/16, o1961 Wil, r1968 SmRo 2/20 +7pf (with pt fr Leith Bonnington), to here 1981 & r SmRo 2/17 +2pf (1ss added 1982)

**Sale Rooms** - see Barr, Bruce (Wm), Dalglish & Forest, Dowell, Stevenson, Tait's Auction House and Taylor

**Salisbury** (Hope Park & Newington South/Newington South/UF/Newington UP/Grange Road UP) Causewayside cld 1993
⟂ (1883 Wad 3/27 +1pf r1904 S&L 3/29 (B&H console & pneumatics), o1958 R&D, o1972 SmRo with new pedalboard, scr 1995-1996

**Salisbury Picture House** South Clerk Street cld 1943
⟂ (1930 Dek 2/42 +19 traps ex6 rem 1934

**Saughton Mains C** 34 Saughton Mains Gardens cld 1969
⟂ (c1910 Sco 1/5 fr Res of A.J. Reid to Constitution Street C, Leith 1926 by Sco, to here 1964 by Wil, rem 1969 to Portobello URC by Wil

**Saughton Park, Scottish National Exhibition 1908**
⟂ (1908 A&S 3/40 rem 1908, for sale
⟂ (1908 N&B 1/ Norvic

**Saughton Prison** Calder Road
⟂ (1968 Osm 1+pd/7 ex2 rem to Dunbartonshire

**Saughtonhall URC** (C) Saughtonhall Drive ch blg cld 1995
⟂ (c1850 Rob 1+pd/7 fr Stewarton Lainshaw House, Ayrshire to St. Cuthbert's Hall pre-1893, rem 1926 and in 1930 to here HCF, inst & r1935 R&D 1+pd/10, o1965 R&D, rem 1995 to St. Monans & r Lig 1/10

**Scandinavian Lutheran** (Norwegian Seamen's Mission) North Junction Street cld 1973 sold 1985 (now Leith School of Art)
⟂ (Cro 1/5 to St. Andrew's E 1857, to here 1868 & r HDT 1+pd/6, o1976 R&D, rem 1987 to Humbie & r Dick

**Scottish Churches Open College** - see Union Advertising Agency Ltd.

**Seafield Crematorium** Seafield Road
⟂ 1939 Ing 2/10 o1985 R&D, o2000 Lig **B-listed**

**57) The organ in Saughtonhall
URC (Congregational)
Church in 1995 prior to its
removal to St. Monance**

**Seventh Day Adventist** (Bristo Place C) Bristo Place (later Edinburgh University Settlement
Forrest Centre, then sold 2014)
  ⅄   1900 IGD 2/16 pt fr Dublin Castle Chapel Royal o1955 Ing, o1965 R&D, o2006 by
      Norwegian visitor, extant 2014 **B-listed**

**Shearer (clock maker)** - see under Residences above

**Slateford Longstone** (Slateford/UF/UP) Kingsknowe Road
  ⅄   1956 Hils 1+pd/11

**Small Bruce & Co.** 101 George Street - see Bruce

**South Leith** - see Leith South

**South Morningside** (UF/F) Braid Road/Cluny Drive cld 1974
  ⅄   (1910 N&B 2/22  rem 1976 to St. Chad's, Holt, Denbighshire, Wales

**Spylaw** nr Colinton
  ⅄   (finger and barrel organ for sale 6v1797

**Stenhouse St. Aidan's** (Stenhouse Saughton/Stenhouse UF) Chesser Avenue
  ⅄   (1897 Vin 2/  fr High (UF/F) 1935 & r Ing 2/20, o1975 SmRo, o1979 Gol, o1998 SmRo,
      scr 2006 by cong

**Stevenson Auctioneers** 2 South Hanover Street
  ⅄   (barrel organ 4ss  sold 22v1834

**Stewart, Neil, Music Shop** Parliament Square
  ⅄   (chamber organ 1/5  for sale 27ii1775
  ⅄   ( Sne 1/5 for sale 29vii1778 & 21vi1780
  ⅄   (organ 1/6  for sale 29vii1778
  ⅄   (barrel organ for sale 6iv1782
  ⅄   (organ 1/6  for sale 6iv1782

**EDINBURGH (Cont.)**

**Stewarts-Melville College** (Daniel Stewart's College) Queensferry Road
  ⊥   1933 Ing 2/12  disused 1980s

**Stockbridge** (UF/F) Deanhaugh Street cld 1977
  ⊥   (1902 Wal 2/16 +2pf  scr 1976 Gol

**Stockbridge** (St. Bernard's) Saxe Coburg Street
  ⊥   (1881 HDT 2/18  1888 moved to new apse by HDT, r1899 HCF 2/19 (5ss replaced & new
       case), r1907 Gle 2/19, r1961 R&D and moved to gallery, case removed, scr 1986
  ⊥   (1985 Lam 1+pd/7  fr Dunfermline Abbey nave 1985 to Altrincham St. Vincent's RC,
       Cheshire, to here 1986, rem 1995 to St. Stephen's Centre for storage
  ⊥   1883 Gern 2/11  fr Monteviot House 1958 to Dryburgh Tweed Horizon Centre (St.
       Columba's College & Monastery) & o R&D, to here 1994 & o 1995 Lig **A-listed**
  ⊥   (c1815 MWo barrel organ 4ss  fr Caister Castle to Wymondham Res of Mrs C. Hill, nr
       Leicester, o1966 Bis (Budgen), rem to St. Annes-on-Sea Res of Brian  Chesters 2014, to
       here 2015 by Chesters, rem & o2016-17  Edm, to Newtonmore Manse 2017

**58) The organ in Stockbridge Parish Church
(St. Bernard's) as built by D.& T. Hamilton
photographed in 1889 and in its rebuilt version
by C. & F. Hamilton photographed 1929**
Photographs kindly supplied by
Stockbridge Church

**Stockbridge** - see also St. Bernard's Davidson & St. Stephen's

**Straiton** - see Res of Johnstone above

**Tait's Auction House** 11 Hanover Street
  ⊥   (finger and barrel organ  for sale 10xii1835

**Taylor's Auction House** 51 George Street
  ⊥   (organ 1/8 + Sw for sale 27iii1845
  ⊥   (barrel organ  fr Res of lady for sale 9vi1845

**Theatre Royal** Princes Street (Shakespeare Square) cld 1859
(title then to theatre in Broughton Street)
⚤ (1753 organ in first blg  rem 1768
⚤ (1775 organ in new blg  extant 1811
⚤ (1828 WSm  rem 1859

**Theological College -** see St. Mary's Music School

**Thymms Warehouse** Canongate
⚤ (chamber organ for sale iii1858

**Tolbooth -** see Highland Tolbooth

**Townsend, William, Music Shop** 9 Greenside Place
⚤ (1844 Tow 2+pd/10 for sale

**Trinity College & Moray Knox** (Trinity College/Collegiate RC), blg rem 1848 fr Leith Wynd and 1872 to Jeffrey Street/Chalmers Close, cld 1959 (old pt later brass rubbing centre)
⚤ (1466 organ  rem 1560
⚤ (1880 Har 2/21  r1926 HCF 2/21, rem 1959

**Tron** High Street/South Bridge cld 1952
⚤ (1888 F&A 2/15  r1913 Ing

**Tron Kirk Moredun** (pt of Tron Kirk: Gilmerton & Moredun) Fernieside Drive
⚤ 1962 Vin 2/23 ex3

**True Jesus Church** (St. Luke's cld 1982) East Fettes Avenue
⚤ 1912 Ing 2/23 (4 Gt ss in box)  o1958 R&D, o2004 For **A-listed**

**59) The 1912 Ingram organ in the
True Jesus Church (St. Luke's Parish)
in 1994**

**EDINBURGH (Cont.)**

**Tynecastle** Gorgie Road cld 1979
   ⅄   (1912 Ing 2/14  o1962 Wil, scr 1984 Gol

**Union Advertising Agency Ltd.** (Scottish Churches Open College cld 2002/St. Colm's College/First Church of Christ Scientist) 18 Inverleith Terrace
   ⅄   1925 HNB 2/18 **B-listed**

**Unitarian Chapel** Young Street cld 1835 (afterwards first St. Luke's cld 1908)
   ⅄   (1823 WSm 1/  with barrels  rem 1835 to St. Mark's Unitarian

**United Reformed -** see St. Margaret's & St. Leonard's and former Congregational churches under each individual name

**University of Edinburgh -** see Alison House, Buccleuch, Chaplaincy Centre, College, Lady Yester's, McEwan Hall, New College, Old College, Reid Concert Hall, St. Cecilia's Hall, Seventh Day Adventist

**Usher Hall** Lothian Road
   ⅄   1914 N&B 4/62 +carillon  electrical repairs 1917-18 HNB, r1926 HNB +12 traps, o1949 R&D, unplayable 1970s, o2000-2003 Har (traps stored) **A-listed**

**60) The Usher Hall organ with the console in original position at a concert in the 1960s**

**Viewforth** (Viewforth St. David's & St. Oswald's/Viewforth St. Oswald's/Viewforth UF/F cld 2009) Gilmore Place (now King's Church)
   ⅄   (1898 B&H 2/23  dest by fire 1898
   ⅄   (1899 B&H 2/23  dismantled 1960s
   ⅄   (1904 F&A 2/29  fr Queen Street to St. David's Viewforth 1958, to here 1976 & r Gol 2/29 incl pt of previous organ, o1987 R&D, rem 2008 (case extant)

**Walker's Agency**
   ⅄   (organ 1/3  for sale 14xii1833

**Wardie -** see Leith Wardie

**Warrender** (Warrender Park UF/F) Whitehouse Loan cld 1972
⊥ (1906 F&A 2/23 rem 1982-87 by Donald Smith

**Warriston Crematorium** Warriston Road
⊥ (1880 Walc 2/10 fr German Church, Rodney Street 1929 & r Ing, rem 1945 to Leith M
⊥ 1936 Wil 2/13 fr McVitties Wedding Parlour 1939 to St. Giles' (temp), & returned 1940,
to here 1945, o1972 SmRo, r1985 Gol 2/14, o1997 R&D

**Water of Leith Mission E** Bell's Brae cld 1976
⊥ (c1890 "Scudamore" Har 1+ppd/3 fr Res of R. Kunz to Res of W.E. Smith, to here 1903
by HCF, rem 1976 by Hugh Ross and friends to St. David of Scotland E

**Waterloo Rooms** Waterloo Place cld
⊥ (1833 SBr large organ
⊥ (1835 HDa large organ

**West Coates** Haymarket Terrace cld 1962
⊥ (1874 HDT 2/20 o1895 McDA
⊥ (1907 S&L 2/24 using 1874 case facade rem 1964 to Sacred Heart RC

**West Port -** see Chalmers

**West St. Giles'** Meadow Place cld 1972
⊥ (1889 IngE 2/20 r1913 Ing 2/22, r1927 Sco 2/22, o1965 R&D, scr 1974

**Wester Coates** (Roseburn/UF/F) Hampton Terrace cld 1973 (Bible Centre)
⊥ (1899 Bin 2/21 rem 1973 to Dundee St. David's North

**Willis, Henry & Sons** (Pleasance cld 1953) The Pleasance/Arthur Street cld 1980
⊥ (various organs in transit under repair

**Willowbrae** (New Restalrig/Restalrig UF/F/Parson's Green F) Willowbrae Road/Piershill Place
⊥ (1903 N&B 2/15 resited 1946, r1951 HNB 2/18, rem 1974
⊥ pre-1870 Wal 2/ fr first Catholic Apostolic, Broughton Street to Mansfield Traquair
Centre (second Catholic Apostolic) & r1876 HDT, o1879 HDT, to Leith St. John's 1884
& r HDT 2/14, r1930 Watt, r Ing, rem 1957 to St. Bride's & r R&D 2/16, to here 1974 & r
SmRo 2/16, 1984 + 1ss SmRo, 1988-89 moved to west end by SmRo

**Wood & Co.** (Wood Small & Co. to 1829) 13 Leith Street/12 Waterloo Place (see also Bruce,
James & Co. workshop)
⊥ ( WSm 3/19 for sale 9i1819
⊥ ( Gre 2/12 for sale 9i1819
⊥ ( chamber organs 1/7 & 1/4 for sale 9i1819
⊥ (organ 1/5 fr family home for sale iii1826 & 5ii1829
⊥ (barrel organ for sale for sale 1vi1846
⊥ (church organ for sale in wareroom July 1846
⊥ (chamber organ 1/5 for sale 24v1847
⊥ (organs to be sold 28iii1854

**Wright's Saleroom**
⊥ (chamber organ for sale 18vii1825

**Edinkillie** (East) nr Forres
⊥　1941 Ing 2/

**Edrom: Allanton**
⊥　1886 Wad 2/11　o1903 Wad **A-listed**

**Edzell Lethnot Glenesk** (Edzell North/Edzell)
⊥　1912 Bin 2/10　r1986 Loo 2/11, o2017 Loo

**Edzell South** (UF/F) cld 1940 (used to 1945 as E chapel)
⊥　(1902 Law 2/12　rem 1946 to Arbroath St. John's M by Bro

**Eglinton Castle** nr Kilwinning, Ayrshire
⊥　(organ extant 1809

**Elderslie**
⊥　1926 B&H

**Elgin High** (UF/F) South Street
⊥　(1914-15 Sco 3/24　r N&B 3/24, r Hils

**Elgin Holy Trinity E** Trinity Place
⊥　(c1790s Patrick Torry fr his Peterhead Res to here, rem pre-1856 to Forgue St. Margaret's
　　E
⊥　(c1853 organ extant 1875
⊥　1881 Wad 2/11　o1915 Wad, r1965 R&D 2/12 and moved, o1980 WoW, r2010 Loo 2/13

**Elgin Res of A.H. Collyer**
⊥　(1887 Har 2/　o Wad

**Elgin Res of A.M. Gregory, Maryhill**
⊥　(1881 Wil 2/　fr Edinburgh Res of Miss Stewart, Learmonth Terrace 1904 by HCF 2/11,
　　rem 1979 to Lhanbryde St. Andrew's by Edm

**Elgin Res of Mr. C.J. Revells, Norman Tower**
⊥　(1899 Wad 3/23　rem 1903 to Glasgow Res of Revells

**Elgin St. Giles' & St. Columba's South** (St. Columba's) Moss Street/Duff Avenue
⊥　(1908 N&B 2+1pf/17+9 pf　6ss added pre-1930
⊥　1890 Har 2/22　fr Perth St. Paul's 1989 & r as new Edm 2/26

**Elgin St. Giles' & St. Columba's South** (St. Giles'/Elgin) High Street
⊥　1884 Wil 2/18　o1901 Wad, r1911 N&B 3/32 +1pf, r1958 HNB, r1981 WoW 3/37
　　(resited), r1983-84 Edm 3/38 (2ss changed)

**Elgin St. Sylvester's RC** Institution Road
⊥　(c1850s Mir extant 1862-94
⊥　1925 Hils 2/9　fr Grantown-on-Spey South

**Elgin South** (UF/F) Moray Street/South Guildry Street cld 1999
  ⚲   1884-1891 F&A 2/18  o1893 Wad, r1908 Wad 2/20, r1930s Sco 3/ , redundant

**Elie** (Old)
  ⚲   (1893 B&F 2/13  fr Polmont Blairlodge School 1906 & r Ing, rem 1965
  ⚲   1965 Wal 2/21 ex3

**Elie St. Michael and All Angels E**
  ⚲   (Kir 1/5 no pd  fr Edinburgh Res of Osmond Lee, St. Alban's Road 1905 & r HCF 2/8, disused by 1955
  ⚲   c1964 Cou 1/4  fr Nottingham St. Mary's 1976

**Elie Wood Memorial** (UF/F) cld 1949
  ⚲   (1901 A&S 2/11

**Ellary House** Knapdale, Argyll
  ⚲   1894 W&M 2/10 (Lorimer case) **A-listed**

**Ellon** The Square
  ⚲   1884 Har 2/16 +2pf  o1901 Wad, o1939 Law +2ss, r1968 to gallery Wal, r Edm 2/15
  ⚲   (1857 Sch 1+pd/5  fr Forgue St. Margaret's E (for temp storage), rem to Aberdeen St. Andrew's Cathedral E 1970 (temp)

**Ellon St. Andrew's** (North/UF) cld 1947
  ⚲   small organ inst 1930s

**Ellon St. John the Baptist RC**
  ⚲   1874 ConJ 1/5  o1917-20 Wad, fr Aberdeen Nazareth House Chapel RC 1991 & r Edm

**Ellon St. Mary on the Rock E** South Road
  ⚲   (organ extant in previous blg 1835
  ⚲   (1876 BBM 2/16  r c1958 Sol, unplayable 1982, rem
  ⚲   1970s Lib 1/5  to here fr Northumberland ch 1982 Lib

**Elvanfoot**
  ⚲   (Mir 1/  extant 1960s

**Enzie: Moray Crematorium** (Enzie South cld by 1997)
  ⚲   1889 Wad 1+pd/6  o1904 Wad, o1924 Wad, o1983 Edm

**Errol** (North) North Back Dykes
  ⚲   1905 MilJ 2/21  r SmRo, r Loo, r2010 Lib

**Errol South** (Errol UF/Grierson Memorial UF/Errol F) Church Lane cld 1938
  ⚲   (MilJ 1/6  rem post-1938 to Kilspindie & Rait

**Errol Grange Hall**
  ⚲   18th C organ encased in mahogany to here 1922 by W&L, gifted by Ogilvie of Watery Butts

**Errol** - see also Megginch Castle

**Erskine** (New Erskine) Rashielee Avenue, Renfrewshire (see also Bishopton and Inchinnan)
⊥  organ o1985 or 1988 HNB, disused

**Eskadale St. Mary's RC** nr Beauly
⊥  (1504 organis to older blg by Goldsmyth
⊥  1884 ConJ 2/9 **A-listed**

**61) The 1884 James Conacher organ at St. Mary's, Eskadale**

**Eskdalemuir**
⊥  1907 Pos 1/5

**Eyemouth** (St. John's UF/F) Victoria Road
⊥  1908 Cou 2/8 no pd

**Eyemouth C** Church Street cld
⊥  organ r1920 Cou

**Eyemouth Masonic Lodge**  (St. Ebbe's) Mason's Wynd
  ⚲   c1830s SBr 1/4  r1903 HCF 1/6, fr Eyemouth Old to Dunglass pre-1954, to storage, to
      here 1957, r1988 Lam 1/4 **A-listed**

**62) The Bruce organ in the Masonic Lodge, Eyemouth**  Photo: Gerard Verloop

**Eyemouth Old** Church Street cld 1954
  ⚲   (c1830s SBr 1/4  to here post-1870, r1903 HCF 1/6, rem to Dunglass pre-1954

**Fairlie** (St. Paul's)
  ⊥  1908 Bro 2/12

**Fairlie Res**
  ⊥  (c1700 Smb  fr church at Cherington, Gloucs, r Wal for Rev. A. Frost, to here 1882, rem
      1952 to University of Edinburgh, to St. Cecilia's Hall 1967

**Fairnilee House** (Res of Alexander Shaw) Yair nr Selkirk
  ⊥  (1933 Ing 2/9  rem 1964 to Aberdeen Northfield

**Falkirk Callendar Park House Museum**
  ⊥  1830s SBr barrel organ 2ss  r1995 Edm, to storage in museum 2014

**Falkirk Camelon** (Camelon Irving UF/Camelon F) Main Street
  ⊥  1922 Gle  to here 1960 from Linlithgow Craigmailen by Hils & r 2/9

**Falkirk Camelon St. John's** (Camelon) Glasgow Road cld 2003
  ⊥  1924 Hils 2/14

**Falkirk Christ Church E** Kerse Lane
  ⊥  (pre-1873 organ
  ⊥  1896 A&S 2/18  o Ing, r1964 R&D 2/18, r1987 Gol, disused

**Falkirk Erskine** Horsemarket Lane (first church, UF/UP) cld 1905
  ⊥  (1889 Har 2/15  o1890 Har, rem 1905 to Falkirk St. Francis Xavier RC

**Falkirk Erskine** (Erskine UF) Cockburn Street cld 2014
  ⊥  1905 N&B 2/24  case 1937, o1989 HNB (action altered) **B-listed**
  ⊥  (1865 HDT 2/10 no pd  fr Dundonald c1906 to Erskine Church Hall, scr 1914

**Falkirk Graham's Road** (UF/UP) cld 1975
  ⊥  (1924 Ing  rem to Slammanan by Gol

**Falkirk Grahamston United** (Grahamston) Bute Street
  ⊥  1903 Ing 2/16  r1966 R&D 2/19

**Falkirk Laurieston** (Laurieston St. Columba's/Laurieston) Polmont Road
  ⊥  (1911 Watt 1/9  to here 1951 fr Paisley Ralston & r1952 Watt, disused 2000, rem

**Falkirk M** James Street cld
  ⊥  (1889 Har 2/15  o1890 Har, fr Falkirk Erskine 1905 to Falkirk St. Francis Xavier RC, to
      here 1919 & r Watt 2/15, rem to Montrose Melville South by Sco 1934

**Falkirk Old** - see Falkirk Trinity

**Falkirk Pavilion/Gaumont/Odeon**
  ⊥  (1920 2/  rem

**Falkirk Res of Russel, Watchmaker**
  ⊥  (organ clock extant 1783-1787, barrel organ extant 1792

**Falkirk St. Andrew's West** (St. Andrew's/UF/Falkirk F) Newmarket Street
  ⊥  1913 Ing 2/24  o1956 Jar

**Falkirk St. Francis Xavier RC** Hope Street (blg replaced 1955)
- ⚓ (organ to here 1843 & r Bru/Wood
- ⚓ (1889 Har 2/15 o1890 Har, fr Falkirk Erskine 1905, rem 1919 to Falkirk M

**Falkirk St. James'** (UF/UP) Thornhill Road
- ⚓ 1905 N&B 1/ fr Queensferry 1972, disused 1990

**Falkirk Salon Theatre** Vicar Street
- ⚓ (1860 Con 2/10 to here post-1920, rem to Dennyloanhead 1932

**Falkirk Trinity** (Old & St. Modan's/Old) Kirk Wynd
- ⚓ (1892 F&A 3/26 o1896 Mir, o1909 Mir
- ⚓ (1936 HNB 2/ r1952 R&D 3/30, r1970 R&D, r1992 Edm, rem 2010

**Falkirk Trinity C** Meeks Road cld 1975
- ⚓ (1893 Ric 2/7 r1923 2/8 Ing

**Falkirk West** (UF/UP) West Bridge Street cld 1990 (became the People's Church)
- ⚓ (1896 Bis 2/22 scr 1991

**Falkland**
- ⚓ 1930 HNB 2/17

**Fa'side Castle Res of Tom Craig** nr Wallyford
- ⚓ (1889 ConP 2/11 r1924 Hils, fr Glasgow Cardonald 1955 to Loanhead East, to here c1980 Tom Craig, rem to Kirkcaldy Res

**Faslane Naval Base**
- ⚓ 1968 R&D "Ardeton" model (submarine base)
- ⚓ 1970 HNB 2/10 o1985 HNB (naval yard "HMS Neptune")

**Fasque St. Andrew's E**
- ⚓ 1846 HDa 1/3 originally with barrel mechanism, disused by 1990 **A-listed**

**Fauldhouse Crofthead** cld 1973
- ⚓ (1908 organ

**Fauldhouse St. John the Baptist RC**
- ⚓ organ gallery from 1873

**Fearn Abbey**
- ⚓ (1441-1485 Flemish organ extant
- ⚓ 1903 Law 1/5 no pd

**Fenton Barns** East Lothian (Charles Davidson collection dest fire 12xii16)
- ⚓ (1969 Wil 1+pd/7 +5pf rem fr Kirkcaldy Torbain 2012 to Haddington Res of Charles Davidson, thence here to storage
- ⚓ (1965 Wil 1+pd/8 ex4 rem fr Musselburgh St. Ninian's 2012 to here
- ⚓ (pre-1938 Wur 3/ ex5 fr Miles Theatre, New Ulm, Minnesota to Workington Ritz Cinema 1938, to storage by Charles Davidson with material from Carlisle Res
- ⚓ (1930s Com r Martin Cross, Grays, Essex, to here

**Ferintosh** (Maryburgh UF/F) nr Conon Bridge
  ⊥   1950s Com 2/11  fr Kirkcaldy Gallatown 1977

**Fernhill & Cathkin** Neilvaig Drive nr Burnside
  ⊥   1962 Wal 1+pd/4

**Ferryden** - see Montrose South & Ferryden

**Ferryport-on-Craig** - see Tayport

**Fetterangus** Ferguson Street (UF/UP) nr Deer cld 1930
  ⊥   (1883 organ

**Fettercairn (West Mearns)**
  ⊥   1886 Wad 1/7  o1919 Wad, r1990 Gol

**Fettercairn House**
  ⊥   (c1850 HDa 1/8  rem to Cambuslang St.Charles RC, Newton c1980 & r McDM 1/6

**63)  The David Hamilton organ after it was moved from Fettercairn House.**

**Fetteresso** - see Stonehaven

**Findo Gask** - see Gask

**Fingask Castle** Rait, Perthshire
  ⊥   (c1868 Ren 1/6  rem 1930s to Halkirk

**Finlarg Chapel** Killin
⅄ (1640 pair of organs

**Fintray** nr Kintore
⅄ 1901 Walc 1/7 o1960 R&D

**Fintry** - see Culcreuch Castle

**Fochabers** - see also Bellie (Parish Church) and Gordon Castle

**Fochabers Gordon Chapel E** Castle Street
⅄ (1834 HDa
⅄ 1874 Hill 1/5 o1988 Edm, o2011 Loo and moved **A-listed**

**Fochabers Pringle Memorial** (UF/F) High Street cld 1947
⅄ (1900 Wad 2/10

**Fochabers Res of Alex Simpson**
⅄ (organ pre-1842

**Fochabers St. Mary's RC** South Street
⅄ 1842-43 Bru 1/6 casework altered 1970s by priest **A-listed**

**64) The Bruce organ at Fochabers RC Church, where it has been located for 175 years. The case veneer was removed in the 1970s**

**Fodderty & Strathpeffer** Strathpeffer
⅄ (1895 Ing 2/15

**Fogo**
⅄ (Pos 1/5 rem 2002
⅄ 1901 Pos 1/5 to here 2002 Julian Bonia

**Folla Rule St. George's E** Rothienorman, nr Fyvie cld 1983
⅄ (1897 Wad 2/10 o1917 Wad, rem 1982 to Aberdeen St. Francis RC & r Edm

**Fordoun (West Mearns)** Auchenblae
- ⊥ (1899 Pos 1/
- ⊥ 19th C organ to here by Gol & r 2/

**Fordyce** Church Street, Fordyce cld 2011 (see also Portsoy)
- ⊥ (1903 Walc 1/
- ⊥ 1902 Bin 2/19 fr Forres Castlehill c1960

**Forfar East & Old** (Old) East High Street
- ⊥ (1900 F&A 4/45 +1pf o1934 Rot, o1958 Wal & console moved, 1 ss changed 1960s by Marr, r1982 Man, disused 2012, rem 2016 to John Paul II Church, Grajewo, Poland by Michal Klepacki

**Forfar Lowson Memorial** Jamieson Street/Montrose Road
- ⊥ ConP & Wat to here & r1914 Wat 2/20, o1966 Wil, r1978 Andrew McHutchison 2/20

**Forfar Res of Richard Finch**
- ⊥ organ 2/8 for sale 2009

**Forfar St. John the Evangelist E** East High Street
- ⊥ (1812 barrel organ fr London (in older blg) extant 1842
- ⊥ (1862 Pil 2/10 in previous ch (organ chamber 1866), rem 1876 & in 1890 to church hall, rem 1908 to Monifieth Holy Trinity E by Wat
- ⊥ 1881 ConP 3/ o1889 Wad, o1900 Wad, o1907 Wad, o1924 Wad, r1951 R&D with new case, r1976 HNB 3/27, o Edm

**Forfar St. Margaret's** (West/UF/F) West High Street
- ⊥ (1921 Hils 2/18
- ⊥ (1901 Wil 3/35 r1911 Vin 3/35, r R&D 3/35, fr Callander St. Kessog's 1987 by Australian amateurs, scr 2012

**Forgan** Newport-on-Tay cld 1980
- ⊥ (1902 MilJ 2/8 rem 1983 to Stonehaven Dunnottar, and Dunfermline Abbey (temp), then to Stirling St. Mary's RC by Loo

**Forglen** nr Turriff cld 1971
- ⊥ (1902 Wad 1/

**Forglen House** nr Turriff
- ⊥ (1820s WSm 2/9 extant here 1889, rem 1936 to Aberdeen All Saints E & r Law

**Forgue** Aberdeenshire cld 1992
- ⊥ 1872 ConP 2/14 o1890 Wad, o1910 Wad, o2001 R&D with motor added **A-listed**

**Forgue St. Margaret's E**
- ⊥ (c1790s Patrick Torry fr Res of Rev. Patrick Torry to Elgin Holy Trinity E, later to here, extant 1856
- ⊥ (1857 Sch 1 +pd/5 rem 1970, to storage at Ellon, then to Aberdeen St. Andrew's Cathedral E (temp), then St. George's Tillydrone 1971 & r P. Wright with new case

**Forres Castlehill** (UF/UP) High Street cld 1972
- ⊥ (1902 Bin 2/19 rem to Fordyce c1960

**Forres C** (Independent) Tolbooth Street (British Legion)
⅄ (1875 organ o1900 Wad

**Forres House** Victoria Road dest 1970
⅄ (chamber organ for sale 1855-56

**Forres Res of Mr. Edwards, Sanquhar House**
⅄ (organ o1899 Wad, o1917 Wad

**Forres St. John the Evangelist E** Victoria Road
⅄ 1869 Bev 2/ r1906 Wad 2/13, r1954 HNB, r1982 Edm 2/14

**Forres St. Lawrence's** (Forres) High Street
⅄ (1877 Har 2/20
⅄ 1906 Law 3/28 in new blg r1964 HNB 3/31, o1989 HNB

**Forres St. Leonard's** (High UF/Cumming Street or Tulloch Park UF/F) High Street
⅄ (1903 N&B 2/16 o1910 N&B, rem 2001/2006 except case

**Forres** - note Forres School is outwith Scotland. See also Kinloss for Seapark House, Forres

**Fort Augustus**
⅄ 1912 Law 2/9 r1982, disused 2010

**Fort Augustus Abbey** cld 1998
⅄ (1875 BBM 4/65 fr London the Hall, Primrose Hill, Regent's Park, Res of Nathaniel Holmes 1884, to London Albert Palace, Battersea, to here 1894, in store until 1915, r Law & the brothers 3/35, r1936-38 Law 4/73, r1958 R&D, r1979 R&D 3/37 (1ss to Stockport, 1ss to Edinburgh Morningside), rem 2000 to Buckie St. Peter's RC  R&D

**Forteviot**
⅄ c1850s HDa 1/10 r1870 HDT 1/10, o1922 & 1925 HCF, fr Edinburgh Napier University Craighouse to Balerno 1975, to here 1992 & o Edm **B-listed**

**Forteviot Workshop of Alexander Edmonstone**
⅄ (c1800 Anon 1/5 fr Letterfourie House nr Buckie 1965 to Cults Res of Charles Davidson, rem 1970 to Aberdeen Res of David Murray, rem 1981 to Burrelton Res of David Murray, c1990 to here, rem 1999 to Blair Atholl St. Adamnan's E
⅄ (many other organs for restoration

**Forth Villa** - see Kirkcaldy Res of John Blyth

**Fortrose** (UF/F)
⅄ (c1850s Ren 1/8 to here & r1914 Cat 1/10, rem 1986 Hugh Ross to Scourie Res of Ross, rem 1987 by Ross to Leithen Lodge

**Fortrose St. Andrew's Episcopal**
⅄ (1799 Don o1834 HDa, rem to here 1915 Law & r 2/13, rem 2007 and replaced with a digital/pipe hybrid

**Fort William Duncansburgh Macintosh** (Duncansburgh)
⅄ 1906 F&A 2/16 + 2pf o1983 McDM, o2000 McDM, r2012 McDM 2/18 (2 ss from Lockerbie Dryfesdale) **C-listed**

**Fort William Macintosh Memorial** (UF/F) cld 2007
⚓ (1926 Watt 2/16 using second hand pipes o1958 R&D, scr 1974

**Fort William Res of Nathaniel Holmes**
⚓ (organ

**Fort William Rosse Chapel** cld 1880
⚓ (c1700 SmB 1/7 r Sne, r c1783 Don, case by Thomas Parker, fr location on east coast post-1817 to here & r 1/10, rem to Duror St. Adamnan's E 1880 BBE/Wardle & r 1/6

**Fort William St. Andrew's E**
⚓ 1880 BBE 2/18 o1911 F&A, o1980, o1997 McDM, o2000/04 McDM following water damage, o2013 For after water damage, disused 2015 following water damage **A-listed**

**Fort William St. Mary's RC**
⚓ (1846 Bru 1/4 fr Edinburgh to here 1913 & r Cat, o1978 R&D, rem 1984 to Glasgow St. Andrew's Cathedral RC McDM
⚓ G&S 2/7 to here c1984 R&D

**Forth Pipe Organs** (Rushworth & Dreaper, Scotland) - see Newton Village and Rosyth

**Fossoway St. Serf's & Devonside** Kinross-shire
⚓ 1892 Wel 1+pd/5 r1992 SmRo 1+pd/6

**Foveran** cld 2008
⚓ 1900 Law 2/10 o1913 Wad

**Foveran** (Holyrood Mission Chapel) Newburgh, Aberdeenshire
⚓ 1913 Wad 2/11

**Foveran South** (UF/F) cld 1931
⚓ (1903 Law

**Fowlis & Liff: Liff** Angus cld 2016 (see also Muirhead of Liff, Liff and Balruddery)
⚓ 1880 You 2/17 **B-listed**

**Fowlis & Liff: Fowlis Easter** (St. Marnock's) Angus
⚓ (c1890 2/15 rem c2003
⚓ c1970 Wal 2/15 ex3 fr Perth Letham St. Mark's 2004 by Edm

**Fowlis Wester** nr Crieff, Perthshire
⚓ 1929 Pos 1/10

**Fraserburgh B** Victoria Street
⚓ 1902 Walc 1/ o1917 Wad

**Fraserburgh Evangelical Union** Manse Street cld 1916
⚓ (organ r1886 Wad 2/ extant 1903

**Fraserburgh Old** (High) Kirk Brae
⚓ 1892 F&A 2/17 o1899 Wad, o Law **A-listed**

**Fraserburgh Our Lady Star of the Sea RC** Commerce Street
- ⚑ (c1850 amateur 1/5  r1876 Wis, to here 1897 fr Boyndie House Chapel & o Wad, o1931 Law, o1980 McDM, r1994 Austin Tobin, rem to Inverness Res of Fr. J. Allen

**Fraserburgh Res of James Fraser**
- ⚑ (c1848-55 James Fraser, joiner  exhibited in Fraserburgh Commissioners' Hall 1855

**Fraserburgh St. Andrew's** (West UF/F/E) Mid Street cld 1961 (now halls)
- ⚑ (1892 Wad 2/11  o1909 Wad, rem 1961 to Aberdeen Mastrick

**Fraserburgh St. Peter's E** (Bishop Jolly Memorial) Charlotte Street
- ⚑ (c1830s Hill in previous blg in Mid Street  for sale 1855
- ⚑ 1880 Hill  to new blg 1892 & r1893 Wad 2/18, o1912 Wad, o1980 R&D

**Fraserburgh South** (UF/F) Seaforth Street
- ⚑ (1914 Wad 2/21  o Law, scr c1972 (facade survives)

**Fraserburgh URC** (Mid Street C) blg replaced 2003
- ⚑ (1880 Por 2/  o1905/1914 Wad, r1919 Law 2/ after fire, rem by minister
- ⚑ organ 2/  fr Yorkshire c1961

**Fraserburgh West** The Hexagon
- ⚑ (post-1905 organ  r1954 HNB, rem pre-1967

**Freuchie** Fife
- ⚑ 1901 Aeo  console scr, rest purchased c1993 Charles Davidson but still on site

**Freuchie UF** cld 1966
- ⚑ (1901 Pos 1/6  rem 1967 to Edinburgh Corstorphine UF

**Friockheim Kinnell** (Friockheim)
- ⚑ (1902 Walc 1/  o1908 following smoke damage, o1936 Wat, rem 1989
- ⚑ c1990 2/12  ex organ

**Fyvie** Aberdeenshire
- ⚑ 1889 Wad 2/11  o1900 Wad,  r1903 Law, o1920 Wad, r1991 R&D

**Fyvie All Saints E** Woodhead
- ⚑ 1850 HDa 2/10  o1887/89 Wad, r1895 Wad, r1919-20 Wad 2/10, r1947 Law, r1979 Dick, o1999 Edm and moved within building **B-listed**

**Fyvie Castle**
- ⚑ 1905 N&B 2/14 with roll mechanism  o1917-18 HNB (new cells), r1923 Hils, o1990 Craig McPherson **A-listed**

**Gairloch Hotel**
- ⚑ 1884 LTC 2/  (est. only)

**Galashiels Ladhope** Ladhope Vale cld 1975 (for Ladhope UF see Galashiels St. Andrew's)
- ⚑ (1874 Gern 2/10  fr Hawick Heronhill, Res of George Wilson 1876 & r HDT
- ⚑ (1898 Gern 2/16  using a little material fr old organ

**Galashiels Old** Church Square cld 1931
- ⚑ (c1890s Gern 2/

**Galashiels Old & St. Paul's** (St. Paul's) Scott Crescent
⚐ 1881 Wil 3/28 o1900, 1932 Choir box added, r1948 Wil 3/31, o1978 Gol, o1989 SmRo, o1999-2002 Lig **B-listed**

**Galashiels Our Lady & St. Andrew's RC** Stirling Street
⚐ 1904 Law 2/24 (organ gallery fr 1873) r1964/1973 R&D 2/24, o1998 Sta, o2016 Lig **A-listed**

**Galashiels St. Aidan's** (St. Cuthbert's/South UP) Gala Park Road cld 2004
⚐ (1928 Sco 1+pd/7 r1964, pipes removed pre-2002

**Galashiels St. Andrew's Arts Centre** (St. Andrew's/Ladhope UF/F cld 1977) Bridge Street
⚐ 1904 Bin 2/20 console rem 1998-2005

**Galashiels St. John's** (UF/F) St. John Street cld 1970
⚐ (1889 Kir 2/12 r1901 Kir 2/13, o1925, o1936 G&D, o1950s, rem 1969 to Edinburgh St. Aidan's by SmRo

**Galashiels St. John's** Langlee
⚐ 1972 Wal 2/18 ex4 disused

**Galashiels St. Mark's** (West) Kirk Brae cld 1962
⚐ (1897 B&F 2/16 o1938 G&D

**Galashiels St. Peter's E** Abbotsford Road/Parsonage Road
⚐ 1881 B&F 2/16 o1999 Sta **A-listed**

**Galashiels Trinity** (West UF/UP) 56 High Street cld 1936
⚐ (1928 A&S 2/10 sold 1937 to Kirkcaldy Raith

**Galashiels Trinity** (St. Ninian's/St. Columba's/East UF/UP) 48 High Street
⚐ 1904 F&A 2/ r1928 Ing 3/32, r1989 SmRo 3/32, o2016 Lig

**Galashiels URC**(C)
⚐ 1880 Har 1/ (est. only)

**Galston** (Old)
⚐ 1913 Bin 3/29 o1927 Bin, o1933 & 1945 BFH, r1959 BinT, o1990 R&D, o2011 MilP 3/29 **A-listed**

**Gamrie** Aberdeenshire cld 1992
⚐ 1900 Law 1+pd/5 Dulsannel design fr display at Marr Wood, Aberdeen, extant 1968

**Gamrie** (UF/F) cld 1932
⚐ (c1900 Walc 1/

**Garlieston Galloway House**
⚐ (c1850 Mir 1/4 r1880 Mir, fr Glasgow Res of Mirrlees, Woodend Drive to here 1959 & o Watt, rem 1966 to Kirkcowan & o Mac/Meek

**Garelochhead** (East) Old School Road
⚐ (1901 Pos 1/
⚐ 1912 Watt r1968 C&C 2/20 ex3, o1994 McDM

**Garelochhead West** (UF/F) cld 1938
⅄ (1919 Watt

**Garmouth** (UF/F) cld 1988
⅄ 1903-04 Walc 1/3

**Garth House Res of Sir D. Currie** nr Aberfeldy/Fortingall
⅄ c1880 Bev

**Gartly** (Gartly St. Andrew's/Gartly) Aberdeenshire cld 1985/1994 sold 2016
⅄ 1911 Wad 2/10 extant 2016

**Gartmore House** nr Aberfoyle
⅄ (c1840s Scottish chamber organ r 1/7, rem 1958 to Port of Menteith R&D

**Gartocharn** - see also Kilmaronock
⅄ (1912 N&B to here fr school in England & r1980s by Pul 1/8

**Gartocharn Res of Dr. Andrew Baxter**
⅄ (1981 Pul 1+pd/5 (lent to Glasgow St. Joseph's RC 1981)
⅄ (1998 Lam 2+pd/7+1pf rem 2000 to Clynder Res

**Gartsherrie** - see Coatbridge New St. Andrew's & Lugar

**Gartshore House Res of William Whitelaw** nr Kirkintilloch
⅄ (1820 WSm
⅄ (1887 Wil 3/25 rem 1947 to Knebworth St. Martin's, Hertfordshire

**Garturk** - see Coatbridge Calder

**Garynahine House** nr Callanish, Lewis
⅄ c1871 organ fr Brenton Church, England

**Gatehouse of Fleet** (Girthon)
⅄ 1880 Fin 2/11 fr Spottes House near Urr 1948, o2000 Clough, Yorkshire, disused 2010

**Gatehouse of Fleet St. Mary's E** Dromore Road
⅄ c1900s Pos 1/5 fr Anwoth 2002 by McDM

**Gattonside Res of J. & E. Wilson** nr Melrose
⅄ 1975 WiB 2/24 ex 3 fr older material (no Sw) 1977 +1ss (half rank), fr Edinburgh Res of Alex & Mary Murray 2017 to here by John Wilson

**Gavinton** (Langton)
⅄ (1912 Ing 2/ r1960s Wal, r1970s Sol, pipes rem 1980s, console removed c2000

**Gavinton Res of Simon Nieminski**
⅄ (1939 Wicks (USA) 2/20 ex3 fr Res of Temple Emeth, Ardmore, Oklahoma 2007

**Giffnock Orchardhill** (UF/UP) Church Road/Claremount Avenue
⅄ (1904 Lew 2/ temp rem
⅄ 1940 HNB 2/17 o1955 HNB, o1990 HNB

**Giffnock Res of George Macfarlane**
⊥ (c1880s Gern 3/27 rem c1925 to Glasgow Royal Scottish Academy of Music & Drama
⊥ (1762 WaJ 1/4 fr Glasgow Res of James Watt to Glasgow Malts Lodging, College 1776,
sold 1815 to Arch. Mclellan, 78 Miller Street, Glasgow, o McLellan & Steven + 1ss, rem
to Mugdock Castle, nr Milngavie, sold 1854 to A.G. Adam of Denovan, Falkirk, rem
1863 to Res of Adam Sim, Coulter Mains, Lanarkshire & o1864 Ren, to here 1918 & o
Simpkin of Paterson's, rem to Glasgow People's Palace Museum

**Giffnock South** Greenhill Avenue
⊥ (1914 Lew 2/10 fr elsewhere to here 1917
⊥ 1956 HNB 3/41 using material fr Hill organ o1976 HNB, o1993 HNB

**Giffnock The Park** Ravenscliffe Drive
⊥ 1966 Vin 2/25 ex3

**Giffnock URC** (C ) Fenwick Road
⊥ 1922/1936 Hils 2/12  r c1983 WoW (Edm), r1986 Edm 2ss changed, o2011 Mac 2/12

**Girthon -** see Gatehouse of Fleet

**Girvan Chalmers** (UF/F) cld 1947
⊥ (chamber organ  fr Edinburgh Res 1920 by Sco, o1921 Brk

**Girvan M** Dalrymple Street
⊥ organ  fr Shotley Bridge Wesleyan M, Co. Durham 1951 by Nel 2/16, o1952-53 Thomas
Reed & HNB

**Girvan North** (Old & St. Andrew's/Old/St. Cuthbert's) Montgomerie Street
⊥ (1886 B&F 2/20  rem 1979, some pipes to Inch, nr Stranraer 1985, case survives

**Girvan Res**
⊥ (1853-55 G&D 3/46  r1856 G&D 4/55, r1877 G&D 4/57 fr Glasgow City Hall to
Glasgow Dixon Halls & r1905 Bin 3/35 (5ss by Bin), to here 1930s & r Watt, rem 1949 to
Greenock St. Mary's RC & r Watt 2/

**Girvan St. Andrew's** (Trinity UF/UP) cld 1973
⊥ (1921 A&S 2/9  r1925 Ing 2/11, pt rem 1977 to Irvine Relief Bourtreehill by McDM

**Girvan St. John's E**  Piedmont Road cld 2009
⊥ 1886 Kir  r1911 Watt 2/9

**Girvan South** Henrietta Street
⊥ 1925 Ing 2/11 **B-listed**

**Gladsmuir** East Lothian
⊥ 1930s Ing 2/10  to here 1940, o1958 R&D, o1978 R&D

**Glamis**
⊥ 1934 BFH 2/12  r Loo, r2010 Lib 2/20

**Glamis Castle Chapel**
⊥ (pre-1627 organ  r1648 1/10 (3 divided), r1737-39 Bris 2/13, rem by 1866

**GLASGOW**

**Abbotsford-Chalmers** (Chalmers UF/F) 100 Pollokshaws Road (pt of Gorbals Church 1973-76) cld 1976
   ⅄   (1900 F&A 2/19 o1914 F&A, dispersed c1978, 1ss to Crosshouse by Mac

**Adelaide Place B** 209 Bath Street
   ⅄   (1898 B&H 2/25
   ⅄   (1934 HNB 3/27 using case of B&H scr post 1978

**Admiral Street M** (Great Wellington Street M) 22 Admiral Street (Great Wellington Street) blg cld c1978
   ⅄   (1874 F&A 2/

**Albert Drive** (Albert Road UF) - see St. Albert's RC

**Alexandra Parade** (UF/UP) 572 Alexandra Parade blg cld 1951
   ⅄   (1904 Watt 2/16 r1936 HNB 2/17, damaged by fire 1951

**All Saints E** 10 Woodend Drive, Jordanhill
   ⅄   (organ fr church hall to church, rem 1910 to St Matthew's Possilpark E
   ⅄   1909 B&F 2/17 extant 2002

**Anderson's Royal Polytechnic** 97 Argyle Street
   ⅄   (1886 Bis rem 1954 to Catholic Apostolic, Camberwell New Road, London

**Anderston & St Peter's** (Anderston St. Martin's/Anderston Est) 880 Argyle Street cld 1968
   ⅄   (1865 Hill 2/16 r1882 Har 2/19, o1903 Mir, o1927 Mir, rem 1969 to Glasgow St Bride's E

65) The 1865 Hill organ at Anderston Established Church, the first pipe organ to be officially opened after the Reformation in the Presbyterian Church of Scotland. It was opened on 15<sup>th</sup> January 1865.
Photograph by James Mackenzie from the Glasgow Society of Organists Archive

**GLASGOW (Cont.)**

**Anderston** - see also Claremont Street M and Gilmorehill

**Anderston Old** (UF/UP) Heddle Place (blg replaced 1965-68)
⚲  (1884 Wil 2/22  scr 1965 stop heads to Knightswood St. Margaret's

**Anniesland Cross** - see Temple Anniesland

**Athenaeum Assembly Rooms** (Ind. Cong) 204 Ingram Street dem 1887 (see also New Assembly Hall and Royal Scottish Academy of Music and Drama)
⚲  (1851 Bev  rem 1853 to Dundas St C

**Augustine Buchanan** - see Hutchesontown

**Baillieston Rhinsdale** (UF/Bailieston UP) Main Street cld 1966
⚲  (1925 Watt

**Baillieston St Andrew's** (replacing Baillieston Old, 35 Church St) 2 Bredisholm Road
⚲  (1974 Vin

**Baillieston St. John's E**
⚲  (chamber organ  r Sol, scr

**Balornock** - see Tron and Wallacewell

**Balshagray Victoria Park** (Balshagray) 218 Broomhill Drive
⚲  (1912 Ing 2/15+6pf  r 2/21, rem except case

**Banquet of Musick (portable organ)** - see Glasgow Res of Robert Lay

**Barlanark Greyfriars** Hallhill Road/Edinburgh Road
⚲  c1964 Vin 2/  ex3

**Barony Hall, University of Strathclyde** (Barony Ramshorn/Barony cld 1985) 2 Castle Street
⚲  (1889 B&F 3/35  o1931 HNB, r1949 Har 3/46, rem 1990 to R&D Liverpool, then to museum in England
⚲  2010 Koe 3/42

**Barony Institute Hall** (Macleod Mission) 22 Black Street
⚲  (1872 F&A 2/  to here fr Macleod 1888, rem c1946

**Barony North** (UF/F) 49 Castle Street cld 1941 (cong to Evangelical Church, blg later school meals centre)
⚲  (1903 Har 2/24  damaged by fire 1941

**Barrowfield** - see Bridgeton and Greenhead

**Bath Street** - see under Blythswood, Renfield, St. Matthew's & St. John's Renfield

**Battlefield** - see Clincarthill and Langside

**BB Cinerama** - see Odeon

**Bearsden** - see Bearsden (outwith Glasgow)

**Belhaven** - see St. Luke's Greek Orthodox and Struthers Memorial

**Bellahouston** - see Ibrox and Steven Memorial

**Bellgrove Young Street** (Bellgrove UF/UP) Bellgrove Street cld 1972
   ⅄  (1924 Bro 2/  scr

**Belmont** 121 Great George Street cld 1950
   ⅄  (1894 Hill  r1933 Wil, rem to Burnside Blairbeth 1954 & r Hils

**Belmont Hillhead** - see Kelvinside Hillhead

**Berkeley Street, Workshop of James Mackenzie** 72 Berkeley Street cld 2010
   ⅄  (c1820s WSm barrel organ remains 4ss  fr Watt workshop to here c1965, rem 2009 to
      Duror Res of Kerr  Jamieson
   ⅄  (c1820s-30s Mir 1/4  fr Res nr Irvine to Uddingston Church of the Nazarene 1959 by
      Watt, to workshop 1961 by Mac, rem 1965 to Hamilton Whitehill, rem 1966 to new blg,
      returned to Mac 1969, temporary inst at Stepps and elsewhere, rem 2009 to Oldhamstocks
      workshop of Lam
   ⅄  (c1810 Astor barrel organ remains  rem 2009 to Oldhamstocks workshop of Lam
   ⅄  (c1840s Mir chamber organ remains  fr Res elsewhere to Muirhead St. Barbara's RC, rem
      1960s to here, scr 2009

**Berkeley Street UF** (UP) 34 Berkeley Street cld 1920
   ⅄  (1883 F&A 2/17  rem to Temple Anniesland 1920

**Bethany C**  Bernard Street
   ⅄  (1873 ConP 2/  with Zimmerman pipes  o1960 Mac, vandalised after dismantling 1972
   ⅄  (1874 ConP (in hall)  sold pre-1950

**Bishopbriggs** - see Bishopbriggs (outwith Glasgow)

**Blackfriars** 9 Westercraigs cld 1982
   ⅄  (1877 ConP 2/16  rem 1902 to Coldstream
   ⅄  (1902 Hard 3/28  r1933 HNB 2/ , dest 1980s (1ss to Neilston)

**Blochairn** (UF/F) Blochairn Road cld 1973
   ⅄  (c1901 Watt 2/  to here 1950

**Bluevale & Whitevale** (Bluevale) 576 Duke Street cld 1975
   ⅄  (1871 F&A 1+pd/11 for Mission Church  rem 1894
   ⅄  (1894 F&A 2/  pt to Kilbarchan East, 1ss to Hurlford McDM

**Blythswood** (Blythswood UF/Bath Street UF/Bath Street UP) Bath Street (S)/Holland St cld 1930
   ⅄  (1877 B&F 2/18  r1898 SmRi, rem to Tollcross Park by Hume 1931

**Bridgeton** (Bridgeton & Newhall/Bridgeton East/Bridgeton) 84 Dale Street cld 1986
   ⅄  (1894 Ing 2/25  scr

**GLASGOW (Cont.)**

**Bridgeton Mission M** (Music Hall/Eastern Mission M) Landressy Street
⊥    (c1929 Hils 2/   scr c1965, pt to Saltcoats North

**Bridgeton West** (UF/F) 46 John Street/Tullis Street/Muslin Street cld 1932
⊥    (1910 Ing 2/15  rem 1932 to Bridgeton West & Barrowfield

**Bridgeton West & Barrowfield** (Edgar Memorial/Barrowfield UF) 10 Landressy Street cld 1962
⊥    (1910 Ing 2/15  fr Bridgeton West to here 1932 Ing, scr c1965 Sol

**Bridgeton** - see also Greenhead, Newhall, Dalmarnock Road  & St. Clements

**Brisby Memorial** (Erskine South Portland Street/Erskine Old/UP/US/Ind) 43 South Portland Street (split c1915, see Erskine Rose) cld 1947
⊥    (1883 Bro 2/  with B&H console, rem by 1920 to Erskine Rose

**Brook, Joseph, organ builder** Rottenrow
⊥    (organ 2/  for sale 7v1906
⊥    (many organs in transit or under repair

**Broomhill Hyndland** (Broomhill/Partick Broomhill UF) 64 Randolph Road
⊥    1915 N&B 2/   o1984 HNB 2/20, r1996 Har 2/21

**Broomhill Trinity C** (Broomhill C/Whiteinch C) 2 Victoria Park Gardens South cld c2003
⊥    (1884 LTC 3/   fr College UF to workshop of SmRi 1903, to here 1911 & r SmRi 3/34, o1927 HNB, rem c2003 (pipes to China)

**Buccleuch** (Garnethill Chapel of Ease) 161 Buccleuch Street, Garnethill cld 1945
⊥    (1911 Lew 2/18  rem 1946 to Bishopbriggs Kenmure

**Buchanan Memorial** (UF/F) 473 Caledonia Road cld 1947 (became factory, then St. Bonaventure's Italian Mission RC in 1953)
⊥    (1907 Walc 1/7  rem c1947 to Hutchesontown & r Watt

**Burnbank** (UF/UP) 19 Carrington Street cld 1968
⊥    (1897 B&F 2/17  r1909 Mir 2/18
⊥    (1935 HNB 2/22 using parts of former organ  rem 1969 to Croftfoot

**Burnside Blairbeth** (Burnside) Church Avenue, Burnside
⊥    1894 Hill  r1933 Wil, fr Belmont 1954 Hils & r 2/24 facade fr St. Gilbert's, o1973 Hils, o1992 Mac, o2007 McDM

**Bute Hall** - see University

**Caledonia Road** - see Hutchesontown

**Calton New** - see St. Luke's & St. Andrew's

**Calton Parkhead** (Calton Old) 122 Helenvale Street
⊥    (1907 Watt  fr former blg in Tobago Street 1935, disused 1960s

**Calton** - see also Unitarian and Ross Street

**Cambridge Street** (UF/UP) 156 Cambridge Street cld 1968
- (1899 Lew 2/   scr

**Cambuslang** - see Cambuslang (outwith Glasgow)

**Campbell Street East UF** - see East Campbell Street

**Camphill Queen's Park** (Camphill/UF/UP) 20 Balvicar Drive cld 1991 (now used by Baptists)
- (1877 You 2/23  r1923 Hils 2/28, rem post-1991

**Candlish Polmadie** (Candlish Memorial UF/F) 513 Cathcart Road cld 1989
- (1903 Walc 2/24  o1954 Watt, scr

**Cardonald** 2155 Paisley Road West
- (1889 ConP 2/11  o1924 Watt, rem 1955 to Loanhead East by Watt
- (1954 Com 2/ ex4  rem 1988 to St. Mary's, Stanwell by M. Mason

**Carmunnock** Kirk Road
- (1893 Wad 2/11  fr St. Peter's E 1948

**Carmyle** (UF) 155 South Carmyle Avenue
- 1956 Com 2/25  ex4

**Carntyne Old** (Shettleston Carntyne UF/F) 862 Shettleston Road cld 2007
- 1892 Hard 2/14  fr Kelso North 1948, for sale 2009

**Carntyne** (High Carntyne) 358 Carntynehall Road
- 1921 Walc 2/  fr Young Street 1937 & r HNB

**Carntyne** - see also St. Michael's

**Castlemilk Lloyd Morris C** Ardmaleish Terrace
- 1907 Watt 1+pd/  r1957 Watt 2/ ex 3 with console in SmRi style from St. Andrew's East, to here fr Henry Drummond Memorial 1968 & r C&C 2/  ex 3

**Cathcart B** 96 Merrylee Road
- (Cou 1/+pd  rem to Bute

**Cathcart C** Garry Street/56 Holmlea Road
- 1896 Wad 2/17  o1901 Wad, o1915 Lew, o c1957 Watt, fr St Kiaran's Dean Park to here 1976 & r McDM 2/17 (2ss changed)

**Cathcart Road M** Cathcart Road cld
- (c1844 chamber organ fr Greyfriars & Alexandra Parade Hall 1861
- (1877 F&A 2/

**Cathcart Old** 119 Carmunnock Road
- 1905 MilJ 2/18  fr former blg 1931 Bro, o1993 Jhn 2/20, r1994 Lib (electrified following theft) 2/20

**Cathcart Trinity** (South/UF/UP) 92 Clarkston Road (see also New Cathcart)
- 1901 F&A 2/25  r1951 R&D 2/25 (1ss changed), o1967 Mac, o1980 Mac **A-listed**

**GLASGOW (Cont.)**

**Cathedral (High or St Mungo's)** Cathedral Square
- ⚲ (1460 1/1   r c1510, ref to organ in 1520, organs rem 1560
- ⚲ (1797 Don  to here 1798 temp organ for Sacred Music Institution Concert
- ⚲ (1797 Don 3/18  fr Trades Hall 1803 for SMI concerts, rem 1812 to St Andrew's by the Green E
- ⚲ (c1830-1835 John Watt 2/12  to here for one concert, rem 1835 to Greenock Res of a Mr Campbell along with two other organs, by John Watt
- ⚲ (1903 Walc 2/8 (temp.) rem to Temple later in 1903
- ⚲ 1879 Wil 3/47  r1903 Wil 4/57 + 18pf, o1913 Wil, o1922 W&L 4/57, r1931 Wil 4/59+16pf, 1948 +2ss Wil, r1971 Wal 4/67, r1996 Har 4/68
- ⚲ box organ 1/ presented 2016

**Cathedral Square** - see Evangelical Church

**Catholic Apostolic** Butterbiggins Road cld early 1950s
- ⚲ ( Bis 2/  r, rem Bis

**Catholic Apostolic** 340 McAslin Street cld c1966
- ⚲ (c1856 Bev 2/  rem
- ⚲ (c1909 Mir 2/  scr
- ⚲ (chamber organ (in hall)

**Causeway -** see Victoria Tollcross

**Central** - see Gillespie Central

**Cessnock** (Paisley Road/UF/F) 15 Edwin St cld 1978
- ⚲ (1898 Vin  pipes scr

**Chalmers** 11 Claythorn Street cld 1954 (for Chalmers UF see Abbotsford Chalmers)
- ⚲ (1904 SmR  destroyed fire 1954

**Christ Church E** Brook Street cld 1978
- ⚲ (c1840 organ 1/  rem 1884 to St James' the Less Springburn E
- ⚲ (1884 ConJ 2/14  r1915 Watt in new ch, rem again to old ch, part rem c1980 to Cumbernauld Holy Name E by Burke

**Christ the King RC** 220 Carmunnock Road, Cathcart
- ⚲ 1961 HNB 2/14 fr old pipework r2016 Lib 2/16

**Christian Scientist 1** (Queen's Rooms) 1 La Belle Place
- ⚲ (1865 ConP (possibly in Trinity C blg)
- ⚲ (1925 HNB  dest c1939 by fire (Com 3/  ordered)
- ⚲ (1958 Wal 2/10 +8pf  o1975 McDM 2/10, rem to St. Bride's RC, Bothwell 1989 McDM

**Christian Scientist 2** (Eglinton Street C cld 1936) 341 Eglinton Street
- ⚲ (1914 Hils 2/14  scr Har

**Christian Spiritualist Church** 26 Holland Street
- ⚲ (c1930 Hils 1+pd/  rem post 1938 to St. Vincent Street F

**Christian Union Church** (EU Hately-Waddell cong fr Trades Hall) 57 East Howard Street
⼅   (1867 ConP 3/27  short compass  fr elsewhere, rem 1873

**Chryston** - outwith Glasgow

**Church of Christ** - see Shawlands URC

**Church of New Jerusalem** - see New Jerusalem, Woodlands M and Seventh Day Adventist

**City F** - see St. Vincent Street Milton F

**City Hall** Candleriggs
⼅   (1853-55 G&D 3/46  r1856 G&D 4/55, r1877 G&D 4/57, rem to Dixon Halls 1905 & r
     Bin 3/35
⼅   (1905 Lew 4/53  rem 1959 Wil to Chesterfield All Saints 1963 as 3/56

**Claremont** (UF/Claremont Street  UP) 18 North Claremont Street cld 1963
⼅   (1856 F&A 3/28+1pf moved upstairs 1858 +1ss F&A, not used on Sundays until 1872 in
     new ch, r1872-74 F&A, o1882 F&A, rem 1899 to Wellpark
⼅   (1899 Hill 3/36  +1ss 1902, o1928 HNB 3/37, r Bell, scr

**Claremont Street M**  (Anderston M) cld
⼅   (1867 F&A 2/  r c1918 Watt 2/ , scr 1958

**Clarkston -** see Clarkston (outwith Glasgow)

**66) Left: The disused 1856 Forster & Andrews at Claremont UP Church probably c.1870,
before replacement in 1899     67) Right: The 1884 Lewis organ in College UF Church
after the fire in 1903, prior to removal by Richard Smith**
Photographs from Glasgow Society of Organists Archive

**GLASGOW (Cont.)**

**Clincarthill** (Battlefield East/UF/Cathcart F) 1216 Cathcart Road
⊥   1914 Ing 2/27  o1963 Watt **B-listed**

**Coliseum Cinerama/ABC** (Coliseum Theatre) 91-97 Eglinton Street
⊥   (1925 Jar 2/23  r1928 Jar, rem 1931 to Greenock Regal/ABC by Com

**College** - see Blackfriars

**College & Kelvingrove** (Kelvingrove UF/UP) Kelvingrove Street cld 1927
⊥   (1880 Wil 2/17  r1913 N&B 3/39, destroyed by fire 1925

**College UF** (F) 40 Lynedoch Street cld 1908
⊥   (1884 Lew 3/22  damaged by fire 1903 & rem to workshop of SmRi, to Broomhill Trinity
     C (Whiteinch C) 1911 SmRi

**Colston Milton** Egilsay Crescent
⊥   (1964 Wil 2/10+1pf  rem 1998 to St Mungo's RC by MilP

**Colston Wellpark** 1378 Springburn Road
⊥   1866 F&A 2/20  fr Tron St Mary's 1951 & rWatt 2/23 new console, o1965 Mac

**Concert Hall** - see New Assembly Hall and University Concert Hall

**Consort of Music** - see Banquet of Music

**Convent of Mercy RC** 62 Hill Street (now pt of St. Aloysius' College)
⊥   Bro 2/

**Convent of Notre Dame RC** - see Notre Dame College

**Convent of the Good Shepherd** 1920 London Road, Dalbeth (moved c1962 to Bishopton)
⊥   (Mir  extant 1862
⊥   (c1920s Bro  2/  disused 1950s

**Convents** - see also St. Mary's RC and Franciscan Convent

**Copland Road** - see St. Columba's Copland Road

**Corn Exchange** 81 Hope Street
⊥   (1896 organ  rem

**Cottier Theatre** (Dowanhill/UF/UP cld 1984) 93 Hyndland Road, Partick
⊥   1876 Wil 3/31  r1954 Wil 3/34 +2pf, Sw damaged 1990, r2007-2014 Har 3/31
⊥   (1902 organ in the hall, rem c1950

**Cowcaddens** (UF/F) 30 Maitland Street/McPhater Street (Garscube Lane) cld 1967 (used as St.
Stephen's Hall to 1974)
⊥   (1888 Bro 2/12  from Kelvingrove International Exhibition 1888 to Cambuslang West by
     Bro, rem 1914 by Vin to Renfield Free Church Mission, to here 1920 by Bro, scr c1970

208

**Cowlairs Somerville** (Cowlairs) 35 Gourlay Street cld 1978
   ⅄  (1905 N&B 2/19 dispersed

**Craigie Hall** 6 Rowan Road, Dumbreck, for sale 2014
   ⅄  1897 B&F 2/12 Mackintosh case extant 2003 but disused, rem 2015 to temp storage McDM

**Croftfoot** (fr Gorbals Macnicol Memorial/Gorbals UF) Croftpark Avenue/Crofthill Road
   ⅄  (1904 Bin 2/14 fr Glasgow Gorbals Macnicol Memorial to here 1936, scr 1969
   ⅄  1935 HNB 2/22 to here 1969 fr Burnbank by C&C, retaining pd fr 1904 Bin

**Crosshill Burgh Halls** - see Dixon Halls

**Crosshill Queen's Park** (Queen's Park High/Queens Park) 40 Queen's Drive cld 2000
   ⅄  (1869 ConP 2/ for temp blg
   ⅄  (1873 ConP 3/29 rem 1926 to Paisley Central M by David Hume
   ⅄  (1926 Bin 3/32 1ss changed 1983 Mac, rem 2003 Six & r2004 3/36 in Chester St Werburgh's RC

**Crosshill Victoria** (Crosshill/Hutcheson UF/F) 34 Dixon Avenue cld 1972 (later studios, then mosque)
   ⅄  (1904 Lew 2/18 scr 1972 1ss to Crosshill Queen's Park

**Crystal Palace Ironmongery Establishment** 67 Buchanan Street
   ⅄  (1854 Bev barrel organ for exhibition

**Cunninghame** (UF/F) Thistle Street cld 1931 (became Hall, then Cash & Carry)
   ⅄  (c1900 organ

**68) The three manual 1926 Binns organ in Crosshill Queen's Park Church
shortly after closure in 2000**

**GLASGOW (Cont.)**

**Dalmarnock** 103 Springfield Road cld 1977
⚓  (1894 Hard 2/22  o1970 Mac, some parts to Larry Maguire, Edinburgh and to Mac

**Dalmarnock Road C** 231 Dalmarnock Road (later F)
⚓  (1910 Rutt 2/18  scr 1986

**Dean Park** - see St. Kiaran's Dean Park

**Dennistoun** 163 Armadale Street cld 1981
⚓  c1910 B&F 2/16

**Dennistoun B** Craigpark Drive/Meadowpark Street blg cld 1999
⚓  (1913 B&H 2/17  o1973 Mac, rem 1999 to Auchterarder Stanley's Antique Shop

**Dennistoun Blackfriars** (South/Whitehill/UF/UP) 12 Whitehill Street cld 2009 (later  Pentecostal)
⚓  1902 SmR 2/24  o1984 Mac, disused 2009, at risk 2016 **A-listed**

**Dennistoun C** Meadowpark Street (later Christian Centre)
⚓  (1910 Bro 2/14

**Dennistoun New** (Dennistoun Central/Rutherford UF/Dennistoun F) 9 Armadale Street
⚓  (1903 N&B 2/16  rem post 1975, scr
⚓  1889 Wil 3/24+1pf  r1911 SmR 3/25, fr Trinity Duke Street 1979 & r1981 McDM 3/26 incl 1ss from Hamilton TH, former case retained **C-listed**

**Dennistoun** - see also St. Barnabas E and Regent Place

**Dixon Halls** Cathcart Road/Dixon Avenue
⚓  (1894 Bro 2/18 electric action  rem 1898 Bro to Our Lady & St. Margaret's RC, Kinning Park
⚓  1905 Bin 3/35 (mostly G&D fr City Hall, some Bin)  rem 1930s to Girvan Res & r Watt, pt to Mearns

**Dowanhill** - see Cottier Theatre and Notre Dame College

**Dowanvale UF** - see Partick Highland Gaelic F

**Drumchapel St. Andrew's** (Drumchapel Old) Garscadden Road
⚓  (c1893 organ
⚓  1961 Hils 2/20 using 1906 SmRi Swell fr St. Peter's r1982 2/22

**Drumchapel St. Andrew's** 404 Kinfauns Drive cld 1995
⚓  (1867 Mir 2/14  moved 1872 Mir in blg, fr St John the Evangelist E 1961 & r Mac (1ss changed), rem 1996 to the Netherlands

**Drumchapel St Benedict's RC** cld
⚓  (1970 RHW 1+pd/5  rem to St. Columba's RC, Maryhill c1980 Mac

**69) The 1867 Mirrlees organ in St. Andrew's, Drumchapel, in 1994**

**Dundas Street C** (Ind) 123 Dundas Street
- ⅄ (1851 Bev  fr Athenaeum Assembly Rooms 1853, rem to Coatbridge C 1899 & r Watt
- ⅄ (1863 F&A 2/8 (18 note pd) in ch hall  for sale 9i1869
- ⅄ (1899 Walc 3/26  scr

**East Campbell Street UF** (UP/Relief) Dennistoun cld 1926 (later Mission)
- ⅄ (1886 F&A 2/   rem 1928 to Dumbarton St. Patrick's RC by Watt

**East End Industrial Exhibitions 1890 & 1903**
- ⅄ (1890 organ
- ⅄ (1903 Lew 2/26  dismantled afterwards

**Eastbank** - see Shettleston

**East Howard Street** - see Christian Union

**Easterhouse** - see Lochwood

**Eastwood** 5 Mansewood Road
- ⅄ (1874 ConP 2/20  rem 1910 to Paisley Greenlaw & r Ing
- ⅄ 1910 Lew 2/23 with encl Gt division  console o1985 Mac **A-listed**

**Eglinton Elgin** (Elgin Street UF) 19 Turriff Street/Elgin Street cld 1953
- ⅄ (1906 Lew 2/16  fr Eglinton Street UF 1921 by Brk, rem 1953 to Bearsden Cross

**Eglinton Street C** - see Christian Scientist 2

**Eglinton Street UF** (UP) Eglinton Street cld 1920
- ⅄ (1906 Lew 2/16  rem 1921 to Eglinton Elgin by Brk

**GLASGOW (Cont.)**

**Elder Park** 100 Golspie Street cld 1970
⊥   (1899 Wal 2/14

**Elder Park C** Elderpark Street, Govan cld
⊥   (1922 Vin 2/

**Elder Park Macgregor Memorial** (Macgregor Memorial) 137 Crossloan Road, Govan cld 1992
⊥   (1904 ConP 2/16  rem 1993, some ss to Huddersfield ConP workshop

**Elgin Place C** 193 Pitt Street/24 Bath Street cld 1962
⊥   (1866 ConP 2/  r1881 Bro 3/31, rem 1909 to St. Aloysius RC, Rose Street & r Bro
⊥   (1902 Wil 3/30 +1pf  rem 1981 to St Andrew's Cathedral RC

**Emmanuel C** Overnewton, Yorkhill
⊥   (Walc 1/

**Emmanuel Haus German Congregation** - see Hyndland

**Empress Playhouse** St. George's Cross (later New Metropole)
⊥   (1913 Hils 2/19 +traps  console rem 1935, some pipes rem 1949 Hils, remainder dest
     1990

**Erskine Rose** (Erskine Old/UF/UP/US/Ind) 20 Cartvale Road cld 1971 (See also Brisby Memorial)
⊥   (1883 Bro 2/ with B&H console  fr previous blg (Brisby Mem) at 43 South Portland
     Street by 1920, rem

**Evangelical Church** (Barony North/Cathedral Square UF/UP cld 1941) 20 Cathedral Square
⊥   1887 F&A 3/26 +1pf o2001 Lig **A-listed**

**Exhibitions** - see
Kelvingrove (1888, 1901 & 1911)
Polytechnic (1866)
East End (1890 & 1903)
Crystal Palace (1854)
Gorbals (1884)

**Ewing Place C** - see Hope Street Gaelic F

**Fairbairn Memorial** (UF/F) 197 Baltic Street, Bridgeton cld 1959
⊥   (1915 Bin 2/23  vandalised, scr

**Fairfield** (Govan Fairfield UF/UP) 80 Golspie Street, Govan cld 1975
⊥   (1895 Ben 2/  scr

**Ferguson Memorial C** Palermo Street, Springburn
⊥   (N&B 2/  inst 1938 Bro fr elsewhere

**Fernhill & Cathkin** - outwith Glasgow

**Finnieston** - see Kelvingrove

70) The 1887 Forster & Andrews organ in the Glasgow Evangelical Church

**GLASGOW (Cont.)**

**Forsyth Memorial C** (Govanhill C) 147 Coplaw Street (later offices)
⊥ (organ inst Hils 2/

**Franciscan Convent** 72 Charlotte Street (blg replaced twice)
⊥ (Mir extant 1862

**Free Gospel** Charlotte Street cld c1900
⊥ (c1866/1875 Grindrod 2/ rem c1900 to Robson Street Free Ind M by Watt

**Gairbraid** (Gairbraid UF/Maryhill UP) 1517 Maryhill Road
⊥ 1894 N&B 2/13 r1899 N&B, r1946 2/13

**Gallowgate** (St. Thomas Gallowgate/Gallowgate UF/Whitevale F/Camlachie F) 760 Gallowgate,
opp Bluevale Street blg dem 1998, hall in David Street used
⊥ (1902 Walc 1/7 rem elsewhere
⊥ (1911 Ing 2/ o1929 Ing, to here 1938 fr St. Thomas, dest 1998 pt to East Kilbride

**Gardiner, T.W. & Condi D.W. Music Shop** 280 George Street
⊥ (1850 Mir 1+pd/4 for sale (amongst other organs)

**Garnethill** - see Milton St. Stephen's and Buccleuch

**Garngad** (UF/St. Rollox UP) 15 Tharsis Street cld 1946 (later Foundry Boys Mission)
⊥ (1887 Bro 2/13 fr Springbank UF c1925

**Gaumont Picture House** Sauchiehall Street
⊥ (1925 Wur 2/ ex8 rem 1958 Watt to workshop, Bourdon to St. Anthony RC

**German Church** Woodlands Road cld c1914
⊥ (1910 Walc 1/7 rem

**German Evangelical** 7 Hughenden Terrace
⊥ (1960s Sol rem
⊥ (1973 Jhn 1/5 rem to Hyndland c2001 with cong

**Giffnock** - see Giffnock (outwith Glasgow)

**Gillespie Central** (Central/St. Luke's & Trinity/Trinity UF/F) Charlotte Street cld 1953
⊥ (1902 Walc 2/22 rem 1953 Hils

**Gilmorehill** (Hillhead UF/Anderston F) 19 University Avenue cld 1959 (now pt of University)
⊥ (1899 Har 3/29 rem 1961 to St Thomas', St. Helens, Lancs by R&D

**Glasgow Cathedral** - see Cathedral

**Gorbals** - see also Abbotsford Chalmers, St. Francis, Buchanan Memorial & Hutchesontown

**Gorbals Exhibition 1884**
⊥ (1884 Bro 2/7 rem 1884 to Rothesay Aquarium by Bro

**Gorbals John Knox** (Gorbals) 34 Carlton Place cld 1973
⚓ (1893 IngE 2/20  scr

**Gorbals Macnicol Memorial** (UF/F) South Portland Street cld 1933
⚓ (1904 Bin 2/14  rem 1936 to Croftfoot by Bro 2/14

**Gordon Park** (Whiteinch UF/F) 1228 Dumbarton Road cld 1981
⚓ (1934 HNB/K&B 2/11 with pt of case of Gern fr Paisley Woodside House  rem c1990 to Coatbridge St Augustine's RC & r SmRo

**Govan** - see also under Linthouse, Elder Park Macgregor Mem, Macgregor Street, St. Columba's Copland Road,  Pearce Institute, St. Kenneth's and St. Michael's E

**Govan and Linthouse** (New Govan/St. Mary's Fairfield/St. Mary's UF/F) Govan Cross
⚓ (1914 N&B 2/18  scr (case & console extant)

**Govan B**
⚓ (1895 Vin 2/8 damaged by fire

**Govan Evangelical Union** location not known, cld
⚓ (1904 Watt

**Govan Old** 866 Govan Road cld 2007 (now run by Trust)
⚓ 1888 B&F 3/  o1895 B&F 3/31, r1939 Sco 3/32, r1990s Lib, o1999 Mac 3/34

**Govan Town Hall** Albert Street
⚓ (1901 N&B 4/44  rem 1934 to Linthouse St. Kenneth's & r HNB

**71) The 1901 Norman & Beard organ in Govan Town Hall prior to its removal.** Photograph by David Hume from Glasgow Society of Organists Archive

**Govan White Street C**
⚓ (1865 ConP 3/30  1870 +2ss ConP, to here 1911 fr Trinity C Watt, r1920 Watt, rem

**Govanhill Trinity** (Govanhill West/UF/UP) 12 Daisy Street cld 2015
⚓ 1912 A&S 2/25  r1958 HNB 2/26

**GLASGOW (Cont.)**

**Govanhill South** (Govanhill) Cathcart Road/Allison Street cld 1952
  ⊥  (1896 B&F 2/18

**Grace B** - see Polmadie

**Great Hamilton Street C** (Ind) cld 1880s
  ⊥  (1850s ConP

**Great Wellington Street M** - see Admiral Street M

**Greenbank** - see Greenbank (outwith Glasgow)

**Greenhead Barrowfield** (Greenhead/Greenhead West) 100 Canning Street/570 London Road, Bridgeton cld 1971 dest 1973
  ⊥  (1886 F&A 2/19 + 2pf +1ss later by F&A, resited 1895 + 1ss Mir 2/21, scr

**Greenhead East** (UF/UP) 31 John Street/Tullis Street/Muslin Street, Bridgeton cld 1937 dem
  ⊥  (1900 F&A 2/19  rem 1937 to Macmillan Calton by Bro

**Greenhead** - see also Bridgeton

**Greyfriars & Alexandra Parade** (Greyfriars UF/UP) 190 Albion Street cld 1966
  ⊥  (1901  IGD 3/27  dest by fire 1918
  ⊥  (1920 Bin 2/  vandalised 1966 during court case, pt rem to Melksham St. Michael & All Angels, nr Bath, pt to Glasgow Res
  ⊥  (c1844 chamber organ in hall/Session house  rem 1861 to Cathcart Road M

**Grosvenor Picture House** 24 Ashton Lane, Hillhead
  ⊥  (1925 B&H 3/16  rem c1935 to a Glasgow ch

**Hamilton Crescent** (St. Mary's) 16 Peel Street, Partick cld 1978
  ⊥  (1884 ConJ 2/21  r1938 Wil 2/33, rem to Partick South 1978 by Reeves

**Henry Drummond Memorial** (Possilpark UF/F) Allander Street cld 1967
  ⊥  (1907 Watt 1+pd/  r1957 Watt 2/  with console fr St. Andrew's East, rem to Castlemilk Lloyd Morris C 1968 & r C&C 2/ ex 3

**High Carntyne** - see Carntyne

**Highlanders' Memorial** (St. Peter's UF) Waterloo Street/Blythswood Street (Mains Street) cld 1941
  ⊥  (1918 Watt 2/13  inst as memorial to Sir Harry Lauder's son, rem 1941 & to Stevenston Livingstone 1944

**Hillhead** - see Kelvinside Hillhead and Salon Cinema

**Hillhead B** Cresswell Street/Cranworth Street blg cld 2011
  ⊥  (1885 Lew 2/13 +1pf  r1930 Watt 2/ , r1980s Wil 2/22, rem 2016 to Belfast, r2017 in Dunmurry St. Colman's E, Co. Antrim

**Hillhead C** University Avenue
  ⊥  (1890 F&A 2/18

**Hillington Park** 24 Berryknowes Road, Cardonald
 ⚒ 1933 A&S 2/23 disused

**Hippodrome (Zoo)** New City Road
 ⚒ (organ extant 1902

**Hogganfield** cld 1931
 ⚒ (organ

**Hogganfield** - see also St. Enoch's Hogganfield

**Holy Cross E** 2064 Great Western Road, Knightswood cld 2013
 ⚒ 1885 Har 2/8 r1934 Bro, fr St Luke's E 1952 Watt, o c1960 Hils

**Holy Cross RC** 109 Dixon Avenue, Crosshill
 ⚒ Bro 1+pd/5 disused 2001
 ⚒ 1895 F&A 2/20 o1906 F&A, o1927 F&A, fr Alva St Serf's 1982 & r1983 McDM 2/23

**Hood Memorial C** Muslin Street, Bridgeton cld 1960s
 ⚒ (1922 Hils 2/ rem

**Hope Street Gaelic F** (Ewing Place C cld 1888) 58 Waterloo Street/West Campbell Street dest 1957
 ⚒ (organ post 1871, pre-1888

**Howard Street Ind** - see Christian Union

**Hutcheson's Boys Grammar School** - see Rose Street

**Hutchesontown** 117 Rutherglen Road cld 1969
 ⚒ (1900 B&F 2/20

**Hutchesontown** (Rutherglen Road/Augustine Buchanan/Augustine UF/F) 284 Rutherglen Road cld 1995 (later B)
 ⚒ (1907 Walc 1/7 fr Buchanan Memorial 1947 by Watt

**Hutchesontown & Caledonia Road** (Caledonia Road UF/UP) 1 Caledonia Road/Cathcart Road cld 1963
 ⚒ (1883 Jar 2/24 o1892 F&A, scr

**Hutchesontown C** 155 Rutherglen Road (cong to Castlemilk)
 ⚒ (organ 2/

**Hutchesontown UF** (UP) 61 Hospital Street cld 1924
 ⚒ (1892 F&A 3/25 rem c1925 to Greenock St. Columba's Gaelic & r Mir

**Hutchesontown** - see also Crosshill-Victoria

**Hyndland** 79 Hyndland Road (now pt of Broomhill Hyndland)
 ⚒ 1887-92 Wil 3/20 +11pf r1913 Wil 3/31, o1954 Wil 3/31, r1974 Wil 3/31 new action
 ⚒ 1973 Jhn 1/5 in aisle fr German Evangelical c1971

**GLASGOW (Cont.)**

**Ibrox** (Bellahouston Steven/Bellahouston) 18 Carillon Road/Clifford Street
⊥  1874 Cav 2/12  r1898 SmRi, r1928 Hils 2/21, r1981 McDM 2/21, disused 2009

**Ibrox** (UF/UP) 534 Paisley Road West cld 1978 (used by Admiral Street M, then climbing centre)
⊥  (1898 B&F 2/17  rem c1958 Watt, scr, facade pipes to St. Anthony's RC

**Immaculate Conception RC** 2049 Maryhill Road
⊥  (1874 ConP 2/  (in former building)  r1936 Mir, damaged by fire
⊥  (1956 Com 2/  ex  r1991, rem

**John Knox & Tradeston** (John Knox's UF/F) 5 Surrey Street cld 1943
⊥  (1925 B&H 2/  rem 1943 to Carriden, Bo'ness

**John Street** (UF/UP/Relief) 18 John Street/Cochrane Street cld 1972
⊥  (1892 IngE 3/28  scr

**John Street M**
⊥  (1863 F&A  rem to St. John's M 1880

**Johnstone Memorial** - see Springburn

**Jordanhill** (UF/F) 28 Woodend Drive
⊥  1906 Lew 3/20  fr Rhu Res of I. Macdonald 1921 & r 1923 by Brk 3/20, r1966 Mac 2/16 (3$^{rd}$ manual retained), o2014 Mac, o2015 Har

**Kelvin** (Wilton) 121 Wilton Street cld 1979
⊥  (1920 Hils 2/20

**Kelvinbridge** (Kelvin Stevenson Memorial/Stevenson Memorial/UF) 62 Belmont Street
⊥  1903 Bin 2/21  o1926 HNB + additions, o2010 MilP

**72) The Binns organ in the Kelvin Stevenson Memorial Church in Belmont Street.**
Photograph by David Hume from the Glasgow Society of Organists Archive

# Kelvingrove (Finnieston/UF) 49 Derby Street cld 1979
⊥  (1930 HNB 2/18  scr 2006

**Kelvingrove UP** - see College & Kelvingrove

**Kelvingrove Art Gallery and Museum**
⅄  1901 Lew 3/48  fr Glasgow International Exhibition, Kelvingrove 1902, o after WW1,
   o1951 Wil, o1989 Man (full restoration), o2008 Man
⅄  1887 Michael Welte of Freiburg 'Orchestrion' (mechanical organ) for William Clark of
   Paisley, to here 1942 & r Robert Dobie, later to Museums Resources Centre, to here 2006
   & o McDM

73) The 1901 Lewis organ at Kelvingrove Art Gallery, played each day at lunchtime

**Kelvingrove International Exhibition 1888**
⅄  (1885 Wal 4/44  fr South Kensington Inventions Exhibition to here 1888, rem 1890 to
   London Exeter Hall, the Strand, then 1907 to Ipswich Public Hall, dest by fire 1948
⅄  (1888 IngE
⅄  (1888 Bro 2/12  rem 1888 to Cambuslang West

**Kelvingrove International Exhibition 1901**
⅄  (1901 Lew 3/48  rem to Kelvingrove Art Gallery & Museum
⅄  (1901 Walc 1/7  in display of Marr Wood  rem

219

**GLASGOW (Cont.)**

**Kelvingrove Exhibition of History, Art & Industry 1911**
  ⅄  (1911 A&S 3/34 + percussion  rem to Victoria Park

**Kelvinhaugh** - see St. Enoch's Kelvinhaugh

**Kelvinside Botanic Gardens** (Kelvinside UF/F) 731 Great Western Road/408 Byres
Road cld 1978
  ⅄  (1886 Wil 219 +2pf r1909 Wil 3/28, r1913 N&B 3/30+1pf, o1917 N&B, o1922 W&L,
     o1929 HNB, o1934 HNB, r1956 Wil 3/31, rem Gol to north of Scotland

**Kelvinside East Park** (Kelvinside Old) 13 Kelvinside Avenue cld 1975
  ⅄  (1892 B&F 2/17  console moved c1920s, o1950s, vandalised, scr

**Kelvinside Hillhead** (Belmont & Hillhead/Hillhead) Saltoun Street
  ⅄  1876 Wil 3/31  r1906 Wil 3/32, o1921 W&L, r1930 Wil 3/47

**Kenmuir Mount Vernon** 2405 London Road
  ⅄  c1951 Watt 2/  ex 3

**Kent Road St Vincent's** (Kent Road UF/UP) 69 Kent Road cld 1977
  ⅄  (1890 George Adams 3/24 (pneumatic)  r1920s, o1939 Bro, rem by Scottish Cinema
     Organ Trust

**King's Park** 242 Castlemilk Road (for King's Park see also Christ the King RC)
  ⅄  1969 HNB 2/14  o1996 HNB

**Kingston Union** (Kingston) Morison Street  building dest 1941, cong in halls until 1953
  ⅄  (1886 H&B 2/19  organ survived blg!

**Kinning Park** (Kinning Park/Kinning Park West) 567 Scotland Street dem 1973 in halls to 1978
  ⅄  (1896 F&A 2/19  rem to Ardrossan St. Andrew's E by amateur

**Kinning Park** (St. Andrew's Plantation/Plantation/Plantation St. Andrew's) 115 Plantation Street,
now Eaglesham Place
  ⅄  (1889 Bro 2/18  r1908 Watt 2/19, scr

**74) The Brook/Watt organ at Kinning Park (Plantation) Parish Church.** Photograph by Edwin
Wyllie from the Glasgow Society of Organists Archive

**Kinning Park East** (UF/F) 376 Scotland Street cld 1957
  ⚲ (1932 Bro 2/

**Kinning Park Town Hall**
  ⚲ (1902 Bin 2/26 rem 1933 to Mosspark by Bro

**Kinning Park** - see also Our Lady & St. Margaret's and Cessnock

**Kingston Union** (Kingston) Morrison Street dest 1941
  ⚲ (1886 H&B 2/

**Knightswood St. Margaret's** Knightswood Cross
  ⚲ 1948 Watt 2/13 with Har pipe facade o1977 HNB 2/13, console dismantled 2002
  ⚲ 1866 Wil 2/15 r1875 Wil, o1961 HNB, fr Townhead Blochairn 1994 Mac, r1999-2002 Mac 2/15 **A-listed**

**Knightswood -** see also St. Ninian's RC and St. David's Knightswood

**La Scala Theatre** 115 Sauchiehall Street
  ⚲ (1928 ChrN 2/28 ex 8 rem 1937 to Stotfold Regent Cinema & rem 1946 to Birkenhead Ritz as 3/ ex8

**Lamond Auctioneers**
  ⚲ (1825 finger organ for sale

**Lancefield** - see St. Mark's Lancefield

**Langside** (Battlefield Erskine/Battlefield West) 167 Ledard Road (blg replaced 1994)
  ⚲ (1914 N&B 2/17 scr 1994

**Langside Avenue** - see St. Helen's RC

**Langside Hill** (UF/F) 122 Langside Avenue cld 1979
  ⚲ (1911 N&B 2/23

**Langside Old** 2 Langside Monument cld 1975
  ⚲ (1905 Bin 2/ r c1954 Watt & console moved

**Lansdowne** (Lansdowne Woodside/UF/UP) 420 Great Western Road cld 2013
  ⚲ (1880 LTC 2/16 +1pf rem 1911 to SmRi workshop, then 1920 to Campbeltown Lorne Street
  ⚲ 1911 N&B 3/40 o1923 HNB, disused 2010 **A-listed**

**Laurieston** 131 Norfolk Street cld 1941
  ⚲ (1876 ConP 2/ dest 1940

**Laurieston Renwick** (Renwick UF/F) 21 Cumberland Street cld 1973
  ⚲ (1912 Watt 2/ used as demonstration organ

**Linthouse St Kenneth's** (Govan Linthouse/UF/F) 9 Skipness Drive cld 2007
  ⚲ 1901 N&B 4/44 fr Govan Town Hall 1934 & r HNB 3/28

**GLASGOW (Cont.)**

**Lloyd Morris C** - see Castlemilk

**Lochwood** Lochend Road, Easterhouse cld 2015
⊥   (1963 Mac 1/4  Hill pipes

**London Road East** (UF/F) 49 Boden Street, Bridgeton cld 1941 (Church House)
⊥   (organ to here 1902 & r SmRi

**London Road St. Clement's** (London Road/UF/UP) 723 London Road, Bridgeton cld 1967
⊥   (1903 SmRi 2/  damaged

**Macgregor Memorial** - see under Elder Park

**Macgregor Street (Ardlaw) C** Govan cld
⊥   (1954 Watt 2/  ex  sold c1958 to Watt, rem to Dundee St. Francis Friary RC, Tullidelph
      Road & r Watt

**Mackenzie, James, workshop** - see under Berkeley Street

**McLellan Galleries** 254 Sauchiehall Street
⊥   (large organ extant fr 1856  rem by 1866

**Macleod** 229 Parliamentary Road cld 1944
⊥   (1872 F&A 2/  rem to Barony Institute Hall (Macleod Mission) 1888
⊥   (1888 Ann 2/28  rem, pt to Jedburgh Trinity 1948 by Wil

**Macmillan Calton** (Macmillan) 302 London Road (Great Hamilton Street) cld 1961
⊥   (1900 F&A 2/19  to here 1937 fr Greenhead East & r Bro 2/22, rem Hils

**Macnicol Memorial** - see under Gorbals

**Majestic Ballroom** (New Savoy Cinema) Hope Street/Sauchiehall Street  cinema cld 1958
⊥   (1916 Hils 3/37 ex 11 + 24 traps  moved and re-erected 1926 Hils 3/35 + traps, rem 1934
      to Hilsdon workshop, 1ss to new organ
⊥   (1929 ChrN 2/  +piano ex7 fr Tivoli, Partick 1937, scr 1958 Bell, reed unit to
      Grangemouth Zetland 1970 by H. Graham
⊥   (organ fr Odeon (BB Cinerama) in store in basement 1931 for a short time

**Malts Lodging** College
⊥   (1762 WaJ 1/4  fr Glasgow Res or workshop of James Watt to here 1776, rem 1815 to Res
      of Archibald McLellan (see Res of James Watt below for full story)

**Marr Wood Music Shop**
⊥   (various small organs, e.g. Walcker Dulsannels c1900

**Martyrs' ("The Martyrs")** (Martyrs East) 25 Monkland Street building cld 1977, cld 2011
⊥   (1885 Bro 2/17  scr

**Martyrs' West** (Martyrs UF/F) 56 Stanhope Street cld 1962
⊥   (1908 Watt 1/  r Bro 2/

**Maryhill** (Maryhill Old/Est) 1956 Maryhill Road blg cld 1988
⚓ (1902 N&B 2/17 r1924 Hils 2/20, dest fire 1980s

**Maryhill** - see Gairbraid, Immaculate Conception RC, St. Columba's RC and St. George's E

**Maryhill Community Centre** (Maryhill or North West Wesleyan M) 304 Maryhill Road
⚓ 1889 LTC 3/25 o1901 Lew, to here 1923 fr St John's UF & r Hils 3/24 o R&D, 1ss rem 1966 Frank Geiger, o1971 Mac

**Maryhill High** (Maryhill UF/F) 7 Sandbank Street cld 1998
⚓ (1912 A&S 2/18 r Watt, scr 2000

**Masonic Hall** 102 West Regent Street cld 1976/1980 (see also Royal Arch Masonic Lodge)
⚓ (1897 B&F 2/c12

**Maxwell** 113 Pollok Street cld 1969
⚓ (1865 ConP 1+pd/ rem to White Memorial (Parkgrove C) 1875 without case
⚓ (1875 ConP 2/23 r c1907 Mir

**Mearns** - outwith Glasgow

**Merrylea** (Holy Trinity) 78 Merrylee Road
⚓ (1890 ConP fr Bothwell Kirkfield 1915, rem 1947 to Milngavie UF
⚓ 1926 HNB 3/ fr Titwood 1947 & r HNB 3/ , r1972 R&D 3/36, r1990 Gol 3/37, 1996 + 3ss electronic, later 1ss changed, disused

**Methodist Central Halls** - see Maryhill Community Centre

**Metropole -** see Empress Theatre

**Millerston** - see Hogganfield

**Milton** 31 Milton Street cld 1957
⚓ (1868 Wil 2/ moved 1878 fr gallery to chamber, rem 1957 Wil

**Milton St. Stephen's** (St. Stephen's Garnethill/Garnethill/Shamrock Street UP) 159a Shamrock Street cld 1964
⚓ (1850 Mir 1/4 + pd, not used, rem, probably sold by T.W. Gardiner
⚓ (1874 Bry 2/18 fr elsewhere originally , scr c1968, but pts reused

**Milton** - see also Colston Milton

**Mirrlees, Robert, John, Alex, Adam organ builders** 23 Cochran Street
⚓ (organ 1/5 for sale 12v1859 (and many other organs under repair)

**Mitchison's Music Saloon** Buchanan Street
⚓ (London-made chamber organ 1/5 for sale 1vi1846

**Monti: de Monti Music Shop** 101 Buchanan Street
⚓ (organ 1/6 for sale 1853 (plus many others at different times)

**Montrose Street C** Montrose Street/George Street
⚓ (1901 SmRi 2/ rem 1956 to Parkhead C by R. Inglis

**GLASGOW (Cont.)**

**Morning Journal Office (c/o)**
  ⋏  (chamber organ 2/9 for sale 14iii1863

**Mosspark** 149 Ashkirk Drive cld 2017
  ⋏  1902 Bin 2/26 fr Kinning Park Town Hall 1933 & r Bro 2/26, o1953 Wil 1ss changed

**Mosspark C** Ladybank Drive
  ⋏  (c1900s Pos 1/ to Nelson Street C 1920, to here c1935 & r Bro 2/

**Mount Florida** (UF/UP) 1123 Cathcart Road cld 2010
  ⋏  1911 Bin 2/23 o1926 HNB, disused **A-listed**

**Museums Resources Centre** Nitshill
  ⋏  (1887 Michael Welte of Freiburg 'Orchestrion' (mechanical organ) for William Clark of Paisley, to Kelvingrove Art Gallery & Museum 1942 & r Robert Dobie, later to here, returned to Kelvingrove 2006 & o McDM
  ⋏  1762 WaJ 1/5 - see People's Palace for history, o2014 McDM, to here 2016 McDM

**Nelson Street C** (South Side C)
  ⋏  (c1900s Pos 1/ to here 1920 rem to Mosspark C c1935 & r Bro 2/

**Netherlee** - see Netherlee (outwith Glasgow)

**New Assembly Hall, Tontine Building** Trongate, Glasgow Cross dem 1911
  ⋏  (c1783 organ

**New Bridgegate** (fr Bridgegate UF/F) 69 Dixon Road cld 1990
  ⋏  (c1920s B&H 1+pd/5 scr

**New Cathcart** (UF) 212 Newlands Road cld 2002 (organ excluded from sale)
  ⋏  (1926 HNB 2/11 rem

**New Cinerama** - see Odeon

**New City Road C** first building (later used as cinema)
  ⋏  (organ rem

**New Jerusalem Church (Swedenborgian)** Cathedral Street
  ⋏  (1875 ConP rem 1909 & pt r SmRi in workshop, to Woodlands M by SmRi

**New Jerusalem** - see also Seventh Day Adventist and Woodlands M

**New Metropole** - see Empress Theatre

**New Public Halls** - see St. Andrew's Hall

**New Savoy Cinema** - see Majestic Ballroom

**Newhall** Main Street, Bridgeton cld 1952
  ⋏  (1875 ConP 2/ r Watt 2/

**Newlands East** (Newlands) 969 London Road cld 1966
   ⅄  (1911 Watt 2/ vandalised, scr

**Newlands St. Peter's College RC** cld 1984
   ⅄  (1846 HDa 1/6 r1857, fr St. Andrews St. Andrew's E to St. Andrews B 1869, to St.
      Andrews C pre-1920, rem to Milngavie St. Joseph's RC 1978 McDM, to here 1979, rem
      1982 to Blantyre St. Andrew's

**Newlands South** (UF/UP) Riverside Road/Langside Drive
   ⅄  (1903 Walc 3/34 r1959 Com, rem 1984

**Newlands** - see also St. Margaret's Newlands

**Newton Place** - see Partick South

**Newton Mearns** - see Mearns and Newton Mearns (outwith Glasgow)

**Nitshill** - see Museums Resources Centre

**North Hanover Street C** cld c1878 organ and church for sale
   ⅄  (1874 G&D 3/

**North Kelvinside** (UF/Kelvinside UP) 153 Queen Margaret Drive cld 2010
   ⅄  (1914 N&B 2/ rem pre-1990

**North Woodside UF** 94 Raeberry Street cld post-1960
   ⅄  (1903 B&H 2/ to here 1930 B&H

**Notre Dame College RC** Victoria Crescent/Observatory Road
   ⅄  (1886 B&F 2/11 fr Kilmacolm Res 1930 by Watt, rem to St. Thomas the Apostle RC,
      Riddrie 1979 McDM & r 2/11

**Oatlands Trinity** (Oatlands St. Bernard's/Oatlands) 17 Pine Street cld 1968
   ⅄  (1893 IngE 2/ r1909 Vin 2/23, scr

**Odeon** (New Cinerama/BB Cinerama) Eglinton Toll cld 1981
   ⅄  (1928 ChrN 2/ ex6 r1931-32 2/ ex8, scr 1964

**Old Partick** - see Partick Old

**Old Rose Street** - see Rose Street

**Our Lady & St. Margaret's RC** 118 Stanley Street, Kinning Park cld
   ⅄  (1894 Bro 2/18 with electric action to here fr Dixon Halls 1898 Bro

**Our Lady of Perpetual Succour RC** 17 Mitre Road, Broomhill
   ⅄  1965 R&D 1+pd/10 ex2

**Paisley Road** - see Cessnock

**Paramount/Odeon** Renfield Street cld
   ⅄  (1934 Com 4/ + traps ex 10 rem 1969 to Porthcawl, S. Wales, console to Coatbridge
      Summerlee Museum

**GLASGOW (Cont.)**

**Park, The** Lynedoch Place cld 1966
  ⅄  (1866 HDT 3/36  r1872 F&A, rem 1889 to Edinburgh Greyfriars New by HDT
  ⅄  (1890 Wil 3/38  o1921 W&L, r1934 Har 3/41, rem 1966 Har some pts used elsewhere

**Parkgrove C** - see White Memorial

**Parkhead** (Parkhead East/UF/UP) 110 Westmuir Street cld 1977 (later other denomination)
  ⅄  (1912 Watt 2/  o1972 Mac, dest by fire c1978

**Parkhead C** Westmuir Street/Ravel Row
  ⅄  (1901 SmRi 2/  to here 1956 fr Montrose Street C by R. Inglis, rem pre-1970

**Parkhead West** (Parkhead/Camlachie) 1159 Gallowgate cld 1965
  ⅄  (1886 Mir 2/7  vandalised

**Partick Anderson** (UF/F) 16 Anderson Street cld 1977
  ⅄  (1929 Bro 2/15

**Partick Broomhill UF** - see Broomhill

**Partick C** 37 Stewartville Street cld 2012
  ⅄  (Walc 1/
  ⅄  (1931 Ing 2/13  disused by 1996, casework remains

**Partick Dowanhill** - see Cottier Theatre

**Partick East**  - see Partick Trinity

**Partick Hamilton Crescent** - see Hamilton Crescent

**Partick Highland Gaelic Free** (Partick Dowanvale UF/F cld 1936) 35 Dowanhill Street
  ⅄  (1905 Watt 2/  rem post-1945 to Cleland

**Partick High & Dowanvale** (High/UF/F) 60 Fortrose Street/70 Peel Terrace cld 1963 (later other denomination)
  ⅄  (1903 Bin 3/  retained after closure, dem

**Partick M** 524 Dumbarton Road
  ⅄  1886 F&A 2/15  r1928 Hils 2/16, o1974 Mac **A-listed**

**Partick Old** (Partick) 11 Church Street cld 1990
  ⅄  (1888 Bin 2/25  moved to chamber in church 1896, r1934 BFH 2/26, o post-1945, scr
  ⅄  (c1850 Mir 1/5  in ch hall  extant 1960s

**Partick Rosevale Cinema** 467 Dumbarton Road
  ⅄  (1928 HNB ChrN 2/  ex7  to storage 1932 HNB, rem to London

**Partick St. Bride's** - see St Bride's

**Partick St. Peter's RC** - see St. Peter's RC

**Partick St. Simon's RC** - see St. Simon's RC

**Partick South** (Partick Newton Place UF/UP) 259 Dumbarton Road, new building 1987
⊿    (1899 SmR 2/ rem 1960s
⊿    (1884 ConJ 2/21 r1938 Wil 2/33, fr Partick Hamilton Crescent 1978 Reeves, rem

**Partick Town Hall** Burgh Hall Street
⊿    (1873 ConP 3/28 rem 1930s

**Partick Trinity** (Partick East & Dowanhill/Partick East UF/UP) 20 Lawrence Street
⊿    1927 A&S 2/23 r1980s Reeves, Stoke 2/27, Har pipes fr St. George's in the Fields, o Nic

**Paterson & Sons Musicsellers**
⊿    (1903-11 N&B six Norvic organs supplied

**Pearce Institute Macleod Hall** Govan
⊿    1906 B&F 2/27 damaged 1981, extant 2001, unplayable

**Penilee St. Andrew's** Bowfield Crescent cld 2017
⊿    1965 Sol 2/ ex 2

**People's Palace Museum** Glasgow Green
⊿    (1762 WaJ 1/4 rem 1776 to Malts Lodging, College, sold 1815 to Archibald McLellan,
     78 Miller Street, o McLellan & Steven +1ss & rem to Mugdock Catle, Milngavie, sold
     1854 to James G. Adam, Denovan nr. Dunipace, sold 1863 to Adam Sim, Coulter Mains,
     Biggar & o1864 Ren, sold 1918 to George MacFarlane, Giffnock, o Simpkin of
     Paterson's, to Glasgow Museums & to here, o1973 Robert Ingles, o2014 McDM,
     displayed at Kelvingrove Art Gallery 2014, rem 2016 to storage at Museums Resource
     Centre, Nitshill

**75) The James Watt organ now stored at Nitshill.**
Photograph by Michael Macdonald

**GLASGOW (Cont.)**

**Plantation Cornwall Street** (Plantation UF/UP) Cornwall Street cld 1953
⚓  (1906 F&A 2/22  rem 1954 to Edinburgh Juniper Green St Margaret's

**Plantation** - see also Kinning Park

**Pollok** (UF/UP) 2091 Pollokshaws Road cld 1976
⚓  (1927 A&S 2/14  o1957 Watt, rem to St. Teresa's RC, Possilpark & r McDM

**Pollok House** (Res of Sir John Stewart Maxwell) 2060 Pollokshaws Road
⚓  (1883 A&S (Abbott) 2/7 no pd  r Wal  rem 1936 to Dunblane Holy Family RC by Wal
⚓  barrel organ

**Pollok Street** (UF/UP) 5 Pollok Street cld 1975 (see also Maxwell)
⚓  (1903 Lew 2/  scr

**Pollokshaws** (Pollokshaws Shawholm/Secession Church) 223 Shawbridge Street
⚓  1968 C&C 2/30  ex 5 using pipes from St. Columba's Copland Road, console moved
   2009 Mac

**Pollokshaws Auldfield** (Pollokshaws) 169 Shawbridge Street cld 1965
⚓  (1895 B&F 2/15  scr

**Pollokshaws Burgh Hall**
⚓  1939 Wur 3/107 ex10  fr Stockport Ritz Cinema to storage 1960s, to Clydebank Town
   Hall 1994, r1994-98 Ian McNaught & team, rem 2006 to storage, to here 2008  **B-listed**

**Pollokshaws Primitive M**  2 Cross Street cld
⚓  ( Walc 1/

**Pollokshaws** - see St. Mary's RC

**Pollokshaws West UF Cont** (UF/F) 181 Shawbridge Street cld 1994
⚓  (1908 Watt 1/  rem

**Pollokshields** (Pollokshields Titwood/St. Kentigern's/Pollokshields) 274 Albert Drive/Shields Road
⚓  (1878 ConP 2/21  rem 1913 to St. Alphonsus' RC
⚓  1913 Har 3/30  r1930 HNB 3/31, o1954 HNB, r1984 Har 3/31 **A-listed**

**Pollokshields** - see also St. Albert's RC, St. Ninian's E and Titwood

**Pollokshields C** 63 Fotheringay Road (now pt of Hutchesons' Grammar School)
⚓  (1903 B&F 2/15  case extant

**Pollokshields Glencairn** (Trinity/UF/UP) 67 Glencairn Drive cld 1977
⚓  (1891 George Adams, case by Rowan  r c1911 Ing 3/ , partially dest then scr 1980s

**Pollokshields Kenmure** (East/Maxwell UF/UP) 60 Leslie Street cld 1977 dest fire
⚓  (1883 F&A 2/  o1896 F&A , r1901 Bin 2/31, dest

**Pollokshields West** (UF/F) 620 Shields Road cld 1963
⊿  (1897 N&B 3/30 +1pf o1900 N&B, r1910 N&B 3/28 +3pf, o1923 Hils, rem to Bedford Christ Church 1966

**Polmadie** (UF/UP) 570 Calder Street cld 1968 (now Zion GBZ/Grace B)
⊿  1903 Watt 2/ vandalised

**Polytechnic Exhibition** 99 Argyle Street
⊿  (1866 Mir 2/ rem 1867 to Coatbridge St John the Evangelist E

**Port Dundas** Dobbie's Loan cld 1916, dest fire
⊿  (1887 Gern 2/ dest

**Possilpark** 157 Bardowie Street cld 1975
⊿  ( Walc 1/ disused 1939, rem 1948 to Tron St. Mary's (Balornock)

**Provincial Grand Lodge** 100 West Regent Street blg cld 1976/80
⊿  (post-1895 B&F

**Qualified Chapel E** - see St. Andrews by the Green E

**Queen's Cross** - see St. Cuthbert's & Queen's Cross

**Queen's Park** (Strathbungo Queen's Park/Queen's Park West UF/F) 168 Queen's Drive
⊿  (1902 Lew 2/17 o1914 Lew, o1980 HNB, scr 2006

**Queen's Park** - see also Crosshill Queen's Park

**Queen's Park B** 180 Queen's Drive (also using Camphill Church)
⊿  1924 Bin 2/19 o1957 BinT

**Queen's Park St. George's** (Queen's Park East UF/Queen's Park UP) Langside Road dest 1946
⊿  (1881 LTC 3/ o1902 Lew, r1925 Wil 3/30, dest c1943

**Queen's Rooms** Claremont Street - see Christian Scientist 1

**Red Hall** - see Res of Anderson, A

**Regal/ABC** 72 Renfield Street
⊿  (1930 Com 3/ ex12 scr 1963

**Regent Place & Cathedral Square** (Regent Place UF/UP) 10 Craigpark Street cld 1960
⊿  (1897 LTC 2/23 rem 1963 to Stamperland by Mac

**Renfield Free Church Mission** 199 Cowcaddens Street.cld c1920
⊿  (1888 Bro 2/12 fr Kelvingrove International Exhibition 1888 to Cambuslang West by Bro, o1899 Bro, o1907 Bro, o1909 Mir, rem 1914 to here by Vin, rem 1920 to Cowcaddens (UF)

**Renfield UF** (F) Elmbank Street/311 Bath Street - see entry under St. John's Renfield

**GLASGOW (Cont.)**

**Renfield St. Stephen's** (Renfield/St. Matthew's Blythswood/Blythswood Est/Bath Street Ind) 260 Bath Street/Holland Street
- ⚓ (1852 Bev 2/18  rem 1925 to St. Bridget's RC, Baillieston
- ⚓ (1926 Ing 2/25, rem 1967 & in 1970s to St James' (Pollok) Mac
- ⚓ 1878 Wil 2/  o1905 Wil, r1923 W&L 3/30, r1960 HNB 3/35, fr Renfield Street 1965 to here 1968 & r 3/37, 1998 console dest, r2001 Well 3/37

**Renfield Street** (UF/UP) 79 Sauchiehall Street/101 Renfield Street cld 1964
- ⚓ (1878 Wil 2/  o1905 Wil, r1923 W&L 3/30, r1960 HNB 3/35, rem 1965-1968 to Renfield St Stephen's

**Renfield** - see also under Blythswood, St. John's Renfield and St. Stephen's

**Renwick** - see Laurieston Renwick

**Residences**

Allen, J.A. Park Gardens:
- ⚓ (1882 Wil 2/15

Anderson, Alex P., Red Hall, 1014 Great Western Road (dem 1968): See also Anderson's Royal Polytechnic.
- ⚓ (c1886 Wal

Anderson, R.B:
- ⚓ (1883 Wil 2/ (est. only)

Anon - see under "Residences" alphabetically below

Baker P, Crosshill:
- ⚓ (pre-1883 organ 2/8

Barr, Samuel, 196 Pitt Street:
- ⚓ (ConP

Berry, Thomas, 46 Grant Street, 40 Rosebank Terrace:
- ⚓ (1879 ConP 3/9 rem to St. Bride's E 1916 J. Blossom

Bickwell, Mr:
- ⚓ (1874 Hill 2/ (ests.)

Bielby, Sir George:
- ⚓ (1924 organ  rem HNB to Hampstead.
- ⚓ (1925 HNB 2/  organ to Technical College, George Street.

Black, Prof/Dr:
- ⚓ (c1760 WaJ 1/

Brodie, James *et al.*, 197 Onslow Drive:
- ⚓ (1887 Wil (ests. only)

Burns *et al.*, 4 Sardinia Terrace:
   ⊥   (1888 Wil (est. only)

Cochran, Archibald, 4 Broompark Circus:
   ⊥   (organ 2/ extant 1890s

Cochran, Miss P. Hillhead:
   ⊥   (ConP

Cochran, Mrs:
   ⊥   (1875 Conp ordered by A.L. Peace

Cochran, Patrick R:
   ⊥   (ConP

Cochran, R, 7 Crown Circus:
   ⊥   (1873 ConP

Curle, Rev. D., G4:
   ⊥   c1830s SBru 1/5 donated to St. Margaret & St. Mungo's E, Rutherglen Road & r c1950
       Watt

Donaldson, R, 6 Princes Square/91 St. Vincent Street:
   ⊥   (1875 Conp

Findlater, A. Kensington Place, Sauchiehall Street:
   ⊥   (1762 WaJ 1/4 bought by James Steven, Music Seller, 35 Wilson St who added 1ss, sold
       1807 to Rev Dr Ritchie for St Andrew's Church, rem fr ch 1807, returned to James
       Steven, then to here, rem c1840 to Perth Res

Frier, Gordon 25 Whittingehame Drive, rem 1997 to 5 Arthurlie Avenue, Barrhead, rem later to
Glasgow, 60 Woodlinn Avenue, Cathcart, rem 2015 to 8 Deanwood Avenue, Netherlee:
   ⊥   (c1914 W.J. Bird 2/8 fr Greenock Res of Cake to Helensburgh Cragdarroch House, to
       here 1969 & r Mac 2/10 with GDB pd, rem 1997 to Rutland Res by MilP
   ⊥   (1969 Brug 1/5 no pd lent to various locations, rem 1978 to Keele University
   ⊥   (1971 Col 1/3 rem to Canterbury Res
   ⊥   (1973 Jhn 1/5 bureau organ hired to various locations, sold 2012 to Edinburgh St. Mary's
       Cathedral E
   ⊥   (1976 Jhn 1/5 rem 2014 to Oundle School nr Peterborough
   ⊥   1979 Brug 1/7 GG compass completed 1982 Mac lent to Kelvingrove Art Gallery 1984
       & 1985
   ⊥   (1986 Jhn 1/5 trumpet regal organ, sold 2016 to Dr. Malcolm Clarke, nr Colwyn Bay
   ⊥   (1987 Jhn 1/4 portative rem 2015 to Deal RC, Kent
   ⊥   (1994 Col 1/3 rem to Cumbria Res
   ⊥   (1998 Col 3/11 box organ rem 2014 to Cathcart Res by V. Woodstock, sold 2015 to
       Edinburgh St. Mary's Music School
   ⊥   (c1852 Bry barrel organ 5ss fr Yorkshire 1990, sold Sotheby's 2016
   ⊥   c1798 DavJ barrel organ 1ss fr Michael Hart Antiques, Edinburgh
   ⊥   2015-17 Vincent Woodstock 4/15

Friskin, J:
   ⊥   (1882 Wil (ests. only)

Glen, Ninian - see Bearsden (outwith Glasgow)

**GLASGOW (Cont.)** Residences

Gordon, Lady:
  ⊥  (Wad  extant 1929-32

Hastie, A:
  ⊥  (1886 Wad  fr Strichen All Saints E 1897

Inglis, John, Hyndland:
  ⊥  (1886 Wil 2/19

Jacob, Dr. Roger - see Eaglesham (outwith Glasgow)

Johnson, David B, 44 Lansdowne Crescent:
  ⊥  (1881 ConP

Laurie, John, 52 Carlton Place:
  ⊥  (1817 MWo 2/c15, rem 1954 to North Wales, by Arthur Jones

Lay, Robert:
  ⊥  1996 Lam 1/3 no pd (Banquet of Music) also stored at St. Bride's E and University

Logue, Tom:
  ⊥  (1900 Pos 1/  fr Kilsyth Anderson c1970, rem to Clydebank Our Holy Redeemer RC 1984

McArthur, Miss:
  ⊥  (c1888 LTC

McConochie, J:
  ⊥  (ConP

Mcfadyen, 30 Wilson Street:
  ⊥  (c1820 organ 1/7 for sale 1825

Macfarlane, George A: see details under Watt below; also under Giffnock (outwith Glasgow)

Macfarlane, J.W: see Bearsden (outwith Glasgow)

MacHair, Mr.
  ⊥  (1897 Wad 1/7

Mackinlay, Dr. John, 1 Thorncliffe, Victoria Circus:
  ⊥  (1842 Mir 1/4 +1ss c. 1870, rem to Pinecotts, Leicester 1971, r R. Godfrey 1981, rem 1988 to St. Saviour's Vicarage, Leicester (Res of Mrs. Gould, née Mackinlay), rem to Folkestone, rem 2011 to Luke Spencer for a school in Cardiff

Maclaurin, R. Thornville, 24 Great George Street:
  ⊥  (1881 LTC 2/

McLellan, Archibald, 78 Miller Street (also at Mugdock Castle, nr Milngavie): see below under Watt, James

76) The 1842 Mirrlees chamber organ originally in the house of Dr. John Mackinlay, Glasgow, photographed in 1993 at St. Saviour's Vicarage, Leicester, but now in Cardiff

Maclure, Hugh:
   ⅄  (Wil (ests. only)

MacNeill, Paul, 55 Courthill Avenue:
   ⅄  (1987 Chu 2/4  sold

Mallock, I: see Kilpatrick (outwith Glasgow)

Mason, Sir Thomas - see Craigie Hall

Miller, A. 56 Brunswick Street:
   ⅄  (1875 Hill 2/  (est. only)

Mirrlees, A. 27 Woodend Drive:
   ⅄  (c1850 Mir 1/4  r1880 Mir, rem 1959 to Galloway House, Garlieston

Morven, 31 Second Gardens, Dumbreck:
   ⅄  (N&B

Muir, James, 8 Burnbank Gardens:
   ⅄  (1871 ConP 3/14

233

**GLASGOW (Cont.)** Residences

Munck, Meg:
⋏ (Rasmussen, Denmark 1/ r Frob 1/2+1pf, for sale 2004

Pattman G.T., 3 Caledonian Mansions:
⋏ (1916 Har 4/28 travelling organ with piano and dulcitone, sold 1922 to Sir John
Priestman, Harrogate, then to Durham School

Peace, Dr. A.L:
⋏ (1881 Wil 2/14 (two ests.)

Primrose, Sir John Ure, Dumbreck:
⋏ (c1900 Walc 2/ rem 1924 to Milngavie St. Joseph's RC (St. Luke's/UF)

Residences (Anon):
⋏ (1901 Walc 1/5
⋏ (1909 Walc 1/5 gifted to St. Margaret's Tollcross but not erected, sold c1948 to Watt, case
used at Greenock St. Mary's RC
⋏ (c1870s Mir/Ewart 2/7 rem by Ren, 1951 to Kinlochleven St. Paul's E
⋏ (c1905 Rutt 2/ rem to Paisley Orr Square

Res at Fleurs Avenue:
⋏ (Hils

Res at Hatfield Drive:
⋏ (organ extant 1940s

Revells, C.J.
⋏ (1899 Wad 3/23 to here fr Elgin Res of J.C. Revells, rem c1914 to Balham, Surrey, Res
of Revells, rem 1916 to All Saints, Hundon Church, East Anglia **A-listed**

Robb, Alexander:
⋏ (ConP

Robb, John:
⋏ (Mir 2/c28 rem to Glasgow St. Andrew's 1866

Roberts or Robertson, Henry:
⋏ (1859 F&A 2/

Scott, R., Morven, Dumbreck:
⋏ (pre-1860 Hill

Senior:
⋏ (Wad

Simpson, James C, Hillside, Partickhill:
⋏ (1871 Con

Steven, James, Wilson Street: see Steven, James, Music Seller

Stewart, R:
⋏ (1857 Hill 2/14

Thomson, George:
⚲ (1864 F&A

Warden, Mr.
⚲ (1845 Hill 2/ (est. only)

Watt, James, St. Andrew's Square, workshop Saltmarket, later Trongate:
⚲ (c1762 WaJ 1/5  fr here to Malt's Lodging, College 1776, sold 1815 to Archibald McLellan, 78 Miller Street & o McLellan & Steven +1ss, rem to Mugdock Castle, Milngavie, sold 1854 to James G. Adam of Denovan, nr Falkirk, rem 1863 to Res of Adam Sim, Coulter Mains, Lanarkshire & o1864 Ren, rem in 1918 to Giffnock Res of George A. Macfarlane, o Simpkin of Paterson's, then to Glasgow People's Palace
⚲ (1771 Morison of Birmingham

White, Alexander, Leverneholme, 51 Aytoun Road:
⚲ (ConP 2/

**Robson Street Independent M** Govanhill
⚲ (c1866/1875 Grindrod 2/  fr Free Gospel, Charlotte Street c1900 Watt, o1920s Watt

**Rose Street** (UF/F) 111 Florence Street cld 1947 (later pt of Hutchesons' Boys Grammar School)
⚲ (1900 Mir 2/  rem c1950

**Rosevale Cinema** 467 Dumbarton Road cld 1965
⚲ (1929 ChrN 2/  ex 7  to store 1932 HNB, rem 1935 to Burnt Oak Savoy, London

**Ross Street Unitarian** - see Unitarian

**Royal Arch Masonic Lodge** cld 1812
⚲ (1762 WaJ 1/

**Royal Conservatoire of Scotland** (RSAMD) Renfrew Street
⚲ (c1880s Gern 3/27  fr Giffnock Res of George Macfarlane, to former blg in St George's Place c1925 & r K&B, r1953 HNB 3/27, fr former blg & r1988 HNB, rem 2007 MilP
⚲ 1978 Hra 2/6 fr former blg 1988
⚲ 1987 Wal 2/22
⚲ 1990 Wal 2/5
⚲ Robin Jennings 1/3 (property of John Langdon)  rem 2004 to Paisley Abbey

**Royal Scottish Academy of Music and Drama** (Athenaeum) St. George's Place (now Nelson Mandela Place)
⚲ (1893 Bro
⚲ (c1880s Gern 3/27  fr Giffnock Res of George Macfarlane, to here c1925 & r K&B, r1953 HNB 3/27, rem to Royal Conservatoire of Scotland 1988 & r HNB

**Ruchill Kelvinside** (Ruchill UF) Maryhill Road/26 Ruchill Street, opposite Shakespeare Street, Maryhill
⚲ 1910 Sco 2/  r Allan Stark 2/16

**Rutherford** - see Dennistoun New

**Rutherglen** - see Rutherglen (outwith Glasgow)

**GLASGOW (Cont.)**

**Sacred Heart RC** Old Dalmarnock Road, Bridgeton
⚞  c1870 ConP  2/  to here fr elsewhere, disused

**Sacred Music Institution - see Cathedral**

**St. Albert's RC** (Albert Drive/UF/Albert Road UP cld 1965) 153 Albert Drive
⚞  1907 N&B 2/  o Hils, organ resited Har post 1965, o1981 McDM 2/22

**St. Aloysius' RC** Hillkirk Street, Springburn
⚞  1884 Kir 2/14  o1956 Watt and moved forward, o1997 **A-listed**

**St. Aloysius' RC** 25 Rose Street
⚞  1866 ConP 2/  r1881 Bro 3/31, to here 1909 fr Elgin Pl C after storage & r1911 Ing 3/33 ,
   r1980 John Corkhill, Wigan 3/34, r2007 For 3/34
⚞  (c1930 Hils 1/+pd  fr Christian Spiritualist Church, Holland Street to St. Vincent Street F
   post 1938, to here c1975 Hils, rem c1980 to England
⚞  1993 Van den Heuvel 2/24  fr London Duke's Hall, Royal Academy of Music to here
   2015 by Van den Heuvel

**St. Alphonsus' RC** 217 London Road, Barras
⚞  (1853 Mir 2/  in previous building (ex-F) in Great Hamilton Street, rem to new building
   1905, rem 1913
⚞  1878 ConP 2/21  to here 1913 fr Pollokshields, r1930 Watt, o1947 Watt after war damage,
   o1988 McDM 2/20, r1997 McDM 2/20 +1pf

**St. Andrew's** St. Andrew's Square cld 1993
⚞  (1762 WaJ 1/4 bought by James Steven, musicseller, 35 Wilson St who added 1ss, sold
   1807 to Rev Dr Ritchie for here, rem fr ch 1807, returned to James Steven, then possibly
   to Res of Alexander Findlater, Sauchiehall St, then c1840 to Perth Res
⚞  (Mir 2/c28  fr Res of John Robb 1866, rem to Greenock St. John's the Evangelist E c1875
⚞  1875 Mir  2/  r1906 Lew 3/32 +2pf, r c1955 Hils 3/33 +3pf, post-2001 console rem, parts
   missing

**St. Andrew's by the Green E** (Qualified Chapel) 33 Turnbull Street cld 1974 (now offices)
⚞  (1757 Sne  fr Leith per ship "Edinburgh" to here 1758
⚞  (1747 Sne 1/7  fr Edinburgh St Andrew's Qualified E, Carrubber's Close to here 1775,
   r1788 Don 2+pd/13  rem 1813 to Unitarian, Union St by Mir
⚞  (1797 Don 3/18  fr Trades Hall 1803 to Cathedral & to here 1812 Mir & volunteers,
   r1898 to chancel Mir 2/23, 1960s vandalised, remainder rem 1977 Mac, later to Tours by
   Martin Renshaw & r

**St. Andrew's Cathedral RC** 90 Dunlop Street/Clyde Street
⚞  (1817 MWo 3+ppd/21 + full pd & o later by Mir
⚞  (1871 Mir 3/41 reusing some material and case of 1817 organ, r B&F, r1950s Bro, mostly
   scr by 1980
⚞  (1902 Wil 3/30 +1pf  fr Elgin Place C 1981 & r McDM 3/30 (with case of 1817 MWo
   organ and 32'), +1ss inst later, 1ss fr Dixon Halls 1990 McDM 3/32, rem to storage 2010
   by Wells **A-listed**
⚞  (1846 Bru 1/4  fr Edinburgh 1913 to Fort William St Mary's RC & r Cat, o1978 R&D, to
   here 1984 & r McDM (1ss fr St. John's RC) **B-listed**

**St. Andrew's East** (St. Andrew's UF/F) 681 Alexandra Parade blg cld, hall used 2002
⚲ (1905 Watt 2/ o1956 Watt, SmRi style console rem 1957 to Henry Drummond

**St. Andrew's Hall** Granville Street/Kent Road dest fire 1962
⚲ (1877 LTC 4/64 r1904-6 Lew 4/75, dest 1962

**St. Andrew's Plantation** - see Kinning Park

**St. Anthony's RC** 62 Langlands Road/839 Govan Road
⚲ (c1880s ConJ 2/7 fr elsewhere rem 1958 to St. Margaret Mary's RC, Castlemilk by R. Quinn
⚲ 1958 Watt 2/ pt from Claremont St M and elsewhere, o1976 McDM 2/20, console moved 1988, disused

**St. Barnabas E** Craigpark, Dennistoun cld (later Christian Centre)
⚲ ( ConP 2/ to here, rem

**St. Benedict's RC** - see Drumchapel

**St. Bernard's** 350 Cumberland Street cld 1931
⚲ (1908 Watt 1+pd/ rem to Saltcoats St. Mary's Star of the Sea RC

**St. Bernard's RC** Nitshill
⚲ (c1960 Com 1/6 scr

**St. Bride's** 23 Rosevale Street, Partick cld 1975
⚲ (1904 Bin 2/20

**St. Bride's E** 69 Hyndland Road
⚲ (1879 ConP 3/9 to here 1916 fr Res of Thomas Berry, Grant Street by J. Blossom, rem 1972 to Leven St. Margaret's E by SmRo
⚲ 1865 Hill 2/16 r1882 Har 2/19, o1903 Mir, r1927 Mir, fr Anderston & St Peter's 1969 inst 1972 Mac & r 2/19, o2017 Har **A-listed**
⚲ (1996 Lam 1/3 Banquet of Musick organ stored here, rem to University Memorial Chapel

**St. Bridget's RC** 15 Swinton Road, Baillieston
⚲ (1852 Bev 2/18 fr Renfield St. Stephen's c1926, scr 1956
⚲ 1957 Com 2/18 ex 4

**St. Catherine's Labouré RC** 90 Lamont Road, Balornock
⚲ 1962 Watt 2/13 ex3 r1991 McDM

**St. Charles RC** 1 Kelvinside Gardens
⚲ (chamber organ inst 1980 McDM 1/10 (temp) rem 1980

**St. Christopher's Priesthill & Nitshill** (Househillwood St. Christopher's) Meikle Road ch blg cld, hall used, cld 2016
⚲ (c1962 Sol 2/

**GLASGOW (Cont.)**

**St. Clement's** 63 Brook Street, Bridgeton cld 1950
   ⋏   (1900 Walc 2/16  case to Portsoy

**77) The Walcker organ of 1900 in St. Clement's Church, Bridgeton.**
Photograph supplied by Gerhard Walcker-Mayer

**St. Columba's (Gaelic)** 300 St. Vincent Street
   ⋏   1905 Walc 3/33  **A-listed**

**St. Columba's Copland Road** (Copland UF/UP) 1505 Govan Road cld 1966
- ♫ (1906 Bin 2/21  o1919 HNB, pipes to Pollokshaws

**St. Columba's E** Baltic Street cld 1960s
- ♫ (Pos 1/    to here 1922 Watt

**St. Columba of Iona RC** 74 Hopehill Road, Maryhill
- ♫ 1970 RHW 1+pd/5  fr Drumchapel St. Benedict's RC 1980
- ♫ (1867 Mir 2/16  o1980 Mac, fr St Joseph's RC (in store here 1985), rem to Clydebank Our Holy Redeemer RC 1997 McDM

**St. Cuthbert's** 45 Doncaster Street cld 1954
- ♫ (1912 SmRi using older organ

**St. Cuthbert's & Queen's Cross** (Queen's Cross UF/F) Queen's Cross/866 Garscube Road cld 1976
- ♫ (1884 Wil 2/10  fr Bearsden Res of J.W. Macfarlane 1921 to here & r Watt 2/10, rem 1978 to Eaglesham

**St. David in the West** (UF/F) Cromwell Street, nr St. George's Cross
- ♫ (1913 Hils 2/12  rem 1936 to St David's Knightswood 1939 HNB

**St. David's (Ramshorn)** - see St. Paul's (Outer High) & St. David's (Ramshorn)

**St. David's Knightswood** (Knightswood West) 66 Boreland Drive
- ♫ 1913 Hils 2/12  fr St David in the West 1936 & to here 1939 & r HNB 2/12, o1956, o1962, o1986, 1994 1ss changed, 1997 1ss changed

**St. David of Scotland E** Lennox Avenue, Scotstoun cld
- ♫ (organ 1/4  to here c1915

**St. Enoch's** St. Enoch Square cld 1924
- ♫ (1901 F&A 2/19  rem to St. Enoch's Hogganfield 1930 by Hils

**St. Enoch's Hogganfield** 860 Cumbernauld Road
- ♫ 1901 F&A 2/19  to here 1930 fr St. Enoch's & r Hils 2/19

**St. Enoch's Kelvingrove** (St. Enoch UF/F) Dumbarton Road/Old Dumbarton Road dest 1943
- ♫ (1904 SmRi  dest 1943

**St. Enoch's Kelvinhaugh** (Kelvinhaugh) 146 Kelvinhaugh Street cld 1935, reopened 1943, cld 1967
- ♫ (1896 F&A 2/19  rem 1936 to Rutherglen Wardlawhill by Hils

**St. Francis' Centre** (St. Francis Xavier RC) 405 Cumberland Street
- ♫ (c1880 Bis 2/  rem Bis
- ♫ 1891 Bis 2/27  r1953 Watt in twin cases with electrics by Vin 2/31, o1978 McDM 2/31, disused 1999, blower rem

**St. Gabriel's E** 40 Greenfield Street, Govan cld 1990s
- ♫ (1908 Sim 2/16  o1958 Watt

**GLASGOW (Cont.)**

**St. George's & St Peter's** (St. George's UF/F) 137 Elderslie Street blg cld 1957
⚜ (1898 LTC 3/ rem to St. Mary & St. Laurence, Bolsover 1958 Wil, r1992 Six 3/34, rem Wil

**St. George's E** 11 Sandbank Street, Maryhill cld & dem 2006
⚜ (1893 Mir 2/10 o1925 Hils, disused, scr 2006

**St. George's in the Fields** 485 St. George's Road cld 1980
⚜ (1883 Har 2/ o1924 Mir, o1972 Mac 2/23, some pipes to Partick Trinity
⚜ (chamber organ 1/ (in hall)

**St. George's Queen's Park** - see Queen's Park St. George's

**St. George's Road** (UF/UP) 406 St. George's Road cld 1971
⚜ (1904 Lew 2/ o1924 Mir, moved within blg 1888

**St. George's Tron** (St. George's) 163 Buchanan Street
⚜ (1888 Har 2/ r Watt 3/ , rem c1945
⚜ (1903 Bin 2/26 fr Tron St Anne's c1946 & r Wil, disused 1990s, rem c2000

**St. Gilbert's** Hamilton Avenue/Sherbrooke Avenue cld 1942
⚜ (1903 Walc 1/ in temp blg
⚜ (1910 N&B 3/31 r1931 HNB +1ss, rem 1946 to Sherbrooke St Gilbert's & r HNB, case front to Burnside Blairbeth

**St. Helen's RC** (Langside Avenue/UF/UP cld 1963) 30 Langside Avenue
⚜ 1902 F&A 2/18 r1968 C&C 2/22, o2002 McDM

**St. James'** (Great Hamilton Street M cld 1820) 216 London Road (30 Great Hamilton Street) cld 1949/1953
⚜ (1903 B&H 2/21 o1932 HNB console moved, rem 1955 to St James' (Pollok) & r Wil

**St. James' (Pollok)** (Pollok St. Aidan's) 183 Meiklerigg Crescent/Lyoncross Road
⚜ (1903 B&H 2/21 fr St James' 1955 by Wil, rem c1970
⚜ 1926 Ing 2/25 fr Renfield St Stephen's 1970 & o Mac 2/25

**St. James' the Less E** Mollinsburn Street, Springburn cld c1979 (cong to Bishopbriggs)
⚜ (c1840 organ 1/ fr Christ Ch E, Brook St, Mile End 1884, rem1899
⚜ (1899 HCF 2/10 rem c1975

**St. James' the Less E** Hilton Road, Bishopbriggs
⚜ 1964 Wal 2/18 ex 3 to here 1996 fr Clydebank St. Columba's E by Mac

**St. John's Chalmers** (St. John's) 343 Bell Street (161 Graeme Street) cld 1963
⚜ (1878 F&A 2/21 r1904 N&B

**St. John the Evangelist E** Houldsworth Street cld 1959
⚜ (organ
⚜ (1850 Mir rem 1867 to Ayr Holy Trinity E
⚜ (1867 Mir 2/14 moved in ch 1872 Mir, rem 1961 to Drumchapel St Andrew's & r Mac (1 ss changed)

240

**St. John's M** 20 Sauchiehall Street dem

- (1863 F&A  fr former John St M 1880, rem ConP
- (1891 ConP 3/c23  Rowan case

**St. John's Renfield** (UF/Renfield UF/Renfield Street F) 22 Beaconsfield Road

- 1893 B&F 3/31  in former ch in Elmbank Street/311 Bath St (SE) to here 1931 & r HNB 3/40, r1972 HNB 3/40, o2018 Nic

**St. John's RC** 90 Portugal Street cld c1980

- (small organ extant 1864
- (1869 Mir 2/19  fr previous blg c1890, r c1920 Bro, some pipework saved, rest scr

**St. John's UF** (F) 201 George Street cld 1923

- (1889 LTC 3/25  o1901 Lew, rem 1923 to Maryhill Community Centre

**St. Joseph's RC** 40 North Woodside Road cld c1979

- (1867 Mir 2/16  o1980 Mac, rem 1985 to store at St. Columba's RC by Mac, 1997 to Clydebank Our Holy Redeemer RC by McDM
- (1981 Pul 1+pd/5  fr Gartocharn Res of Dr. Andrew Baxter 1981, rem
- (1820s-30s Anon Scottish 1/  fr Irvine Res to Uddingston Church of the Nazarene 1959 Watt, to workshop 1961 Mac, 1965 to here Mac, 1966 new blg,1969 to Stepps, to here 1976 by Mac, returned to Mac workshop, Berkeley St, rem 2009 to Lam

**St. Jude's Independent E** 278 West George Street cld 1877

- (1839 organ  rem 1877 to Belfast Res by ConP

**St. Jude's Free Presbyterian** (Woodlands UF/Woodlands Road UP cld 1974) 137 Woodlands Road

- (1878 You 2/24
- (1912 Lew 2/  case survives

**St. Kenneth's** 10 St. Kenneth's Drive, Govan cld 1976

- (1907 Vin 3/40 (some pf)  pt rem 1976 to Edinburgh George Watson's College, mostly scr 1982

**St. Kenneth's** - see also Linthouse St. Kenneth's

**St. Kiaran's Dean Park** (Dean Park) 28 Copland Road, Govan cld 1976

- (1896 Wad 2/17  o1901 Wad, o1915 Lew, o c1957 Watt 2/17, rem 1976 to Cathcart C

**St. Luke's & St. Andrew's** (Calton New/St. Luke's) Bain Square cld 2010, sold 2012

- (1891 Ann 2/25  dest fire 1925
- 1926 HNB 2/18

**St. Luke's E** 13 Grafton Street, Townhead cld 1952

- (organ to here fr Rev. W.E. Bradshaw 1877  rem
- (1885 Har 2/8  r1934 Bro, rem post-1952 to Holy Cross E by Watt

**St. Luke's Greek Orthodox Cathedral** (Belhaven/UF/UP cld 1960) 29 Dundonald Road

- (1877 LTC 2/22  r1899 Hill 3/32, o1924 HNB, r1947 HNB, rem 1964 to Chipperfield St Paul's, Herts by S. Shaw

**GLASGOW (Cont.)**

**St. Luke's UF** (F) 131 Great Hamilton Street cld 1919
⅄ (1868 Ren fr Arbroath Inverbrothock to Arbroath West 1882, to here & enlarged 1898 MilJ 2/ , rem c1923 to Millport East without case

**St. Margaret & Mungo E** 167 Rutherglen Road, Gorbals cld 1974
⅄ (c1835 SBru 1/5 + barrels r c1860s + Sw, fr Res of Rev. David Curle to here c1950 Watt (minus barrels), Sw rem fr 1950s, organ hired, rem 1973-76 to storage at University, inst 1975 in Concert Hall by Mac

**St. Margaret Mary's RC** 99 Dougrie Road, Castlemilk
⅄ c1880s ConJ 2/7 fr elsewhere to St. Anthony's RC, Govan, to here1958 R. Quinn

**St. Margaret's Newlands E** 351 Kilmarnock Road
⅄ (1913 B&H 2/15
⅄ 1924 B&H 3/ r1963 Wil 3/34, r 2014 Well 3/34

**St. Margaret's Polmadie** 110 Polmadie Road cld 1984
⅄ (1908 Hill 2/ scr

**St. Margaret's** - see also Our Lady & St. Margaret's and Knightswood St. Margaret's

**St. Margaret's Tollcross Park** (St. Margaret's Tollcross) 179 Braidfauld Street cld 2016
⅄ (1901 N&B 1/ Norvic
⅄ (1930s Percy Beard 2/ ex fr Res on Clyde to here c1956 Hils, vandalised

**St. Maria Goretti RC** 259 Bellrock Street, Cranhill
⅄ c1870s organ fr London to Edinburgh North Merchiston 1897 & r Ing 2/9, r1921 HCF, to here c1956 Watt, o1972 Wal

**St. Mark's** 21 Cheapside Street cld 1959
⅄ (1875 F&A 2/14 r1912 Mir + 1ss, rem 1959, pt to Uddingston Burnhead by Mac

**78) The Forster & Andrews/Mirrlees organ in St. Mark's Parish Church.**
Photograph by James Mackenzie, 1958, from the Glasgow Society of Organists Archive

**St. Mark's E** 430 Scotland Street/Shields Road blg cld 1953 (cong to East Kilbride)
⚲ (organ

**St. Mark's Lancefield** (St. Mark's West/UF) 721 Argyle Street cld 1968
⚲ (1904 Walc 2/6 rem 1951
⚲ 1955 BinT 2/27 rem 1968 to Clydebank Kilbowie St. Andrew's by C&C

**St. Mark's RC** Muiryfauld Drive, Carntyne cld 1970
⚲ ( Mir chamber organ 1/ to here c1930, o1962 Mac, dest by fire 1970

**St. Martin's E** 139 Dixon Road cld (later housing)
⚲ (1913 Watt 2/ o1974 Wal

**St. Mary's** - see Hamilton Crescent

**St. Mary's and St Anne's** nr Trongate - see also Tron St. Mary's
⚲ (ref to organ c1539-90

**St. Mary's Chapel E** (in Grammar School) George Street
⚲ (organ extant 1822

**St. Mary's E** 30 Renfield Street (later to Great Western Road below)
⚲ (1825 WSm 3+ppd/19 to here 1825, +pd later, rem 1871 to St Mary's RC, 89 Abercromby Street by Mir

**St. Mary's Cathedral E** Great Western Road/Holyrood Crescent
⚲ 1871 Hill 3/31 r1909 Har 3/53 +1pf, o1947 Har 3/53 +1pf, r1967 HNB 3/59, r1990 HNB 3/59

**St. Mary's Fairfield** (St. Mary's UF/F) - see Govan and Linthouse

**St. Mary Immaculate RC** Shawhill Road, Pollokshaws
⚲ (organ gallery extant 1866
⚲ (1920 Watt 2/ rem 1929 to Rutherglen St. Stephen's E

**St. Mary's RC** (Convent) 89 Abercromby Street, Calton
⚲ (1825 Bru 3+ppd/19 to St. Mary's E 1825, +pd later, to here 1871 Mir, r1906 Wilk 3/28, dest fire c1946
⚲ 1914 N&B 2/ to here 1947 fr Tower Cinema, Peckham & r HNB 2/24

**St. Matthew's Blythswood** - see Renfield St. Stephen's

**St. Matthew's** William Street/North Street cld 1926
⚲ (1897 B&F 2/19 rem 1926 to Edinburgh St Mary's Star of the Sea RC

**St. Matthew's Highlander Memorial** (St. Matthew's UF/F) Bath Street/Newton Street damaged by fire 1952, dem (fell into Bath Street)cld 1953
⚲ (1899 B&H 3/32 o1903-09 SmRi, r1914 Ing 3/35, o1928 Ing, o1942 Ing, rem 1953 to Dalry St Margaret's & r HNB 3/35

**St. Matthew's Possilpark E** 200 Balmore Road
⚲ (organ fr All Saints E, Jordanhill 1910

**GLASGOW (Cont.)**

**St. Michael's Carntyne** 50 Edrom Street cld 1965
⋏ (Pos 1/

**St. Michael's E** (Public Baths) Whitefield Road, Ibrox cld
⋏ (organ sold to Watt
⋏ (1914 N&B 2/14  additions 1916 HNB

**St. Michael's Mission** - see St. Peter's E

**St. Mungo's** - see Cathedral

**St. Mungo's RC** 52 Parson Street
⋏ (pre-1850 mech organ  maintained Mir
⋏ 1951 Com 3/47  extant
⋏ 1964 Wil 2/10+1pf  fr Colston Milton 1998 MilP

**St. Ninian's** (Crown) 427 Crown Street/Kidston Street cld 1934 (later used by Wynd UF)
⋏ (c1892 A&S 2/18  vandalised

**St. Ninian's E** 1 Albert Drive, Pollokshields
⋏ 1879 S&B 2/11+7pf  1887 +7ss Bro  r1903 Bro, r c1972 Gro 2/24 (reed unit), disused 1997, 1ss to Crichton 2011 Wil

**St. Ninian's RC** Knightswood Cross
⋏ 1915 B&H 2/  to here fr Stranraer St. Margaret's 1959 & r Hils 2/12, o WoP

**St. Ninian's Wynd** (Wynd UF) 427 Crown Street/Cathcart Road cld 1973
⋏ (1934 HNB/K&B 2/

**St. Oswald's E** 260 Castlemilk Road
⋏ (ConP  fr elsewhere (in hall ch)
⋏ (1966 Sol 2/  ex

**St. Patrick's RC** Hill Street, Anderston
⋏ (1870 LTC 2/  Bentley case  o1905 Lew, extant 1922, rem 1899 to St. Patrick's RC, North Street

**St. Patrick's RC** North Street/William Street, opened 1898
⋏ (1870 LTC 2/  fr St. Patrick's RC, Hill Street 1899 SmRi, o1905 Lew, r1939 Wil 2/15, rem 2008 McDM
⋏ 1969 Wal  to here fr London B ch 2008 McDM & r with case & console fr Swiss convent & LTC pipework fr old organ 2/20 ex 5

**St. Paul's (Outer High)** (St. Paul's/Outer High/East) 97 St. John Street cld 1953 (now Strathclyde University Chaplaincy Centre)
⋏ (1882 F&A 2/16  fr previous blg at 72 John St, to here 1908 Lew, rem HNB

**St. Paul's (Outer High) & St. David's (Ramshorn)** (St. David's (Ramshorn)) 98-102 Ingram Street opp Candleriggs cld 1982 (now Strathclyde University Theatre)
⋏ (1887 F&A 2/16  o c1909 Ing, dismantled McDM

244

**St. Paul's E** Buccleuch Street cld c1888 (later used by Garnethill Chapel of Ease until 1916)
   ⚮  (1874 Hun 2/18  rem 1888 to Cadder

**St. Paul's Protestant E** Duke Street
   ⚮  (small organ

**St. Paul's RC** 1213 Dumbarton Road, Whiteinch
   ⚮  1960 Watt 2/  ex  r McDM 2/13 ex 3

**St. Paul the Apostle Shettleston RC** 1653 Shettleston Road
   ⚮  1874 ConP 2/20  fr Glasgow Eastwood to Paisley Greenlaw 1910 & r Ing 2/20, r1987 McDM 2/20, rem 1999 to here & r2000 SmRo 2/19

**St. Peter's** (Brownfield Chapel of Ease) 72 Brown Street cld 1951
   ⚮  (1906 SmRi  Sw rem to Drumchapel St. Andrew's & r 1961 Hils

**St. Peter's College RC** - see Glasgow Newlands and Cardross

**St. Peter's E** Burnside Street (later St. Michael's Mission fr St. George's)
   ⚮  (1893 Wad 2/11  rem 1948 to Carmunnock

**St. Peter's E** St. Peter's Street (Gardner Street) cld 1963
   ⚮  (1903 Wad 3/24  r pre-1921 3/26, o1961 Mac, rem 1964 to Ayr Good Shepherd Cathedral RC

**St. Peter's Partick RC** 46-50 Hyndland Street
   ⚮  (organ  fr St. Vincent's RC, Duke Street to here 1903 (temp), rem, possibly to St. Simon's RC c1914
   ⚮  1914 Law 3/34  r1952 Wil, r1969 C&C 3/44, o1987 McDM 3/45, r1999-2003 McDM 3/28 using N&B pipes fr Paisley St. John's

**St. Philomena's RC** 1255 Royston Road, Provanmill
   ⚮  (1963 Watt 2/19 ex 3  rem 2017
   ⚮  2017 McDM ex

**St. Robert Bellarmine RC** 310 Peat Road, Househillwood
   ⚮  1958-59 R&D 2/28 ex 4

**St. Roch's RC** 311 Royston Road (Garngad Road)
   ⚮  (Walc 1/  to here 1956 Watt, scr post-1980

**St. Rollox** (UF/UP) 9 Fountainwell Road/153 Springburn Road (for earlier blg see Garngad)
   ⚮  (1903 Mir  dest fire 1982

**St. Saviour's Mission E** Port Dundas Road cld 1950s
   ⚮  (Ric 2/9

**St. Serf's E (Petrie Memorial)** 1464 Shettleston Road
   ⚮  (organ 2/  no case

**St. Silas' English E** Eldon Street/Park Road
   ⚮  1864 Bev 2/  r1877 ConP 3/25 & to gallery, o1958 R&D, disused

**GLASGOW (Cont.)**

**St. Simon's RC** (Bridge Street Chapel/St. Peter's RC) 33 Bridge Street, Partick
⏃  (organ possibly fr St. Peter's Partick RC c1914, rem by 1945

**St. Stephen's** (St. Stephen's Blythswood/St. Stephen's Buccleuch/St. Stephen's) 24 Cambridge Street cld 1974 (see also Milton St. Stephen's)
⏃  (1885 Har 2/20 moved in blg 1890 Mir, r1933 Watt 2/22, o1965 Mac (1ss changed), scr, pt rem 1976 to Invergordon by Gol

**St. Stephen's Garnethill** - see Milton St. Stephen's

**St. Stephen's West** (UF/F) 213 New City Road cld 1941
⏃  (1902 F&A 2/ rem to Port Glasgow Clune Park post-1941

**St. Teresa's RC** Saracen Street, Possilpark
⏃  (1961 Watt 2/ ex 5 scr
⏃  1927 A&S 2/14 o1957 Watt, to here 1977 fr Pollok (UF) & r McDM 2/15, disused

**St. Thomas'** Campbellfield Street/nr 790 Gallowgate cld 1938
⏃  (1911 Ing 2/20 o1929 Ing, rem to Gallowgate (St. Thomas' Gallowgate) 1938

**St. Thomas' Gallowgate** - see Gallowgate

**St. Thomas' Wesleyan M** 600 Gallowgate/Orr Street
⏃  (1871 Nicholson of Walsall 2/ rem to Millport: Cumbrae 1893 by Mir
⏃  (1893 Har 2/17 scr

**St. Thomas the Apostle RC** Smithycroft Road, Riddrie
⏃  1886 B&F 2/11 to here fr Notre Dame College, Hillhead 1979 McDM 2/11

**St. Vincent de Paul RC** - see Thornliebank (outwith Glasgow)

**St. Vincent Street Milton F** (Hope Street Gaelic F/City use to 1971/Spiritualist National Church/St. Vincent Street UF/UP cld 1939) 265 St. Vincent Street (SE)
⏃  1904 N&B 3/29 case and other parts survive
⏃  (c1930 Hils 1+pd/ fr Christian Spiritualist, Holland Street post 1938, rem to St. Aloysius' RC, Rose Street c1980

**St. Vincent's** Dover Street cld 1934
⏃  (1897 Wad 2/19 o1926 Watt, rem to North Ayrshire by Hils

**St. Vincent's RC** (Duke Street Gaelic F) Duke Street cld 1900s
⏃  (organ rem 1903 to St. Peter's RC, Hyndland Street, Partick (temp)

**Salon Cinema** 17 Vinicombe Street, Hillhead cld 1992
⏃  (c1913 B&H (slider chests) rem by 1945

**79) The Wadsworth organ at St. Vincent's, Dover Street**
Photograph by David Hume, from the Glasgow Society of Organists Archive

**Sandyford Henderson Memorial** (Sandyford) 13 Kelvinhaugh Street
⋏   1866 Wil 3/30 + 2pf (added 1872)  o1905 Wil, r1922 Ing 3/32 +5pf and moved into
    chancel, o1975 Mac, disused

**Sandyhills** (UF/F) 28 Baillieston Road
⋏   (A&S 2/  in previous blg dem 1982

**Sang Schule** nr College
⋏   (c1600 organ

**Savoy Cinema** - see Majestic Ballroom

**Scotstoun** (Scotstoun Whiteinch/Scotstoun East/UF) 70 Earlbank Avenue
⋏   1927 Hils 2/21  r1969 HNB 2/22, o1990 HNB

**Scotstoun** - see also Gordon Park

**Scotstoun West** (Scotstoun) 8 Queen Victoria Drive/Dumbarton Road cld 1988
⋏   (1923 Hils 2/20  dest fire

**Scottish Early Music Consort** - see University Music Department

**Seventh Day Adventist** (New Jerusalem Swedenborgian) 174 Queens Drive cld 1998
⋏   (1898 Bin 2/18  rem to SDA Church, Heidelberg post-1996

**Shamrock Street** - see Milton St. Stephen's

**Shawlands** (Shawlands Cross/UF/F) 1114 Pollokshaws Road
⋏   1904 SmR 2/  r1960 HNB 2/24, o1983 HNB

247

**GLASGOW (Cont.)**

**Shawlands URC** (Church of Christ) 111 Moss Side Road
⚲ 1910 Pos 1/7

**Shawlands Old** (Shawlands) 1114 Pollokshaws Road cld 1998 (now Independent ch)
⚲ (Cat 2/
⚲ (1922 Hils 2/20 scr 1999

**Shawlands** - see also South Shawlands

**Sherbrooke St Gilbert's** (Sherbrooke/UF/F) 240 Nithsdale Road
⚲ (1900 B&F rem by 1946, some material to new organ
⚲ (1910 N&B 3/31 fr St. Gilbert's 1946 & r HNB 3/ , dest fire 1994
⚲ 1997 Lam 3/32 +2pf

**Shettleston New** (Eastbank/UF/Shettleston UP) 679 Old Shettleston Road/Annick Street
⚲ 1904 A&S 2/19 r1948 Hils 2/19

**Shettleston Old** 111 Killin Street cld 2016, sold with organ 2017
⚲ 1903 Lew 2/22 r1965 Hils 2/24 **B-listed**

**Shettleston UF Cont** 191 Sandyhills Road/Amulree Street cld
⚲ (1926 organ

**Shettleston** - see also St. Paul the Apostle RC and Sandyhills

**Sighthill** (UF/F) 1/7 Mollinsburn Street/Springburn Road cld 1978
⚲ (1915 Hils 2/20 scr

**Smith, Richard, Workshop** Charing Cross
⚲ (1902 SmiRi 2/24 on display iii1902
⚲ (and many other organs in transit - see individual entries)

**South Glasgow Exhibition** - see Gorbals

**South Shawlands** (UF) 14 Regwood Street cld 2017
⚲ 1921 Hils 2/21

**Springbank UF** (UP) 654 New City Road cld 1925
⚲ (1887 Bro 2/13 to Garngad c1925

**Springburn Johnstone Memorial** (UF/UP/Springburn UP) Springburn Road at Queenshill Street cld 1978
⚲ (1900 SmRi 2/17 r1930s Watt, scr 1976, some pipes to Stepps

**Springburn North** (UF/F) Springburn Road at Elmvale Street dest/cld 1967
⚲ (1874 ConP 2/22 fr Ayr Cathcart 1901 by Mir with new console, scr

**Springburn North Hill** (Hill/Springburn) 40 Hillkirk Street/Springburn Road cld 1967
⚲ (1875 F&A 2/ fr elsewhere r1898-99 F&A, r1913 N&B 2/30 (3 depts), o1916 HNB, o1924 HNB, scr

**Springburn Public Hall** 46 Keppochhill Road cld 1985 dem 2012
  ⊥  (1905 Bin 3/47  case survived until 2012

**Springburn Wellfield** (UF/UP) 24 Balgrayhill cld 1978
  ⊥  (1903 Lew 2/  some pipes rem by Six

**Springburn** - see also St. James' the Less E, St. Aloysius' RC and Sighthill

**Stamperland** - see Stamperland (outwith Glasgow)

**Stepps** - see Stepps (outwith Glasgow)

**Steven, James, Music Seller** 35 Wilson Street
  ⊥  (1762 WaJ 1/4  1ss added by Steven, sold 1807 to Dr. Ritchie at St. Andrew's, rem 1807 to here again, then to Res of Findlater, Sauchiehall Street

**Steven Memorial** 61 Gower Street, Bellahouston cld 1969
  ⊥  (1915 Hils 2/22

**Stevenson Memorial** - see Kelvinbridge

**Strathbungo** 603 Pollokshaws Road cld 1979
  ⊥  (1888 Wil 2/14  r1934 Wil 2/22, o1968, rem 1980 to Mauchline by Wil

**Strathbungo Queen's Park** - see Queen's Park

**Strathclyde University** - see Barony Hall, Technical College and St. Paul's (Outer High)

**Struthers Memorial Independent** (Belhaven Westbourne/Westbourne UF/F cld 1980) 52 Westbourne Gardens
  ⊥  (1884 Gern 2/20  r1902 N&B 2/22
  ⊥  1913 N&B 3/38 using some pipes fr Gern  o1928 HNB, o1963 R&D, disused

**Swedenborgian** - see Woodlands M, New Jerusalem and Seventh Day Adventist.

**Sydney Place** - see Trinity Duke Street

**Technical College** George Street (now part of Strathclyde University)
  ⊥  1925 HNB 2/  (per Sir George Bielby)

**Temple** 964 Crow Road cld 1984 dem
  ⊥  (1903 Walc 2/8  fr Cathedral 1903

**Temple Anniesland** (Anniesland Cross/UF/UP) 869 Crow Road
  ⊥  1883 F&A 2/17  fr Berkeley Street UF 1920, r c1962 Hils 2/21

**The Park** - see Park

**Thornliebank** - see Thornliebank (outwith Glasgow)

**Titwood** Glencairn Drive cld 1941 (see also Pollokshields)
  ⊥  (1895 B&F 2/16 +8pf  added later
  ⊥  (1926 HNB 3/  rem 1947 to Merrylea & r HNB 3/

**GLASGOW (Cont.)**

**Tivoli/Classic** 53 Crow Road, Partick
⟂ (1929 ChrN 2/ + piano ex 7 rem 1937 to Majestic Ballroom

**Tolbooth Mission** Spoutmouth Street
⟂ (organ

**Tollcross** - see also St. Margaret's Tollcross Park & Victoria Tollcross

**Tollcross Central** (Tollcross UF/UP/Relief) 1088 Tollcross Road cld 1987
⟂ (1904 B&F 2/20 r1939 HNB 2/ , scr

**Tollcross Park** (UF) 16 Drumover Drive cld 1994
⟂ (1877 B&F 2/18 r1898 SiRi, fr Blythswood 1931 by Hume

**Townhead Blochairn** (Townhead) 178 Roystonhill cld 2000
⟂ (1866 Wil 2/15 r1875 Wil removed fr gallery, o1961 HNB, rem 1994 to Knightswood St Margaret's & inst & o Mac 1999-2002

**Trades' Hall** Glassford Street
⟂ (1797 Don 3/18 rem 1803 to Cathedral

**Trinity C** 71 Claremont Street cld 1978 (later Henry Wood Hall)
⟂ (1865 ConP 3/30 +2ss 1870s ConP, to Govan White St C 1911 Watt
⟂ (1911 N&B 3/36 o1929 HNB, 1972 some pipes to Woodlands M, scr

**Trinity Central** - see Gillespie Central

**Trinity Duke Street** (Sydney Place & East Campbell Street/Sydney Place UF)) 176 Duke Street cld 1975 (later day centre)
⟂ (1889 Wil 2/24+1pf r1911 SmR 3/25, rem 1979 to Dennistoun New by McDM

**Trinity Possil & Henry Drummond** (Trinity Possil) 2 Crowhill Street/Broadholm Street
⟂ (organ 1/
⟂ ( Bro 2/ scr

**Trinity UF** - see Gillespie Central

**Tron St Anne's** (Tron St. Anne's/Tron UF/F) Dundas Street cld 1940
⟂ (1903 Bin 2/26 rem to St George's Tron c1946

**Tron St Mary's** 71 Trongate cld 1951 (see also St. Mary's & St. Anne's)
⟂ (1866 F&A 2/20 rem 1951 to Colston Wellpark & r Watt

**Tron St Mary's** (Balornock Tron/Laigh) 128 Red Road
⟂ (Walc 1/ fr Possilpark 1948 to new ch hall by Watt, o1956 Watt, rem 1964
⟂ 1964 Vin 2/25 ex 4 in new ch

**Unitarian** 34 Ross Street (South St, Mungo Street) cld c1950
⟂ (1881 organ
⟂ (1911 Watt 2/ rem Watt case to Falkirk

**Unitarian** 287 St. Vincent Street cld 1982
 ⚭ (1747 Sne 1/7 fr Edinburgh St Andrew's Chapel, Carrubber's Close E, 1775 to St. Andrew's by the Green E, r1788 Don 2+pd/13, to former Unitarian, Union St 1813 by Mir, to Soho workshop 1853 Bev, inst here & r1856 Bev 2/13, moved and r1887 2/14, o1920s Hils, o1959 Mac, r1974-76 Mac, rem 1982 Mac to store, to University Concert Hall 1985

**Unitarian** 72 Berkeley Street
 ⚭ 1978 Brug 1/3 to here 1984 fr Bellshill Sacred Heart RC (temp) by Mac

**University Bute Hall** Gilmorehill
 ⚭ (1870 ConP 2/21 fr University Hunter Hall 1883 by Wil, rem 1905
 ⚭ 1905 Lew 4/50 r1907 Lew 4/52, r1962 HNB 4/70, o1975 HNB, o1985 HNB, o2018 Nic

**University Concert Hall** Gilmorehill
 ⚭ c1835 SBru 1/5 +barrels Sw added, r c1860s plus Sw, fr Res of Rev. David Curle to St. Margaret & St. Mungo's E, Rutherglen Road c1950 Watt (barrel mechanism removed), Sw rem fr 1950s, organ hired, rem to storage here 1973 and r1975 Mac 1/5 **A-listed**
 ⚭ 1747 Sne 1/7 fr Edinburgh St Andrew's Chapel, Carrubber's Close E, 1775 to St. Andrew's by the Green E, r1788 Don 2+pd/13, to former Unitarian, Union St 1813 by Mir, to Soho workshop 1853 Bev, inst at Unitarian, St. Vincent Street & r1856 Bev 2/13, moved in blg and r1887 2/14 o1920s Hils, o1959 Mac, r1974-76 Mac 2/13, rem 1982 Mac to store, to here 1985 by Mac **B-listed**

**80) The 1830s James Bruce organ in the Concert Hall, University of Glasgow**
Reproduced with permission of the Music Department, Glasgow University

**GLASGOW (Cont.)**

**University Hunter Hall** (Museum Lower Hall)
⚓ (1870 ConP 2/21 rem 1883 to University Bute Hall

**University Memorial Chapel** Gilmorehill
⚓ 1928-29 Wil 3/45, o1938 Wil, r1978 Wil 3/47, r2005 Har 3/49
⚓ (1996 Lam 1/3 stored at St. Bride's E, to here, rem to Glasgow Res of Robert Lay

**University Music Department** 14 University Gardens
⚓ 1983 G&G 1/3 kept here for use of Scottish Early Music Consort

**University of Strathclyde** - see Barony, Technical College and St. Paul's (Outer High).

**Victoria** (UF/F) Victoria Road/Eglinton Toll cld 1930
⚓ (1901 Walc 3/32 dest fire 1929

**81) Photograph of the 1901 Walcker organ in Victoria Church.**
Photograph reproduced with kind permission of Gerhard Walcker-Mayer

252

**Victoria Park** (UF/UP) 35 Balshagray Avenue blg cld 1967
- ⅄ (1911 A&S 3/34 plus percussion to here 1911 fr Kelvingrove Exhibition, o1960 R&D, rem

**Victoria Park** Broomhill Drive cld 1991
- ⅄ (1970 R&D 2/ fr older material, scr

**Victoria Tollcross** (UF/Tollcross F) 1134 Tollcross Road (now Causeway: Tollcross)
- ⅄ 1912 N&B 2/20 disused 2009

**Wallacewell** (Balornock North) 57 Northgate Road
- ⅄ c1850 Mir 2 +ppd/ r Law1+ppd/ fr Alloa St Mungo's RC 1961 & to here 1963 & r Mac 1/5

**Watt, Andrew & Sons, workshop** (Polmadie Road/North Portland Street/Pollokshaws Rd)
- ⅄ (1884 ConP 2/17 r1902 N&B (TWLewis), fr Prestwick New Life 1926 to here
- ⅄ (many other instruments in transit or under repair

**Waverley/ABC Picture House** 18 Moss-side Road
- ⅄ (1928 ChrN 2/ ex 6 scr 1953 HNB

**Wellfield** - see under Springburn

**Wellington** (UF/UP) 76 University Avenue (fr Wellington Street 1884)
- ⅄ 1884 F&A 3/34 r1912-13 F&A 3/35, r1951 R&D 3/48, o1962 R&D, r1977 Nic 3/44

**Wellpark** (UF/F) 165 Duke Street cld 1949
- ⅄ (1856 F&A 3/28+1pf 1858 +1ss F&A, r1872-74 F&A, o1882 F&A, fr Claremont 1899 & r SmRi 3/c38, rem 1953 to Dundee Coldside by Watt

**Wellpark** - see also Colston Wellpark

**West Regent Street Masonic Temple** - see Masonic Hall

**Westbourne** - see Struthers Memorial

**West End Playhouse** - see Empress Playhouse

**Western Infirmary Alexander Memorial Chapel**
- ⅄ 1924 HNB 2/11 disused

**White Memorial** (White Memorial UF/Parkgrove C) Paisley Road dest fire 1954 cld 1958
- ⅄ (1865 ConP 1+pd/ to here 1875 from Maxwell & r with new case 1876

**White Street** - see Govan

**Whitehill** - see Dennistoun Blackfriars

**Whiteinch** (Jordanvale/Whiteinch) 25 Squire Street cld 1992
- ⅄ (1891 Walc 1/ in former ch
- ⅄ (1921 HNB/K&B with 1860s pipes scr

**Whiteinch** - see also Gordon Park, Broomhill Trinity and Scotstoun

**Whitevale** (UF/UP) Whitevale Street, Dennistoun cld 1961
⊥   (1903 SmRi 2/

**82) The Richard Smith organ at Whitevale Church.**
Photograph by David Hume, from the Glasgow Society of Organists Archive

**Wilton** - see Kelvin

**Windsor Place M**  164 Great Western Road cld pre-1922
⊥   ( F&A fr elsewhere

**Woodlands M** (New Jerusalem Church) 229 Woodlands Road/Park Drive
⊥   1908 SmRi 2/ with pt ConP (1875)  fr New Jerusalem (Swedenborgian) Church,
    Cathedral Street as larger 2/ , o1961 HNB, r1973 Claypole 2/19 pipes stolen and replaced
    from Trinity C

**Woodlands Road** - see St. Jude's Free Presbyterian

**Woodside** (St. Oswald's) 341 Great Western Road cld 1959
⊥   (1882 Har 2/21+1pf  o1953 BFH, rem Watt

**Yoker** (Yoker Old) Hawick Street/Dumbarton Road
⊥   (1913 organ
⊥   (1896 Dob (Watt) 2/9 fr Cupar Boston 1918

**Young Street** (UF/F) cld 1937
⊥   (c1902 Walc 1/
⊥   (1921 Walc 2/  rem to Carntyne 1937 by HNB

**Glass** (St. Andrew's) Aberdeenshire cld 2007
- ⚐ 1906 Kir 1+pd/8 +1pf (gift of Sir F. Bridge)  o1979 R&D, organ excluded from sale of ch

**Glassburn -** see Marydale

**Glenalmond Trinity College Chapel** Perthshire
- ⚐ (1851 Hol  fr Res of Sir Frederick Bridge to here, rem 1879 to hall, scr c1950
- ⚐ (1880 F&A 3/  r1932-44 G&D 3/27, o1955 R&D, o1961 R&D, r1975 HNB with pipework fr Alyth added 1978 3/28, rem 2003
- ⚐ 2007 Har 2/26

**Glenapp** nr Girvan cld but occasionally used
- ⚐ 1928 organ

**Glenaray & Inveraray -** see Inveraray

**Glenbervie (West Mearns)**
- ⚐ 1923 Law 2/

**Glenboig** nr Coatbridge
- ⚐ c1870 Ren 1/c7  fr Res to Larkhall Chalmers & r with pd by Ing, to here 1962 & o Mac

**Glencairn & Moniaive** (Glencairn) Dumfriesshire
- ⚐ (1902 Vin 3/24  disused 1938, case extant 1996

**Glencarse -** see Pitfour Res of Sir John Richardson

**Glencoe St. Mary's E**
- ⚐ (1914 N&B 1/5  o1917 Law for N&B, disused c2000, case extant

**Glencorse** Midlothian
- ⚐ 1904 N&B 1/6

**Glencorse Res of Mr. Somerville**
- ⚐ (1903 N&B 1/  (Norvic)

**Glencruitten House** nr Oban
- ⚐ 1928 Ing 2/16  Welte player mechanism & Lorimer case **A-listed**

**Glenfinnan St. Mary & Finnan RC**
- ⚐ (c1850 Bev 1/5  fr London Res of Mr. Hood 1975 Wal, disused c2000, rem

**Glengairn** nr Ballater blg sold 2014
- ⚐ c1900s Pos 1/5  fr Kincardine O'Neill c1968 HNB

**Glengarry**
- ⚐ 1898 IngE 2/  r1985 Six and relocated, o2012

**Glenmuick** Church Square, Ballater
- ⚐ 1889-92 F&A 2/17  o1906 F&A, o1973, o2002  Nob **A-listed**

**Glenrothes St. Columba's** Church Street/Rothes Road
- ⚓ 1961 Wal 1/4 ex3

**Glenrothes St. Luke's E** (B until 1979) Ninian Quadrant
- ⚓ Cou 1/ to here 1962

**Glenrothes St. Ninian's** Durris Drive
- ⚓ 1967 R&D 1+pd/10 ex 2 **B-listed**

**Glenrothes** - see also Leslie

**Glentanar House** nr Aboyne
- ⚓ (1924 Har 4/61 rem 1954 to London Temple Church & r 4/62

**Glentanar House St. Lesmo's Chapel E**
- ⚓ (1860 organ supplied by de Monti for adjacent tower house, to here post-1871, rem pre-1936
- ⚓ 1874 Hill 2/12 fr Strathfieldsaye House, Basingstoke 1936 & r Law 2/9, r1953 Har 2/9 (1ss changed), disused 1997

**Gordon Castle** nr Fochabers (for Gordon Chapel see Fochabers)
- ⚓ (organ to here 1804 fr Peterhead
- ⚓ (1852 Bev

**Gordon St. Michael's** Berwickshire
- ⚓ 1895 F&A 2/12 fr Prestonkirk St. Andrew's 1996 & r 1998/2003 Sta 2/14 **B-listed**

**Gordonstoun School** nr Lossiemouth
- ⚓ 1967 R&D 2/26 (St. Christopher's Chapel)
- ⚓ 1964 R&D 1+pd/10 ex 2 o1978 R&D (Michael Chapel)

**Gorebridge Struthers Memorial Ind** (St. Paul's/UF/F cld 1975)
- ⚓ organ to here fr Galashiels area & r1952 Bell

**Gosford House** nr Longniddry
- ⚓ 1745 Sne 1/5 with Kirkman harpsichord (claviorganum) **A-listed**

**Gourock Ashton** (UF/UP) 56 Albert Road cld 1989
- ⚓ (1885 ConJ 2/14 2ss added later, r1910 N&B 3/21 +1pf, dest fire 1923
- ⚓ (Wil 3/24 to here 1928 fr cathedral in England, rem to Ireland c1990 Gol

**Gourock Castle Levan Res of C.M. Mann**
- ⚓ (1898 F&A 3/15 rem to Kilbarchan East 1914 by F&A

**Gourock: Old Gourock & Ashton** (Gourock Old) 41 Royal Street
- ⚓ (1882 F&A 2/ o1900 F&A, r c1909 Ing 3/28, o1959 R&D 2/28, case extant

**Gourock St. Bartholomew's E** Barrhill Road
- ⚓ (1857 2/ o1877
- ⚓ (1882 ConJ 2/11 r 1910 Watt 3/ , case extant

**Gourock St. John's** (UF/F) Bath Street
 ⚓ (1897 Bin 2/18 rem 1933 to Innellan West
 ⚓ (Hils 2/ ex pt rem c1990, case extant

**Grange** (St. Ninian's) Aberdeenshire
 ⚓ 1903 Wad 1+pd/7 o2008

**Grangemouth Abbotsgrange** (Kerse) Abbot's Road
 ⚓ 1915 Bin 2/21 disused 2001

**Grangemouth Charing Cross & West** (Charing Cross/UF/F) Charing Cross cld 2002
 ⚓ 1902 A&S 2/23 o1920, 1959 R&D, o1988, extant 2004

**Grangemouth Dundas** (UF/UP) Bo'ness Road cld 2006 (now funeral parlour)
 ⚓ 1894 Mir 2/20 +1pf o R&D

**Grangemouth Grange** (UF/UP) Park Road cld 1991
 ⚓ (1955 Com 2/18 rem 1990s to Daventry Monastery

**Grangemouth Kirk of the Holy Rood** Bowhouse Road
 ⚓ (1963 Wil 1+pd/8 ex3 rem 1991 to Ladykirk by Julian Bonia, Norham

**Grangemouth Old** - see Grangemouth Zetland

**Grangemouth Public Institute Hall**
 ⚓ (organ opened 1877

**Grangemouth St. Mary's E** Ronaldshay Crescent
 ⚓ (1876 Hewins of Stratford 2/7 to here 1941 fr Edinburgh & inst Sco, r1976 Gol, rem
   1980 to North Queensferry by SmRo

**Grangemouth West** (UF/F) Dalgrain Road cld 1978
 ⚓ (1914 Law 2/14 (incl 32') redundant 1979

**Grangemouth Zetland** (Old) Ronaldshay Crescent
 ⚓ (1911 N&B 1/ rem 1951
 ⚓ (1882 BBE 4/49 reopened 1895, r1921 HNB, o1938 HNB, fr Paisley Town Hall 1951 &
   r1953 Bell 2/27 +2pf, 1958 1ss rem, r1960 Hugh Graham with ChrN pt fr Glasgow
   Majestic Ballroom, r1967 Hils, rem 1982
 ⚓ 1890 Wil 3/22 fr London Willesden, St. George's Presbyterian, Brandesbury to store at
   London St. Michael's, Chester Square, to here 1983 Man & r 3/22 **A-listed**

**Grantown-on-Spey** - see Inverallan

**Grantown-on-Spey B**
 ⚓ 1902 Pos 1/8 o1913 Wad, disused 1999, extant

**Grantown-on-Spey Castle Grant**
 ⚓ (1766 Byf 1/6 rem 1957 to Cullen House

**Grantown-on-Spey St. Columba's E**
 ⚓ (1712 organ 2/ (no pd) fr Edinburgh Old St. Paul's E 1716, to Duke Street URC 1854,
   sold to Andrew Jupp 1867, later possibly to here, organ extant 1925, rem

**Grantown-on-Spey South** (UF/F) cld 1960
⤷ (1925 Hils 2/9 rem to Elgin St. Sylvester's RC

**Grantshouse & Houndwood** (Houndwood) cld 2003 (now crematorium)
⤷ organ presented 1902

**Greenbank** Busby nr Glasgow
⤷ (1903 B&H 2/ r Bro to chancel, r Hils, r c1990 Har (recabled), console rem

**Greenbank** - see also under Edinburgh

**Greengairs** nr Airdrie
⤷ (1902 Cou 1+pd/6 to here 1931 fr Greengairs UF, rem 1966 to Greenock St. Margaret's
by Mac

**Greengairs UF**
⤷ (1902 Cou 1+pd/6 rem to Greengairs 1931

**Greenlaw** Berwickshire
⤷ 1904 ConP 2/12 o1970s R&D, r1992 Sta 2ss changed

**Greenlaw New Palace Centre (Scottish Theatre Organ Preservation Trust)**
⤷ 1929 Hils 2/58 +17 traps ex8 fr Edinburgh Palace Cinema 1953 to store in Hils works, 4
Dorset Street, Glasgow, 1975 pt to store in Edinburgh Playhouse, 1985 pt to Edinburgh
Res of G. Lucas & L. Maguire, r post-1985 STOPS 4/ ex12 +traps, incl additions fr
Edinburgh Playhouse, to here 1991 & r1994 STOPS 4/49 ex +6 traps, r1995-99 STOPS
with parts fr Edinburgh Playhouse, Paisley Picture House & parts fr 4 ch organs 4/187 ex
+200pf + 51 traps + 17 traps pf, r2003-present 5/625 ex 125 + 95 traps (16 tonal
percussion units & 4 sets of effects)

**Greenock Ardgowan** (St. Andrew's 1967-92/Trinity/Trinity UF/UP) 31 Union Street, fr 2011 pt of
Greenock Lyle, blg retained
⤷ 1908 Ing 2/20 r1951-52 Wil 2/27 + 1pf in west gallery with Bin material, o1986 McDM,
disused 2002, console rem

**Greenock Ardgowan Picture House** (Salon/George Square UP cld 1882) George Square cld 1922
⤷ (c1920 organ

**Greenock Augustine** Belville Street cld 1929 (later Elim Foursquare Gospel Alliance) dem
⤷ (1904 Walc 1/

**Greenock B -** see Greenock George Square B

**Greenock C -** see Greenock East C, Greenock West URC and Greenock Nelson Street C

**Greenock Cartsdyke** (Cartsburn Augustine/Cartsburn) 14 Crescent Street blg cld 2003, ruined
(became Greenock East End, no blg)
⤷ (1874 Mir 1+pd/7 o1885 Mir, o1923 Mir
⤷ (Bro 2/ inst here 1933 o1950 Bro, o1959 Wil, r1960s Dan 2/20, extant 1985

**Greenock East** Regent Street/Antigua Street cld 1973 dem
- ⚓ (1889 Wad 2/ o1936 Mir

**Greenock East C** Bawhirley Road
- ⚓ (1900 Hard in previous blg in St. Lawrence Street (cld 1968) r1920 Watt

**Greenock Elim Pentecostal** (Greenbank/UF/UP cld 1955) Kelly Street/Newton Street
- ⚓ (1921 Watt 2/19 rem 1963 to Bellshill St. Andrew's by Watt

**Greenock Finnart** (UF/Madeira Street UP) Madeira Street cld 1978
- ⚓ (1883 Gern 2/18 moved within ch and divided 1934 & r HNB (K&B), rem to Netherlands

**Greenock Finnart St. Paul's** - see Greenock Lyle

**Greenock Gaelic** West Stewart Street/Westburn Street cld 1966
- ⚓ (1905 ConP rem 1967 to Edinburgh Leith St. Andrew's Place

**Greenock George Square B** cld (now dance studio, cong using Waterfront Cinema/St. Andrew's UF Cont.)
- ⚓ (1907 ConP

**Greenock George Square C** - see under Greenock West UR

**Greenock Greenbank** - see Greenock Elim Pentecostal

**Greenock Ladyburn** Pottery Street/Port Glasgow Road cld 1969
- ⚓ (organ in use 1899
- ⚓ (1920 Ing 2/15 o1947 R&D, o1964 R&D, rem post-1969 to Greenock Nelson Street C

**Greenock Lyle** (Finnart St. Paul's/St. Paul's) Newark Street/Bentinck Street
- ⚓ (1878 Har 2/7 in previous blg (St. Paul's)
- ⚓ (1894 Wil 3/25 +2pf o1909 Wil, o1923 Wil + 1ss, r1936 Wil 3/28 + 3pf, scr 2014

**Greenock M** (first West F blg) 4 Ardgowan Street
- ⚓ 1905 Kea 2/20 **A-listed**

**Greenock Martyrs & North** (North UF/F) Westburn Square cld 1983
- ⚓ (1902 Bis 2/18 r Bro, extant 1985

**Greenock Mearns Street C** dem c1985
- ⚓ (1866 ConP 2/15 fr Perth C 1899 & r Mir, r1920 Watt

**Greenock Mid Kirk** - see Greenock Wellpark Mid Kirk

**Greenock Middle UF** - see Greenock St. George's North

**Greenock Mount Kirk** (Mount Pleasant/UP) 95 Dempster Street
- ⚓ (1922 Watt 2/ using material fr earlier house organ rem c1989, case extant

**Greenock Mount Park** - see Greenock South Park

**Greenock Nelson Street C** cld 2005
- ⚓ (1865 ConP 2/18
- ⚓ 1920 Ing 2/15  o1947 R&D, o1964 R&D, fr Greenock Ladyburn 1970, o R&D

**Greenock North** (Greenock/Greenock West Kirk cld 1841, rest 1864) Nicolson Street blg moved 1928 to Esplanade - see Greenock Old West
- ⚓ (1874 Hill 2/12  o1900, moved to gallery 1908, rem 1928 with blg to Greenock Old West by Mir 1930

**Greenock Old West** (North 1928-1979) Esplanade (fr 2011 part of Greenock Lyle, blg retained)
- ⚓ (1874 Hill 2/12  o1900, moved to gallery 1908, to here 1928-30 by Mir with North Church blg, rem 1988 to Linlithgow St. Michael's RC by McDM

**Greenock Regal Cinema/ABC**
- ⚓ (1925 Jar 2/23  r1928 Jar, fr Glasgow Coliseum Cinerama/ABC 1931 Com & r 3/ , rem 1946 Watt, pt (Sw chest) to Paisley St. Mirin's RC Cathedral 1948 & r Watt

**Greenock Res of Cake**
- ⚓ (1914 W.J. Bird 2/8  rem to Helensburgh Cragdarroch House

**Greenock Res of Mr. Campbell**
- ⚓ (c1830-1835 John Watt 2/12  to here fr Glasgow Cathedral 1835 by John Watt with two other organs

**Greenock Res of John D. Gillies**
- ⚓ (1880 Har 2/12

**Greenock Res of R.W. Jamieson**
- ⚓ (1887 Har 2/  (est. only)

**Greenock Res of C. Lyle**
- ⚓ (1881 Wil 3/21

**Greenock Res of Mr. Poulter**
- ⚓ 1872 Hill 2/  (est. only)

**Greenock Res of Sir Michael R. Shaw Stewart** - see Ardgowan House (nr Inverkip)

**Greenock Res of James Watt**
- ⚓ (c1762 WaJ 1/

**Greenock St. Andrew's** (UF/F) Ardgowan Street/Margaret Street cld 1967 (cong to Trinity blg as "St. Andrew's" later called Ardgowan)
- ⚓ (1897 Vin 2/22  o1928 Mir

**Greenock St. Andrew's RC** Auchmead Road
- ⚓ 1966 R&D 2/20 ex4

**Greenock St. Bartholomew's E Chapel**  - see Gourock

**Greenock St. Columba's Gaelic** (Gaelic UF, St. Thomas UF/F 1857-1907, cong to Middle UF) West Blackhall Street/Grey Place/Patrick Street cld 1979
   ⚒ (1892 F&A 3/25 fr Glasgow Hutchesontown UF c1925 by Mir, rem post-1979 to the Netherlands, then c1992 to Helsinki Sibelius Academy

**Greenock St. George's North** (St. George's/St. George's UF/Middle UF/F) George Square cld 2006
   ⚒ (1897-99 Wil 2/22 o1922 W&L, r1947 Wil, damaged by fire, r1951 Wil 2/23 +6pf, o1967 Wil, rem, pt to Edm, pt to McDM

**Greenock St. John the Evangelist E** Union Street
   ⚒ (c1800 Don in previous building to here 1823 possibly fr Res of Houldsworth, rem to new blg 1878, rem 1879 by Mir
   ⚒ Mir 2/c28 fr Glasgow Res of John Robb to Glasgow St. Andrew's 1866, to here 1879 & r Mir 2/30 with 3 divisions, r1914 Mir 3/32 , o2007 Lib **A-listed**

**Greenock St. Laurence RC** 6 Kilmacolm Road
   ⚒ (pre-1850 organ (GG pd) r 3/9, extant 1920s in previous blg, dest WW2
   ⚒ (1941 Wil 2/22 rem c1990

**Greenock St. Luke's** - see Greenock Westburn

**Greenock St. Margaret's** Finch Road
   ⚒ 1902 Cou 1+pd/6 fr Greengairs UF to Greengairs 1931, to here 1966 Mac

**Greenock St. Mark's Greenbank** (St. Marks fr 1929/West UF/F) Ardgowan Street/Kelly Street cld 1987 dem
   ⚒ (1889 B&F 2/21 r1951 Bro 2/28

**Greenock St. Mary's RC** Patrick Street
   ⚒ (organ post-1822
   ⚒ (1864 ConP
   ⚒ (1853 G&D 3/47 r1856 G&D 4/55, r1957 4/57, fr Glasgow City Hall to Glasgow Dixon Hall & r 1905 Bin 3/35 (5ss by Bin), rem 1930s to Girvan Res & r Watt, to here 1949 & r Watt 2/ with casework fr Glasgow Res by Walc , o1966 Wal, r1976 McDM 2/23, rem 2005 McDM

**Greenock St. Ninian's** (Larkfield) Warwick Road
   ⚒ Watt 2/ to here pre-1963 R&D, disused

**Greenock St. Patrick's RC** 5 Orangefield Place
   ⚒ (c1960 Watt 2/ ex
   ⚒ 1923 A&S 2/13 fr Dumfries South and Townhead 1985 & r McDM 2/11 ex

**Greenock St. Paul's** - see Greenock Lyle

**Greenock Salon Picture House** - see Greenock Ardgowan Picture House

**Greenock Sir Michael Street** (UF/UP) cld 1949
   ⚒ (1901 Ing 2/22 rem 1949 to Bro workshop minus tubing, 1953 to Alexandria North (former ch) & r1955 Bro

**Greenock South** Ann Street cld 1965
⚒ (1878 F&A 2/17  o1902 F&A & moved to chamber

**Greenock South Park** (Mount Park/UF/F) Trafalgar Street cld 1982
⚒ (1914 B&H 2/14

**Greenock The Old Kirk** - see Greenock Westburn

**Greenock The Union Church** (Union Street/UF/UP) 3 Union Street cld 1992 dem
⚒ (1912 Bin 2/15  scr, 1ss to Kirn McDM

**Greenock Town Hall** Cathcart Square
⚒ (1862 F&A 3/36  r1865 F&A, o1883 F&A (pt replaced), rem pre-1966

**Greenock Trinity** - see Greenock Ardgowan

**Greenock Wellpark** (UF/F) 5 Lynedoch Street cld 1979 dest fire later
⚒ (1921 Watt 2/c20

**Greenock Wellpark Mid Kirk** (Mid Kirk) Cathcart Square
⚒ 1867 F&A 3/28  r1886 Mir 3/32, r1912 Mir, o1957 HNB 1ss changed, o2008 Lib

**Greenock Wellpark West** (Wellpark) Regent Street cld 1996 dem 1999
⚒ (organ fr London 1899 2/18
⚒ (1926 Hils 2/17  scr 1996

**Greenock West** - see Greenock Old West, North, St. Mark's Greenbank and Westburn

**Greenock West URC** (George Square C) George Square
⚒ 1861 ConP 2/17  r1880 Mir 2/21 (moved fr gallery to chancel ), o1887, r1897, r1911 N&B 2/21, o1926 HNB 2/22, Gothic case 1935, o1979 HNB

**Greenock Westburn** (St. Luke's/The Old Kirk/West Kirk) 5-9 Nelson Street
⚒ (1889 ConJ 2/25
⚒ 1912 Bin 2+1pf/31 +9 pf using most of the pipework fr old organ  o1960 BinT, r1974 R&D 2/31, o2000 For

**Gretna All Saints E**
⚒ c1890s Pos 2/5 no pd  fr Annan St. John the Evangelist E 1931 & r Thu, r2000

**Gretna Old**
⚒ 1910 Ing 2/9

**Gretna St. Andrew's** (UF)
⚒ 1890 F&A  to here after 1917

**Guardbridge** (UF/UP) Fife cld 1999
⚒ (organ  rem c1992

**Gullane Res of John Clare** - details under Edinburgh Res

**Gullane St. Adrian's E**
⚲ 1880s Wil 1/7 (no pd) to here 1952 fr Bristol Res

**Haddington Holy Trinity E** Church Street
⚲ (1841-42 HDa barrels added 1848, o1863 HDa, sold 1877
⚲ 1877 Har 2/17 +3pf +1ss 1892 Har, r1989 R&D after fire

**Haddington Res of Charles Davidson** (rem to East Saltoun 2015)
⚲ (1969 Wil 1/3 +5pf ex2 fr Kirkcaldy Torbain 2012 to here, and then to storage at Fenton Barns
⚲ (1965 Wil 1+pd/8 ex4 fr Musselburgh St. Ninian's 2012 to here and to storage at Fenton Barns

**Haddington Res of Walter H. Ferme**
⚲ (c1872 Holt 2/9 rem 1937 to Penicuik St. James the Less E

**Haddington** - see also Standingstone Farm

**Haddington St. Mary's** Sidegate
⚲ (1892 F&A 3/29 +1pf o1963 R&D 3/30, rem to storage c1972, parts dispersed later
⚲ (1972 Wal 2/16 ex4 rem 1990 to Winchburgh by R&D
⚲ 1990 Lam 2/24 **A-listed**

**83) The Lammermuir organ at St. Mary's, Haddington** Photograph by Peter Backhouse

**Haddington St. Mary's RC** Poldrate
⚲ (Bru/Mir 2/5 fr Lothian Res to here, rem 1992 to Thurso Res of Fr. John Allen, rem to Inverness Res
⚲ F&A to North Berwick Carlekemp School RC, rem 1978, to here 1992, o1998 R&D

**Haddington West** (St. John's UF/F) Court Street
⚲ 1930 Ing 2/14 **B-listed**

263

**Haddington West** (UF/UP) Court Street cld 1932
⚓ (1903 F&A 2/14 rem 1933 to Edinburgh St. Colm's

**Haddo House** Aberdeenshire
⚓ 1881 Wil 3/24 (Chapel) o1950 R&D, o1976 Man, o Edm **A-listed**
⚓ (1888 LTC 2/ chamber organ rem 1891
⚓ 1975 Man 1/3 (Theatre)

**Halkirk** Caithness
⚓ (c1868 Ren 1/6 fr Fingask Castle, Perthshire to here 1930s, vandalised 1970s & rem to Budge Bank House, Halkirk, rem to Maine, USA 1996, r c2010 Thomas R. Thomas 1/6, rem to Epsom, New Hampshire, Res of Jeremy Cooper

**Hamilton Auchingramont** Auchingramont Road/Union Street cld 1982
⚓ (1866 BBE 2/20 +4pf engine added 1902, r Bro 2/26, dest

**Hamilton Auchingramont North** (UF/UP) Auchingramont Road cld 1944 blg rem to Holytown
⚓ (1914 Hils 2/15 rem 1950 to Holytown

**Hamilton Avon Street** - see Hamilton St. Andrew's

**Hamilton Brandon** (UF/UP) Brandon Street cld 1967
⚓ (1902 Kir 2/12

**Hamilton Burnbank** Udston Road/High Blantyre Road cld 2013 (now Coptic Orthodox)
⚓ 1913 Sco 2/17 r1922 Hils, r1934 HNB 2/

**Hamilton Cadzow** Woodside Walk
⚓ 1889 F&A 2/17 r1927 Hils 2/19, r1984 McDM (2 ss changed), r2000 Lib 2/23 with reed unit

**Hamilton Gilmour and Whitehill** (Gilmour Memorial/Burnbank UF/UP) Purdie Street
⚓ 1912 Watt 2/11 fr Bothwell Wooddean 1946 Watt 2/11 +2pf, o c1956 Watt, o1981 McDM

**Hamilton North** (Saffronhall Associate Antiburgher) Windmill Road cld 2013 for sale
⚓ 1902 A&S 2/17

**Hamilton Old** Church Street/Leechlee Road
⚓ 1897 Ing 2/24 1926 case, r1950s Wil, r Hils, r1980 SmRo 2/26

**Hamilton Primitive M** Keith Street cld
⚓ (1916 B&H

**Hamilton St. Andrew's** (Avon Street/UF/UP) Avon Street cld 2013
⚓ 1906 B&H r Ing, o Wil

**Hamilton St. John's** (UF/F) Duke Street
⚓ (1900 Walc 2/18 r1908 Walc in chamber +ss, r1970s Sol 2/20, disused 1999 case extant

**Hamilton St. Mary's E** Auchingramont Road
⊼ (1842 Holland fr Duke of Hamilton to here G&D
⊼ (1868 ConP 2/13
⊼ 1889 F&A 2/19 o1999-2012 Mac **A-listed**

**Hamilton St. Mary's RC** Cadzow Street
⊼ (1852 organ
⊼ (1877 You 2/8 o1980 McDM, rem

**Hamilton South** (UF) Strathaven Road/Mill Road
⊼ 1957 Watt 2/ ex3 disused

**Hamilton Victoria Hall** (Town Hall)
⊼ (1871 ConP 3/31 o1920 Mir, rem 1949 to Blantyre St. Andrew's & r Hils

**Hamilton West** (UF/F) Burnbank Road
⊼ 1902 Hill 2/15 o1909 B&F **A-listed**

**Hamilton Whitehill** Abbotsford Road, Whitehill blg cld 2001
⊼ (c1820s-30s Mir 1/4 fr Res nr Irvine to Uddingston Church of the Nazarene 1959 Watt, to workshop 1961 Mac, 1965 to here Mac, rem 1966 to new blg, returned 1969 to Glasgow Berkeley Street, workshop of Mac

**Hardgate** - see Urr

**Harthill M** - in Yorkshire

**Hatton Castle** nr Turriff
⊼ 1773-91 chamber organ, moved within house 1783

**Hatton House** nr Ratho
⊼ (organ for sale 21iv1846

**Hatton of Fintray** - see Fintray

**Hawick Allars** (UF/UP) cld 1948
⊼ (1926 A&S 2/15 o1946 Ing, rem 1949 to Musselburgh Bridge Street & r Ing

**Hawick B** North Bridge Street
⊼ (1928 Cou 1/6 o1949 Ing, fr Hawick Orrock 1951, rem WiB, pt 1976 to Denholm

**Hawick C** Bourtree Place
⊼ 1925 A&S 2/17

**Hawick Old** (Buccleuch/Hawick) Buccleuch Road cld 1989
⊼ (1897 F&A 3/28 r1912 Ing 3/33, o1972 R&D, rem 1991 to Belfast Antrim Road B by Gol & r 2/34

**Hawick Orrock** (Orrock Place UF/UP) Orrock Place cld 1951
⊼ (1928 Cou 1/6 o1949 Ing, rem 1951 to Hawick B

**Hawick Res of George Wilson, Heronhill** (later school, then factory)
⤣ (1874 Gern 2/10 rem 1876 to Galashiels Ladhope by HDT

**Hawick Res of M. Webb, 52 Fraser Avenue**
⤣ (1830s SBr barrel organ 3ss rem post-1958 to Burnley, Res of W. Blakey, Lancs, rem post-1992 to Botany Bay Res of George Crutchley, Enfield, Middlesex, rem 1999 to Edinburgh Broughton St. Mary's Church Centre

**Hawick Res of Prof Dove Wilson**
⤣ (organ 1/8 (GG compass) rem 1903 to Aberdeen St. Andrew's Cathedral E

**Hawick St. Andrew's** (UF/F) cld 1959
⤣ (1904 A&S 2/ dest by fire 1922
⤣ (1924 A&S 2/15 rem 1960 to Edinburgh St. John the Evangelist RC, Portobello & r1961 R&D 2/15

**Hawick St. Cuthbert's E** Slitrig Crescent
⤣ (1852 HDa fr St. Cuthbert's E School to here 1858, rem 1875
⤣ 1875 F&A r1891 F&A 2/15, r1908 N&B 3/26, o c1925 Hils, o1952, r1984 WiB 2/17

**Hawick St. John's** cld 1959
⤣ (1880 ConP 2/20 r1912 Sco 3/25, organ sold to Edinburgh piano dealer 1960

**Hawick St. Margaret's** Wellington Street cld 1940
⤣ (c1896 Har 2/ (est. only)

**Hawick St. Margaret's & Wilton South** (Wilton South/Wilton UF/UP) Commercial Road cld 1987
⤣ (1893 B&F 3/26 r1910 Sco 2/ , fr Edinburgh Hope Park 1941 & r Ing 2/22, o c1980 WoP, scr 2001

**Hawick St. Mary & David RC** Buccleuch Street
⤣ c1840s HDa 1/ r here c1883 HDT, r1914 Law 2/13, o2007 Lam, o2012 KK **B-listed**

**Hawick Teviot** (St. George's West/St. George's UF/F) Free Church Lane
⤣ 1920 Hils 3/29 o1973 WoW, r1993 WoP 3/29

**Hawick Trinity** (East Bank UF/UP) Brougham Place
⤣ 1911 Bin 2/21 o1931 BFH, o c1951-54 R&D, console reversed 1959 R&D, o1974 WoW, o2009 For **A-listed**

**Hawick West Port** (UF/F) cld 1959
⤣ (1902 Watt 1/ r1912 Watt 2/11

**Hawick Wilton** Princes Street/Dickson Street
⤣ (1886 C&M 2/19
⤣ (1910 Sco 4/31 +3pf in west gallery, using material from old organ r1956 Wil 3/35 r1987 WiB 3/45 ex in new case, using older material

**Heads of Ayr (Butlin's)** Ayrshire
⤣ (1924 Verbeeck of London player organ rem c1970 & o Jack Weir (Law)

**Helensburgh** (St. Andrew's/West/Old & St. Andrew's/St. Andrew's/West UF/F) Colquhoun Square
  ⋏  (1894 Hill 3/24  damaged by fire
  ⋏  1925 HNB 3/  using material fr old organ, r1968 HNB 3/34, o1992 HNB

**Helensburgh Cairndhu, Res of John Ure, Lord Provost of Glasgow**
  ⋏  (1866 ConP  2/8  rem to Silloth St. Andrew's

**Helensburgh Cragdarroch House**
  ⋏  (c1914 W.J. Bird 2/8  fr Greenock Res of Cake,  rem 1969 to Glasgow Res of Gordon
     Frier 1969 & r Mac

**Helensburgh Old** East Clyde Street cld 1956
  ⋏  (1900 F&A 3/

**Helensburgh Park** (UF/F) Charlotte Street cld 2014
  ⋏  1900 IGD 2/22  r1917 Ing, o1922 Myers, o1936 HNB, o1952 Hils, r1963 Hils

**Helensburgh Res of Captain Proudfoot**
  ⋏  (post-1860 Bev

**Helensburgh Res of Dr. Andrew Baxter**
  ⋏  2013 Lam 2+pd/6

**Helensburgh St. Bride's** (West) John Street cld 1981
  ⋏  (1898 LTC 2/15  r1922 Hils 2/17 in gallery, r1966 Hils 2/24, rem 1985, scr

**Helensburgh St. Columba's** (UF/UP) - see Helensburgh The Tower

**Helensburgh St. Michael's & All Angels E** (Holy Trinity) William Street
  ⋏  1882 Gern 2/23  r1906 IngE 3/31, r1927 Hils 3/31, r1969 Hils 3/39, o WoP, r2001 Lib
     2/27

**Helensburgh School E**
  ⋏  (organ in use 1856-59

**Helensburgh The Tower** (St. Columba's/UF/UP cld 2011) 77-81 Sinclair Street
  ⋏  1878 Har 2/22  o1902 IngE +1ss, r1912 Lew 3/31, o1978/81 Mac, console to store 2014
     **B-listed**

**Helensburgh URC** (C/Tabernacle) 35 West Princes Street
  ⋏  (1867 ConP 2/11
  ⋏  1902 Hill 2/19  o1926 HNB **A-listed**

**Helensburgh West -** see entries under Helensburgh (St. Andrew's) and Helensburgh St. Bride's

**Heriot** Midlothian
  ⋏  c1890 "Scudamore" Har 1+ppd/3  fr Edinburgh Res of  Kunz to Res of W. E. Smith, rem
     to Edinburgh Water of Leith E Mission 1903 by HCF, rem 1976 & r later by Hugh Ross
     & friends at Edinburgh St. David of Scotland E, o1984, rem 1995 to Edinburgh
     Broughton St. Mary's Church Centre, rem to here 2005 & o Sta **B-listed**

**Hillside** nr Montrose
⚓ 1925 Ing  disused c2015

**Hoddom** nr Ecclefechan cld 1956 dest fire 1975
⚓ (1923 Com

**Holm** Orkney (now called East Mainland)
⚓ 1910 organ

**Holm Norwood Collection** Graemeshall House, Orkney
⚓ (Cle barrel organ 1ss & 2 traps, 3 barrels, auctioned 2007

**Holyrood** - see Foveran and Edinburgh

**Holytown**
⚓ 1914 Hils 2/15  fr Hamilton Auchingramont North 1950

**Holywood** Dumfriesshire
⚓ 1896 Wilk 1/  to here 1920, for sale 2009

**Hopeman** (UF/F) Moray
⚓ (organ fr London r Not 3/  rem 1960s by Norman Marr, case extant

**Hoswick Visitor Centre** Sandwick, Shetland
⚓ (organ 1/7  extant 2001

**Houston & Killellan** (Houston)
⚓ (1938 Ing  damaged by fire 1963
⚓ 1981 Chu 2/12 (no Sw)

**Howgate** (UF/UP) Midlothian
⚓ c1830s SBr 1/3  fr Res to Edinburgh Willis, Henry & Sons, 1951 to here Wil **B-listed**

**Howwood** Beith Road, Renfrewshire
⚓ 1904 N&B Norvic  r 1953 Watt & Vin 2/18 ex3, o1976 McDM

**Hoy Melsetter House**
⚓ (organ  dest 1940s

**Hoy Rackwick Res of Peter Maxwell Davies**
⚓ (1982 Man 1/4  rem 1997 to Sanday Res

**Humbie** East Lothian
⚓ c1850 Cro 1/5  to Edinburgh St. Andrew's E 1857,  to Scandinavian Lutheran, Leith 1868 & r HDT 1+pd/6, o1976 R&D, to here 1987 & r Dick 1/5 (no pd)

**Humbie Stobshiel House Res of Peter Ferguson-Smyth**
⚓ (1792 Hugh Russell  rem 1991 to Crichton Manse
⚓ (1987-89 Lam 1/5  rem 1991 to Crichton Manse by Lam
⚓ (18th C South German  fr Amsterdam, rem 1991 to Crichton Manse

**Huntly Cairnie Glass** (Huntly) Church Street
⚓ 1894 IngE 2/20  r1961 R&D 2/23

**Huntly** - see also Strathbogie Drumblade

**Huntly Christ Church E** Provost Street
- ⊥ (c1900 Walc 1/ rem 2012
- ⊥ c1860 Mir 1/4 fr Edinburgh Res to Kinneff 1910, rem 2010 to Cambusbarron Loo workshop, to here 2012 & o Loo **B-listed**

**Huntly C**
- ⊥ (organ extant 1865 r1890 Wad for Mr. Spence (enlarged)

**Huntly Masonic Hall** (Huntly F c1840/St. John's RC to 1834) Meadow Street
- ⊥ (1833 German organ to Aberdeen Res of James Reid 1834 by Wis, to here 1834 by Wis, rem later to Huntly St. Margaret's RC

**Huntly St. Margaret's RC** Chapel Street
- ⊥ (1833 German organ to Aberdeen Res of James Reid 1834 by Wis, to Huntly Masonic Hall (Huntly RC) by Wis, later to new blg here, o pre-1862 Mir
- ⊥ 1871 ConP 1/7 o1890 Wad, r1992 Edm 1/7 **B-listed**

**84) St. Margaret's RC Church, Huntly. a) the Conacher organ in the gallery
b) the altar with painting by Romero. Octagonal interior by William Robertson**

**Hurlford** (Hurlford Reid Memorial/UF/F) nr Kilmarnock
⅄   1875 F&A 2/17 + 2ss 1896 F&A, o1924 F&A, r1978 McDM 2/18, fr Hurlford Kirk 1996 McDM & r 2/18

**Hurlford Kirk** (Hurlford) cld 1995
⅄   (1875 F&A 2/17 +1ss 1896 F&A, o1924 F&A, r1978 McDM 2/18, rem to Hurlford (Reid Memorial) 1996 McDM

**85) The 1875 Forster & Andrews organ at Hurlford**

**Hutton & Fishwick** (Hutton) Berwickshire
⅄   Pos 1/8

**Inch** nr Stranraer
⅄   (1890 organ damaged by fire
⅄   (1909 2/7 r1980 John Wilson 2/8
⅄   1898 B&F 2/23 r1970 Hils 2/25, fr Ayr Darlington New 1985 & r John Wilson 2/26 with material fr Girvan North

**Inchbrayock** (Ferryden/Craig UF/F) - see Montrose South & Ferryden

**Inchinnan** Renfrewshire Old Greenock Road
⅄   1886 Bev 2/12 donated by Sir Archibald Campbell for first ch blg, 1908 to next blg (cld 1965) & r Ing, to present blg & r1968 R&D, r1975 R&D, o1994 R&D, o2006, disused

**Inchmahone** Lake of Menteith
⅄   (organist in 1548

**Inistrynich, Res of W. Campbell Muir** nr Dalmally
⅄   (1880 Wad 3/18 rem to Lochawe St. Conan's 1887 by Wad

**86) The Bevington organ at Inchinnan, now in its third building here**

**Innellan** (Matheson) Argyll
⚓ (Watt 2/12 to here 1933 fr monastery  r later, pt rem c2000

**Innellan Res**
⚓ (organ  for sale 1967

**Innellan West** (North UF/F) cld 1972
⚓ (1897 Bin 2/18  fr Gourock St. John's 1933, r1950s R&D, rem 1970s

**Innerleithen** Leithen Road
⚓ 1889 Bro 2/14  r1898 Bin 2/18, o1920 G&D, o1934 G&D  **B-listed**

**Innerleithen C** High Street (later bike shop)
⚓ (c1910 Ing 1/   +2ss 1912

**Innerleithen Craigside** (Law UF/Innerleithen UP) Pirn Road cld 1960
⚓ (organ inst c1935

**Innerwick** East Lothian
⚓ 1911 N&B 1/6 **B-listed**

**Insch** (West/Insch) Western Road, Aberdeenshire
⚓ 1907 Wad 2/15

**Inverallan** Grantown-on-Spey
⚓ 1920 Hils 2/16  r1981 Edm 2/17

**Inveraray**
⚜ c1855 HDa 1/6 fr Jedburgh Res 1967 **B-listed**

**87) The small Hamilton organ in Inveraray Parish Church in 1993**

**Inveraray All Saints E**
⚜ (1840 Hol 1/3

**Inveraray Castle**
⚜ (1757 Cum dest by fire 1877

**Inveravon** nr Ballindalloch, Speyside
⚜ 1876 Hill 1/5 inst Wel in gallery r1911 Law 1+pd/7, o2009 Walc **B-listed**

**Inverbervie** - see Bervie

**Inveresk** - see Musselburgh

**Invergordon** (UF/F)
⚜ (1914 N&B fr Portree St. Columba's E 1923
⚜ 1885 Har 2/20 r1933 Watt 2/22, o1965 Mac (1ss changed), pt fr Glasgow St. Stephen's 1976 & r Gol 2/24, disused

**Invergordon Castle Res of Sir John Gordon**
⚜ (chamber organ for sale 11viii1784

**Invergowrie** (Invergowrie St. Columba's/Invergowrie)
⚜ 1906 Wad 2/13 +3pf fr Carnoustie Erskine to here 1934 & r Bro, r1956 Wil 2/22, o1960 Wil, o1996 Lib, r2009 Lib 2/16

**Invergowrie All Souls E**
⚜ (1912 MilJ 2/15 +4pf 1ss added later, scr except case post-1990

**Invergowrie East** (Longforgan UF/F) cld 1945 (now hall)
⚜ 1906 organ

**Inverkeilor & Lunan** (Inverkeilor)
- ⚒ (Com 2/  ex  scr

**Inverkeithing St. John's** (UF/UP) Church Street cld 2006
- ⚒ 1903 Cou 1/6 no pd ("Premier")  latterly disused

**Inverkeithing St. Peter's** Church Street
- ⚒ 1912 Bro 2/10  fr Dunfermline Chalmers Street-Headwell 1943 by Ing, o1952 R&D, disused

**Inverkeithney** Banffshire cld 1992 (run by Trust)
- ⚒ 1914 Walc 1/

**Inverkip** (see also Ardgowan House)
- ⚒ 1909 Mir 2/10 **A-listed**

**Inverness Bishop's Mission House** Bank Street cld
- ⚒ ("Scudamore" 1+ppd/4  for sale 24i1870

**Inverness Central M** (music hall) Union Street  dest fire 1961 - see Inverness M
- ⚒ (1935 A&S 2/19 +1pf

**Inverness Crown** (UF/F) Kingsmills Road
- ⚒ (1879 F&A 3/  o1900 F&A, fr Taymouth Castle, nr Aberfeldy 1923 3/23, r1958 HNB 3/23 (moved to gallery), rem 1987, case survives

**Inverness Dalneigh** (St. Mary's Dalneigh) blg cld 1979
- ⚒ (organ 1/  fr Inverness St. Mary's Gaelic 1951

**Inverness East** (UF/F) Academy Street
- ⚒ (F&A  2/  to here 1948 & r R&D 2/19, o1986 R&D, rem

**Inverness Infirmary Chapel** Ness Walk
- ⚒ (1899 Pos 1/6

**Inverness M** Huntly Street
- ⚒ 1965 R&D 2/20 ex4  o c2005

**Inverness Ness Bank** (UF/UP) Ness Bank
- ⚒ 1903 Bin 2/17  r1980 R&D 2/17 (3ss  fr Inverness West) **C-listed**

**Inverness Old High** Church Street
- ⚒ (organ in 1539
- ⚒ 1892 Wil 2/18 +1pf  o1907 Wad, r1923 Hils 2/23, o1948 Hils, o1977 R&D, r2010 Nic 2/19

**Inverness Res**
- ⚒ (c1850 Ren barrel organ 4ss  sold by Phillips to Hugh Ross, Leithen Lodge

**Inverness Res of Fr. John Allen** St. Ninian's, Culduthell Road/Hill Park
- ⚒ Bru/Mir 2/5  fr local Res to Haddington St. Mary's RC, to Thurso Res 1992, to here
- ⚒ c1850 amateur 1/5  r1876 Wis, fr Boyndie House Chapel to Fraserburgh RC & o1879 Wad, o1931 Law, o1980 McDM, r1994 Austin Tobin, rem to here 2016

**Inverness Res of Miss Leith**
⚓ (1893 Wad

**Inverness Res of Mr. Luss**
⚓ (organ o1899 Wad

**Inverness St. Andrew's Cathedral E** Ardross Street
⚓ (1869 Hill 3/26 +1pf o1920 Wad (new pd), r1927 HNB 3/29, scr 2004, pt to Caithness

**Inverness St. Columba High** (High UF/F) Bank Street blg cld 2009
⚓ (1923 Ing 2/ damaged by fire 1943
⚓ 1928 Ing 2/13 +6pf fr Edinburgh Davidson 1946 & r1953 2/19

**Inverness St. John's the Evangelist E** Church Street/Southside Road
⚓ (c1772 organ fr France to first blg c1792, rem to second blg 1801, rem to third chapel 1839, sold 1840
⚓ 1840 Bru 2/14 r1889 Wad 2/13 +1pf, rem to fourth blg in Southside Road 1903 Wad & r 2/12 +2pf, o1992 Har 2/12 +2pf **B-listed**

**Inverness St. Mary's Gaelic** blg cld 1951
⚓ (organ 1/ rem 1951 to Inverness Dalneigh

**Inverness St. Mary's RC** Huntly Street
⚓ (1837 SBr 1/5 no pd
⚓ (1894 Bis
⚓ 1928 Law 2/13 fr Aberdeen Res of A.G.Wilson, King's Gate 1960s
⚓ 1981 Jhn 1+ppd/8 ex2

**Inverness St. Michael & All Angels E** Abban Street
⚓ 1913 Whi 2/12 o c1920s, o2000 MilP, r2009 Edm

**Inverness St. Stephen's** Old Edinburgh Road
⚓ 1902 Wad 2/13 o1987, r2001 Edm 2/12 +1pf (2ss changed)

**Inverness West** Huntly Street blg cld 2003
⚓ (1902 Law 2/16 +2pf r Law 2/20, r1935 R&D 2/31, r1979 Gol (3ss to Inverness Ness Bank), rem 1980-88

**Inverurie Immaculate Conception RC** North Street
⚓ (1855 Wis r ConP 1/15

**Inverurie St. Andrew's** (South/Auld Kirk) High Street
⚓ (organ in hall 1886-1900
⚓ 1898 ConP 2/18 r1933 Law 2/22, r1965 R&D 2/24 & resited, disused

**Inverurie St. Mary's E** High Street
⚓ (1900 Law 2/13 o1919 Wad, o1966 R&D

**Inverurie West** (UF/F) West High Street
⚓ 1935 Com/R&D 2/31 ex5 o1990s, blg reconstructed 2008, organ extant

**Irongray, Lochrutton & Terregles** (Irongray) Dumfriesshire
⚒ (1903 Cou  rem by 1970s

**Irvine Fullarton** Church Street
⚒ (1897 ConP 2/  o Watt, fr Irvine St. Paul's c1974 & r Gol, case rem 2015

**Irvine Old** (St. Inan's) Kirkgate
⚒ (1878 ConP 2/21  r1912 Ing 3/28, pipework extant 1980s

**Irvine Relief** (UF/UP/Relief) West Road blg cld 1977 (now Christian Centre)
⚒ 1921 Hils 2/16

**Irvine Relief Bourtreehill**
⚒ 1921 A&S 2/10  r1925 Ing 2/11, fr Girvan St. Andrew's 1977 & r McDM 2/17

**Irvine Res**
⚒ (c1820s-30 Mir 1/  rem to Uddingston Church of the Nazarene 1959 Mac

**Irvine St. Mary's RC** West Road
⚒ (organ 2/  rem 2007

**Irvine St. Paul's** (Wilson Fullarton/Fullarton UF/F) Waterside cld 1974
⚒ (1897 ConP 2/  o Watt, rem to Irvine Fullarton c1974 & r Gol

**Irvine Trinity** (UF/UP) Bridgegate cld 1963
⚒ (1915 Ing 2/21

**Isla** - see Airlie

**Jamestown** Dunbartonshire
⚒ (1887 ConP 3/24  r1933 HNB 2+1pf/19 after fire, disused, only case extant

**Jedburgh Old & Trinity** (Old) Newcastle Road
⚒ (1875 F&A 2/22  r1912 Sco 3/34, o1950s R&D, disused 1993

**Jedburgh Res**
⚒ (c1855 HDa 1/6  rem 1967 to Glenaray & Inveraray (see Inveraray)

**Jedburgh St. John the Evangelist E** Pleasance
⚒ (1844 HDa 2/
⚒ (1882 BBE 2/8+1pf  rem 1990s

**Jedburgh The Immaculate Conception (St. Mary's) RC** Old Bongate
⚒ 1978 WiB 1/6  with Har pipework & older Gedact

**Jedburgh Trinity** (Boston Blackfriars/UF/Blackfriars UF) High Street cld 2007
⚒ (organ  pt fr Glasgow Macleod to here 1948 & r Wil, o1950s  Wil, most rem late 1960s by SmRo

**Johnstone East** (UF/UP) cld 1965
⚒ (1907 N&B 2/16  +1pf

**Johnstone High** (Johnstone) Ludovic Square
⚒ (1901 Lew 2/17  o1910 Lew, console moved 1938, scr 1989

**Johnstone Public Hall** (Working Men's Institute)
⊥ (1868 ConP 3/27 rem pre-1925 to Edinburgh Res of Rev. R.C. Strang by Watt

**Johnstone St. Andrew's Trinity** (Trinity/UF/F) blg cld 1978
⊥ (1903 Bro  scr

**Johnstone St. John the Evangelist E** Floors Street
⊥ 1883 Hew 2/11+1pf o1964 Hils, damaged

**Johnstone St. Margaret's RC** Graham Street
⊥ (Gray 3/  fr Huddersfield St. Paul's 1879 by Mir 3/ , r1894 HCF 2/16, r Watt 2/13  with new console, r Wil 2/13

**Johnstone St. Paul's** (West/UF/UP) blg cld 1989
⊥ (1899 organ  in previous blg
⊥ (1905 Hill 2/
⊥ (1923 Hils 2/22  r1976 Gol 2/36, pt to Burntisland Erskine UF 1989 by Loo

**Kames**  Argyll - see Kilfillan and Kyles

**Keig** (North/Keig) nr Alford cld 1999
⊥ 1912 Wad 1/6  r1964 R&D, available 2002

**Keith Holy Trinity E** Seafield Avenue
⊥ (Tytler 1/4  for sale 1811. inst here1815 fr Peterhead Res of James Argo by John Morison, o1842 Bru, o1866
⊥ 1887 Wad 1+pd/8 +1pf (gifted by Mr. & Mrs. George Kynoch), o1909 Wad 1+pd/10

**Keith North** (UF/F) Church Road/Mid Street
⊥ (1902 N&B 2/14  rem by 2003

**Keith St. Rufus** (Keith) Church Road
⊥ 1892 IngE 2/20  r c1930 Ing, r1987 Nic 2/23

**Keith St. Thomas RC** Chapel Street
⊥ (1835 Wis
⊥ (c1870 ConP  r1916 Law 2/9, disused 2001

**Keithhall** Aberdeenshire
⊥ 1907 Law 1/c8

**Keithock**  nr Brechin
⊥ (organ  o1820 WSm

**Kells** New Galloway
⊥ 1890 Har 2/9  organ chamber built 1910, o1949 Har, o1996

**Kells St. Peter's RC**
⊥ 1959 Wal

**Kelso Abbey**
⊥ (ref to organ in 1517

**Kelso North** cld 1940
A   (1892 Hard 2/14  rem 1948 to Glasgow Carntyne Old

**Kelso North & Ednam** (St. John's Edenside/St. John's/UF/North UF/F) 42 Bowmont Street
A   1935 R&D 2/29 ex4  o1949 R&D, o1990 R&D

**Kelso Old** Abbey Row
A   (1904 IHJ 3/  disused fr 1964, pt to Kelso St. Andrew's E, pipes rem

**Kelso St. Andrew's E** Abbey Court
A   (organ extant c1790-1820 in previous blg
A   (1871 F&A 2/14  r1903 F&A, r1964 2/32 by rector with pts fr Kelso Old and Edinburgh
Portobello St. Philip's Joppa, rem 1994, some pipes to Westruther by Sta

**Kelso St. Mary's RC** Bowmont Street
A   (1873 organ  presented by Lady Douglas

**Kelso Trinity North** (Trinity UF/UP) East Bowmont Street, cld 1980 (hall then Res of Dean
Warwick, for sale again 2014)
A   1900 Wal 2/17  extant 2007, keyboards removed by 2014

**Kelton** nr Castle Douglas (pt of Bengairn Parishes)
A   1895 F&A 2/16  o1986 McDM

**Kemnay** (East) Fraser Place, Aberdeenshire
A   1907 Law 2/10  r1964 R&D 2/10, o1982 R&D

**Kemnay House Res of Mrs. Milton**
A   Cle barrel organ

**Kemnay St. Anne's E** Kendal Road
A   1816 Ell 2+ppd/11 fr Castle Fraser 1938 & r Law 2/11, o1978 R&D, o1996 Har **A-listed**

**Kemnay** - see also Castle Fraser

**Kenmore & Lawers** (Kenmore) nr Aberfeldy
A   pre-1924 Gle 1/5 rem to gallery 1924, o McDM

**Kenmore** - see also Taymouth Castle

**Kenmure Castle** New Galloway dest by fire 1950
A   (Gray  fr elsewhere to here 1834

**Kentallen St. Moluag's Chapel E** cld 2017
A   (c1830s SBr 1/7  for sale fr Res 1861, to Edinburgh Res of Dr. McArthur, Beachcroft,
Trinity by 1883, to Kirkcaldy West End C 1898 & r King 1+pd/8, rem to Dundee Morison
C 1920 & r MilJ, rem 1928 to Aberfeldy C, rem 1988 to Leithen Lodge, Peeblesshire and
inst Hugh Ross, rem to Largs St. Columba's 1995 by SHOT volunteers, to here 2006, rem
2017 to Portnacroish Holy Cross E by SHOT

**Kettle** Fife
A   1902 F&A 2/  fr Uddingston C c1979

**Kilbarchan C** cld
⊥   (1904 SmRi 2/12  o c1926 Watt, rem 1957 to Paisley St. Columba's Foxbar

**Kilbarchan** (East/UF/UP)
⊥   1898 F&A 3/15  fr Gourock Castle Levan, Res of  C.M. Mann 1914 by F&A 3/15, o1960
     B&H, r1975 McDM 3/15 (2ss changed, fr Glasgow Bluevale & Whitevale)

**Kilbarchan Glentyan House Chapel, Res of Hunters**
⊥   (organ  rem

**Kilbarchan West** (Kilbarchan) cld 2015
⊥   1904 Hill 3/38  o1936, o1954 HNB, o1968 & 1ss changed, o1982 HNB, o1985 (1ss
     changed), o1990 HNB, o2011 Har, redundant **A-listed**

**Kilbirnie Auld** (Barony/Kilbirnie) Dalry Road
⊥   1911 Ing 2/13  o1982 McDM, o1990s McDM

**Kilbirnie St. Columba's** (East UF/F) Glasgow Street
⊥   1903 ConP 2/c12  o1970s Wal, o1997 McDM, disused

**Kilbirnie West** (UF/F) cld 1964 (now ch hall)
⊥   1899 ConP

**Kilbowie** - see Clydebank

**Kilbrandon** (Seil)
⊥   (c1960 Cou 1/5  o1993, rem 2012 to Bearsden Cross (temp) by Matthew Hynes

**Kilchrenan** Argyll
⊥   1925 organ

**Kilconquhar** (Kinneuchar) Fife (now pt of East Neuk Trinity)
⊥   1900 Pos 1/7  disused fr 1990s

**Kilcreggan Res of James McCoard, Greenhill**
⊥   (1926 Wil 2/11  rem 1945 to Edinburgh Kirk Memorial C by Ing

**Kilcreggan** - see also Craigrownie

**Kilfinan** West Cowal
⊥   (c1900s Pos 1/6  o1970s R&D, fr West Linton 1996 and later to here by Murray
     Campbell & David Kellas, redundant 2015

**Killearn**
⊥   c1930 Ing 2/12  disused

**Killin** (St. Fillan's)
⊥   (c1900s N&B 1/
⊥   1925 Ing 2/8 +1pf   fr Killin Breadalbane 1932, r1993 Edm 2/9, o2010 McDM

**Killin Breadalbane** (Killin UF/F) cld 1932
⊥   (1925 Ing 2/8 +1pf  rem to Killin 1932

**Kilmacolm** - see also Bridge of Weir Quarrier's

**Kilmacolm Hydro** dem
  ⚓ (1879 organ

**Kilmacolm Old** High Street/Port Glasgow Road
  ⚓ (1903 B&F r1938 Wil 2/24, disused 1984
  ⚓ 1995 Col 2/26 using some pipework from old organ

**Kilmacolm Res**
  ⚓ (1886 B&F 2/11 rem to Glasgow Notre Dame College 1930 by Watt

**Kilmacolm St. Columba** (Kilmacolm St. James'/UF/UP) Duchal Road
  ⚓ 1896 B&F 2/11 rem to new blg 1903 by B&F, r1927 HNB 2/ , o1978 HNB 2/28

**Kilmacolm St. Columba** (UF/F) cld 1957
  ⚓ (1906 Lew 2/14 fr London exhibition 1906, rem to Comrie 1959

**Kilmadock** (Kilmadock East/Kilmadock) Main Street, Doune blg cld
  ⚓ (1896 IngE 2/15 o1951 Bell
  ⚓ 1908 Ing 2/16 fr Kilmadock West c1959 by Neil Dorward (undertaker) & r R&D, o1981 WoW, for sale 2008

**Kilmadock West** (Doune UF/Kilmadock F/Doune F) Balkerach Street, Doune cld 1958
  ⚓ (1908 Ing 2/16 rem to Kilmadock c1959 by Neil Dorward (undertaker) & r R&D

**Kilmadock** - see also Doune

**Kilmarnock** - see also Coodham House

**Kilmarnock Corn Exchange** London Road/9 Green Street (fr 1902 Palace Theatre)
  ⚓ (1871 F&A 3/31 (4 depts) r1887 F&A 3/33, rem c1906 to Coatbridge St. Augustine's RC by Watt

**Kilmarnock Dean Castle** off Dean Road
  ⚓ c1500s English regal 1/1
  ⚓ c1600s Italian positive 1/2

**Kilmarnock Glencairn** (UF/Holm UP) West Shaw Street cld 1967
  ⚓ (1920 Law 2/19

**Kilmarnock Grange** (UF/F) Woodstock Street cld 2009
  ⚓ 1902 F&A 2/20 o1912 F&A, o1956 Watt (case rebuilt), for sale 2011

**Kilmarnock Henderson** - see Kilmarnock Kay Park

**Kilmarnock Holy Trinity E** Dundonald Road/2 Portland Road
  ⚓ (1857 Hill 2/ rem 1876
  ⚓ 1876 Hill 3/22 r1939 HNB 2/21

279

**Kilmarnock Howard St. Andrew's** (Howard/Portland Road/UP) 5 Portland Road blg cld 1971/2008 (now ch hall)
   ⅄  (1896 F&A 2/18 rem by 1971

**Kilmarnock Kay Park** (Henderson/UF/F) London Road
   ⅄  1907 N&B r1928 HNB 3/26, o1987 HNB

**Kilmarnock King Street** (UF/UP) King Street cld 1965
   ⅄  (1894 Walc 2+1pf/23+7pf 7ss added 1899, rem 1966, pt to Kilmarnock South

**Kilmarnock Martyrs** (UF/F) Mill Lane cld 1958
   ⅄  (organ fr house nr Dreghorn to here 1934 & r Watt 2/8 ex3, r1953 Watt, rem 1958 to Kilmarnock South by R&D

**Kilmarnock New Laigh Kirk** (Laigh West High/Laigh/Kilmarnock)) John Dickie Street
   ⅄  (1878 Har 2/21 r1888 Mir, r Watt 2/22
   ⅄  (1921 Law 3/35 (4 divisions) disused 1985, case (1878) extant

**Kilmarnock Old High** (High) Soulis Street/Church Street cld 2012
   ⅄  (1869 Hun 2/14 r1924 Watt 2/17, disused 1992, case extant

**Kilmarnock Princes Street** (UF/UP) cld 1968
   ⅄  (1905 B&F 2/15

**Kilmarnock Riccarton** Old Street
   ⅄  (1884 Har 2/18 r1911 Ing 2/18, r1936 HNB, rem 1999

**Kilmarnock St. Andrew's & St. Marnock's** (St. Marnock's) St. Marnock Street
   ⅄  1872 F&A 2/16 r1886 F&A 2/18, r1908 Watt 3/24, 2ss changed 1997 Wil 3/24

**Kilmarnock St. Andrew's Glencairn** (St. Andrew's) St. Andrews Street cld 2002
   ⅄  (1899 Mir 2/17 scr post-2006

**Kilmarnock St. Andrew's North** (St. Andrew's UF/F) Fowlds Street cld 1984
   ⅄  (1896 ConJ 2/20

**Kilmarnock St. John's** (UF/F) John Finnie Street blg cld 1937 (cong to Morven Avenue, then 1955 to Wardneuk Street, Onthank)
   ⅄  (1914 organ rem 1928
   ⅄  (1928 organ

**Kilmarnock St. Joseph's RC** Portland Street/Hill Street
   ⅄  (1847 small but powerful organ
   ⅄  1903 Har 2/17 o1971 Wal, 1986 McDM

**Kilmarnock St. Kentigern's** Dunbar Drive
   ⅄  (1972 Wal ex console rem 2001, pipes remain

**Kilmarnock South** (St. Ninian's Bellfield) Whatriggs Road
   ⅄  organ fr house nr Dreghorn 1934 to Kilmarnock Martyrs & r1953 Watt 2/8 ex3, to here 1958 R&D, r1966 R&D 3/ , material added by minister fr Kilmarnock King Street, o Mac 2/29

**Kilmarnock West High** (High UF/F) Portland Street cld 2000
  ⅄  (1878 Hard  dest by fire
  ⅄  (1887 You 2/18  rem 1897 to Dumfries Maxwelltown West by N&B
  ⅄  (1897 Jar 3/30  o1919 Jar, o1930 Jar, r1969 ConP 2/30, rem apart from case

**Kilmarnock Winton Place C**
  ⅄  (c1864 ConP  in gallery
  ⅄  1884 ConJ 3/26  o1904 Wad, o c1910 SmRi **A-listed**

**Kilmaronock Gartocharn** (Kilmaronock) - see also Gartocharn
  ⅄  B&T 2/9  r Law, to here fr Res c1962 & r Hils 2/10, r late 1980s 2/10 (ss changed)

**Kilmartin St. Columba's E** Poltalloch, Argyll
  ⅄  1855/1862 G&D 2/13  o1927 HNB **A-listed**

**Kilmartin** - see also Poltalloch House

**Kilmaurs Maxwell UF Cont.** Crosshouse Road
  ⅄  W. Young  inst 1927 Watt 1+pd/5

**Kilmaurs St. Maur's Glencairn** (St. Maur's) Kilmarnock Road
  ⅄  1913 Ing 2/13  o1984 WoP, disused 1997

**Kilmaurs Glencairn** (Smyton UF/Kilmaurs UP) Fenwick Road cld 1963 (now workshop)
  ⅄  (1950 Watt 2/  ex 3

**Kilmorack** nr Beauly
  ⅄  (1903 Law 2/10

**Kilmore & Oban** - see Oban

**Kilmun (St. Munns)** nr Dunoon
  ⅄  (1899 Bro 1/1  for sale fr N&B 1910
  ⅄  1909 N&B 2/16  o2007 MilP **A-listed**

**Kilpatrick** - see Old Kilpatrick

**Kilpatrick Res of I. Mallock, Norwood**
  ⅄  1882 Wil 2/10

**Kilrenny** Fife
  ⅄  (1926 organ presented by Woman's Guild

**Kilspindie & Rait** Perthshire
  ⅄  MilJ 1/6  fr Errol South post-1938

**Kilsyth Anderson** (UF/UP) Kingston Road
  ⅄  (1900 Pos 1/  rem c1970 to Res of Tom Logue, Glasgow
  ⅄  (Ing  fr cinema to Neilston South by Watt, rem by Watt, 1965 to here by C&C

**Kilsyth Burns** (High UF/Kilsyth F) cld 1975, dem 2002
  ⅄  (1901 SmRi 2/13

**Kilsyth Burns & Old** (Old) Backbrae Street
⋏    1930-32 ConP 2/20  o1980 Mac, o2014 Mac

**Kiltarlity** (East) nr Beauly
⋏    1906 Walc 1/5  o1987 McDM 1/5

**Kilwinning Erskine** (UF/UP) Garden Square Lane cld 2005 (now FIEC)
⋏    (1875 Hill 3/15  to here from Auchincruive House 1922 & r,  rem 1995, 2ss to Paisley
       Sandyford

**Kilwinning Mansefield** (UF/F) Howgate blg cld 1999 (now childcare centre)
⋏    1902 SmRi 2/15  intact 2002

**Kilwinning Old** (Abbey/Kilwinning) Main Street
⋏    1897 F&A 3/28  o1960 HNB  **A-listed**

**88) The 1897 Forster & Andrews at Kilwinning Old Church.** Photograph by Andrew Hayden

282

**Kincardine** Fife - see Tulliallan

**Kincardine O'Neil** North Deeside Road cld 2012
⋏   (c1900s Pos  o c1968 HNB, rem 1998 to Glengairn by Marshall Sykes

**Kincardine O'Neil Christ Church E** Pitmurchie Road
⋏   (1866 organ  rem 1873
⋏   1850s organ  to here 1998

**Kinghorn** (St. Leonard's)
⋏   (1903 MilJ 2/9 +2pf (in Laird's loft)
⋏   1982 WiB 3/c40 ex8 (in rear gallery)  Sw pipes fr old organ

**Kinghorn Rosslands** (UF/UP) cld 1961 (later ch hall)
⋏   1907 Cou 1/6

**Kingsbarns**
⋏   1883 F&A 2/11  fr Cambo House 1953 by R&D, o1980s R&D 1ss changed **A-listed**

**Kingskettle** - see Kettle

**Kingussie St. Andrew's** King Street cld 1959 sold 2002
⋏   (1936 Com 2/13  o1959 R&D, rem 2000 to Athlestaneford by Gol

**Kingussie** (St. Columba's)
⋏   (1915 Vin  dest by fire 1924
⋏   1926 E&B 2/21  o1951 Bell, o1994 R&D 1ss changed, o2016 Walc **B-listed**

**Kingussie St. Columba's E** Spey Street cld c2000
⋏   (1951 Bell

**Kinloch Castle** Rhum
⋏   1887 Imhof & Mukle Orchestrion (paper rolls) 4ss  to here c1900

**Kinlochleven**
⋏   (Bro 2/7 using  pipes fr Bute Res and Sanquhar, to here 1931 by David Hume, pt rem 1995 McDM, pt scr

**Kinlochleven St. Paul's E**
⋏   (c1870s Mir/Ewa 2/7  fr Glasgow Res by Ren, to here 1951, rem 1993 to RC School in Brentwood, Essex by McDM, then to Kirkintilloch St. Flannan's RC 1994 McDM

**Kinloss Abbey**
⋏   (organ  rem 1482
⋏   (1500s organ  rem pre-1540 to Forres

**Kinloss & Findhorn** (Kinloss)
⋏   1879 Har  r1904 Wad, o1988 Edm 1/7

**Kinloss Seapark House Res of J & A Dunbar**
⋏   (organ  o1899 Wad

**Kinneff** Kincardine cld 2010
⚓ (c1860 Mir 1/4 fr Edinburgh Res to here 1910, rem to Cambusbarron workshop 2010 Loo, to Huntly Christ Church E 2013 & o Loo **B-listed**

**Kinnoull** - see Perth

**Kinross** (West/Kinross) Station Road
⚓ (1911 N&B 2/17 o1926 HNB, o1980 McDM, scr 1993

**Kinross East** (West UF/Erskine UF/West UP) High Street cld 1979
⚓ (1895 HCF 2/15 o1926 HNB, rem 1982 to Rosyth

**Kinross St. Paul's E** The Muirs, Kinross
⚓ (1893 B&F 2/9 r1962 Sol 2/15 ex2, rem post-1967

**Kintore** The Square, Aberdeenshire
⚓ 1927 War 2/12 r1979 Loo, o2011 Loo

**Kintore UF** cld 1929
⚓ (1910 Law 1+pd/7 rem 1929 to Culsalmond & Rayne

**Kippen**
⚓ 1928 HNB 2/10 adjusted 1930 HNB, o1979 HNB, o1988 HNB 2/10 **B-listed**

**Kirkcaldy Abbotshall** Abbotshall Road
⚓ (1872 Holt 2/12 o1883 Rbt
⚓ 1899 Bin 2/22 o1956 Bin, o1974 R&D, o2001 R&D **A-listed**

**Kirkcaldy Bennochy** (St. John's) 3 Elgin Street
⚓ (c1938 Ing
⚓ 1909 N&B 2/12 +4pf fr Kirkcaldy St. Peter's E to here 1978 & r 2/17

**Kirkcaldy Beveridge Memorial Hall** (Adam Smith Memorial Hall) St. Brycedale Avenue
⚓ (1901 N&B 4/42 +1pf r Sco +1ss, rem to storage 1948 Ing, scr 1957 Wil after fire

**Kirkcaldy Dunnikier** - see Kirkcaldy Our Lady RC

**Kirkcaldy Gallatown** (UF/F) cld 1977
⚓ (1950s Com 2/11 ex rem 1977 to Ferintosh by SmRo

**Kirkcaldy Linktown** (Bethelfield/UF/UP) Nicol Street
⚓ 1930 Ing 2/17 console moved 1970s, disused 2009

**Kirkcaldy Loughborough Road** (UF/UP) cld 1969
⚓ (1904 Ing 2/11 +1pf r1954 Ing 2/12, r1959 R&D 2/12

**Kirkcaldy MGM Cinema** (ABC/Regal/Opera House/Kings Theatre) 25 High Street
⚓ (1925 Jar 2/19 + traps +1ss later, rem 1935 without traps to Wishaw Thornlie

**Kirkcaldy Old** Kirk Wynd cld 2010 (now Trust)
⚓ 1885 Gern 2/21 o1904 Gern, r1911 Wel, r1951 R&D 2/23 new console, r1964 Jar 2/21, console moved 1968 Hils, o1987 Edm 2/23, o2010 Edm **B-listed**

**Kirkcaldy Our Lady of Perpetual Succour & St. Marie's RC** (St. Mary's RC/Dunnikier/UF/F cld 1972) Victoria Road/Dunniker Road
⊥ 1931 Hils 2/17 r1975 Loo, disused

**Kirkcaldy Pathhead** (East/Pathhead) Harriet Street
⊥ (1913 Ing 2/ o c1924, r R&D, dest fire 1953
⊥ 1921 ConP 2/15 to here 1958 fr Kirkcaldy Pathhead West by R&D

**Kirkcaldy Pathhead West** (UF/F) St. Clair Street cld 1958
⊥ (1921 ConP 2/15 rem 1958 to Kirkcaldy Pathhead by R&D

**Kirkcaldy Raith** (Abbotshall UF/F) 32 High Street cld 1964 (became play centre)
⊥ (1903 Walc 2/7 fr Kirkcaldy Union UF 1928 by Sco
⊥ 1928 A&S 2/10 to here 1937 fr Galashiels Trinity & r 1938

**Kirkcaldy Res of John Blyth, Forth Villa** Loughborough Road, Sinclairtown
⊥ (1887 Har 2/8 rem 1892 to Broxburn SS John Cantius & Nicholas by Har (1ss to Silsden M, West Yorkshire)
⊥ (1893 Har 3/27 r1926 Har 3/28, rem 1936 to Crail

**Kirkcaldy Res**
⊥ (1889 ConP 2/11 r1924 Hils, fr Glasgow Cardonald 1955 to Loanhead East, rem c1980 to Fa'side Castle by Tom Craig, then to store here, rem to Crail Res

**Kirkcaldy Res of T.K. Lockhart** East Fergus Place
⊥ (1926 Wur 2/53 +17 traps ex10 fr Baltimore Embasssy Theatre to Edinburgh Odeon 1930, to here 1964, rem 1979 to East Kilbride Civic Centre, console to St. Alban's Organ Museum

**Kirkcaldy St. Andrew's** (Victoria Road UF/UP) Victoria Road cld 2010 (later Pentecostal)
⊥ 1925 HNB 3/28 r1970s

**Kirkcaldy St. Bryce** (St. Brycedale/UF/F) St. Brycedale Avenue
⊥ (1893 B&F 3/25 +10pf r1903 B&F 3/34, r1924 Hils 3/34, scr 1988 (console on display)

**Kirkcaldy St. Columba's E** Linktown cld 1946 (RC 1946-1979)
⊥ (1909 organ

**Kirkcaldy St. Michael's Mission E** Kidd Street, Pathhead cld 1966
⊥ (1812 Gothic barrel organ converted to finger 1815, fr Kirkcaldy St. Peter's E 1909

**Kirkcaldy St. Peter's E** Townsend Place
⊥ (1812 Gothic barrel organ inst Routledge, Glasgow, converted to finger 1815, to here fr old church in Coal Wynd 1844, rem 1909 to St. Michael's E
⊥ (1909 N&B 2/12 +4pf rem 1978 to Kirkcaldy Bennochy
⊥ 1967 GDB 2/8 fr St. Alban's Abbey (Festival) to Oxford New College, to Nottingham St. Mary's, to Nottingham St. Ann's 1974 & r Wal, o1979 GDB, to new blg here 1980 & r Gol

**Kirkcaldy Sinclairtown** - see Kirkcaldy Viewforth

**Kirkcaldy Torbain** Lindores Drive
⊥ (1968 Wil 1+pd/7 +5pf ex2 rem 2012 by Charles Davidson, to store at Fenton Barns

**Kirkcaldy Town Hall** - see Kirkcaldy Beveridge Memorial Hall

**Kirkcaldy Union UF** (UP) cld 1928
  ⊥  (1903 Walc 2/7  rem 1928 to Kirkcaldy Raith by Sco

**Kirkcaldy Viewforth** (Sinclairtown) Viewforth Street/Terrace
  ⊥  (1955 Hils 2/16  case extant

**Kirkcaldy West End C** High Street
  ⊥  (c1830s SBr 1/7  for sale fr Res 1861, to Edinburgh Res of Dr. McArthur, Beachcroft, Trinity by 1883, to here 1898 & r King 1+pd/8, rem 1920 to Dundee Morison C  MilJ
  ⊥  (1920 Bro 2/14

**Kirkcaldy Whyte's Causeway B** Whytescauseway
  ⊥  1927 B&H 2/13

**Kirkconnel**
  ⊥  (1923 Watt 2/17  fr Dumfries Townhead 1953 & r Watt 2/17, rem, case survives

**Kirkcowan** Wigtown
  ⊥  c1850 Mir 1/4  r1880 Mir, fr Glasgow Res of Mir, Woodend Drive to Galloway House, nr Garlieston 1959 & o Mac, to here 1966 by Robert Meek, o1975 J. Wilson

**Kirkcudbright** (St. Cuthbert's)
  ⊥  1886 Har 2/27  r1953 Wilk 3/30, o1999 R&D

**Kirkcudbright Greyfriars E** St. Cuthbert Street
  ⊥  (c1964 Sol 1/5 ex1  rem by 2005

**Kirkcudbright St. Andrew's & St. Cuthbert's RC**
  ⊥  1901 Bis 1/7

**Kirkcudbright St. Mary's** (UF) cld 1983
  ⊥  (1915 N&B 2/

**Kirkintilloch Hillhead** Newdyke Road
  ⊥  (1964 R&D 1+pd/10 ex2  rem 1994 to Yetholm

**Kirkintilloch Holy Family and St. Ninian RC** Union Street
  ⊥  (1947 HNB 3/  dest by fire 1980s
  ⊥  1886 Wil 2/16  fr Ardgowan St. Michael & All Angels Chapel nr Inverkip to Port Glasgow St. Mary the Virgin E 1921 & r Mir, o1930 Wil, o1973 R&D, to here 1985 & r McDM 2/15

**Kirkintilloch Park** (UF/UP) Kerr Street cld 1991
  ⊥  (1903 SmRi 2/13

**Kirkintilloch** - see also Gartshore House

**Kirkintilloch St. David's & St. Andrew's** (St. David's) Ledgate/Kilsyth Road blg cld 1969 (cong to St. Columba's, Waterside Road, new blg)
  ⊥  (1911 N&B 2/  o1925 HNB, rem 1969, some pipes to Kirkintilloch St. David's Memorial Park

**Kirkintilloch St. David's Memorial Park** (St. David's Memorial/UF/F) Alexandra Street
⊥    1899 Ann 2/16  fr former blg to here & r1926 Ing 2/21, o1960 R&D, r1969 R&D 2/21,
     r1975 Gol 2/31 +1pf, r1979 Gol 2/31 +1pf, r1989 Gol 2/33

**Kirkintilloch St. Flannan's RC** Hillhead Road
⊥    (c1870s Mir/Ewa 2/7  fr Glasgow Res 1951 to Kinlochleven St. Paul's E by Ren, rem
     1993 to RC School in Brentwood, Essex by McDM, to here 1994 McDM, rem 1998 to
     Res of Joseph Cullen, Crick, Northamptonshire, c2000 to Otley nr. Leeds & o G&G **A-
     listed**

89) The Anonymous Scottish-made organ, possibly the work of Mirrlees or Will Ewart,
when it was located at St.Paul's Episcopal Church, Kinlochleven. More recently it was
located at Kirkintilloch St. Flannan's

**Kirkintilloch St. Mary's** (Kirkintilloch) Cowgate
⊥    1915 N&B 3/27  o1929 HNB, r 1976 Gol (1ss changed), o1998 Lig, o2016 Lig

**Kirkliston** (Old) nr Edinburgh
⅄  1925 Ing 2/11 rem to gallery 1960 R&D, o1984 R&D

**Kirkmabreck** nr Creetown
⅄  1912 Ing 2/12 disused

**Kirkmichael** Banffshire
⅄  (1910 Wad 2/9 dest fire 1950

**Kirkmuirhill** Lanarkshire
⅄  1956 organ disused 1996

**Kirknewton House Res of J. Maconochie** (Meadowbank House) dem 1950s
⅄  (1881 Har fr Melrose Res of Maconochies 1893 by Har

**Kirkoswald** (St. Oswald's) Ayrshire
⅄  (1902 N&B 2/11 r c1935 HNB +ss, damaged, rem 2010, case extant

**Kirkpatrick Irongray** - see Irongray, Lochrutton & Terregles

**Kirkton of.....** filed under following name

**Kirkwall East** (Paterson/UF/UP) School Place blg cld 2000
⅄  (1921 Ing 2/18 o1950s, o1970s, o1988 R&D, rem 2002 to Papa Stronsay Golgotha
Monastery to storage

**Kirkwall East** (King Street UF/F) cld 1968, used as hall, reopened as Kirkwall East 2000
⅄  (1937 Yal 2/13 rem c1980
⅄  IngE 2/8 fr All Saints RC, Oxted, Surrey 2002

**Kirkwall High School Hostel**
⅄  WoP 1/1 fr Cambridge

**Kirkwall Our Lady & St Joseph RC** Junction Road
⅄  Hol 1/6

**Kirkwall St. Magnus Cathedral** Broad Street
⅄  (organ extant 1544
⅄  1926 Wil 3/34 r1971 Wil 3/42, o1993 Wil, o2001, 2007 & 2017 Wil
⅄  (c1810s Cle 1/4 (temp) rem 1971 to Orphir

**Kirkwall St. Olaf's E** Dundas Crescent
⅄  1881 Hol 1+pd/5 o1980s R&D, o c1990 Edm

**Kirn & Sandbank** (Kirn/Kirn St. Andrew's) Marine Parade, Argyll
⅄  1923 Ing 2/14 o1992 McDM +1ss fr Greenock The Union

**Kirn St. Margaret's** (UF/UP) Hunter Street cld 1970
⅄  (1898 Lew rem, pt to Kirn

**Kirriemuir Old** (Barony) High Street/Bank Street
⅄  (1876 ConP 2/ r1923 (enlarged), rem 1988, pipe facade survives

**Kirriemuir St. Andrew's** (Livingstone/South UF/F) Glamis Road
⅄   (1913 MilJ 1+pd/7 (2/11 pf)  r1995 SmRo 2/11, rem 2006

**Kirriemuir St. Anthony's RC**
⅄   1983 Edm 1/3

**Kirriemuir St. Mary's E**
⅄   (1853 Edinburgh-made organ in former blg
⅄   1906 HCF 2/13  o1938 **A-listed**

90) The Comper-designed St. Mary's Episcopal Church, Kirriemuir with the 1906 C.&F.
Hamilton organ in swallow's nest position. The case was said to be a copy of a 16th century
original

**Kirriemuir St. Ninian's** (First UF/West UF/UP) cld 1972
⅄   (1905 MilJ 2/16

**Kirtle-Eaglesfield**
⅄   (1890 Pos 1/   rem 2011 to Middlebie by Sav

**Knockando**
⅄   (1906 Law 2/13  dest by fire 1991

**Kyles** West Cowal
⅄   (1932 Hay 1+pd/5  to Dundee St. Margaret's Barnhill 1932 & r Wat, to Edinburgh
     Richmond Craigmillar 1974 by Douglas Galbraith 1+pd/5, rem to Strathkinness 1977, to
     here 1998, rem towards Glasgow

**Ladhope** - see Galashiels

**Ladybank** (St. Mary's/UF/F/Collessie F) Fife
⊥    1900 Vin o1931 Wel, r1959 Com 2/13, r R&D

**Ladykirk** Berwickshire cld 2016
⊥    (18th C chamber organ rem 1970s
⊥    1963 Wil 1+pd/8 ex3 fr Grangemouth Kirk of the Holy Rood 1991 & r Julian Bonia, o2014 Bonia

**Laggan** Badenoch
⊥    1901 Pos 1/6 o1985 R&D

**Lainshaw House** - see Stewarton Lainshaw House

**Lamlash** Arran
⊥    1934 HNB 2/12

**Lamlash Res**
⊥    1993 Lam 2/10

**Lanark Christ Church E** Hope Street
⊥    (1726 organ r1781, r Bru, fr Douglas Support to Coatbridge St. John the Evangelist E & r1844 Bru and Baker, pt to here 1867 by Mir, pt rem c1916 K&B
⊥    1923 Watt 2/8 using some material fr old organ o1984 McDM, r1990 R&D 2/10

**Lanark C** West Port
⊥    c1900 organ extant

**Lanark Greyfriars** (Cairns/Bloomgate/UF/UP) Bloomgate
⊥    (1901 Pos 1/ sold
⊥    1931 Ing 2/17 o1996 R&D, disused 2015

**Lanark St. Kentigern's** (UF/F) Hyndford Road cld 1993
⊥    (1901 Pos 1/

**Lanark St. Mary's RC** (Vincentian) St. Vincent Place
⊥    (1859 G&D 1/ rem 1861
⊥    (c1900 ConP
⊥    1912 Mag 2/ in new blg r1959 ConP 2/23 with new console and action, o1987 McDM

**Lanark St. Nicholas'** (Old/St. Nicholas) Bloomgate
⊥    1892 F&A 3/31 o1899 F&A, o1930 HNB, r1974 SmRo 3/32, r1995 Wal 2/30 following blg archaeology **B-listed**

**Langbank** (West/UF/UP)
⊥    1903 LTC 2/13 o1979 HNB

**Langholm** (Old)
⊥    1893 Wil 3/19 o1921 Lew, r1970-80s Sol 3/19, 1ss changed 2001 Wil **B-listed**

**Langshaw House** - see Stewarton Lainshaw

**91) The 1912 Magahy organ, rebuilt by Conacher, in St. Mary's RC Church, Lanark.**
Photograph by John Riley

**92) The 1892 Forster & Andrews organ in St. Nicholas Parish Church, Lanark.**
Photograph by John Riley

**Langton & Lammermuir** - see Gavinton

**Lanton Coachhouse Res** nr Jedburgh
⊥  1970 Marshall Sykes 2/26 ex3  r WiB

**Larbert East** (UF/F) Main Street/Kirk Avenue (see also Stenhouse & Carron)
⊥  1902 A&S 2/14  o c1973 Wal, o c1975, o1984 McDM, o1995 Lig, o2000 McDM, r2016
Lib

**Larbert Old** Denny Road
⊥  1887 Wilk 2/  r1912 Ing 3/33, o c1980 L&B/Nic, o1985 Mac & HNB 3/34 **B-listed**

**93) Left: The organ at Larbert Old Church, as rebuilt by Ingram. Right: Part of the original
Wilkinson facade, now concealed inside the instrument**

**Larbert St. Thomas E**
⊥  1907 Sco

**Larbert West** (UF/UP) Main Street
⊥  1903 N&B 2/13 +1pf  1ss added later, o1965 R&D (console moved), o c2000s Loo **B-
listed**

**Largo** (Largo & Newburn/Largo)) Upper Largo, Fife
⊥  (1895 Pos 1/8  rem c1950s
⊥  1981 Loo 2/25 using Bin pipes fr Dunfermline St. Margaret's and other material

**Largo St. David's** (UF/UP) Lower Largo cld 2017
⊥  1920 1/  o1934 Wel

**Largs Clark Memorial** (John Clark UF/UP) Bath Street
⊥  1892 Wil 2/20  r1927 Wil 2/22 + 2 couplers, Sw pd converted 1947, o1976 Mac **B-listed**

**Largs House** Twynholm, Kirkcudbright
  ⊥    Lew 2/8  fr Largs Res by HNB

**Largs Res**
  ⊥    (Lew 2/8  rem to Largs House, Twynholm by HNB

**Largs St. Columba's** Gallowgate Street
  ⊥    1892 Wil 2/24  o1951 Wil, o1980s Mac **A-listed**
  ⊥    (c1830s SBr 1/7  for sale fr Res 1861, to Edinburgh Res of Dr. McArthur, Beachcroft,
        Trinity by 1883, to Kirkcaldy C 1898 & r King 1+pd/8, 1920 to Dundee Morison C, 1928
        to Aberfeldy C, 1988 to Leithen Lodge, to chapel here 1995, rem 2006 to Kentallen St.
        Moluag's E

**Largs St. Columba's E** Aubrey Crescent
  ⊥    1892 Har 2/12  new case 1930, r1947 Har 2/12, o1999 Har **B-listed**

**Largs St. John's** (UF/F) Bath Place
  ⊥    1891 Wal 2/11  r1950 Wil 2/15 + 2pf, r1995 Lib 2/15

**Larkhall Chalmers** (UF/F) blg cld 1961
  ⊥    (c1870 Ren 1/c7  to here fr Res & r with pd by Ing, rem to Glenboig 1962 by Mac

**Larkhall Chalmers** (Chalmers Strutherhill)
  ⊥    1915 Vin 2/21 + 2 pf added later  o1944 Mir, fr Cambuslang West 1961 & r BinT, disused

**Larkhall St. Machan's** (Larkhall)
  ⊥    (1902 B&F  case extant

**Larkhall Trinity** (UF/UP)
  ⊥    1902 N&B 2/20  o1916 N&B, o1975 HNB 2/20, o2006 **A-listed**

**Lasswade** (Lasswade Strathesk/UF/UP)
  ⊥    organ 2/  inst 1980s

**Lasswade Old** (Lasswade) blg cld 1950
  ⊥    (1897 MilJ 2/19 +2pf  rem post-1950 to Dundee St. James' & r Rot

**Lasswade St. Leonard's E** Dobbie's Road
  ⊥    c1860 Cro 2/10 no pd (Hill pipes)  rem fr Edinburgh Res of John Croall, 21 Broughton
        Street, r c1880 HDT 2/10, to Edinburgh Marshall Street Baptist 1916 & r HCF +pd 2/11,
        rem to here 1945 by Sco, r1962 Wil 2/14, r1983 R&D 2/14

**Lauder**
  ⊥    1903 Law 2/9  r1912 Law 2/12, fr Aberdeen John Knox's (Mounthooly) to Cowdenbeath
        Cairns 1975 & r R&D, rem 1999 to here & r2003 2/12 by Sta

**Laurencekirk**
  ⊥    (1896 Wad 2/14  r Law
  ⊥    c1970 Wal 2/10 ex

**Laurencekirk St. Laurence's E**
  ⊥    (1878 Har  r1889 Wad 2/11
  ⊥    1909 Wad 2/11  o1916 Wad

**Laurieston** - see Falkirk Laurieston and Balmaghie, Kirkcudbrightshire

**Lecropt** Bridge of Allan
- ⌁ 1905 B&H 2/7 case presented by Stirling of Keir o1938 G&D, disused at different times fr 1988 **B-listed**

**Leithen Lodge** (Res of David Lumsden of Cushnie and Hugh Ross) nr Innerleithen
- ⌁ (1850s Ren 1/8 to Fortrose & r1914 Cat 1/10, rem 1986 to storage in Scourie Res of Mrs. Careen Ross, rem to here 1987 Hugh Ross 1/8, case and pt rem 1995 to storage at Edinburgh Broughton St. Mary's and Stow, pt lost, pt 2006 to Lam
- ⌁ (c1830s SBr 1/7 for sale fr Res 1861, to Res of Dr. McArthur, Beachcroft, Trinity, Edinburgh by 1883, to Kirkcaldy West End C 1898 & r King 1+pd/8, rem 1920 to Dundee Morison C & r MilJ, rem 1928 to Aberfeldy C, to here 1988 Hugh Ross, rem 1995 to Larg's St. Columba's by SHOT volunteers
- ⌁ (1884 Rich 2/19 fr Strathbrock to here 1989, scr 1995, pt to Sta
- ⌁ (1888 Fai 2/9 fr Res to St. Andrew's E, Newcraighall 1904 by Ing, o1950s, to Edinburgh Res of Hugh Ross 1982, rem to here 1989, scr, pt to Sta
- ⌁ (1892 Wil 3/34 fr Birkenhead St. Mark's, Claughton by Hugh Ross 1991, rem 1994 to Rijnsaterswoude Res of Henk Kooiker, rem to Leiden Hooglandse Kerk & r2014-2017 Wil 3/34
- ⌁ (1850s Ren barrel organ 4ss fr Inverness Res, sold at Phillips 1993 to Hugh Ross, to here, sold 1994 to National Museum of Scotland, stored in Depository, Leith, Edinburgh (rem 2015 to Granton)
- ⌁ (1902 Watt 2/11 fr Bishopton Rossland 1993 to here, rem 1995 to storage in Broughton St. Mary's, Bellevue Crescent, rem 1996 to Lutten "De Opgang" Kerk, the Netherlands & r de Feenstra 2/12

**94) The Renton finger and barrel organs in the Music Room at Leithen Lodge in 1993**

**Leitholm** Berwickshire
- ⌁ 1882 Bev 1+pd/7 o1937 Har, fr Coldstream Rodger Memorial 1951

**Lennoxtown** - see Campsie

**Lenzie Old** Garngaber Avenue/Kirkintilloch Road
⚓ 1874 ConP 2/17  r1931 HNB 2/21, o1966 Mac

**Lenzie St. Cyprian E** Beech Road
⚓ (1874 Holt 1/   r1892 Mir 2/ , o1931

**Lenzie Union** (UF/UP) Moncrieff Avenue/Kirkintilloch Road
⚓ (1887 Mir 2/17  r1921 Hils 2/21, dest fire 1923
⚓ 1925 ConP 3/29  r1971 Wal, r1981 Gol, r1991 Gol

**Lerwick & Bressay** (St. Columba's) Greenfield Place
⚓ (1872 Bry 1+pd/8
⚓ 1895 Wad 2/15 incorporating Bry as Gt  r1900 Law 2/17, o1964 R&D, r2009 Nob, r2011 Edm 2/17

**Lerwick B** Clairmont Place blg cld 2010
⚓ (c1880 Bry 1+pd/7  fr Lerwick M, o1978 R&D, for sale 2010, pts rem

**Lerwick C** Clairmont Place
⚓ (1907  Law 2/12

**Lerwick Library** (St. Ringan's UF 1958-96, St. Olaf's & St. Ringan's cld 1955/St. Ringan's/UF/UP) Lower Hillhead
⚓ (1888 Har 2/7  o1895 Wad

**Lerwick M** (Adam Clarke Memorial) Hillhead
⚓ (c1880 Bry 1+pd/7  rem to Lerwick B
⚓ 1897 Har 2/9  rem 1898 Wad to chamber, o1895 Wad, o1950 R&D, fr Lerwick St. Olaf's c1960, extant 2001

**Lerwick St. Magnus E** Greenfield Place
⚓ (1864 Hol  o1895 Wad rem to chamber, r1900 Law 2/15, rem pre-1975

**Lerwick St. Olaf's Hall** (St. Olaf's UF cld 1958/St. Olaf's/UF/F cld 1931) Annsbrae Place (now occupied by businesses)
⚓ (1897 Har 2/9  rem 1898 Wad to chamber, o1950 R&D, rem c1960 to Lerwick M

**Leslie & Premnay** Aberdeenshire - see Premnay

**Leslie Christ's Kirk on the Green** nr Glenrothes, Fife (transported 1991 to Glenrothes)
⚓ (1911 Sco 2/  o1920 F&A, o1968 R&D

**Leslie St. Mary Mother of God RC** Fife (Logan Martin/Logan UF/F cld 1956)
⚓ 1905 Watt

**Leslie Trinity** Fife (West & Prinlaws/West/UF/UP)
⚓ 1903 Har 2/7

**Lesmahagow Abbeygreen** (UF/F)
⚓ 1902 Watt 2/  o c1957 Hils

**Lesmahagow Old**
⚓ 1889 B&F 3/25  o1985 McDM, r2002 Wil 3/25

**Letterfourie House Res of G. Gordon** nr Buckie
- ⚲ (c1800 Anon 1/5 used at Buckie St. Peter's RC (temp), rem 1965 to Cults Res of I. & C. Davidson

**Leuchars St. Athernase**
- ⚲ c1890s Wad r here 1918 MilJ 2/17, o2004 Lib **B-listed**

**Leven** (Scoonie)
- ⚲ 1884 Gern 2/17 rem to new blg 1904 Gern, disused 1960s, o1992 R&D, used again **A-listed**

**95) The Gern organ in Scoonie Kirk, now Leven Parish Church**

**Leven Linnwood Hall Res of Charles Augustus Carlow**
- ⚲ (1909 N&B 2/
- ⚲ (1933 Hils 2/19 +6 traps o1943 Hils, rem 1946 Hils

**Leven St. Andrew's** (Forman/UF/F) cld 2001
- ⚲ 1912 Ing r1958 BinT 2/24 ex, org excluded fr sale 2005

**Leven St. Margaret's E**
- ⚲ (HDT 2/7 fr Edinburgh Granton House 1907 HCF 2/7, rem c1970
- ⚲ (1879 ConP 3/9 fr Glasgow Res of Thomas Berry to Glasgow St. Bride's E 1916 by J. Blossom, to here 1972 by SmRo, rem c1992 Loo

**Leven St. Peter's RC** (St. John's/UF/UP cld 1975)
- ⚲ 1907 Wad 2/14 o1921 Wad

**Lhanbryde** (St. Andrew's)
- ⚲ (1881 Wil fr Edinburgh Res of Miss Stewart, Learmonth Terrace to Elgin, Maryhill House, Res of A.M. Gregor by HCF 1904 & r 2/11, rem to Elgin B, to here 1979 & r Edm (1ss changed), rem 2005 to store MilP, to Shalfleet St. Michael's, Isle of Wight 2009 & r Andrew Cooper

**Liddesdale** - see Newcastleton

**Liff** - see also Fowlis, Muirhead of Liff and Balruddery

**Liff Poorhouse**
⋏  (barrel organ purchased 1866 for psychiatric wards

**Lilliesleaf** Roxburgh
⋏  (1978 WiB 1/8  rem
⋏  1985 Lam 1+pd/7  fr Dunfermline Abbey 1986, to Altrincham St. Vincent's RC (temp), rem 1986 to Edinburgh Stockbridge, rem to store in Edinburgh St. Stephen's Centre 1994, to here 1998 & r Sta

**Limekilns**
⋏  c1970s Wal 2/  ex  extant 2017

**Linlithgow Craigmailen** (UF/Trinity UF/West UP) cld 1954
⋏  (1877 organ  rem 1924
⋏  (1922 Gle  rem 1960 to Falkirk Camelon & r 2/9 Hils

**Linlithgow Palace**
⋏  (organis to here 1504 & 1512 by Carwour and Branwood
⋏  (1513 Gilyem of France

**Linlithgow Res of Philip Sawyer and Anne McAllister, 10 Whitten Lane**
⋏  (1985 Lam 2+ppd/2  fr Edinburgh Res of Anne McAllister, Portobello, to here 1988, rem 2002 to Stonehouse Res of David Hamilton

**Linlithgow St. Michael's**
⋏  (pre-1546 organis
⋏  (1878 Har 2/28  r1894-96 IngE 3/31 in larger blg, r1912 Ing 3/40, + 3ss later by Ing, r1960 R&D 3/40, r1979 Gol 3/57, rem 2000, console to Edinburgh Duke Street URC, Leith
⋏  1912 Wil 2/20  o1958 Har, o1973 Har,  fr Harrogate Queen Ethelburga's College 1998 by WoP & r here 2001 Cop 2/25

**Linlithgow St. Michael's RC** Blackness Road
⋏  (1894 organ 3/  rem pre-1950
⋏  1874 Hill 2/12  o1900, moved within Greenock North 1908, to new blg 1928-30 Mir, fr Greenock Old West 1988 & r McDM 2/12, o1990s Loo **A-listed**

**Linlithgow St. Ninian's Craigmailen** Falkirk Road (St. Ninian's/High UF/F)
⋏  1902 A&S 2/22  r1997, disused

**Linton House Chapel -** see Cluny South

**Linnwood Hall -** see Leven

**Linwood**
⋏  1957 Com 2/19 ex3

**Linwood St. Conval's RC**
⋏  1967 C&C 2/20 ex

**Little Dunkeld -** see Dunkeld Cathedral

**Livingston St. Columba's Craigshill** blg cld 2010
⊥   (1969 Wal 2/18 ex  rem to store

**Loanhead** (West) The Loan
⊥   1905 F&A 2/23  fr Edinburgh Bristo 1967 R&D, o1993 R&D

**Loanhead East** (UF/South UF/F) Polton Road cld 1978
⊥   (1889 ConP 2/11  o1924 Watt, fr Glasgow Cardonald 1955 by Watt, rem c1980 to Fa'side Castle, Wallyford

**Loanhead Res of Tom Craig**
⊥   (early 19$^{th}$ century English organ 1/3  fr Argyll  rem to Edinburgh Res of Tom Craig

**Lochaline -** see Morvern

**Lochawe St. Conan's**
⊥   (1880 Wad 3/18  fr Inistrynich Res of W. Campbell Muir & r1887/90 Wad 3/19, derived case facades survive only

**96)  The photograph shows the remnants of  Walter Campbell's casework designed for the Wadsworth organ in the private chapel at St. Conan's, Lochawe.**
Photograph by Kerr Jamieson

298

**Lochcraig** Fife cld, dem
⚘ (1903 Law 1+pd/5 extant 1997

**Lochgelly St. Andrew's** Bank Street cld 2006
⚘ (1901 Wad 2/10 moved in ch 1915-17 & 1ss changed Wad, rem 2007 to Burntisland St.
Serf's E & r Edm

**Lochgelly St. Serf's** (Macainsh/UF/F)
⚘ (1908 Watt 1/8 no pd extant 1950s, rem by 2008

**Lochgelly** - see also Benarty

**Lochgilphead** Argyll Street/Oban Road
⚘ 1913 Cou 1/6

**Lochgilphead Christ Church E** Bishopton
⚘ (1851 organ in rectory
⚘ 1876 Hill 2/8 to chamber 1888 & r, o1990 Edm **A-listed**

**Lochgilphead** - see also Kilmartin and Poltalloch

**Lochinch Castle** nr Stranraer
⚘ pre-1883 LTC 2/6

**Lochmaben** (St. Magdalene's)
⚘ 1903 Walc 2/13 o1994 Har **A-listed**

**Lochryan** cld 1985
⚘ (1960s Sol 1/5 ex1 rem 1986 to Portpatrick by John Wilson

**Lochside** - see Ayr St. Columba's Lochside

**Lochwinnoch Collegiate Church**
⚘ (ref to organs in 1504

**Lochwinnoch** (St. John's)
⚘ 1885 F&A 2/ r1958 HNB 2/21 with new action **B-listed**

**Lochwinnoch** location unknown
⚘ (Hill 2/20 rem c1939 to Arrochar Ardmay House Hotel

**Lochwinnoch West** (UF/F) cld 1947
⚘ (1926 Watt 2/12

**Lockerbie Dryfesdale** (Dryfesdale & Trinity/Dryfesdale) Townhead Street
⚘ 1905 F&A 2/18 r Pen 2/18 all unencl, disused, r2001 1ss changed, 2ss rem 2012 to Fort
William Duncansburgh Macintosh by McDM

**Lockerbie Holy Trinity RC** (Trinity/UF/UP cld 1973) Arthur's Place
⚘ 1915 Ing 2/13 console moved 1973

**Lockerbie St. Cuthbert's** (UF/F) Bridge Street cld 1986 (later craft centre)
⚘ 1907 Sco 2/13

**Logie** nr Cupar cld 1972
⚓ 1910 J.G. Gibb 2/11

**Logie** nr Stirling
⚓ (1901 Ing fr house to here per Gibb of Glasgow pre-1950, r Loo with other pts
⚓ 1997 Edm 2/19 using the older material

**Logie Pert** nr Montrose cld 1982
⚓ (1867 Holt 2/11 +4pf fr Edinburgh St. Michael's & All Saints E 1893 & r HCF 2/11
+4pf, rem 2001 to Millport Cathedral of the Holy Spirit E & r2004 WoH

**97) The 1867 Holt organ when located at Logie Pert, some years after the church closed: an unusual adaptation of a church gallery**

**Longforgan**
⚓ 1923 Com 2/10 (mechanical) r1989 Lib

**Longridge** West Lothian cld 2000
⚓ (c1870 Ewa 1/7 o1900, fr Polkemmet House 1960s R&D, o1994 McDM, damaged by heat, rem by 2005 to Bearsden New Kilpatrick & o Matthew Hynes

**Longriggend** (UF/F) cld 1973
⚓ (c1890 Kir 1/6 rem 1975 to Cumbernauld Condorrat by Mac

**Longside St. John the Evangelist E** Aberdeenshire
⚓ (1727 Bris for sale 1872
⚓ (1872 Hill 2/12 r1960 Sol ex4

**Lonmay St. Columba's E** cld 1957 (house fr 1990s)
⚓ (1869 HDT/Holt 2/11 no pd o1889 Wad, rem c1960 by Sol

**Loretto School** - see Musselburgh

300

**Lossiemouth St. Gerardine's High** (Drainie St. Gerardines 1918-60/Drainie)
Prospect Terrace
- (1901 Walc 1/
- (Walc fr Dick at Leeds to here & r1985 Edm 2/7 +2pf, rem 1999 David Shepherd for Keith Bance

**Lossiemouth St. James'** (UF/UP) James Street blg cld 1966
- (1909 Walc 2/7 rem 1968 to Portlethen by Norman Marr

**Lossiemouth St. James'** (Lossiemouth High/UF/Drainie F cld 1960) Prospect Terrace
- (1908 N&B 2/9 dest fire
- 1934 BFH 2/12 o1981 Edm

**Loudon -** see Newmilns

**Luce Valley -** see Old Luce

**Lugar** Ayrshire
- 1867 G&D 1/5

**Macduff** (Doune/Macduff) Church Street
- (organ presented by Earl of Fife, inst 1806 MWo, rem 1816, inst Banff Our Lady of Mount Carmel RC 1820
- 1903 Law 2/19 r1911 Wad 2/19, o1951, o1962 R&D, o1977 **B-listed**

**Macduff Arts Centre** (Macduff Gardner Memorial/UF/F) Duff Street cld 1989
- 1912 Wad 2/18 o R&D

**Manderston House Res of Lord Palmer** nr Duns
- 1907 Aeo 2/20 + mechanism for paper rolls and chimes, inst by Dav, + harp 1908, o1991 William & Derek Hutcheson **A-listed**

**Manor** nr Peebles
- (1965 Sol 1/3
- 1889 ConP 2/7 fr Pencaitland 2003 & o Lig **A-listed**

**Marchmont House** (Res of Burge/Sue Ryder Home/Res of McEwen/Hume-Campbell) nr Greenlaw
- 1919 HNB (Hill) 3/28 +1pf o1974 R&D, o1986 R&D, o2017-18 For **A-listed**

**Markinch** (St. Drostan's/Markinch)
- 1914 A&S 2/15 +1 coupler 1934, o1955

**Markinch St. Mark's** (Brunton/UF/Markinch F) cld 1969
- (1948 Hils 1+pd/6

**Marlee House** (Res of Captain Kenneth Lumsden/A.J. Meacher) nr Blairgowrie
- 1914 Har 2/16 disused **B-listed**

**Marnoch** Cairnhill, nr Aberchirder cld 1991
- 1914 Wad 1+pd/7 o1917 Wad, r R&D, extant 2012

**Maryburgh -** see Ferintosh

**Maryculter Trinity** (Maryculter)
ᴧ 1883 Wad 1+pd/8 o1901 Wad, o1920 Wad, o1937 Law, o1978 R&D **A-listed**

**Marydale Our Lady & St. Bean RC** nr Cannich
ᴧ Mir to here 1868 fr old chapel at Glassburn

**Mauchline** (Old)
ᴧ (organ to here 1882 by James Andrew (amateur)
ᴧ (1912 Sco 2/22 r1958 Watt, rem 1980
ᴧ 1888 Wil 2/14 r1934 Wil 2/22, o1968, fr Glasgow Strathbungo 1980 & r Wil 2/22

**Mauchline Castle** (Res of Gavin Hamilton)
ᴧ (large organ rem to Mauchline Temperance Hall 1871 & inst by Hector Alexander

**Mauchline Temperance Hall**
ᴧ (large organ fr Mauchline Castle 1871, inst by Hector Alexander

**Mauldslie Castle** nr Carluke
ᴧ (organ rem by 1935

**Maxwelton House Chapel** nr Moniaive (for Maxwelltown see Dumfries)
ᴧ c1845 John Blacklock 1+pd/3 to here 1969 by Har, o Har **A-listed**

**Maybole Cargill-Kincraig** (Cargill/Cargill UF/F) cld 1978
ᴧ (1925 B&H scr 1978

**Maybole Kincraig** (UF/UP) cld 1949
ᴧ (small organ extant 1947

**Maybole Old** Cassillis Road blg cld 2005
ᴧ (1891 F&A 2/19 o1979 HNB, o1986 Har 2/19, o2003 Har, rem 2007 to Holland by de Feenstra, inst in Forchheim St. Johannes Baptista, Germany 2011 & o de Feenstra

**98) The Maybole organ by Forster & Andrews in its new home at Forchheim**

302

**Maybole St. Oswald's E** Cargill Road
⊥   1892 Kir 2/5  o1956 Jar, o1991 McDM

**Maybole West** Coral Glen cld 2003
⊥   (1920 Hils 1/9  rem 2005 by L. Sikkema to Holland

**Meadowbank House** - see Kirknewton

**Mearns** Newton Mearns
⊥   (c1904 N&B 1+pd/7
⊥   ( organ 1+pd/8  inst 1932 HNB using N&B & G&D material fr Glasgow Dixon Hall
⊥   1983 R&D 2/23 ex  case fr old organ

**Mearns** nr Glasgow - see also Newton Mearns

**Mearns Coastal** (St. Cyrus) Kincardine
⊥   1902 Ing 2/9

**Megginch Castle Res of Captain Humphrey Drummond & Baroness Strange** nr Errol
⊥   (organ early 18th C German 1/7  r1856 Rob, fr Snaresbrooke, Mozarbe Lodge, collection
      of Captain Lane to Mottispont Abbey Res of Raymond Russell, rem to Dilke Street, then
      to Pitfour 1955 & r Man, to here & r1966 Chu, rem & o2013 Lam
⊥   (two English barrel organs

**99) The small German-made organ which stood in Megginch Castle**

**Meigle St. Margaret's E** cld 1953
⊥   (1869 G&D 1/4
⊥   (1909 MilJ 2/9  rem 1954 to Alyth St. Ninian's E

**Meiklefolla St. George's E** nr Rothienorman, Aberdeenshire
⅄  (1849 organ

**Meldrum & Bourtie** (Meldrum South) Oldmeldrum
⅄  (1898 Wad 2/11  o1914 Wad, rem 1953 to Aberdeen Gilcomston B

**Meldrum North** (UF/F) cld 1939
⅄  (1900 Pos 1/
⅄  (1936 Law 2/8

**Meldrum St. Matthew's & St. George's E** Urquhart Road
⅄  (1863 organ or organ chamber
⅄  1903 Law 2/9  o c1983 Edm

**Melrose** (St. Cuthbert's/Old) Weirhill
⅄  (1889 B&F 2/17  dest by fire 1908
⅄  1911 B&F 3/32  r1956 R&D, r1976 Gol 3/33

**Melrose Holy Trinity E** High Cross Avenue
⅄  (1854 organ  in schoolroom  rem to ch
⅄  (1872 ConP 2/16  to transept 1900
⅄  (1931 Ing 2/24  o1979 Gol, r1987 Gol 3/24, rem 2015

**Melrose Independent**
⅄  (1878 organ

**Melrose Res of J. A. Maconochie**
⅄  (1881 Har  rem 1893 to Kirknewton Meadowbank House

**Melrose Res of Mr. Robson**
⅄  (organ clock  extant 1936

**Melrose St. Aidan's** (UF/F) cld 1946
⅄  (1903 Cou 1/

**Melrose St. Cuthbert's RC** (High Cross/UF/UP cld 1984) High Cross Avenue
⅄  c1900 N&B Norvic 1/5  to here 1927 by Gle, o1999 & 2005 Sta

**Menstrie**
⅄  1910 Lew 2/10  fr Biggar Gillespie-Moat Park 1980 & r Loo

**Methil Wellesley** Wellesley Road, Fife
⅄  1926 R&D 2/19  o1959 R&D, o1962 R&D, o2011 For

**Methilhill & Denbeath** (Methilhill) Fife
⅄  Sol 1/

**Methlick** Aberdeenshire
⅄  1879 Wil 2/10  o R&D, o2010 Wil **B-listed**

**Methven & Logiealmond** (Methven)
⅄  1866 F&A 2/20  fr Dupplin Castle 1914 & r MilJ 2/18 +1pf, r SmRo, disused

**Midcalder -** see Calder, Kirk of

**Midcalder Res of A. & C. Buchan, 21 Bank Street**
⊥ (1830s SBr barrel organ 3ss fr Hawick Res of M. Webb post-1958 to Burnley Res of W.
Blakey, rem post-1992 to London Botany Bay, Enfield, Middlesex by George Crutchley
& o 1990s, to Edinburgh Broughton St. Mary's Church Centre 1999, to here 2000, rem
2002 to Stow Manse

**Middlebie**
⊥ 1890 Pos 1/ fr Kirtle Eaglesfield 2011 by Sav

**Midmar** Aberdeenshire
⊥ 1910 Vin 2/9

**Millearn House Res of John G.Home Drummond** nr Auchterarder, Perthshire dem 1969
⊥ (1841 Hill 2+ppd/13 with barrel mechanism r1842 Bru 2/30 possibly rem pre-1867 to
Edinburgh Albany Street C

**Millport Cathedral of the Holy Spirit** E College Street
⊥ (1849 Rob fr St. Andrew's Chapel E (temp) to here 1851, o1854 G&D, o1856 Archibald
Lumsdaine, moved within ch 1931 HNB
⊥ (1935 Com 2/11 ex2 r1982 Gordon Harrison 2/20 ex3, rem c2002 to Bridgend St.
Columba, Islay
⊥ 1867 Holt 2/11 +4pf fr Edinburgh St. Michael's & All Angels to Logie Pert 1893 & r
HCF 2/11 +4pf, rem 2001, to here & r2004 WoH 2/15

**Millport: Cumbrae** (Millport West/Millport Abbey/Cumbrae) Bute Terrace blg cld 2014
⊥ 1871 Nic of Walsall 2/ to here fr Glasgow St. Thomas' Wesleyan M 1893 by Mir 2/16,
r1983

**Millport East** (UF/F) Glasgow Street cld 1971
⊥ 1868 Ren fr Arbroath Inverbrothock to Arbroath West 1882, to Glasgow St. Luke's UF
1898 & r MilJ 2/ to here c1923 without Ren case

**Millport West** (UF/UP) cld 1932 dem
⊥ (1893 F&A 2/17 rem 1948 to Alva

**Millseat** C nr Turriff cld 1972
⊥ (organ rem 1900

**Milngavie Cairns** (UF/UP) Cairns Drive/Buchanan Street
⊥ 1908 N&B r1926 HNB 2/17, o1980 HNB, o2002

**Milngavie St. Joseph's RC** (St. Luke's/Milngavie & Baldernock UF, now in new blg) Station
Road/Buchanan Street
⊥ (c1900 Walc 2/ fr Glasgow Res of Sir John Ure Primrose to here 1924
⊥ (1957 Watt 2/ ex using pipework fr previous organ, rem by 1970s
⊥ (1846 HDa 1/6 r1857, fr St. Andrews St. Andrew's E to St. Andrews B 1890, rem to St.
Andrews C pre-1920, to here 1978 & r McDM, rem 1979 to Glasgow Newlands St.
Peter's College. Photographs with St. Andrews listing on page 341

**Milngavie St. Paul's** (Milngavie) Strathblane Road/Baldernock Road
⊥ 1914 Bin 2/23 r post-1975 Six 2/23

**Milngavie UF Cont.** Craigdhu Road
⊥ (1890 ConP fr Bothwell Kirkfield to Glasgow Merrylea 1915, to here 1947 Mir

**Minnigaff** - see Monigaff

**Minto** nr Hawick
- ⊿ (1904 Ing 2/14 mostly rem c1980
- ⊿ 19th C chamber organ 1/5 fr St. Ives Res, Cornwall to here 1985 & r McDM with pt of Ing case, some pipes rem 2009

**Mochrum**
- ⊿ c1904 Walc 1/6 fr Thornhill Virginhall 1972 & r1975

**Moffat** (St. Andrew's)
- ⊿ 1894 IngE 2+1pf/22 +6pf completed 1899 3/28 o1962 Watt, r1974 Wal 3/28, o2005-2007 Edm **A-listed**

**Moffat Hydropathic** dest fire 1921
- ⊿ (organ extant 1892

**Moffat St. John the Evangelist E**
- ⊿ 1872 Wil 2/14 opened by Henry Willis o1990s JoG, o2005 Edm **A-listed**

**Moffat St. Mary's UF** (St. Mary's/UF/F cld 1931) cld 1999
- ⊿ (1912 N&B 2/16

**Moffat Well Road** (UF/UP) cld 1960 dem
- ⊿ (1889 Bev 2/19 rem Watt

**Moffat Well Road Centre** (Warriston School cld 1985)
- ⊿ (c1920s Ric 2/10 rem 1936 to Cranstoun by Ing

**Moniaive** - see Glencairn & Moniaive

**Monifieth** (St. Rule's) Church Street
- ⊿ (1908 Sco 2/13 rem 1969 to Dundee Broughty Ferry St. James'

**Monifieth Holy Trinity E** Panmure Street
- ⊿ (1862 Pil 2/10 fr Forfar St. John the Evangelist E 1908 by Wat, rem 1932 to Dundee St. Luke's E, Downfield
- ⊿ 1909 Wat 2/12 fr Dundee Belmont House 1932, r1975 by Jim Bremner, disused

**Monifieth South** (UF/F) Hill Street blg cld 2008
- ⊿ 1926 Wat 2/12 console moved by Mac 1966
- ⊿ (1909 Har 2/15 fr Coldstream Community Centre 1998 by Lib, stored then rem 2004

**Monigaff** nr Newton Stewart
- ⊿ 1872 Bry 2/12 r1890s 2/13 (4ss changed) **B-listed**

**Monikie & Newbigging** (Monikie)
- ⊿ Wal fr Devon to Dundee Res of Rev. Wm. Miller 1960s, to here 1973 by Michael Miller

**Monimail** - see Bow of Fife

**Monkland** - for Old Monkland see Coatbridge, for New Monkland see Airdrie

**Monkton** - see Prestwick

**Monktonhall House** East Lothian
    ⅄ (clock organ

**Monquhitter and New Byth** (Monquhitter) Aberdeenshire (See also Cuminestown)
    ⅄ 1885 Scot 2/21 fr Dundee Tay Square 1954

**Monteviot House Res of Marquis of Lothian** Ancrum
    ⅄ (1883 Gern 2/11 rem 1958 to Dryburgh Tweed Horizons Centre (St. Columba's College,
    White Fathers Monastery) & o R&D

**Montrose Knox UF** (Montrose St. Luke's/UF/Mill Street UP cld 1953) Mill Street
    ⅄ 1890 IngE 2/17 o1892 Wad, case extant 2015

**Montrose Melville** - see Montrose Town Hall

**Montrose Melville South** (South/St. Paul's UF/F) Castle Street cld 2017
    ⅄ 1889 Har 2/15 o1890 Har, fr Falkirk Erskine 1905 to Falkirk St. Francis Xavier RC, to
    Falkirk M 1919 & r Watt 2/15, to here 1934 by Sco & r 2/16

**Montrose Old & St. Andrew's** (Old) High Street
    ⅄ 1885 B&F 3/27 r1934 Hils 3/26, r1954 Wil & Wal 3/27 new console

**Montrose Res of W. Beattie**
    ⅄ (organ inst 1848 by G&D

**Montrose Res of M. Law**
    ⅄ (organ extant 1900-06

**Montrose St. Andrew's** (St. George's & Trinity/UF/St. George's UF) George Street/Baltic Street
cld 2004 sold
    ⅄ 1902 Wad 2/19

**Montrose St. Luke's** - see Montrose Knox UF

**Montrose St. Luke's & St. John's** (St. John's/UF/F) Mill Street/John Street cld 1977
    ⅄ (1904 N&B o1914 Wad, r1922 Hils rem

**Montrose St. Mary's E** Panmure Place cld 1927 (later church hall, now day care centre)
    ⅄ (1868 HDT 2+pd/15 o1887 Wad
    ⅄ (1910 B&H 2/18 rem 1927 to Montrose St. Mary's & St. Peter's E

**Montrose St. Mary's & St. Peter's E** (St. Peter's English E) Panmure Place/Mid Links
    ⅄ (1734 Bris/Jordan 1/ o1759 F. Schuniman, r1777 Crole with Sw, o1798 Moo, o1799,
    o1831 HDa rem 1834 by SBr
    ⅄ (1834 SBr 2+pd/18 ch & organ dest by fire 1857
    ⅄ (1870 F&A 2/18 +1pf rem 1924 to Stonehaven South by Ing
    ⅄ 1910 B&H 2/18 to here fr Montrose St. Mary's E 1927 & r B&H 2/19 with pt F&A,
    r1963 D&R 3/42 with pt of M. Forsyth-Grant Res organ, o1985 GDB, o2016 Lib

**Montrose South & Ferryden** (Inchbrayock/Ferryden/Craig UF/F) Ferryden, Montrose
⃥   (1929 Pos 1/
⃥   1939 Walc 2/10  fr Edinburgh Moray UF to Edinburgh Moray Knox 1910 & r 2/14 Ing, to here 1939 Ing

**Montrose Town Hall** (Melville cld 1951) Melville Gardens
⃥   1880 F&A 2/19  o1902 Wad, o1906 F&A, o1940 Wad

**Montrose URC** (C/Ind) Baltic Street/Museum Street
⃥   (1812 MWo 2/  fr Dundee St. Paul's Cathedral E 1865 by Ren, rem to Rosslyn St. Matthew's E by 1870
⃥   1891 ConP 2/16  r1909 Wad,  new action later

**Montrose** - see also Hillside

**Monymusk**
⃥   1932 Law 1/6

**Monymusk Arts Centre** (furniture store/E chapel 1801-1939/lapidary mill)
⃥   1760 Rostrand 1/5 + barrels  r1834 Lin (new case) 1/5, o1890 Wad, r1908 into chamber, r1992 Edm 1/6 with some new pipes **B-listed**

**Monymusk House Res of Archibald Grant**
⃥   (organ pre-1748  rem post-1801

**Monzie** Perthshire
⃥   1913 N&B 2/

**Monzie South** (UF/F) Gilmerton, Perthshire cld 1938
⃥   (1904 MilJ 1/10  rem 1949 to Ardoch

**Moonzie** Fife cld 1971 but occasionally used
⃥   F&A  fr elsewhere & r here 1947 R&D, r1959 R&D 2/11

**Moray Crematorium** - see Enzie

**Morebattle** (St. Lawrence)
⃥   organ to here & r1978 SmRo 2/17 ex

**Morham** - see Standingstone Farm

**Morningside** Lanarkshire (See Edinburgh for the suburb of Morningside)
⃥   (Walc 1/

**Mortlach & Cabrach** (Mortlach) Dufftown
⃥   1888 Wad 2/18  o1916 Wad, r1930 HNB 2/23, o1980s R&D, r SmRo

**Morton** - see Thornhill

**Morven**
⃥   (Pos 1/  o1980 Renn, redundant 1995-2002

**Mossend -** see Bellshill

**Motherwell B**
⊥   1881 LTC 2/13 (all encl)  fr Coltness House (nr Wishaw), Res of Walter Houldsworth to
here c1951 by BFH, o1979 HNB  **A-listed**

**Motherwell Brandon** (UF/Brandon Street UP) West Hamilton Street cld 1971
⊥   (1903 Law 2/18  r1921, r1956 Wil 2/22, o1967 Wil, rem to Motherwell Crosshill

**Motherwell C** Brandon Street
⊥   1902 Bro  to here fr elsewhere, o2012 Wil

**Motherwell Coltness House** - see Coltness

**Motherwell Crosshill** (Cairns/UF/UP/Dalziel UP) Brandon Street/Airbles Street
⊥   (1921 W&L (Lew) 2/20
⊥   1903 Law 2/18  r1921, r1956 Wil 2/23, o1967 Wil, fr Motherwell Brandon

**Motherwell Dalziel North** (UF/F) Muir Street cld 1970 (now Gospel Outreach Centre)
⊥   (1902 B&H  r1915 Sco 2/16 in new blg, r1956 Watt 2/  with new console

**Motherwell Dalziel St. Andrew's** (Dalziel/Dalziel High) 43 Merry Street/Muir Street
⊥   (1874 Hill 2/12  rem 1898 to Thornliebank by Mir
⊥   1900 Walc 2/23  o2004, o2011/2013 Walc 2/23 **A-listed**

**Motherwell Holy Trinity E** Crawford Street
⊥   (Mon  r IngE 2/9, to here fr London 1892 by F&A 2/9
⊥   (1864 Mir  fr Motherwell Primitive M to Motherwell M & r 1918 B&H 2/  (3ss pf), to
here c1980 by Burke (Wal, S. Africa)

**Motherwell M** (Primitive M to 1932) Hamilton Road/Avon Street cld c1980
⊥   1864 Mir  fr Motherwell Primitive M & r1918 B&H 2/  (3ss pf), rem c1980 to
Motherwell Holy Trinity E

**Motherwell Our Lady of Good Aid Cathedral RC** Coursington Road
⊥   1900 MilJ 2/  o1929, r1975/79 SmRo 3/33, r2005-09 Lib 4/57 (4ss electronic)

**Motherwell Primitive M** Milton Street blg cld c1912
⊥   (1864 Mir  rem  to Motherwell M & r1918 B&H

**Motherwell St Mary's** Avon Street
⊥   1906 N&B 1/6  fr Rosskeen East to here & r1952 Bell with pts fr Midlands, r1959 BinT
2/14, r1984 R&D 2/14, disused

**Motherwell South Dalziel** (Dalziel South/Dalziel until 1874) 504 Windmillhill Street cld 2007
(now studios)
⊥   (1926 Bro 2/17
⊥   (1930 Ing 2/15 fr Edinburgh Liberton 1973 to here 1979 & r SmRo with case fr old organ
and other ss, disused 2003, rem

**Moulin** - see Pitlochry

**Mount Stuart Res of Marquis of Bute**
⊥   1781 H.H. Hess, Gouda  rescued fr Dutch dyke, rem to Cardiff Castle pre-1848, rem to Llandough c1868 & r Vow 2/13,  to here (hall) 1893 (case, facade, 2 ss and keyboards survive fr 1781) **B-listed**
⊥   1898 LTC 1/5 (old chapel)
⊥   1905 Lew 1/4 (chapel)  r1990 Wil (1ss changed), o2016 Wil **B-listed**
⊥   c1880s organ (crypt) 2/5  no case

**Muchalls Castle**
⊥   (organ

**Muchalls St. Ternan's E**
⊥   (c1852-62 organ 1/6  fr elsewhere, rem outside ch 1882
⊥   1882 Wad 1/8  o1917 Wad, r1985 Edm

**Mugdock Castle** nr Milngavie
⊥   (c1762 WaJ 1/4  fr Glasgow Res of James Watt to Glasgow Malt's Lodging, College 1776, 1815 to Glasgow Res of Archibald McLellan, 78 Miller Street, o McLellan & Steven +1ss, to here, rem 1854 to Denovan House nr Falkirk

**Muirhead St. Barbara's RC**
⊥   (c1840s Mir 1/  fr Res elsewhere to here, rem to Glasgow Berkeley Street Workshop of Mac, scr 2009

**Muirhead** - see also Chryston

**Muirhead of Liff** (Liff UF/F)
⊥   (1901 MilJ 1/4

**Muirkirk** (Old)
⊥   (1901 IGD
⊥   1903 Watt 1+pd/3  fr Muirkirk Wellwood c1953

**Muirkirk Kames Mission** cld 1953
⊥   (1904 Pos 1/

**Muirkirk Wellwood** (UF/Chalmers UF/F) cld 1949
⊥   (1903 Watt 1+pd/3  rem to Muirkirk c1953

**Mulben** - see Boharm Mulben

**Murroes & Tealing**
⊥   c1830s chamber organ 2/  (Gt pipes, Sw harmonium) fr Dundee Res of Christie to Dundee Balgay 1906 by Lind, to here 1924, o c2000.

**Murthly Castle**  Perthshire
⊥   (1841 powerful organ in first chapel  rem, possibly to Arbroath
⊥   (1845 Ren 1+Sw/8 in new chapel  rem to Crieff St. Fillan's RC 1871 & r Ren

**Musselburgh** - see also Carberry Tower and Fa'side Castle

**Musselburgh Bridge Street** (UF/UP) cld 1960-62
 ⊥ (1926 A&S 2/15  o1946 Ing, fr Hawick Allars 1949 & r Ing 2/16, rem 1962 to Musselburgh St. Andrew's

**Musselburgh C** Links Street, Fisherrow
 ⊥ 1860 Hol  fr Appleby Castle 1885 to Appleby St. Michael's & r 2/14, to here 1977 Gol, o2000 R&D **B-listed**

**Musselburgh High** (UF/F) Mall Avenue/Dalrymple Loan cld 1985-90
 ⊥ (1933 BFH 2/17  o1961 Wil, rem 1990 to storage at Edinburgh Lockhart Memorial

**Musselburgh Loretto School Chapel** Linkfield Road
 ⊥ (NicF 2/17  to here 1880 by You, r1892 Vow 3/16 +9pf for new chapel, r1912 Bin 3/28, r1965 Wil 3/28 console moved, r1972/77 R&D 3/28, rem 1988
 ⊥ 1989 JoK 3/32  with 9 ss fr old organ & 3 ss fr Ireland

**Musselburgh Northesk** Bridge Street
 ⊥ 1905 A&S 2/18  to chamber 1913 A&S 2/18, r2004 Lig 2/18 **B-listed**

**Musselburgh Our Lady of Loretto & St. Michael's RC** Newbigging
 ⊥ 1905 N&B 2/9

**Musselburgh Res** Grove Street
 ⊥ (organ for sale 1811

**Musselburgh Res of Rev. Donald Lindgren** 8 The Grove
 ⊥ barrel organ to here 1978

**Musselburgh St. Andrew's High** (St. Andrew's/Millhill/UF/UP) 70 Millhill
 ⊥ (1895 organ
 ⊥ (1908 Sco  fr Biggar Gillespie 1952
 ⊥ (1926 A&S 2/15  o1946 Ing, fr Hawick Allars 1949 & r Ing 2/16 to Musselburgh Bridge Street, to here 1962 by Wil, rem 1989, scr

**Musselburgh St. Michael's Inveresk**
 ⊥ (1871 ConP 2/  rem 1894 to Edinburgh Canongate
 ⊥ (1892 Lew 3/31  opened 1894, altered 1897 Lew, o1913 Gle, r1925 Ing, r1932 Ing, o1963/74 R&D, o2017-18 Lig **A-listed**  Photograph on page 22

**Musselburgh St. Ninian's** Macbeth Moir Road, Levenhall cld 2012
 ⊥ (1965 Wil 1+pd/8 ex4  rem 2012 by Charles Davidson to store at Fenton Barns, East Lothian

**Musselburgh St. Peter's E** High Street/Linkfield Road
 ⊥ (c1785 1/  r with pd (in former ch)
 ⊥ (1866 Holt 1+pd/7  r1884 Bis 2/ , rem 1943
 ⊥ (Har 2/12 experimental organ to here 1943 by Har  most rem c2008

**Muthill St. James's E**
 ⊥ (barrel organ  rem 1856 to Drummond Castle
 ⊥ (organ  fr Drummond Castle Res of A. Drummond 1856, moved fr gallery to aisle 1874
 ⊥ 1888 Wad 2/9  o1896 Wad, o2000s Edm **B-listed**

**Myres Castle** nr Auchtermuchty
⟡ (c1850 Bru/Ren 1/4 fr Craufurdland Castle, Ayrshire, to chapel here 1890, moved to drawing room 1921, rem 1966 to workshop of Wal, rem to Athelhampton House, Dorset & o Wal

**Nairn Old** Academy Street
⟡ 1903 N&B 2/20 r1964 Hils 2/22, r2006 Loo 2/26

**Nairn Rosebank** (UF/UP) Academy Street cld 1974
⟡ (1900 Law 2/15 rem to storage, then scr

**Nairn St. Columba's E** Queen Street
⟡ 1889 F&A 2/9 o1912 Wad, r c1934 HNB +ss, o1965 R&D, o R&D, o1989 Edm

**Nairn St. Mary's RC** Academy Street
⟡ (1888 James Graham to Carnoustie Res of Graham c1892, rem post-1925 to Aberdeen Res of Doctor, rem to here, rem c1965 to Pluscarden Abbey by monks

**Nairn St. Ninian's** (High UF/F) High Street/Queen Street
⟡ 1924 W&L 2/20 o1934 Wil, o1956 Wil, o1986 Wil, o1994 Har, o2015 MilP **A-listed**

**Nairn URC** (C ) Crescent Road
⟡ (1878 Har 2/10 r1906 Wad 2/13 & moved, o1930 Wad, o1988-95 R&D, scr c2000

**Neilston** (Old) Main Street
⟡ 1888 ConP 2/16 o1940, o1980-82, o1987 Mac (1ss replaced, fr Glasgow Blackfriars)

**Neilston South** (UF/F) High Street cld 1964
⟡ (Ing cinema organ to here by Watt, rem by Watt moved 1965 to Kilsyth Anderson by C&C

**Neilston St. Thomas's RC**
⟡ (1861 organ

**Nenthorn Workshop of David Stark** The Old Schoolhouse, nr Kelso
⟡ 1936 Com 2/11 ex 2 o1988, damaged slightly by fire, fr Edinburgh St. Margaret's 2002, dism
⟡ 1879 ConJ 1+pd/6 1954 + blower, o1979 R&D, fr Edinburgh Royal Infirmary Chapel 2005
⟡ various organs at different times for repair

**Netherlee** Glasgow
⟡ 1938 HNB 3/41 r1969 HNB 3/37, o1983/88 HNB, r2003 Well 3/37

**Netherlee** - see also Glasgow Res of Gordon Frier

**New Abbey** Dumfriesshire
⟡ (1886 organ
⟡ (1926 organ

**Newbattle** Newbattle Road, nr Dalkeith
⟡ (1886 HDT 2/ o1892-94 McDA
⟡ 1895 IngE 3/19 moved fr gallery 1937 by G&D, 3ss (reeds) rem **B-listed**

**Newbattle Abbey College** Newbattle Road
⅄ (1822 Ell 2/10 no pd moved 1830s HDa, r1862 HDa 2/11, r1871 HDT 2/12, case and stop handles survive

**100) The surviving casework from the 1822 Elliot organ at Newbattle Abbey**

**Newburgh** Cupar Road, Fife (for Newburgh, Aberdeenshire see Foveran)
⅄ 1906 MilJ 2/15

**Newcastleton Heritage Centre** (Newcastleton C cld 1993/South UF/UP cld 1934)
⅄ 1903 Cou 1/5 extant 2004

**New Cumnock** (Old/Martyrs) Ayrshire
⅄ 1928 Hils 2/17

**New Cumnock Afton UF** (F) cld 1918
⅄ (1906 N&B 1/

**New Cumnock Arthur Memorial** (UF/F) cld 1982
⅄ (N&B 1/ extant 1933

**New Cumnock Res of R. Kennedy**
⅄ organ extant 1933

**New Deer North** (UF/F) cld 1958
⅄ (organ inst 1923 rem 1960 to Strichen by Watt

**New Deer St. Kane's** (New Deer South/New Deer)
⅄ 1878 Wil 2/12 rem 1879 by Wil fr Edinburgh St. Mary's Cathedral E, to Canterbury Cathedral 1885 as 2/12 then to Gloucester Cathedral 1885, to here 1887 2/13, o Wad, o1975 Loo, o2006 after damage Loo **A-listed**

**New Erskine** - see Erskine

**New Galloway** - see Kells and Kenmure Castle

**Newhills** - see under Bucksburn

**Newlands** Peeblesshire
⊥  c1880s organ 1/4  extant 2005

**New Leeds** (UF/UP) cld 1940
⊥  (1903 Wal 1/

**Newmachar** Aberdeenshire
⊥  (c1914 Kir 2/  rem 1975, blower to Boharm Mulben

**Newmachar West** (UF/F) cld 1932
⊥  (1901 Pos 1/

**Newmains Coltness Memorial**
⊥  1878 LTC 2/21 o1896 LCT, r1911 Smri 2/23 **B-listed**

**Newmilns Loudon** (Loudon Old)
⊥  1898 B&F 2/20

**Newmilns East** (Loudon UF/F) cld 1980
⊥  (1901 Pos 1/5

**New Monkland** - see Airdrie

**New Pitsligo** (North)
⊥  1904 Law 2/17 o1995 Edm **A-listed**

**New Pitsligo St. John the Evangelist E**
⊥  (1842 HDa
⊥  1898 B&H 2/11

**Newport-on-Tay** (St. Thomas) Blyth Street (for Newport see also Forgan)
⊥  1902 Wil 2/15  +1ss 1908 Wil, r1935 MilJ 2/18, o2010 Edm **A-listed**

**Newport-on-Tay C** (Ind) Kilnburn cld 1986
⊥  (1869 F&A 2/9  scr

**Newport-on-Tay St. Fillan's** (UF/F) Hillside Place cld 1978
⊥  (1897 Vin 2/22  r SmRo, rem

**Newport-on-Tay St. Mary's E** High Street
⊥  1904 MilJ 2/10 +1pf o1920 MilJ, r1948 Rot, o1966 Mac, o1997 Edm

**Newport-on-Tay Trinity UF** (UP) High Street/Boat Road cld, for sale 2017
⊥  1911 MilJ 2/17  extant 2017

**Newton** - see Cambuslang

**Newton Mearns** (Mearns UF)
⊥  (1909 Walc 1/5
⊥  1965 Wal 3/34 r1988 HNB

**Newton-on-Ayr** - see Ayr

**Newtonmore Res of Buchan, Manse**
- ⋏ 1830s SBr barrel organ 3ss fr Hawick Res of M. Webb post-1958 to Burnley Res of W. Blakey, rem post-1992 by George Crutchley to London Botany Bay, Enfield & o1990s, rem 1999 to Edinburgh Broughton St. Mary's Church Centre, rem 2000 to Midcalder Res of Buchan, rem 2002 to Stow Manse, to here 2009
- ⋏ c1815 MWo barrel organ 4ss fr Caister Castle to Wymondham Res of Mrs. C. Hill nr Leicester, o1966 Bis (Budgen), rem to St. Annes-on-Sea Res of Brian Chesters 2014, to Edinburgh Stockbridge 2015 by Chesters, rem & o2016-17 Edm, to here 2017

**Newtonmore St. Bride's** (St. Andrew's, blg replaced 1955-58)
- ⋏ (organ by amateur fr Edinburgh New College to here 1937, rem c1956

**Newton Stewart All Saints E** Challoch
- ⋏ (1872 Tel 1/7
- ⋏ 1878 Hars 2/15 inst here 1881 o1992 McDM **A-listed**
- ⋏ (temp organ following flood inst 1895, rem

**101) The 1878 Harston organ at All Saints, Challoch** Photograph published with kind permission of All Saints Church, Challoch, Newton Stewart

**Newton Stewart Chapel of Rest** (St. Andrew's E cld)
- ⋏ 1910 Ebr 2/10

315

**Newton Stewart Penninghame** (Penninghame St. John's/Penninghame)
⋏   1878 Hars 3/27 r1962 HNB 3/27 **C-listed**

**Newton Stewart St. John's** (St. John's UF/York Road UF/UP) cld 1971
⋏   (1907 Cou 2/9 pipework re-used elsewhere

**Newton Stewart** - see also Monigaff

**Newton Village Workshop of Forth Pipe Organs** (Rushworth & Dreaper cld 2002) nr Danderhall, rem 2013 to Rosyth, Liberty House, Cromarty Campus
⋏   (1893 G&D 2/7 fr Edinburgh Res of J.S. Sturrock to Edinburgh Gillis Centre RC 1894, o1900 G&D, o1956 Wal, disused 1994, rem here 2009 to storage, then Rosyth
⋏   (many other organs under repair

**Newtown** Newtown St. Boswells
⋏   1896 Bin 1+pd/8 to here 1958 fr Bramley Holy Trinity, Hough End by Marshall Sykes **B-listed**

**Newtyle** Kirkton Road/Dundee Road
⋏   (c1850s 1/ r1913 Cat 1+pd/10, rem
⋏   1938 HNB 2/10 r1977 Loo 2/17

**Newtyle East** (UF/F) Castle Street cld 1938 (ch hall)
⋏   (1901 Pos/MilJ 1/5 moved later within blg

**North Ballachulish** - see Onich

**North Berwick Abbey** (UF/UP) High Street
⋏   1912 Sco 2/13 disused fr 1976

**North Berwick B** (Blackadder/UF/F cld 1990) 1 Victoria Road
⋏   (1895 F&A 2/13 o1921 F&A, r1976 Gol 2/23, rem 1990 to Dingwall Castle Street by McDM

**North Berwick Carlekemp School RC** Abbotsford Park cld c1980
⋏   (F&A fr elsewhere rem c1978, later to Haddington St. Mary RC

**North Berwick Our Lady Star of the Sea RC** Law Road
⋏   c1900s Pos

**North Berwick St. Andrew Blackadder** (St. Andrew's/North Berwick) St. Andrew Street
⋏   (1886 F&A 2/14 o1897 F&A, r1914 Ing 2/22, rem 1999 (blg altered)

**North Berwick St. Baldred's E** Dirleton Road
⋏   (1866 F&A moved 1884 to chamber by F&A, o1899 F&A, r1907 N&B 3/23 +1pf r1931 Hils, rem c1976
⋏   (1891 Wad 2/15 r1935 G&D 2/18, o1965 Wil, fr Anstruther Chalmers Memorial 1983 & r Gol 2/23, disused, rem 2017

**North Bute** - see Port Bannatyne

**North Queensferry**
⋏   1876 Hew 2/7 fr Edinburgh 1941 & inst Grangemouth St. Mary's E by Sco, r1976 Gol (1ss changed), to here 1980 & r SmRo

**Noth** Rhynie
   ⚒  1899 Law 2/14  o2008 HNB **A-listed**

**Nunraw Sancta Maria Monastery** East Lothian
   ⚒  1970 Man 1/3

**Oban** - see also Glencruitten House

**Oban Christ's Church Dunollie** (Dunollie Road/UF/UP) Corran Esplanade blg cld 2013
   ⚒  (1902 Walc 1+pd/5 (in former blg cld 1956)
   ⚒  (1956 Wal 1/11 ex4  fr Edinburgh St. Cuthbert's (temp) 1957 to here, o1976 McDM and moved downstairs, rem 2014 to Bishopton, Renfrewshire & r McDM

**Oban Old** Glencruitten Road/Soroba Road
   ⚒  (1914 Cou 1+pd/9 + Solo  scr 1988
   ⚒  (1927 Ing 2/14  to here fr Oban St. Columba's Argyll Square 1988 & r McDM 2/14, innards scr 2009

**Oban Res of Col Malcolm** - see Poltalloch

**Oban St. Columba's** George Street cld 1949
   ⚒  (1898 B&F 2/15  r 2/20, rem 1950s

**Oban St. Columba's Argyll Square** (Argyll Square/UF/F) Argyll Square cld 1983
   ⚒  (1927 Ing 2/14  rem to Oban Old 1988 by McDM

**Oban St. Columba's RC Cathedral** Corran Esplanade
   ⚒  1886 LTC 1/5 (in tin blg)  o1893 Wad, to new blg here 1936 Watt

**Oban St. John the Divine Cathedral E** George Street
   ⚒  (Bev  o1888-93 Wad, for sale 1915
   ⚒  (1915 B&H 2/18 +1pf  +1ss later, r1994 J. Wood & Sons, rem 1990s

**Old Cumnock C** Auchinleck Road
   ⚒  1894 ConP 2/12  o c1980 Mac 1ss changed

**Old Cumnock Old** The Square
   ⚒  (1881 LTC 2/12 +4pf (added later)  rem 1966, facade survives

**Old Cumnock St. John's RC** Glaisnock Street
   ⚒  1884 LTC 2/13 +1pf  r c1970 Hils 2/13 (1ss changed), case altered **B-listed**

**Old Cumnock Trinity** (Crichton West/Crichton Memorial) Ayr Road
   ⚒  1899 Ing 2/  r Wil 2/  , disused

**Old Cumnock West** (UF/UP) New Bridge Street cld 1949
   ⚒  1909 Bro 2/18

**Old Dailly** - see Dailly

**Old Deer** - see Deer

**Oldhamstocks Workshop of Lammermuir Pipe Organs**
- ⚘ c1820s-30s Anon Scottish 1/4 fr Res nr Irvine to Uddingston Church of the Nazarene 1959 Watt, to Glasgow Berkeley Street workshop 1961 Mac, 1965 to Hamilton Whitehill, rem 1966 to new blg, returned to Mac 1969, temp organ at Stepps, to here 2009
- ⚘ c1810 Astor barrel organ rems to here 2009
- ⚘ c1850s Ren 1/8 to Fortrose & r1914 Cat 1/10, rem 1986 to Scourie Res of Ross, 1987 to Leithen Lodge by Hugh Ross, rem 1995, case and pt to Edinburgh Broughton St. Mary's and in 2002 to Stow Manse, to here 2006 (incomplete)
- ⚘ 2011 1/3 Lam box organ
- ⚘ 2008-17 Lam 2/14
- ⚘ 2018 Lam 1/4 for sale

**Old Kilpatrick Barclay** (Barclay UF/F) cld 1990
- ⚘ (1937 Hils 1+pd/6

**Old Kilpatrick Bowling** (Old Kilpatrick)
- ⚘ (1898 Vow 3/21

**Old Luce** Church Street, Glenluce (now pt of Luce Valley Parish)
- ⚘ 1968 C&C 2/19 ex3 pipework from Colmonell UF

**Old Meldrum** - see Meldrum

**Old Monkland** - see Coatbridge

**Onich St. Bride's E** North Ballachulish
- ⚘ 1879 Wad 1+pd/9 moved 1889 Wad to loft, r1911 Fer, r 1950s (Oboe replaced), o1975 McDM **A-listed**

**Ordiquill & Cornhill** (Cornhill & Ord/Ordiquill & Ord UF/F) Banffshire
- ⚘ (1933 Law 1/

**Orphir** Orkney
- ⚘ c1810s Cle 1/4 altered, to here 1971 fr Kirkwall St. Magnus Cathedral

**Oxnam** Roxburghshire
- ⚘ (1960s WiB
- ⚘ 1991 Lam 1/3 no pd

**Oyne** (St. Ninian's) Aberdeenshire cld 1990
- ⚘ (1907 Wad 1/6 o1911 Wad, scr following fire

**Oyne Westhall Manor**
- ⚘ (1778 Gre 1/5 rem to Aberdeen St. Mary's E 1946 by Law

**Paisley Abbey** Cotton Street
- ⚘ 1874 Cav 2/24 o1888 LTC, to another gallery 1902 SmRi, r1928 HNB 4/66, r1968 Wal 4/66, o1998 Nic, r2009 Har 4/67 **A-listed**
- ⚘ (1968 Wal 2/17 ex3 (temp) rem 1968 to Paisley School Wynd C
- ⚘ Robin Jennings 1/3 (property of John Langdon) to here 2004 fr Glasgow Royal Conservatoire of Scotland

**Paisley Abbey Close** (UF/UP) Abbey Close cld 1965
⼈ (1906 N&B 2/ o1925 HNB, rem to Cumbernauld Sacred Heart RC & r C&C

**Paisley Adam, John, shop** 67 Bromlands Street/2 New Street
⼈ (organs 1/4 and 1/3 for sale 29i1875

**Paisley Castlehead** (Canal Street/UF/UP) Canal Street cld 2011
⼈ (1899 Bis 2/14 o1925 +1ss, o1970s HNB, o2003 MilP 1ss changed, organ redundant 2011, rem by 2017

**Paisley Central B** 14 Lady Lane
⼈ (c1900s B&H 2/16 part of case remains

**Paisley Central Hall Methodist** Gauze Street
⼈ 1873 ConP 3/29 fr Glasgow Crosshill Queen's Park 1926 by Hume, disused, mixtures rem 1990 and later to Paisley Sandyford by McDM 1998, blowing plant later removed **B-listed**

**Paisley Coats Memorial B** - see Paisley Thomas Coats Memorial B

**Paisley C** - see Paisley School Wynd C and Paisley New Street C

**Paisley George Street B** George Street cld
⼈ 1866 ConP 2/ to here fr Paisley Storie Street B 1911 & r1913 Hils 2/13

**Paisley Glenburn** Nethercraigs Drive
⼈ 1962 Wil 2/10 + 4ss and traps by minister 1960s, o MilP

**Paisley Greenlaw** Greenlaw Avenue cld 1997
⼈ (1874 ConP 2/20 fr Glasgow Eastwood 1910 to here & r Ing 2/20, r1987 McDM 2/20, rem 1999 to Glasgow St Paul the Apostle Shettleston RC & r SmRo 2/19

**Paisley High** - see Paisley Oakshaw Trinity

**Paisley Holy Trinity and St. Barnabas E** (Holy Trinity) Moss Street
⼈ (1833 HDa 1/4 disused 1846, for sale c/o Murdoch, 1 Maxwell Street, rem 1849 to England with Mrs. Wade, wife of first rector
⼈ 1887 ConP 2/16 r1908 SmR 2/18, r1967 Wil 2/21, r1982 Gro 2/21 after fire, o R&D

**Paisley Laigh** - see Paisley Stow Brae and Paisley New Street C

**Paisley Life Church** (Lylesland/UF/UP cld 1983) 56 Stock Street
⼈ (1912 N&B 2/17 o1926 HNB

**Paisley Lylesland** Rowan Street
⼈ 1983 Chu 2/14 all unencl

**Paisley Martyrs'** Broomlands Street cld 1979 (now hall)
⼈ 1905 Ing 2/15

**Paisley Martyrs'** (Martyrs' Memorial/UF/F) King Street
⼈ 1909 Watt 2/ disused, case extant

**Paisley Merksworth** (Paisley North) Love Street cld 1983
⚓ (1906 Har 2/12 rem 1948 to Richmond, Res of Sir Frederick Cook, Doughty House by HNB
⚓ (1948 HNB 2/ (Hill organ) case rem 1991 to Wick Pultneytown McDM, keyboards to Alan Rodger

**Paisley Methodist** - see Paisley Central Hall M

**Paisley Middle** Church Hill cld 1975
⚓ (1875 B&F 2/20 r c1925 Watt 2/18

**Paisley Middle UF** - see Paisley St. John's

**Paisley Moredun House Res of J.A. Brown** Stanely Road
⚓ (c1890 Hun 2/10 rem to Stocksfield M, Co. Durham

**Paisley Museum & Library** High Street
⚓ 1888 Gern 3/29 from Paisley Woodside House 1932 by HNB (K&B) (back of case to Glasgow Gordon Park) **A-listed** Photograph on page 21

**Paisley New Jerusalem (Swedenborgian)** (M chapel 1810-60) 17 George Street
⚓ (1886 Gern 2/13 disused 1970s, console to Paisley Museum; case & pts extant 2006

**Paisley New Street C** (USC/OLB/Laigh) New Street cld 1980 (now Arts Centre)
⚓ (c1900s N&B Norvic 1/11 scr post-1980

**Paisley North** - see Paisley Merksworth

**Paisley Oakshaw East & Gaelic** (Oakshaw East/UF/UP) 6 Oakshaw Street cld 1951
⚓ (c1900s N&B 1/
⚓ (1933 Com 2/11 ex2

**Paisley Oakshaw Trinity** (High Kirk) Church Hill
⚓ 1899 Hill 2/24 r1923 HNB, r1950 HNB 2/28, o c1979, r2004 Pri 2/30
⚓ (1968 Wal 2/17 ex3 (temp) fr Paisley Abbey to Paisley School Wynd C 1969, to here 2003 McDM, rem to Caldercruix 2004 McDM

**Paisley Orr Square** (High UF/F) Orr Square/High Street cld 1994
⚓ (c1905 Rutt 2/ fr Glasgow Res, rem 1960 to Bishopton Convent of the Sisters of the Good Shepherd

**Paisley Picture House** (Capitol Theatre) 23 High Street (later bingo hall)
⚓ (1930 Hils 3/76+27 traps ex11 rem 1980-84 to East Kilbride Civic Centre, console and other pts later to Edinburgh Playhouse, pt to STOPS, Greenlaw 2001

**Paisley Primitive M** (St. James' UP, cong moved 1880) St.James Street cld c1961
⚓ (1899 Bis 2/ rem Bis to school in England by 1964

**Paisley Ralston** (UF/UP) Violet Street cld 1945
⚓ (1911 Watt 1/9 rem 1951 to Falkirk Laurieston

**Paisley Regal/ABC** High Street
⚓ (1934 Com 3/ ex6 rem 1958 to Dunning St Serf's

**Paisley Res of J. Roy Fraser** Terrace Buildings
⊥   (ConP 2+pd/10 for sale 12ii1875

**Paisley Res of Wm Clark**
⊥   (1887 Michael Welte of Freiburg 'orchestrion' player organ rem 1942 to Glasgow
    Kelvingrove Art Gallery & Museum & r Robert Dobie, piano tuner

**Paisley Royal Alexandria Hospital** Corsebar Road
⊥   (c1900 Kir 1+pd/6 rem 1994 by Hugh Ross, to store at Edinburgh Portobello Old Manse
    1995, rem 1996 to Norham Res of Julian Bonia, Northumberland, pipe facade to Wooler
    URC, keyshelf to Swinton, rest scr after damage

**102) The Kirkland organ in the
Royal Alexandria Hospital prior to its removal**

**Paisley St. Barnabas E** Castle 103 blg cld
⊥   (1896 ConJ

**Paisley St. Columba Foxbar** (St. Columba's/Gaelic) Amochrie Road (ch previously in Oakshaw
Street)
⊥   1904 SmRi 2/12 o c1926 Watt, fr Kilbarchan C to here 1957 by R&D, o1958 Hils, o
    Ma⬤ire, disused

**Paisley St. George's** George Street cld 1985
⊥   (1874 ConP 2/23 r Ing 2/23, scr

**Paisley St. George's East** (UF/F) Weighhouse Close, New Street (cong to St. Matthew's)
⊥   (1887 ConP 2/21 r Ing 2/23, rem 1907 to London, Wood Green, Bowes Park M by N&B

**Paisley St. James'** (UF/UP) Underwood Road cld 2016 (see also Paisley Primitive M)
⊥   1884 Wil 2/23 r1903 Wil 3/39, o1946, r1967 Wal 2/36

**Paisley St. James RC Church** 50 Greenock Road
⊥   (c1895 Mir 2/c10 in previous blg, rem 1958 Watt to workshop, material reused

**Paisley St. John's** (Middle UF/F) School Wynd cld 1991 (now Wynd Centre)
⊥   (1908 N&B 2/15 material rem 1999 to Glasgow St. Peter's Partick RC & r2003 McDM
    3/26

**Paisley St. Luke's** (Paisley South) Neilston Road
  入   1902 A&S 2/15 (mechanical) 1ss changed 1938 A&S

**Paisley St. Mary's RC** George Street
  入   1916 Watt 2/12  o1972 Wal, o2004 McDM
  入   (1975 L&B 1/6  rem 1990 to Mytholmroyd Good Shepherd RC by David Rhodes

**Paisley St. Matthew's Church of the Nazarene** (St. Matthew's/St. George's East/F cld 1988)
Gordon Street/Orchard Square - see also Paisley St. George's East
  入   1907 N&B 2/25+2pf  o1924 HNB, o1948 HNB **A-listed**

**103) The 1907 Norman & Beard organ in the Church of the Nazarene (St. Matthew's) in
Paisley with Art Nouveau case by William McLennan**
Reproduced with kind permission of the Church of the Nazarene, Paisley

**Paisley St. Mirin's Cathedral RC**
  入   (c1815 organ in previous blg nearby  extant 1852
  入   (1948 Jar/Wur/Watt 2/28 (3 divisions, pt fr Greenock Regal ABC), o1956 Watt, rem 1983
  入   1884 ConP 2/17  r1902 N&B (TW Lewis), fr Prestwick New Life (Monkton &
       Prestwick) 1926 to Watt workshop, then Stepps St Andrew's & r 2/21, 1983 acquired
       McDM, to here 1986 & r McDM 2/24 with some ss and cases fr old organ, o2001 McDM

**Paisley St. Ninian's Ferguslie** Blackstoun Road
  入   c1890s Bro 2/7  to here 1963 Watt, unplayable, disused

**Paisley St. Ninian's RC**
  入   (organ extant 1877

322

**Paisley Sandyford** (Thread Street UF/UP) Thread Street blg cld 1969
⚓ (1890 Hill 3/26  o1915 HNB,  r1949 HNB, rem to new ch in Gallowhill 1970 HNB

**Paisley Sandyford** Gallowhill/Montgomery Road blg cld 2011, dem
⚓ (1890 Hill 3/26  o1915 HNB, r1949 HNB, fr former ch 1970 HNB, o1998 McDM 3/27 with mixtures fr Paisley Central Hall M

**Paisley School Wynd C** Oakshaw Street East/School Wynd  cld 2002
⚓ (1879 Wad 2/  to here 1900, disused 1966
⚓ (1968 Wal 2/17 ex3  rem fr Paisley Abbey (temp organ) 1968 Wal, to here 1969 Wal, o1982 McDM, rem to Paisley Oakshaw Trinity 2003 by McDM (temp)

**Paisley Sherwood Greenlaw** (Sherwood/UF/F) Glasgow Road
⚓ 1893 Lew 2/17+1pf (electric action)  r1947 HNB 2/18 **B-listed**

**Paisley South** - see Paisley St. Luke's and Paisley Stow Brae

**Paisley Storie Street B**
⚓ (1866 ConP  rem to Paisley George Street 1911 & r Hils 2/

**Paisley Stow Brae** (Laigh/St. Andrew's/South UF/F) Causeyside Street
⚓ (1901 Walc 1/  dest fire
⚓ (1902 Bis 2/17  r Gol, rem 1988-89
⚓ 1989 Lam 2/19

**Paisley Thomas Coats Memorial Baptist** High Street
⚓ 1889 Hill 4/47 installed 1894  o1901 Hill, +1ss pre-1947, r1985 HNB, o1995 HNB 4/50 **A-listed**

**Paisley Thread Street** - see Paisley Sandyford

**Paisley Town Hall** (George Aitken Clark Hall)
⚓ (1882 BBE 4/49  reopened 1895, r1921 HNB, o1938 HNB, pt rem 1951 to Grangemouth Zetland by Bell, pt scr

**Paisley Wallneuk North** (Wallneuk) Abercorn Street/North Croft Street
⚓ 1931 A&S 2/24

**Paisley Woodside Res of Sir P and A Coats**
⚓ (c1850 Bev 2/9 rem 1896 to Bishopton by Mir +1ss changed
⚓ (organ  rem 1858 by F&A
⚓ 1858 F&A 2/12  finger and barrel, one stop from old organ, extant 1887
⚓ (1888 Gern 3/29  rem 1932 to Paisley Museum by HNB (rear case to Glasgow Gordon Park)

**Panbride** - see Carnoustie

**Papa Stronsay Golgotha Monastery** Orkney
⚓ (1921 Ing 2/18  o1950s, o1970s, o1988 R&D, fr Kirkwall East to here 2002 to store

**Patna UF Cont.** (UP)
⚓ 1903 Kir 1/5

**Peathill** - see Pitsligo

**Peebles Old** High Street/Tweed Bridge
  ⊥   1887 Gern 2/18 r1890 Gern 3/24, +2 pd ss 1898, r1906 Ing, r1937 Wil 3/27, r1972 R&D, r1987 Gol 3/47, r2003 Lig 3/44

**104) The 1883 Gern organ in Peebles Old and the 1912 Ingram in the Leckie Memorial, now St. Andrew's Leckie. The Gern organ in rebuilt form is now confined to the left side of the chancel, without its fine cases, and the Ingram is long gone**

**Peebles Res of Colin Mackenzie** - see Portmore

**Peebles Res of Mr. R. Pattison, Kingsmeadows**
  ⊥   (1898 Ing

**Peebles St. Andrew's UF** (F) Eastgate, High Street cld 1918
  ⊥   (1902 F&A 2/19 rem 1922 to Edinburgh Leith Kirkgate by Sco

**Peebles St. Andrew's** (St. Andrew's UF/West UF/UP) cld 1976
  ⊥   (1897 Bin 2/21

**Peebles St. Andrew's Leckie** (Leckie Memorial/UF/East UP) Tweed Green/High Street
  ⊥   (1912 Ing 2/13 rem 1960s

**Peebles St. Joseph's RC** Young Street
  ⊥   (1880 ConJ 2/9 rem 1889 to Edinburgh St. Columba's RC

**Peebles St. Peter's E** Eastgate
  ⊥   (c1700 SmB 2/10 no pd fr Edinburgh Charlotte Chapel, rem 1819 WSm to Bruce workshop, to here 1828 (cong in town ballroom), to present blg 1832, rem 1882
  ⊥   (1882 B&F 2/10 r Ing 2/12, rem 1909 to Evenwood St. Paul's, Co. Durham
  ⊥   1909 Har 3/16 o1947 Har, o1995 Lig **A-listed**

**Pencaitland** East Lothian
  ⊥   (1889 ConP 2/7 rem 2003 to Manor by Lig

**Penicuik Beeslack House**
  ⊥   (1820s WSm 1/9 +Sw rem to Edinburgh Res of John & Sheila Barnes pre-1974

**Penicuik North** (UF/UP) 95 John Street
⊥  (1908 Sco 2/11  rem 1960 to Worksop College Chapel, Ranby School, Retford, Notts

**Penicuik St. James the Less E** Broomhill Road
⊥  1872 Holt 2/9  fr Haddington Res of Walter H. Ferme 1937, 1ss changed 1982 by SmRo, o1996 SmRo 1ss changed

**Penicuik St. Mungo's** 63 Carlops Road
⊥  1887-91 C&M 2/20  r1901 HCF 2/21, r1993 R&D, o2010 Loo

**Penicuik South** (UF/F) Bridge Street, Peebles Road
⊥  1901 HCF 2/17  o1959 R&D, r1989 SmRo **B-listed**

**Penpont** Dumfriesshire
⊥  1875 F&A 2/14  o1977 McDM, o1996 McDM **B-listed**

**Penpont Virginhall** - see Thornhill

**Perceton** - see Dreghorn

**Perth B** 151 South Street (now Gospel Hall)
⊥  (1866 organ

**Perth Bridgend** (UF/UP) Main Street cld 1965
⊥  (1894 organ gifted
⊥  (1903 W. Johnstone  r Sco 2/

**Perth C** (New C/Kinnoull Street C) Kinnoull Street/Murray Place (fr Mill Street 1896)
⊥  (1866 ConP 2/15 (previous blg)  rem 1899 to Greenock Mearns Street C by Mir
⊥  1899 Wad 2/16  o1905 Wad, r1950s Wil 2/19

**Perth City Hall** King Edward Street
⊥  (1887 C&M 3/32  fr previous hall 1911 & r MilJ 3/31, r1957 Wil 4/54, r1979 R&D 4/54, rem 2006 McDM for Perth Organs Pty Ltd, Western Australia, to Melbourne Haileybury College School & r 4/63

**Perth Craigend** (UF/UP) cld 1974 dem
⊥  (1913 Wat 1+pd/8 gifted or lent by minister  o1922, o1923 Cat

**Perth East**  - see St. John's Kirk of Perth

**Perth Kinnoull** Dundee Road nr Queen's Bridge
⊥  (1882 JoH 2/12  rem 1896 to Perth St. Andrew's & St. Stephen's
⊥  (1896 H-J 2/20  rem 1930 to north west corner with new case, r1957 Wil 2/19, o1993 Wil, rem 2009

**Perth Kinnoull Street Chapel** (East Kirk chapel)
⊥  (1809 MWo 1+ppd/8  fr Perth St. John's E (chapel) 1849 by Bru, returned 1851

**Perth Kinnoull Street C** - see Perth C

**Perth Kinnoull Street UF** 43 Kinnoull Street blg cld 1990s cong 2013 (hall now Oasis)
⊥  (1936 Ree 2/17

**Perth Letham St. Mark's** (Letham) Rannoch Road
  ⅄ (c1970 Wal 2/15 ex3 all unenclosed rem 2004 to Fowlis Easter (St. Marnock's) by Edm

**Perth M** Scott Street
  ⅄ BinT 2/16 ex3 to here 1965 R&D

**Perth Menzies, John, Bookseller** George Street
  ⅄ (chamber organ 1/4 for sale 21x1786

**Perth Middle** (UF/F) Tay Street cld 1965
  ⅄ (1901 MilJ 2/24 r Sco 3/

**Perth Middle** - see also Perth St. John's Kirk of Perth

**Perth Mill Street C** - see Perth C

**Perth Murray Royal Hospital** (Asylum) Kinnoull
  ⅄ (1906 MilJ
  ⅄ 1963 Wal 2/29 ex6

**Perth North** (North UF/UP) Mill Street
  ⅄ (1894 H-J/MilJ 2/21 r Wil, o1960 R&D, o1980 R&D, disused 1990s

**Perth Res**
  ⅄ (1762 WaJ 1/4 fr Glasgow Res of James Steven (where 1ss added), to Glasgow St. Andrew's 1807 (temp), returned to Steven, rem to Glasgow Res of J. Findlater, Sauchiehall Street, c1840 rem to here

**Perth Res**
  ⅄ (c1850s Mir 1/5 repaired R. Thomson (Yorks), o Bro, rem 1930s to Edinburgh Fettes College

**Perth Res of A.F. Edmonstone** Tullylumb House
  ⅄ c1715 organ 1/5 in 19$^{th}$ century case fr Aberdeen Res of John Whiteley, Bedford Row & r Edm 1985 **C-listed**

**Perth St. Andrew's & St. Stephen's** (St. Andrew's) Atholl Street/Balhousie Street blg cld 1999 cong transported to Riverside
  ⅄ (1882 JoH 2/12 fr Perth Kinnoull 1896 & r MilJ 2/15, r1930 Sco 2/16 case divided

**Perth St. John's Kirk of Perth** (St. John the Baptist) St. John's Place
Pre-Reformation Kirk:
  ⅄ (ref to organs in 1511 and 1521, dest 1559
East Kirk:
  ⅄ (1874 ConP 3/30 r1893 H-J 3/30, r1905 S&L 3/30, pt used 1928 by Rot
Middle Kirk:
  ⅄ (1887 Scot 1/10
West Kirk:
  ⅄ (1904 MilJ 2/16 twin cases
United Church (fr 1926):
  ⅄ (1928 Rot 3/37 (Lorimer Case) r1961 R&D 3/39
  ⅄ 1986 Edm 3/47 using older material o2003 Edm (2ss changed)

**Perth St. John the Baptist E** (English E to 1848) Princes Street
- ⚞ (1809 MWo 1+ppd/8  rem 1849 (temp) to chapel in Kinnoull Street, 1851 to new  chapel, for sale 1856
- ⚞ (1857 Bev 2/18  o1861 Wis, o1871 ConP, o1886 Wad
- ⚞ (1889 Har 3/28  using material fr old organ
- ⚞ (1908 Bin 2+1pf/  r1915 Bin in ch, r1924 Bin 3/33, rem 1971 to Ipswich St. John's
- ⚞ (1971 Har 2/23  o1979 Har, rem 2011 to Edinburgh Sacred Heart RC by For

**Perth St. John the Baptist RC** Melville Street
- ⚞ (1836 organ  extant 1854
- ⚞ (1867 F&A 2/18  r1910 N&B 2/ , r1950s/1960s R&D
- ⚞ 2004 McDM fr other sources

**Perth St. Leonard's** King Street cld 1985
- ⚞ (1892 MilJ

**Perth St. Leonard's in the Fields** (St. Leonard's in the Fields/UF/F) Marshall Place
- ⚞ (1896 G&D 2/20  r1935 G&D 3/30, rem 1969
- ⚞ (1952 Kin 2/40 ex9  fr Res in Orpington, Surrey to here 1969 by Arn, rem 1985 to Simon Langton School, Kent
- ⚞ 1881 BBE 2/25  r1899 Ing, r1931 R&D 2/27, r1969 R&D 2/29, o1977 R&D, fr Edinburgh North Morningside 1985 & r Loo 2/40

**Perth St. Mark's** (second charge fr St. John's) Feus Road cld 1977
- ⚞ (1924 MilJ

**Perth St. Mary's Monastery RC** Hatton Road, Kinnoull
- ⚞ 1870 F&A 2/13 +1pf (3 Pedal ss derived fr Gt) +1ss by Bro **A-listed**
- ⚞ (1902 Walc 1/7

**Perth St. Matthew's** (West/UF/F) Tay St
- ⚞ 1896 Wal 2/18  r1973 Gol 2/27, r1991 Gol 2/33, r2002 Edm 2/22

**Perth St. Ninian's Cathedral E** Atholl Street/North Methven Street
- ⚞ 1850 SmB/Rob 2/34  fr elsewhere  r1873 ConP, r1894 IngE 4/37 +4pf,  r1901-05 MilJ 4/39 +4pf in new chamber, o1907 MilJ, o1949 R&D, r1964 R&D 3/42 with new console, r1982 Nic 3/43, r1996 Edm 4/49 +2pf with console fr Edinburgh St. Giles' Cathedral, +3ss fr Dunblane Cathedral
- ⚞ (c1700 SmB  fr elsewhere  extant 19$^{th}$ century
- ⚞ (1986 Nic 1/3 (temp) on loan to Edinburgh St. Michael & All Saints 1997-2000

**Perth St. Paul's** High Street/Methven Street cld 1988
- ⚞ (1890 Har 2/22  rem 1989 to Elgin St. Columba's

**Perth St. Stephen's** (UF/F) Paradise Place blg cld 1954 (ch to Ainslie Gardens cld 1991)
- ⚞ (1902 MilJ

**Perth Trinity Church of the Nazarene** (Trinity/York Place/UF/UP cld 1982) York Place
- ⚞ (1914 MilJ 2/19

**Perth West**  - see St. John's Kirk of Perth and also St. Matthew's

**Perth Wilson** (UF/UP) High Street/Scott Street cld 1965
- ⚞ (1896 MilJ 2/19

**Peterculter** (Kelman Memorial/UF/F) North Deeside Road
⊥ (1900s Pos o Law

**Peterculter Rudolf Steiner School**
⊥ 1976 Col 1/3

**Peterculter St. Peter's** (Peterculter) Howie Lane cld 1999 (now Heritage Centre)
⊥ 1914 Ing 2/11

**Peterhead C**
⊥ 1907 Walc 1/5 extant 2015

**Peterhead New** (Peterhead Trinity/West Associate/St. Peter's UF/F)
⊥ 1898 Wad 2/14 o1926 Wad, disused

**Peterhead Non-Jurors Chapel E** Geary's Close, Broadgate cld 1812 (later used by Trinity)
⊥ (c1791 organ rem 1814

**Peterhead Old** (St. Peter's) Erroll Street cld 2016
⊥ (1874 Hill 2/12 r1894 Wad
⊥ 1911 B&F 2/29 using older material o1929 Law
⊥ 1966 R&D 2/ ex5

**Peterhead Res of James Argo**
⊥ (Tytler 1/4 for sale 1811, probably rem 1815 to Keith Holy Trinity E by J. Morison

**Peterhead Res of Thomas Arbuthnott, Bath House** Bath Street
⊥ (organ r1868 Holt, for sale 3xi1868 (see Peterhead St. Peter's E)

**Peterhead Res of Alexander Clarke**
⊥ 1914 Ebr 2/12

**Peterhead Res of Rev. Dr. Wm. Laing**
⊥ (1788 Laing & Beattie pt to Aberdeen Res of Beattie, pt to Aberdeen Song School

**Peterhead Res of John Morrison**
⊥ (organ 1/3½ for sale 1805

**Peterhead Res of Mr. Sutherland**
⊥ (organ extant 1920

**Peterhead Res of Rev. Patrick Torry**
⊥ (c1790s Torry (amateur) rem to Elgin Holy Trinity E

**Peterhead Res of Wm Tytler**
⊥ (Tytler/Laing 1/4 sold 1808 perhaps to James Argo (other organs by amateurs made here, one to Gordon Castle, Fochabers 1804)

**Peterhead St. Andrew's** (East) Queen Street
⊥ 1902 Wad 2/17

**Peterhead St. Mary's RC** St. Peter's Street
⊥ (c1847 organ to new chapel 1852 by Wis
⊥ organ extant 1890-1918

**Peterhead St. Peter's E** Merchant Street
- ⚜ (1749 Sne 1/8 fr Edinburgh St. Paul's Qualified Chapel E, Skinners Close to here 1775 by Joh, r1820 WSm 2/ in new chapel, r1867 Holt 2/13, for sale 1904
- ⚜ (1904 Wad 2/21 o1932 Wad, scr 1970s

**Peterhead South Pentecostal** (South/UF/F cld 1961) Chapel Street
- ⚜ (1901 Wad 2/ o1919 Wad, organ sold 1966

**Peterhead Spa Pump Room** (Masonic Hall) cld 1818
- ⚜ (two organs 1806-15

**Pitfour House** nr Mintlaw dest 1927
- ⚜ (organ extant 1890

**Pitfour Castle Res of Sir John Richardson** Glencarse, Perthshire
- ⚜ 1853 Bev 1/6 fr Crieff St. Margaret's College 1863

**Pitfour** (location unknown)
- ⚜ (organ early 18$^{th}$ C German 1/7 r1856 Rob, fr Snaresbrooke, Mozarbe Lodge, collection of Captain Lane to Mottispont Abbey Res of Raymond Russell, rem to Dilke Street, to here 1955 & r Man, rem 1966 to Megginch Castle

**Pitlochry East** (Moulin UF/F) cld 1992
- ⚜ (1916 Watt 1/6

**Pitlochry Holy Trinity E** Perth Road
- ⚜ 1903 Hele 2/11 o Edm **A-listed**

**Pitlochry** (Pitlochry West/Mission Church) Church Road
- ⚜ (1902 MilJ 2/16 scr 1998

**Pitsligo** Peathill, Aberdeenshire cld 1997
- ⚜ 1899 ConP 2/11 +2pf redundant 2002

**Pitsligo** (Rosehearty UF/UP) Aberdeenshire
- ⚜ pre-1918 Wad 2/20

**Pitsligo** - see also New Pitsligo and Sandhaven

**Pittenweem St. John's E** Marygate
- ⚜ (barrel organ 4ss sold 1853
- ⚜ 1848 Ren/ChrE 1/4 glass swell shutters o1995 Lig, 2001 moved within blg **A-listed**

**Plean** - see Cowie & Plean

**Pluscarden Abbey RC**
- ⚜ (organ extant between 1454 and 1577
- ⚜ (1888 James Graham (amateur) to Carnoustie Res of Graham c1892, rem post-1925 to Aberdeen Doctor's Res, rem to Nairn St. Mary's RC, to here c1965 and inst, r1977 Loo, rem 2000 to Buckie St. Peter's RC (temp) by Loo
- ⚜ (Pos 1/5 fr Aberdeen St. Joseph's RC
- ⚜ (1899 Law 2/12 fr Boharm to Boharm Mulben 1976 by Philip Wright, o1979 R&D, to storage here by Loo, rem
- ⚜ 1999 Tic 2/10

**Polkemmet House** West Lothian
⋏ (c1870 Ewa 1/7 o1900, rem to Longridge 1960s by R&D

**Polmont Blairlodge School**
⋏ (1893 B&F 2/13 rem 1906 to Elie by Ing

**Polmont Old** (North)
⋏ 1931 Ing 2/17

**Polmont Wallacestone M** Shieldhill Road, Reddingmuirhead
⋏ Kir 2/ fr Beeston M, Notts 1914 & r A&S 2/10

**Poltalloch House** Kilmartin, Argyll dem 1959 (see also Kilmartin)
⋏ (1862 G&D 2/18 altered 1865 G&D, r1907 G&D, rem 1958 and then to Stamford
School, Lincolnshire 1961 & r Long Crendon 2/21, r DavA

**105) The 1862 Gray & Davison organ in the stairwell at Poltalloch House.**
Reproduced with the kind permission of Mr. Robin Malcolm of Duntrune

**Port Bannatyne** (St. Bruoc/North Bute UF/F) Bute cld 1956
⋏ (1920 Watt

**Portessie M**
⋏ 1920 Law 2/13

**Port Glasgow Clune Park** (UF/UP) Robert Street cld 1972 (derelict)
⋏ (1902 F&A 2/ fr Glasgow St. Stephen's West post-1941

**Port Glasgow Hamilton** (UF/F) Princes Street blg cld 1958
⋏ (1900 Lew 2/21 o1911 Lew, o1922 W&L/Brk

**Port Glasgow Hamilton Bardrainney** (Hamilton) Bardrainney Avenue
⚲ (1960s Vin 2/22 ex3

**Port Glasgow Holy Family RC** 2 Parkhill Avenue
⚲ 1959 R&D 2/ ex4

**Port Glasgow Newark** Glen Avenue cld 1987 (converted)
⚲ (1902 Walc 2/19 moved within ch 1922, dism 1938

**Port Glasgow Princes Street** (UF/UP) 12 Princes Street cld 1972
⚲ (1902 ConP 2/18 rem

**Port Glasgow St Andrew's** (Old) Princes Street/Church Street
⚲ 1873 ConP 2/17 r1898 Bin 3/25 +1pf, +1ss post-1940
⚲ (Mir 1/6 (in ch hall)

**Port Glasgow St. John the Baptist RC** 23 Shore Street
⚲ (1854 organ rem
⚲ (1891 Bis 2/12
⚲ (c1953 Watt ex o McDM, rem
⚲ 1912 A&S 2/10 r1978 McDM 2/13, fr Coatbridge Coatdyke 1994 by McDM

**Port Glasgow St. Martin's** Mansion Avenue
⚲ (Pos 1/4 vandalised, rem
⚲ Watt 2/ to here by R&D fr Greenock

**Port Glasgow St Mary the Virgin E** Bardrainney Avenue blg cld 1984
⚲ (organ extant 1872
⚲ (c1891 ConJ 2/c15 rem 1921 to Port Glasgow West by Mir
⚲ (1886 Wil 2/16 fr Ardgowan St Michael's and All Angels Private Chapel E 1921 & r Mir, o1930 Wil, o1973 R&D, rem 1985 to Kirkintilloch Holy Family RC & r McDM

**106) The 1886 Willis organ from Ardgowan while at St. Mary's, Port Glasgow.**
Photograph by Michael Macdonald

331

**Port Glasgow Town Hall**
⅄ (1902 Bin 3/34 rem 1960 to Newport Tabernacle C, Monmouthshire 1962 & r BinT 2/24

**Port Glasgow West** (Newark UF/F) Brown Street/Jean Street cld 1983 (flats)
⅄ (c1891 ConJ 2/c15 fr Port Glasgow St. Mary the Virgin E 1921 by Mir, extant 1960s

**Portlethen** Kincardine
⅄ ( pre-1876 Wis valued 1893 by Wad, to here 1898 by Law fr Aberdeen Song School, extant 1919
⅄ (1909 Walc 2/7 fr Lossiemouth St. James' 1968 by Norman Marr, rem 1980s

**Portmore House** nr Eddleston
⅄ (1882 Har 3/22 dest by fire 1883
⅄ (1886 Har 3/22 unplayable by 1952, vandalised 1980s
⅄ 1992 R&D 2/12 using some pipework fr the Harrison
⅄ c1820 Bry barrel organ **A-listed**

107) The 1992 Rushworth rebuild of the organ at Portmore, originally by Harrison

**Portnacroish Res of Brigadier Stewart** Appin, Argyll
⅄ (c1810 Cle barrel organ 4ss + 2 traps rem 1978 to Cumbernauld Res of Joseph Cairney

**Portnacroish Holy Cross E**
⅄ (barrel organ extant post WW2
⅄ (early 19th century English organ fr Loanhead Res of Tom Craig to Edinburgh Res (temp) 1973, returned to Edinburgh Res of Craig, Colinton
⅄ 1830s SBr 1/7 for sale fr Res 1861, rem to Edinburgh Res of Dr. McArthur, Beachcroft, Trinity by 1883, rem to Kirkcaldy West End C 1898 & r King 1+pd/8, rem to Dundee Morison C 1920 & r MilJ 1/8, rem 1928 to Aberfeldy C, rem 1988 to Leithen Lodge, Peeblesshire and inst Hugh Ross, rem 1995 to Largs St. Columba's by SHOT volunteers, rem 2006 to Kentallen St. Moluag's E, to here 2017

**Port of Menteith**

⊥ (c1840s Scottish chamber organ r later 1/7, fr Gartmore House 1958 & r R&D, scr 2005, case survives

**108) The chamber organ at Port of Menteith prior to the removal
of its pipework and action in 2005**

**Portpatrick**

⊥ (1960s Sol 1/5 no pd ex1 to here fr Lochryan 1986 by John Wilson, rem by 2012

**Portree St. Columba's E**

⊥ (1914 N&B rem 1923 to Invergordon

**Portsoy** (Fordyce/West/UF/F)

⊥ 1954-60 Watt 2/20 ex4 disused 2015

**Portsoy** - see also Fordyce

**Portsoy East** (Portsoy) cld 1955 (hall, to be reopened as ch)

⊥ (organ erected 1894 Wad r1938 Law 2/9, r Watt (case fr Glasgow St. Clement's, Bridgeton)

**Portsoy Church of the Annunciation RC** cld c2005

⊥ (1806 MWo fr Macduff to Banff Our Lady of Mount Carmel RC 1820, to here 1829, o1846 Bru, extant 1891, rem later

**Premnay** Aberdeenshire cld 1973
⊥ (1900 Law 2/10

**Premnay Waukmill** (Leslie & Premnay UF/F) cld 1935
⊥ (1899 Pos 1/

**Preshome St. Gregory's RC** nr Buckie
⊥ 1820 WSm 2/10 moved to gallery 1822 WSm & back again 1848 by Wis, r c1896 1ss changed, o c1910, o1959 Watt **A-listed**

**109) The 1820 Bruce organ at Preshome, from the side**

**Prestonkirk** (St. Baldred's) nr East Linton
⊥ 1910 Vin 2/18 fr Newcastle Festival to here 1911, o1976/83 R&D, r2004 Lig 2/17, r2015 Lig after vandalism

**Prestonkirk St. Andrew's** (UF/F) East Linton cld 1959 (ch hall to 1990)
⊥ (1895 F&A 2/12 rem 1996 to Gordon, Berwickshire & r1998/2003 Sta

**Prestonpans** (Prestongrange/Preston/Prestonpans) Kirk Street
⊥ 1899 Ing 2/ r Wal 2/19, r John Thomson and Bob Hooker

**Prestonpans Grange** (UF/F) Ayres Wynd cld 1981 (later St. Andrew's E cld 2014, now Lighthouse Central B)
⊥ (organ 2/ for sale 1950, rem
⊥ (1901 Watt 2/ fr Chryston West 1951 & o Ing, rem 1963 to Sam Burns yard

334

**Prestwick: Monkton & Prestwick North** (Prestwick Nth/UF/Prestwick F)
   ⚶   (1910 N&B 1/  o1922 Hils, o1951 Hils or Bro, disused 1966

**Prestwick New Life** (Monkton & Prestwick/St. Cuthbert's cld 1981) Monkton Road
   ⚶   (1884 ConP 2/17  r1902 N&B (TW Lewis), rem 1926 to Watt workshop, then to Stepps St. Andrew's
   ⚶   1926 Hils 2/23  organ case extant 2013

**Prestwick St. Nicholas** Main Street
   ⚶   1910 N&B 2/20  o1986 HNB

**Prestwick St. Ninian's E** Maryborough Road
   ⚶   (1926 Wad 2/
   ⚶   1948-50 Jar 2/24

**Prestwick South** (UF/Prestwick UP) Main Street
   ⚶   1902 F&A 1/7  (first "Kingston" model organ)  moved within blg 1957, rem c1985 to Ayr St. Columba's Lochside

**Quarrier's Village** - see Bridge of Weir

**Queensferry** (St. Andrew's/UF/UP) The Loan
   ⚶   (1905 N&B 1/  rem 1972 to Falkirk St. James'
   ⚶   (1972-74 Bell 2/10  fr pt of several organs, scr 1984

**Queensferry: Priory Church E** (St. Mary's Carmelite Priory RC) Hopetoun Road
   ⚶   (1902 Walc 2/17  r1959 Bell 2/21, fr Edinburgh Hopetoun 1974 to storage here by Bell, then scr

**Rackwick Res of Peter Maxwell Davies** Hoy, Orkney
   ⚶   (1982 Man 1/4  rem 1997 to Sanday Res of Peter Maxwell Davies

**Raemoir House** nr Banchory - see Aberdeen St. Clement's E and Banchory Res of Innes

**Rankeillor House** (Res of Sir Michael Nairn) nr Springfield, Fife
   ⚶   (1910 N&B 2/21 + solo division & barrel mechanism  rem 1960 to Edinburgh Canongate without barrels

**Ratho** nr Edinburgh
   ⚶   (1884 ConP
   ⚶   1964 Sme 2/28 ex4

**Ratho** - see also Hatton House

**Rathven** nr Buckie
   ⚶   1909 Wad 2/9

**Rayne** Aberdeenshire - see Culsalmond & Rayne

**Renfrew North** (UF/F) Renfield Street
   ⚶   1899 B&H 2/  r1933 HNB, o1987 HNB, r2012 Loo

**Renfrew Old** High Street cld 2012
   ⚶   1910 Bin 2/25  r1929 HNB 2/25 1ss changed, o1987 HNB

**Renfrew St. Margaret's E** Oxford Road/Paisley Road
⚒ c1850 Ren 1/5 o1983 McDM, redundant 2007 **B-listed**

**Renfrew Trinity** (UF/UP) Paisley Road
⚒ organ r1924 HNB 2/15

**Renton Trinity** (Old) Alexander Street, Dunbartonshire
⚒ 1911 Bin 2/20 r R&D

**Renton** - see also Alexandria

**Rerrick** (Dundrennan) Kirkcudbright cld 2010
⚒ (1898 Pos 1/
⚒ 1960s Sol 1/5

**Rescobie** Angus
⚒ 1908 MilJ 1/5

**Rhu & Shandon** (Rhu)
⚒ 1880 F&A 2/20 r1904 Hill 2/28 +1pf, r1957 R&D 3/31 (new console), r2006 Lib 3/30, 2012 pipes stolen, o2013 Lib 3/30

**Rhu Res of I. Macdonald**
⚒ (1906 Lew 3/20 rem 1921, 1923 to Glasgow Jordanhill by Brk

**Rhum** - see Kinloch Castle

**Rhynie** - see Noth

**Riccarton** - see Kilmarnock

**Rosehearty** - see Pitsligo

**Rosewell** Midlothian
⚒ 1903 Ing 2/12

**Rosewell St. Matthew RC**
⚒ 1864 HDT 2/15 +1pf 1s added later, r1890 LTC 2/19 +1pf, o1963 R&D 2/20, fr Edinburgh St. James the Less E, Leith 1980 by John Anderson 2/18 +1pf (pd 16' rem) **C-listed**

**Roslin** (UF/F) Midlothian
⚒ (1922 Pos 1/4 to here 1926, o1994 Gol, rem 1997
⚒ 1929 HNB 1/6 +1pf, o1940s R&D, o1991 Loo, to here fr Torryburn 2016 by Loo

**Rosneath St. Modan's** Dunbartonshire
⚒ 1873 Hill 2/11 r1895 Hill (resited) 2/17 **A-listed**

110) The 1873 Hill organ at Rosneath

**Rosskeen East** nr Rosskeen House/Auchintool blg cld 1943

⚞ (1906 N&B 1/6  rem 1951 to Motherwell St. Mary's by Bell

337

**Rosslyn Chapel: St. Matthew's E** Roslin, Midlothian
- ⋏ (1862 HDa 1/ rem c1865
- ⋏ (1812 MWo 2/ no pd fr Dundee St. Paul's Cathedral E 1865 to Montrose URC, to here by 1870 Ren, rem 1872 to Wingate Parish, Co. Durham by HDT
- ⋏ 1872 HDT 2/11 to new gallery 1880, r1902 HCF 2/11, o1957 R&D, o1983 R&D, r2010 Lam 2/13
- ⋏ (1987-89 Lam 1/5 fr Humbie Stobshiel to Crichton Manse 1991, to here 2005, rem 2010 to Edinburgh Mayfield Salisbury

**111) Rosslyn Chapel. These two photographs show two successive organs installed in the chapel during the 1860s. During Christmas festivities can be seen the 1862 organ by David Hamilton. This was displaced by 1870, probably by the Muir Wood organ from St. Paul's Dundee, although the builder's name is illegible. Photographs reproduced courtesy of Historic Environment Scotland (Gerald Cobb). Copyright SC1546068.**

**Rosyth** Queensferry Road
- ⋏ (1895 HCF 2/15 o1926 HNB,fr Kinross East & r1982 SmRo, disused 2011, scr 2013

**Rosyth Cromarty Campus Workshop of Forth Pipe Organs**
- ⋏ (1893 G&D 2/7 fr Edinburgh Res of J.S. Sturrock to Edinburgh Gillis Centre RC 1894, o1956 Wal, rem 2009 to Newton Village Workshop by For, to here 2013, scr
- ⋏ (various organs in transit or under repair

**Rosyth Dockyard St. Margaret's E**
- ⋏ (c1932 BFH 2/32 ex5 r1980 ConP 2/33, redundant 1996, some pipework rem to storage at Edinburgh Res of Charles Davidson

**Rothes** Moray
- ⋏ (1899 Wad 2/9 o2001 Nob, rem

**Rothesay Aquarium**
- ⋏ (1884 Bro 2/7 fr Glasgow Gorbals Exhibition 1884 by Bro, rem 1900 to Stepps

**Rothesay Bridgend** (UF/UP) Bridge Street/Bridgend Street cld 1942
⅄ (organ r Sco 2/14, rem 1946 to Wishaw Craigneuk (UF) by Hils

**Rothesay Craigmore High** (Craigmore UF/UP) Crichton Road cld 1942
⅄ (1903 Brow 2/16

**Rothesay Craigmore St. Brendan's** (Craigmore) Mount Stuart Road blg cld 1999
⅄ 1903 Walc 2/19

**Rothesay St. Andrew's RC** Columsshill Street
⅄ (1867 ConP
⅄ 1922 Pos 1/5 to here 1925

**Rothesay St. John's** (New) Argyle Street cld 1973
⅄ (1878 ConP 2/13 r1920s Watt

**Rothesay St. Paul's E** Victoria Street/Deanhood Place
⅄ (1854 HDa rem by 1920s pt used elsewhere

**Rothesay Trinity** (UF Parish/Rothesay F) Castle Street
⅄ 1904 B&F 2/18 all unenclosed disused 1988

**Rothesay: United Church of Bute** (The High Kirk/Rothesay) High Street
⅄ 1930 Watt 2/12 +1pf +1ss 1978 McDM, disused

**Rothesay West** (UF/F) Argyle Street cld 1979
⅄ (1901 B&H 2/ rem to South Ronaldsay 1986 & r

**Rothiemay** Aberdeenshire
⅄ (1928 organ

**Rothiemay Res**
⅄ (1923 Mortier (Antwerp) dance organ (automaton) r1946 Decap (Antwerp), fr France to St. Alban's Organ Museum, to here 1967 & o, rem to Alford Grampian Transport Museum 1983

**Rothiemurcus St. John's E** Aviemore
⅄ 1982 Dick 1/6 no pd (pt fr Aberfeldy St. Margaret's E) case modified 2013

**Rothienorman** - see Folla Rule

**Roxburgh**
⅄ 1992 Lam 1/4

**Ruberslaw** - see Bedrule, Denholm and Minto

**Rushworth & Dreaper** - see Newton Village

**Rutherglen East** (UF/F) Farmeloan Street cld 1981
⅄ (1904 N&B 2/16 o c1980 HNB (console moved)

**Rutherglen Greenhill** (UF/UP) Greenhill Road cld 1966
⅄ (1904 Bro 2/

**Rutherglen Old** Main Street
⋏  1902 B&F 3/28  o1954, o2010 MilP 2/23 (Choir extant but disused) **C-listed**

**Rutherglen Res of Mr. Gardner, Ingleneuk, 3 Rodger Drive**
⋏  (1904 Watt 2/

**Rutherglen Res of J. Pinkerton, Grosset Hall** (later rhubarb centre)
⋏  (ConP  rem c1870s

**Rutherglen Res of Mr. Potter**
⋏  (organ  extant until c1904

**Rutherglen St. Columkille's RC** 2 Kirkwood Street
⋏  (1893 Mir 2/  fr previous blg 1930s, rem by 1953
⋏  1966 HNB 2/21

**Rutherglen St. Stephen's E** Melrose Avenue cld c1970 (later Masonic Lodge)
⋏  (1920 Watt 2/  to here 1929 fr Glasgow St. Mary Immaculate RC, Pollokshaws & r
   1+pd/5

**Rutherglen Stonelaw** (UF/UP) Stonelaw Road/Dryburgh Avenue
⋏  (1903 Bro  in previous blg in King Street, rem 1912 to new blg & r Bro 2/20
⋏  1931 Com 3/59 ex (incl some of old organ's pipework)  o1990 Edm, r1993 HNB
   (playback system) **B-listed**

**Rutherglen URC** (C) Johnston Drive
⋏  (1903 Walc 1/7
⋏  larger organ  r Sol, disused 2011, pt rem

**Rutherglen Wardlawhill** (C) Hamilton Road cld 2007 (now Hindu temple)
⋏  (1886 H&B 2/12
⋏  1896 F&A 2/19 fr Glasgow St. Enoch's Kelvinhaugh 1935 & r1936 Hils 2/18, o1976
   McDM

**Rutherglen West & Wardlawhill** (West/Munro/Munro UF/West F) 3 Western Avenue
⋏  1899 Ing 2/20 with German pipework  o1933 Hils, r1960s Hils 2/23

**St. Abbs The Mount** Berwickshire
⋏  ( HDT 1/8  rem 1907 to Duns South & r HCF

**St. Andrews All Saints E** North Castle Street
⋏  1923 HNB 2/15  o1990 HNB, o2004 MilP **A-listed**

**St. Andrews B** South Street
⋏  (1846 HDa 1/6  r1857, fr St. Andrews St. Andrew's E 1869, rem pre-1920 to St. Andrews
   C

**St. Andrews C** Bell Street cld 1966 dem 1983
⋏  (1922 MilJ
⋏  (1846 HDa 1/6  r1857, fr St. Andrews St. Andrew's E to St. Andrews B 1869, to here pre-
   1920, rem 1978 to Milngavie St. Joseph's RC by McDM

112) a: The 1846 Hamilton organ at St. Andrews Congregational before its move to Milngavie. This organ was originally at St. Andrew's Episcopal Church. b: the same organ at St. Joseph's Milngavie, shortly before the destruction of its casework

**St. Andrews Cathedral** cld 1560
⋏   (c1450-1546 organs large and small  rem c1560

**St. Andrews Holy Trinity** South Street
⋏   (1909 Wil 3/24 + 8pf added 1912  o1921 W&L, r1937 Com 3/45
⋏   1966/69 Har 3/49  later using some older material, r1974 Har 3/54, o2008 Har

**St. Andrews Hope Park and Martyrs** (Hope Park/UF/USC) St. Mary's Place
⋏   (1890 F&A 2/15  rem 1925 to Northampton Christ Church
⋏   (1924 HNB 2/19  rem 1956 to gallery & r 2/21 +1pf, disused 2008

**St. Andrews Martyrs** (UF/F) North Street cld 2010
⋏   (1904 MilJ 2/   r in new blg 1928, r1966 R&D 2/23, rem 1991

**St. Andrews Res of  R.E. Curwen, Westerlee**
⋏   (1870 Vow 3/23  rem 1900 to Edinburgh St. Martin's E by Ing

**St. Andrews St. Andrew's E** Queens Terrace
⋏   (1833 organ  sold to HDa 1846
⋏   (1846 HDa 1/6  (previous blg in North Street) r1857, rem 1869 to St. Andrews B
⋏   1869 F&A 3/23  r1909 MilJ 3/27, o1955 R&D, r1968 Har 2/31, 2ss changed 1988 Har

341

**St. Andrews St. James RC** The Scores
- ⊥ (1912 MilJ 2/ rem
- ⊥ 1880 ConJ 2/8 fr Peebles St. Joseph's RC 1889 to Edinburgh St. Columba's RC, o1949 R&D, o1984 R&D +1ss changed, to here 1997 & r Edm 2/8 (1ss reinstated) **B-listed**

**St. Andrews St. Leonard's (Church)** Hepburn Gardens
- ⊥ 1889 Wil 3/20 fr St. Andrews St. Salvator's Chapel 1904 by Wil, o1910 Wil, r1935 Wil 3/30, r1967 Wal 3/29

**St. Andrews St. Leonard's School** off South Street
- ⊥ 1896-97 Wil 3/26 o1920 Lew, r1935 Wil 3/31 (1ss fr Liverpool St. George's Hall), r1979 McDM 3/31, r1980 R&D 3/31, o2004 For

**St. Andrews St. Leonard's Chapel** off South Street
- ⊥ (c1900 Pos 1/5 rem 1994 to Perthshire Res
- ⊥ 1994 Wal 2/9

**St. Andrews St. Salvator's Chapel** (parish ch 1761-1904) North Street
- ⊥ (1889 Wil 3/20 rem 1904 to St. Andrews St. Leonard's Church
- ⊥ (1904 Wil 2/15 o1922 W&L, r1926 Wil 2/22, r1955 Wil 3/32, rem 1973
- ⊥ 1974 Hra 4/40 case altered 1990s by Lam, o2000 Edm
- ⊥ 2012 Robin Jennings 1/4

**St. Andrews University** - see St. Andrews St. Salvator's Chapel, St. Leonard's Chapel and Younger Hall

**St. Andrews Younger Hall**
- ⊥ 1975 Har 2/21 fr Cambridge Selwyn College 1990 & r Edm, 2ss changed 1998 Edm

**St. Boswells** (St. Modan's/UF/F)
- ⊥ 1959 Marshall Sykes 2/11 fr Bin material r2005 Sta 2/11 ex2

**St. Cyrus** (now Mearns Coastal)
- ⊥ 1902 Ing 2/9

**St. Cyrus West** (UF/F) cld 1933
- ⊥ (Ing 2/14

**St. Madoes** Perthshire blg cld 2017
- ⊥ 1908 MilJ 1/5 **A-listed**

**St. Monans** St. Monance, Fife
- ⊥ c1850 Rob 1+pd/7 fr Stewarton Lainshaw House, Ayrshire post-1893 to Edinburgh St. Cuthbert's Hall, rem 1926 and in 1930 to Edinburgh Saughtonhall C & r HCF, r1935 R&D 1+pd/10, to here 1995 & r Lig 1+pd/10 **B-listed**

**St. Mungo** Kettleholm nr Lockerbie
- ⊥ 1906 A&S 2/14

**St. Quivox** - see Ayr

**St. Vigean's** - see Arbroath

**Saltcoats B** (Saltcoats South Beach/UF/Gaelic F cld 1964)
  ⊥  (1914 Bin 2/14 r1960s Wil, rem 1999

**Saltcoats Landsborough & Trinity** (Trinity/UF/UP) Dockhead Street cld 1993
  ⊥  (1893 ConP 2/10 +1pf redundant 1995, scr by 2000

**Saltcoats New Trinity** (Erskine/UF/Middle & West UP/Middle UP) Chapel Brae (now called Ardrossan & Saltcoats: Kirkgate)
  ⊥  1899 F&A 2/16 **A-listed**

**Saltcoats North** Hamilton Street (new blg Dalry Road 1955)
  ⊥  19th C organ fr Glasgow pre-1953, r in new blg here 1954 by Bro, r1964 in extended pt of blg with Hils fr Glasgow Bridgeton M

**Saltcoats St. Cuthbert's** (St. Cuthbert's South Beach/St. Cuthbert's/Ardrossan Parish)
  ⊥  1912 Hils 2/27 o1924 Hils, r1945 Hils +1ss, o1953, r1966 R&D 3/ , o1985 HNB

**Saltcoats St. Mary Star of the Sea RC**
  ⊥  1908 Watt 1+pd/ to here fr Glasgow St. Bernard's post-1931, moved in ch 1975 by Mac

**Sanday Res of Peter Maxwell Davies** Orkney
  ⊥  1982 Man 1/4 to here 1997 from Rackwick Res

**Sandhaven** nr Fraserburgh
  ⊥  (c1910s Wad 2/9 with older material rem 1995, facade survived

**Sanquhar: St. Bride's**
  ⊥  (Bro 2/7 rem 1931 to Kinlochleven
  ⊥  1931 Hils 2/18 **A-listed**

**Sauchen** - see Cluny South

**Sauchie & Coalsnaughton** (Sauchie)
  ⊥  (1905 S&L

**Savoch** (Savoch East/Savoch) Aberdeenshire cld 1996
  ⊥  (1907 Walc 1/11 o1917 (after water damage), rem 1980s

**Savoch West** (UF/UP) cld 1933
  ⊥  1903 Walc 1/

**Scalloway** Tingwall, Shetland
  ⊥  1902 Watt 1+pd/6 to here 1903 o1923, o1938 Law, o1981 R&D, o2009 Loo **B-listed**

**Scalloway C** cld c2000
  ⊥  (organ o1938 Law rem 2001

**Scone New** (Abbey/UF/Scone F) Angus Road/Balformo Road
  ⊥  (pre-1912 organ in gallery o1941 Lang, extant 1952, rem
  ⊥  1905 MilJ o1925-27 MilJ, fr Scone West 1952

**Scone Old** Burnside
- ⊥ (1890 MilJ 1+pd/8
- ⊥ (1966 Wil

**Scone Palace**
- ⊥ 1813 Ell 2+ppd/15 (12 note pd) o1836 & 1843 Alexander Buckingham, o1851 Wis, o1975 C. Stevens **A-listed**

**Scone West** (UF/UP) Abbey Road cld 1952
- ⊥ (1905 MilJ o1925-27 MilJ, o1939/41 MilJ, o1942 Larg, rem 1952 to Scone New

**Scourie Res of Mrs. Careen Ross** Sutherland
- ⊥ (1850s Ren 1/9 to Fortrose & r1914 Cat 1/10, rem 1986 to storage here by Hugh Ross, rem 1987 to Leithen Lodge by Hugh Ross

**Selkirk** (Lawson Memorial/UF/UP) High Street
- ⊥ 1901 Bin 2/20 console moved 1953, o1959 BinT 1ss changed **B-listed**

**Selkirk Heatherlie** cld 1986
- ⊥ (1887 B&F 2/17 o1906 B&F, rem pre-1972

**Selkirk Res of James Lewis**
- ⊥ (1884 G&D
- ⊥ (1889 organ fr Old Mentham by N&B

**Selkirk St. John the Evangelist E** Bleachfield Road
- ⊥ (1869 ConP rem
- ⊥ 1876 Jar 2/ fr Holehird, Windermere Res of Major Dunlop to here 1897 Wilk, r1908 Sco 3/ , o1920 Sco, r1928 Ing 2/18, disused 2017

**Selkirk St. Mary's West** (St. Mary's/Selkirk) Ettrick Terrace cld 1986
- ⊥ (1888 B&F 2/17 o1959 R&D
- ⊥ (Tow 1/ (in hall) rem c1961

**Selkirk West** (UF/UP) Chapel Place cld 1963
- ⊥ (1908 A&S 2/20 o1959 R&D

**Seton Collegiate** cld post-1580
- ⊥ (organ rem 1544 by soldiers to England by sea

**Shotts Calderhead Erskine** (Calderhead)
- ⊥ 1904 B&F 2/15

**Shotts Erskine** (UF/F) cld 1989
- ⊥ (1923 organ

**Shotts: Kirk o' Shotts**
- ⊥ (1914 Sco 2/13 r1967 C&C, scr 2005-07

**Skelmorlie & Wemyss Bay** (South)
- ⊥ (1865 ConP 2/ (in current hall, former ch)
- ⊥ 1905 Bin 3/30 in new pt of blg o1977 HNB **A-listed**

**Skelmorlie & Wemyss Bay North** (UF/UP) cld 1972 (see also Wemyss Bay)
⚓ (1878 You 2/16  r1892 Mir,  r1912 N&B 2/

**Skibo Castle** (Res of Andrew Carnegie) nr Dornoch
⚓ 1904 B&F 2/21  o c1978 Nic, o1996 R&D **A-listed**

**Slains** nr Ellon, Aberdeenshire
⚓ (1930 Law 2/9  rem c1998

**Slamannan** (St. Laurence) nr Falkirk
⚓ (1924 Ing  fr Falkirk Graham's Road post-1975 by Gol, scr 2015

**Slamannan Balquatston** (Slamannan UF/F) cld 1945
⚓ (c1900 Walc 1/

**Smailholm** Roxburgh
⚓ 1903 Pos 1/6  fr Edinburgh Oddfellows Hall exhibition, r1979 Sta, o2001 R&D, r2010
Sta with Bru chest 1/5

**Sorbie** Wigtownshire
⚓ 1877 Ren 2/10  rem fr Cally House nr Gatehouse 1936,  o1960s Wal, o1987 W-K

**Sorn** Ayrshire
⚓ 1910 Walc 2/8

**Sorn Castle Res of Mr. T.W. McIntyre**
⚓ organ  r c1915 Hils 2/18 with player mechanism, o1970s WoW (Edm)

**South Knapdale** Achahoish, Knapdale, Argyll
⚓ c1800 All 1/5  in London Res of W. Kelly c1820, fr 2002 at Liverpool Res of Fritz Spiegl,
o2015 G&G for Harry Bicket, to here 2015 G&G

**South Queensferry** - see Queensferry

**South Ronaldsay & Burray** (St. Margaret's UF/UP)
⚓ (1901 B&H 2/  fr Rothesay West 1986 & r

**Southwick** Dumfriesshire
⚓ (1958 Sol 1/5 ex1  o1977 HNB, rem 1989

**Speymouth** nr Fochabers
⚓ (1850s Hol 1/  fr London Res of Hol, rem & r1894 here IngE 2/12, o1973, scr 2007

**Spottes House** nr Urr
⚓ (1880 Fin 2/11  rem 1948 to Gatehouse

**Springfield** - see Rankeillor House

**Stair** nr Cumnock
⚓ 1904 Ing 2/11  1ss altered

**Stamperland** nr Glasgow
⊥    1897 LTC 2/23  fr Glasgow Regent Place & Cathedral Square 1963 & r by Mac 2/21, disused 2016

**Standingstone Farm** Morham, nr Haddington
⊥    (1975 San 1+pd/6  rem 2011 to Edinburgh New College Martin College by Lam

**Stanley St. James'** (UF/F) Perth Road cld 1959 (now hall)
⊥    1901 Bro 1/5 Dulsannel design

**Stenhouse & Carron** (Maclaren Memorial) Church Street, Stenhousemuir
⊥    1902 Bin 2/22  o1984 Loo, o2012 Edm **A-listed**

**Stenton** East Lothian
⊥    1981 Pul 1+pd/6  fr Southsea Church of the Holy Spirit 1990s to Wells Res of Rupert Gough, to here 2009 & r Lam 1+pd/7

**Stepps** (Stepps Whitehill/Stepps) Whitehill Avenue
⊥    (1820s-30s Mir 1/  fr Glasgow Berkeley Street Mac workshop c1970 (temp)
⊥    1884 Bro 2/7  fr Glasgow Gorbals Exhibition 1884 to Rothesay Aquarium by Bro, rem to here 1900 & r Watt 2/9, r1976 Mac 2/11 (case redesigned)

**Stepps St. Andrew's** (Stepps UF) Blenheim Avenue cld 1983
⊥    (1884 ConP 2/17  r1902 N&B (TW Lewis), fr Prestwick New Life (Monkton & Prestwick) 1926 to Glasgow Watt workshop & r, later to here & r 2/21, rem 1983 to Paisley St. Mirin's RC Cathedral & r McDM 1986

**Stevenston High** Schoolwell Street
⊥    1894 Bev 2/13  r1915 Hils 2/18, disused

**Stevenston Livingstone** (UF/F) New Street
⊥    1918 Watt 2/13  fr Glasgow Highlanders Memorial 1941, to here 1944, o c2000

**Stevenston St. John's RC**
⊥    1963 Com "Augmentum" 1+pd/7  r2003 McDM 2/15, pt fr Aberfeldy St. Andrew's

**Stewarton Cairns** (UF/UP) cld 1961
⊥    (1895 F&A 2/  engine inst 1898

**Stewarton John Knox** (UF/F) Main Street
⊥    1903 Watt 2/11  o1970 Mac **A-listed**

**Stewarton Lainshaw House**
⊥    (c1850 Rob 1+pd/7  rem post-1893 to Edinburgh St. Cuthbert's Hall

**Stewarton St. Columba's** Lainshaw Street
⊥    1911 Jar 2/24  o1916 & 1923 Jar, r1923 Jar, r Houseley Atkins, Derby, disused 1980s, console moved

**Stewarton URC** (F/OLB cld 1841) Avenue Street
⊥    c1900 Walc 1/5  disused **B-listed**

**Stirling Albert Hall** - see Stirling Town Hall

**Stirling Allan Park South** (Allan Park/UF/UP) Dumbarton Road
⅄ 1898 F&A 2/21 r1905, console moved 1960 R&D, disused 1993 **B-listed**

**Stirling B** (South/UF/North UF/F until 1902, cld 1970) Murray Place
⅄ (Ing 2/20 dest vandals 1972, case rem to Cambusbarron pub

**Stirling Castle Chapel Royal**
⅄ (regals to here 1497
⅄ (3 pairs of organs extant 1505 , one o 1506 by a canon from Holyrood, o1511 & 1512 Gilleam, o1532-33, extant 1566, two rem c1567, one dest 1571
⅄ (1594 organ dest 1651

**Stirling Church of the Holy Rude** St. John Street/Castle Wynd
⅄ (1889 Bro 2/20 (in East Church here) o1892, r1925 Ing 3/28, rem 1936 to Edinburgh Murrayfield
⅄ 1940 R&D 4/82 o1967 R&D, r1973-76 Loo 4/82, r1992-95 R&D 4/82 **A-listed**

**Stirling Craigforth House Res of J. Callander**
⅄ (organ rem 1763 to Edinburgh St. Cecilia's Hall by John Johnston

**Stirling Erskine Marykirk** (Erskine UF Cont/UF/UP) St. John Street cld 1969 (now hostel)
⅄ (1911 Bin 2/21 scr c1970

**Stirling Holy Trinity E** Albert Place/Dumbarton Road
⅄ (1867 Hill 2/13 in former blg in Barnton Street, rem to St. Michael and All Angels, Cockerham, Lancashire & r 2/15
⅄ 1878 ConP 3/23 r pre-1910 Bin, r1935 BFH 3/33, r1981 Loo 3/47

**Stirling Marykirk** cld 1934
⅄ (organ rem to Bannockburn Allan 1938

**Stirling North** Murray Place blg cld 1967 (cong to new ch at Braehead)
⅄ (1890 Bro 2/22 scr c1970

**Stirling Res of D.L. Murdoch, Northumberland House**
⅄ (1893 F&A 2/10 rem to store 1903 F&A

**Stirling Res of Arthur Nicol**
⅄ (1927 ChrN 3/ ex5 + 1traps to here 1971 from Stratford Empire Theatre, Essex, o1975, rem 1985 to Blackridge Res of Robert Leys

**Stirling St. Columba's** (UF/North Craigs UF/Peter Memorial F) Park Terrace
⅄ 1903 Bin 2/21 o Loo, o2008 MilP **C-listed**

**Stirling St. Mark's** Drip Road
⅄ 1966 Wal 1/4 r Loo 1/4

**Stirling St. Mary's RC** Upper Bridge Street
⅄ 1902 MilJ 2/8 fr Forgan to Stonehaven Dunnottar (temp) 1983 Loo, to Dunfermline Abbey 1984 (temp), to here & r1991 Loo 2/11

**Stirling St. Ninian's Old** Kirk Wynd, St. Ninian's
  ⊥   1924 Ing 3/28 ex8 + chimes fr Edinburgh St. Andrew Square Cinema 1939 & r Ing 2/28, o1981 R&D, disused

**Stirling South** - see Stirling B

**Stirling Town Hall** (Albert Hall)
  ⊥   (1883 Wil 3/41 rem 1951 Wil, pipes later to Southampton St. Mary's

**Stirling Viewfield Erskine** (Viewfield/UF/UP) Barnton Street/Irving Place
  ⊥   1912 Lew 2/17 fr Edinburgh Holy Trinity E 1949 & r R&D 2/17 **C-listed**

**Stobo Castle** Peeblesshire
  ⊥   (organ rem 1905 to Glasgow for reconstruction by N&B

**Stobshiel** - see Humbie

**Stonehaven C**
  ⊥   (c1935 Com 2/11 ex2

**Stonehaven Dunnottar**
  ⊥   1903 Wad 2/23 r1983 by K. A. David, r1991 & 1999 Loo 3/34
  ⊥   (1902 MilJ 2/8 fr Forgan 1983 by Loo (temp), rem to Dunfermline Abbey 1984 (temp) Loo, to Stirling St. Mary's RC 1991 Loo

**Stonehaven Fetteresso**
  ⊥   1876 Wil 2/17 +5pf o1886 Wad, o1904 Wad, o1909 Wad, r1912 Wil 2/22, r1974 Wal 2/23, o1984 McDM, r2008 McDM 2/23

**Stonehaven** (location unknown)
  ⊥   (c1900 Pos 1/ rem to Addiewell c1950

**Stonehaven Mackie Academy**
  ⊥   Ing 3/ ex3 fr house of Dr. Mackie (original school) to later school and to here by John Fraser, Rector, r by technical dept. with help of Loo 3/18 ex 3

**Stonehaven Res of Charles Davidson**
  ⊥   (c1840s Ren 1/4 to Aberdeen Scandinavian 1948, to here 1970, rem c1979 to workshop of Martin Cross, Essex, then to Basildon Workshop of Ian Stewart & o2011, rem

**Stonehaven Res of Dr. J.G. Mackintosh**
  ⊥   (1888 Wad 1/ r1912 Law, r1920 Com 2/14, rem 1936 by George Blacklock to Aberdeen St. Ninian's E & r by the Rev. Ian Begg

**Stonehaven Res of John Riddoch**
  ⊥   (c1900 John Riddoch 1/3 fr Arbuthnott Manse c1909

**Stonehaven St. James the Great E**
  ⊥   (c1830s SBr 1/5 in previous blg rem 1877 to Cowie House, Res of Major W. D. Innes
  ⊥   1881 Wad 2/17 r1885 Wad 2/18 to chamber, r1912 Wad 2/20, o1980 WoW, o1991 Edm, o2000 McDM **A-listed**

**Stonehaven St. John's Chapel of Ease** blg cld
⚊ (1866 HDT 2/12 r1877 HDT 2/13 (with pd)

**Stonehaven South** (UF/F)
⚊ 1870 F&A 2/18 +1pf fr Montrose St. Mary & St. Peter E 1924 by Ing, r1935 G&D 2/19,
r1973 R&D 2/19

**Stonehouse Hamilton Memorial** (UF/F) cld 1946
⚊ (1900 Bin 1/9

**Stonehouse Paterson UF cont** (UF/UP)
⚊ (c1901 Walc 1/

**Stonehouse Res of David Hamilton**
⚊ (1985 Lam 2+ppd/2 fr Edinburgh Res of Anne McAllister, Portobello to Linlithgow Res
of Philip Sawyer & Anne McAllister 1988, to here 2002

**Stonehouse St. Ninian's** (Stonehouse) Lanarkshire
⚊ 1922 HNB 2/14 disused 2005, revived 2017

**Stonehouse URC** (C) Angle Street cld 2010
⚊ 1935 Com 2/11

**Stoneykirk** Wigtownshire cld 1974
⚊ 1910 B&H r1964 R&D

**Stoneykirk Ardwell** (Ardwell-Sandhead/Ardwell) Ardwell, Wigtownshire cld 2016 (now run by
Trust)
⚊ 1902 Walc 1+pd/7 o1981 R&D, r1996 Loo ex

**Stoneywood** Aberdeenshire cld 1989 (see also Bucksburn)
⚊ 1902 A&S 2/20 r1980s Edm

**Stornoway Martin's Memorial** Francis Street
⚊ 1949 Har 2/10 o2001 Gro

**Stornoway St. Columba's** Lewis Street
⚊ 1902 Bro 2/ r1954 Wil 2/10

**Stornoway St. Peter's E** Francis Street/Matheson Road
⚊ 1888 Bev 2/12 o1892 Wad, o Gro, r1985 Jhn (Derby), o2015

**Stow Manse, Res of Buchan** 209 Galashiels Road
⚊ (1830s SBr barrel organ 3ss fr Hawick Res of M. Webb post-1958 to Burnley Res of W.
Blakey, rem post-1992 to London Botany Bay, Enfield, Middlesex by George Crutchley
& o1990s, rem 1999 to Edinburgh Broughton St. Mary's Church Centre, 2000 to
Midcalder Res, to here 2002, rem 2009 to Newtonmore Manse
⚊ (1850s Ren 1/8 to Fortrose fr Res & r1914 Cat 1/8, rem 1986 to Scourie Res of Ross,
rem 1987 to Leithen Lodge by H. Ross, rem 1995 case & pt to Edinburgh Broughton St.
Mary's and in 2002 to here, rem 2006 to Lam (other parts scr)
⚊ (1841 Hill r1842 Bru fr Auchterarder Millearn House possibly to Edinburgh Albany
Street C & o 1867 Ren, rem to Edinburgh Dalry C c1875, r1892 King 2/13, to storage
here 2005 by For, rem 2008 to storage at Dublin workshop of Stephen Adams

**Stow Res of Gilbert Innes, Pirntaton** nr Fountainhall - see Edinburgh Res of Innes

**Stow St. Mary of Wedale**
⊥   1905 Ing 2/20  o2000 Sta  **B-listed**

**Strachur**
⊥   1906 Walc 1/6  fr Edinburgh 1906, o1922 Hils, o Gordon Harrison

**Strachur** - see also Strathlachan

**Straiton** - see Edinburgh Res of Johnstone

**Stranraer High Kirk** (Sheuchan) Leswalt High Road
⊥   1912 N&B  o1926 HNB, r1981 HNB

**Stranraer** - see also Lochinch Castle and Stoneykirk

**Stranraer Ind** (Stranraer Old/Stranraer cld 2004) Church Street
⊥   1850 Bev 2/12  fr London, fr a Public Hall to here 1882 & r Bev 2/14, r1957 HNB 2/15 (rem to north gallery), o c1975

**Stranraer Res of F.W. Lew**
⊥   pedal attachment to organ 1916 by HNB

**Stranraer St. Joseph's RC** Lewis Street
⊥   (1871 organ

**Stranraer St. Margaret's** (Sheuchan UF/F) cld 1956
⊥   (1915 B&H 2/  rem 1959 to Glasgow St. Ninian's RC, Knightswood & r Hils

**Stranraer St. Ninian's** (UF/West UP/Bridge Street UP) Lewis Street cld 2013
⊥   1884 ConP 2/16  r1959 R&D 2/16, r1978 R&D, r1992 McDM 2/16

**Stranraer Trinity** (Town Kirk/St. Andrew's/UF/Ivy Place UF/UP) London Road
⊥   (c1898 ConP
⊥   1928 Bin 2/16  r Bin 2/17, o1957 HNB, r1967 Dan/Sol 2/22 +8pf, o1984 Har with console fr Ayr Cathcart (Auld New), r1994 with new console WoP 2/21

**Strathaven Avendale Old**
⊥   1934 Hils 2/20  o1993 Mac, o2009 Mac **B-listed**

**Strathaven East** (UF/UP)
⊥   (1903 Walc  case extant

**Strathaven Rankin** (UF/F)
⊥   c1934 Com 2/11 ex 2

**Strathaven West** (UF/UP) cld 2011
⊥   (c1900s M&S

**Strathblane**
⊥   1910 Ing 2/16 (3 divisions)  o Wil **B-listed**

**Strathblane: Blanefield** (UF/F) cld 1934 blg cld later
⚲ (1884 Har 2/ dest fire 1905
⚲ (1907 Sco 2/10

**Strathblane** - see also Mugdock Castle

**Strathbogie Drumblade** (Strathbogie/UF/Huntly F) Bogie Street, Huntly, Aberdeenshire
⚲ 1904 Lew 2/18 resited 1912 & r Law, o1914 Lew, o1987 HNB, 2ss changed 1994

**Strathbrock (St. Nicholas)** (Uphall North) Uphall, West Lothian
⚲ (1885 Ric 2/10 rem 1988 by Hugh Ross, scr

**Strathbrock** - see also Ecclesmachan

**Strathkinness** Fife
⚲ (1954 organ
⚲ (1932 Hay 1+pd/5 to Dundee Barnhill St. Margaret's 1932 & r Wat, to Edinburgh
Richmond Craigmillar 1974 by D. Galbraith, to here 1977, rem 1998 to Kyles

**Strathlachlan** Argyll
⚲ c1920 Pos 1/4 o c1970s Gordon Harrison

**Strathnairn St. Paul's E** Invernesshire
⚲ (organ o1896 Wad, o1905 Wad, rem

**Strathpeffer** - see Fodderty & Strathpeffer

**Strathpeffer St. Anne's E**
⚲ (1905 S&L 2/10 r1936 HNB 2/ , rem 1990s

**Strichen** (North/ Strichen UF/F) Aberdeenshire
⚲ (Wish o1898 Wad, r Wil, rem 1960
⚲ organ to here 1960 from New Deer North by Watt, disused 2008

**Strichen All Saints E**
⚲ (1886 Wad in previous blg rem 1897 to Glasgow Res of Mr. Hastie
⚲ 1893 Wad 2/10 o2004 Edm **A-listed**

**Strichen Res**
⚲ (1828 organ by amateur completed 4viii1828

**Stromness** (St. Peter's & Victoria Street/Victoria Street/UF/UP)
⚲ 1906 Bin 2/11 o1961 BinT, o1985 R&D

**Stromness St. Peter's** (Stromness) cld 1950 (Community Centre)
⚲ (1902 Pos 1/ scr pre-1950

**Stromness Town Hall** (Academy Hall/North/UF/F cld 1971)
⚲ 1910 N&B 2/7

**Stuartfield** - see Deer

**Summerlee** - see Coatbridge

**Sutherland Res of S. Walker**
   ⅄   (c1881 Bis

**Swinton** Berwickshire
   ⅄   (Pos 1/7 o1977 R&D, rem c2006
   ⅄   c1800s organ r1862 E. Hitchin 1/5 fr Barrow M to Saughall M, Cheshire 1975, to here
       2000s & r Julian Bonia 1/5

**Swinton West** (Swinton UF/F) cld 1932
   ⅄   (1903 Walc 1/

**Symington** Ayrshire
   ⅄   (1927 Hils 2/14 console moved c1949, disused 1999, facade survives

**Symington** - see also Dankeith Castle

**Tain** (Queen Street UF/F) Easter Ross
   ⅄   1931 Law 2/25 r 2/17, o Nob

**Tain Duthac Centre** (Tain Town Hall/Tain cld 1942)
   ⅄   (1906 F&A 2/15 rem 1944 to Avoch C

**Tain St. Andrew's E** Manse Street
   ⅄   1913 HCF 2/10 o1986 **B-listed**

**113) The 1913 C. & F. Hamilton organ in St. Andrew's Episcopal Church, Tain. This was the Hamilton firm's last completely new organ after a steady output of 90 years**

**Tarbolton** (Old) Ayrshire
   ⚰  1908 N&B 2/19 **B-listed**

**Tarff & Twynholm** - see Twynholm

**Tarves** Aberdeenshire
   ⚰  1892 Wad 2/13  o1910 Wad

**Taymouth Castle Hall** nr Aberfeldy
   ⚰  (1879 F&A 3/23  o1900 F&A, rem 1923 to Inverness Crown

**Taymouth Castle St. James Chapel E**
   ⚰  (1880 F&A 2/11  o1899 F&A

**Tayport** (Queen Street/UF/F) Fife
   ⚰  1895 Vin 2/13  disused 1937, revived 1963 L&B (new console), disused

**Tayport Auld Kirk (Trust)** (Erskine Ferryport-on-Craig/Ferryport-on-Craig/Auld cld 1978) Castle Street
   ⚰  1899 MilJ 2/16 **A-listed**

**Teviothead**
   ⚰  1990 WiB 1/14 ex

**Thornhill** (Morton) East Morton Street, Dumfriesshire
   ⚰  1885 Har 2/21  o1915 F&A, r1958 Com 2/21, disused 2004

**Thornhill Virginhall** (UF/Thornhill UF/UP) West Morton Street cld 1963/73
   ⚰  (c1904 Walc 1/6  rem 1972 to Mochrum via Newton Stewart Res of Wilson

**Thornliebank** (Speirsbridge/UF/UP) Rouken Glen Road, nr Glasgow
   ⚰  1883 You 2/9  o Watt

**Thornliebank St. Vincent de Paul RC** Main Road
   ⚰  1961 HNB 2/14  o1988 HNB

**Thornliebank Woodlands** (Thornliebank) Woodlands Road cld 1992
   ⚰  (1874 Hill 2/12  fr Motherwell Dalziel St. Andrew's 1898 by Mir, o1973 Mac 2/17

**Thurso Res of Fr. John Allen** (rem to Inverness 2015)
   ⚰  (Bru/Mir 2/5  fr Lothian Res to Haddington St. Mary's RC 1992, rem to Inverness Res 1992
   ⚰  (other organ pts at various times

**Thurso St. Peter's & St. Andrew's** (St. Peter's/Thurso) Princess Street
   ⚰  1914 N&B 2/12  o1918 HNB, o2009 John Allen **A-listed**

**Thurso St. Peter's E** Sir George's Street
   ⚰  1894 Ben 2/10  fr Temple M, Glazebrook, Cheshire 1973 & r Pen, r1999 & 2001

**Thurso URC** (C) Castle Street
   ⚰  1901 Bro  r1970s, 2004 new blower, partially usable

**Tillicoultry** Dollar Road
   ⚰  (1922 Hils 2/21  scr 1997

**Tillycoultry C** High Street
⊥ (c1880 ConP 2/8  o1961 R&D, scr 1997

**Tillymorgan St. Thomas' E** cld 1960
⊥ (1855 organ
⊥ (1902 Wad 1+pd/8  rem 1961 to Dalbeattie Christ Church E & r Sol

**Tingwall** - see Scalloway

**114) The Peter Conacher organ in Tillicoultry Congregational Church immediately before its destruction in 1997**
**115) The 1896 James Conacher organ at Tombae RC Church prior to its removal to the Lebanon in 2017**

**Tobermory** Mull
⊥ (1903 Cou 1/9  o1964 R&D

**Tombae Church of the Incarnation RC** Banffshire cld 2013
⊥ (1896 ConJ 2/8  rem 2017 by Walc to Johann Ludwig Schneller School, St. Michael's Chapel, Khirbet Qanafar, Lebanon

**Tomintoul**
⊥ 1903 Walc 1/6  o2009 Walc **B-listed**

**Tomintoul St. Michael's RC**
⊥ (1866 ConP  case only survives

**Tongland** Kirkcudbright cld 1988
⊥ (c1900 Pos 1/5  rem 1989 to Balmaghie

**Torphins** Aberdeenshire
⊥ 1913 A&S 2/13  disused 1994, revived & o2004 Lib **B-listed**

**Torryburn** Fife cld 2014
  ⚓ (1929 HNB 1/6 +1pf o1940s R&D, r1991 Loo, rem 2016 to Roslin by Loo

**Torthorwald** Dumfriesshire
  ⚓ 1904 Law 1/6

**Touch, Res of Mr. Seton** nr Stirling
  ⚓ (1771 Joseph Hollman 1/8 for sale 6ii1787, rem to Edinburgh Res of Seton

**Toward** Cowal, Argyll
  ⚓ (organ 1/ to here 1948 by Hils, disused 1995

**Tranent** Church Street, East Lothian
  ⚓ 1909 Sco 2/12 rem to east end 1953, disused 1983

**Tranent Wishart St. Andrew's** (Wishart/UF/UP) cld 1980 (later ch hall)
  ⚓ (1920 R&D 2/10 o1951 Bell

**Traprain** - see Prestonkirk, Stenton and Standingstone Farm

**Traquair** nr Innerleithen
  ⚓ (1912 Walc 1/ rem c1979

**Troon Marr College Hall** Dundonald Road
  ⚓ (1931 Hils 2/15 r R&D, rem 2015 to storage McDM, console only survives

**Troon Old** Ayr Street
  ⚓ 1895 Hill 2/18 r1965 HNB 2/23, o1984 R&D, r2008 MilP 2/23

**Troon Our Lady & St. Meddan's RC** St. Meddan's Street
  ⚓ 1934 R&D ex4 disused

**Troon Portland** (Portland Street UF/Troon F) St. Meddan's Street, South Beach
  ⚓ (1893 Vin in first blg
  ⚓ (1903 Bin
  ⚓ 1914 Har 2/18 for present blg r1970 Har 2/21, o2010-13 Har

**Troon Res of D.L. Murdoch, Warrix**
  ⚓ organ r1910 N&B 3/

**Troon St. Meddan's** (UF/UP) St. Meddan's Street/Church Street
  ⚓ 1889 Mir 2/19 r1930s Watt, r Dan, disused

**Troon St. Ninian's E** Bentinck Drive
  ⚓ 1921 Bin 3/33 +2pf r1959 BinT, r1988 Six, o2013 Har

**Troqueer** - see Dumfries

**Tulliallan Castle**
  ⚓ organ extant 1980s

**Tulliallan & Kincardine** (Tulliallan)
  ⚓ 1894 F&A 2/18 r Sco 2/ , o1935 Hils, o1969 R&D 2/21, o1982/1990

**Turriff St. Andrew's** (UF/F) Balmellie Road
  ⅄  1910 Wad 2/12 +1pf o1919 Wad

**Turriff St. Congan's E** Deveron Street
  ⅄  (1889 organ
  ⅄  1906 Wad 2/12

**Turriff St. Ninian's & Forglen** (St. Ninian's) Gladstone Terrace
  ⅄  (1876 F&A 2/11 o1898 Wad, r1899 F&A
  ⅄  (1914 Ing 2/27 (3 divisions) scr 2009

**Turriff** - see also Forglen House and Hatton Castle

**Twatt** Orkney
  ⅄  Pos 1/5 o M. Cross for Dr. Colin Fothergill, Eve's Cottage, Danbury, Essex, to here
    1986 by Alex Bain

**Twechar** nr Kilsyth
  ⅄  1903 Wil 2/15 o1934 HNB, o1996 local organist **A-listed**

**116) The Willis II organ at Twechar Parish Church**

**Tweed Horizons Centre** - see Dryburgh

356

**Twynholm** (now Tarff & Twynholm)
⋏   c1963 HNB 1/5

**Twynholm** - see also Largs House

**Tynet St. Ninian's RC** Auchenhalrig, Moray
⋏   (c1800-15 Fr. George Mathison  lent to Aberdeen St. Peter's RC 1814-15 , o1817, r1824
    with Bru pipes by Mathison, rem 1853 Wis

**Tyrie** nr Strichen, Aberdeenshire
⋏   1903 Law 1/6

**Uddingston Burnhead** Laburnam Road
⋏   (1959 Mac 1/7 using material fr 1875 F&A 2/15 at Glasgow St. Mark's

**Uddingston Chalmers** (UF/F) Main Street cld 1982 dem
⋏   (1902 Lew 2/17  o1909 Lew, console moved 1937

**Uddingston Church of the Nazarene** Old Mill Road
⋏   (c1820s-30s Mir 1/  fr Irvine Res to here 1959 Watt, rem 1961 to storage by Mac then to
    Hamilton Whitehill 1965 by Mac

**Uddingston C** Sheepburn Road cld
⋏   (1902 F&A 2/  rem c1979 to Kettle

**Uddingston Old** (Chalmers Trinity/Trinity/Uddingston) Old Glasgow Road
⋏   1888 F&A 3/27  o1995 HNB, +1ss 2011 by MilP **A-listed**

**Uddingston Park UF** (Uddingston Park to 2007/UF/UP) Main Street/Church Street
⋏   1887 F&A 2/11  o1959 R&D **A-listed**

**Uddingston St. Andrew's E** Bothwell Road
⋏   1895 B&H 2/14  damaged by fire 1993, o2011 Mac **A-listed**

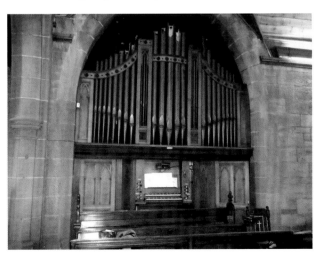

**117) The 1895 Blackett & Howden organ at St. Andrew's Episcopal Church, Uddingston**

357

**Udny & Pitmedden** (Udny) Aberdeenshire
⚒ 1891 Har 2/13 o1914 Wad, o1979 R&D, o2000 Edm

**Unst: Uyeasound** (UF/F) Shetland
⚒ 1964 Sol 1+pd/9 ex2 fr local Res to here, disused

**Uphall South**
⚒ (c1914 Sau 2/13 to here c1940 fr Ballater North, rem 1995 to Bearsden All Saints E & r by Ian McNaught

**Uphall** - see also Strathbrock and Ecclesmachan

**Upper Clyde** - see Crawford & Crawfordjohn

**Upper Largo** - see Largo

**Urquhart** Moray cld 1988
⚒ (1935 Rot 2/7 o1978 R&D, rem 1991 to Braes of Rannoch & r Loo

**Urr** Kirkcudbright
⚒ 1897 Bro 2/11 r1914 Ing 2/20, r1994 Vin 2/19, disused

**Urr: Hardgate** (Urr UF/UP) cld 1932
⚒ (1911 Bin 2/13

**Viewpark** - see Uddingston

**Walkerburn** Peeblesshire cld 2009
⚒ 1896 Ing 2/19 o SmRo

**Wallacestone** - see Polmont

**Wallyford St. Clement's**
⚒ (1908 organ o Gle

**Weem** (St. David's E cld 1918) Perthshire
⚒ 1875 Wal 2/9 +2 pf +2ss 1876, opened here 1878, o1994 R&D **A-listed**

**Wemyss** Fife - see East Wemyss and West Wemyss

**Wemyss Bay English E** cld pre-1970
⚒ (1879 F&A 3/20 o1904 F&A

**Wemyss Bay** - see also Skelmorlie

**Wemyss Castle** Fife
⚒ 1899 B&T inspected 1909 Wad, r1986 Edm 1/8

**West Calder High School**
⚒ 1902 IHJ 2/15 fr Edinburgh Prestonfield 1976 & r 2/14

**West Calder Our Lady & St. Bridget's RC**
⚒ (Ren 1/6

**West Calder West Kirk of Calder**
⊥   1902 B&H 2/18  r1968 SmRo, r1988 SmRo

**Wester Gartshore House** - see Gartshore

**Westerkirk** Dumfriesshire
⊥   2005 JoG 2/10  with pt by Walc & pt fr Dundee Baxter Park

**Westhall** - see Oyne

**West Kilbride** (St. Andrew's/St. Bride's/UF/F) Main Street
⊥   (1913 Hils 2/13  rem

**West Kilbride Barony** (West Kilbride) Main Street cld 1974 (later Church Centre)
⊥   (1903 B&H  r1913 B&H 3/24

**West Kilbride Overton** (UF/UP) Ritchie Street cld 2010
⊥   1921 Bin 2/13

**West Linton St. Andrew's** Peeblesshire
⊥   (c1900s Pos 1/6  o1970s R&D, rem 1996 by Murray Campbell, later to Kilfinan, Argyll

**West Mearns** - see Fettercairn, Fordoun and Glenbervie

**Westray** Orkney
⊥   1967 Sol 1/6 ex1

**Westruther** Berwickshire
⊥   1994 Sta 1/6  with pt of organ fr Kelso St. Andrew's E

**West Wemyss** (St. Adrian's, disused 1960s, reopened 2008)
⊥   (c1840 Bis 1+ppd/8  fr elsewhere, rem 1983 to Bridge of Don St. Columba's & r Edm

**Whitburn South** Manse Road, West Lothian
⊥   (1911 Sco 2/11  dest by fire 1955

**Whitekirk & Tyninghame** (Whitekirk) East Lothian
⊥   (c1887 ConP  2/14  o1952 Bell
⊥   c1950s Com 2/18 ex3  fr Dunbar Abbey 1972, o1994 Wil

**Whithorn St. Ninian's Priory** Bruce Street
⊥   1974 Wal 2/16 ex 2

**Whittingehame Res Chapel**
⊥   2006 Har 1/3

**Wick B** (Central/Pulteneytown Central/UF/F cld 1990) Dempster Street
⊥   (1967/1975 L&B 2/15  rem 1992 to Wick Pulteneytown by McDM

**Wick Bridge Street** (Wick UF/F) cld 2009
⊥   1880 Whiteley 2/8  o1993 McDM, on e-bay 2014, but not sold

**Wick Pulteneytown** (St. Andrew's/Pulteneytown St. Andrew's/Pulteneytown) Argyle Square
⳽ 1967/1975 L&B 2/15 fr Wick B (Central) 1992 by McDM with case fr Paisley Merksworth, o2004 McDM

**Wick St. Fergus** (Old/North/Wick) High Street
⳽ 1883 Wad 2/18 o1974 R&D, o2007 McDM **A-listed**

**Wick St. John the Evangelist E** Moray Street
⳽ (c1855 Bev (Scudamore) 1/ (in hall) rem to ch c1870
⳽ 1948 Har 1+pd/5 o1978 R&D

**Wigtown** Bank Street
⳽ (1878 Har 2/14 moved & r1924 Ing 2/17, r1968 Dan/Sol, rem 2002

**Wigtown Church of the Sacred Heart RC** South Main Street
⳽ (1879 Hill

**Wigtown Res of Earl of Galloway**
⳽ Swe

**Wigtown Res of H. Bowen**
⳽ 2011 Lam 2/7
⳽ 2016 Lam 1/5

**Wilton** - see Hawick

**Winchburgh** West Lothian
⳽ (1936 G&D rem 1989
⳽ 1972 Wal 2/16 ex4 fr Haddington St. Mary's 1990 by R&D

**Wishaw Cambusnethan North** (UF/F) Cambusnethan Street
⳽ (1903 organ o1908, o1931 Ing o1935 Watt, o1947 Bro
⳽ 1966 Wal 2/18 ex 3 o1994 McDM, o2015 McDM

**Wishaw Cambusnethan Old & Morningside** (Cambusnethan Old) Greenhead Road/Kirk Road blg cld 2016 (temp)
⳽ (1876 F&A 2/14 +1pf o1893 F&A +1ss, sold
⳽ (c1979 Sol 2/ using F&A material, court case, rem
⳽ 1913 Wal 2/8 fr London Greek Orthodox (ex-Golders Green C of E) 1981 & r Man 2/10

**Wishaw Coltness House** - see Coltness

**Wishaw Craigneuk** Clamp Road cld 1975
⳽ (1951-54 Bro 2/ using material fr elsewhere o1955 BFH

**Wishaw Craigneuk & Belhaven** (Belhaven Craigneuk/Craigneuk UF/F) Craigneuk Street
⳽ organ r Sco 2/14, fr Rothesay Bridgend to here 1946 by Hils, o1962 & 1966 R&D

**Wishaw Old** 110 Main Street
⊥ 1892 F&A 2/20 o1985 McDM, o2009 McDM **A-listed**

**Wishaw Primitive M** Caledonian Road cld 1976
⊥ 1910 B&H

**Wishaw St. Andrew's E** Belhaven Terrace
⊥ 1903 Job r Sol 1+pd/7 ex1

**Wishaw St. Ignatius RC** Young Street
⊥ (1907 Cou rem by 2008

**Wishaw St. Mark's** Coltness Road
⊥ 1962 Wal 2/ ex3

**Wishaw St. Patrick's RC** 71 Shieldmuir Street, Craigneuk
⊥ 1903 B&H r Watt 1+pd/9, r c1990 Lib

**Wishaw South** (Wishaw Chalmers/UF/F) East Academy Street
⊥ (1915 Ing 2/19 r1978 R&D 2/19, o1980s, scr 2012, case survives

**Wishaw Thornlie** (Thornlie UF/Wishaw UP) West Thornlie Street/Caledonian Road cld 2004
⊥ (1925 Jar 2/19 +traps +1ss later, fr Kirkcaldy MGM Cinema (Opera House) 1935 & r
Watt 2/20, r1959 R&D 2/21, r1962 Kin 2/40, vandalised, pt sold c2000, pt to South
Africa, 1ss to Birmingham

**Wolfhill** (Cargill UF/F) nr Blairgowrie cld 1932
⊥ (1903 Walc 1/

**Woodhead -** see Fyvie

**Woodhill -** see Ballintuim

**Woodside -** see Paisley

**Wormit** (UF/F) Riverside Road, North Fife
⊥ 1913 Wat/ConP 2/16 o1960s, r pre-2005 Lib

**Yair -** see Fairnielee

**Yarrow** nr Selkirk
⊥ 1961 Sol 1/5 ex

**Yetholm** Roxburgh
⊥ (organ 1/8 rem 1994
⊥ 1964 R&D 1+pd/10 ex2 fr Kirkintilloch Hillhead 1994 & r R&D

**Ythan Wells** Aberdeenshire cld 1992
⊥ 1912 Wad 1/7 o1919 Wad